OPENING JAPAN'S FINANCIAL MARKETS

OPENING JAPAN'S FINANCIAL MARKETS

J. Robert Brown, Jr.

London and New York

First published 1994
by Routledge
11 New Fetter Lane, London EC4P 4EE

Simultaneously published in the USA and Canada
by Routledge
29 West 35th Street, New York, NY 10001

Typeset in Garamond by LaserScript Limited, Mitcham, Surrey

Printed and bound in Great Britain by
Mackays of Chatham PLC, Chatham, Kent

British Library Cataloguing in Publication Data
A catalogue record for this book is available from the British Library

ISBN 0-415-05750-7 (hbk)   ISBN 0-415-10604-4 (pbk)

Library of Congress Cataloging in Publication Data
Brown Jr, J. Robert (James Robert), 1957-
Opening Japan's financial markets : shared responsibilities / J. Robert Brown, Jr.
p.   cm.
Includes bibliographical references and index.
ISBN 0–415–10844–6
1. Investments, Foreign–Japan. 2. Banks and banking, Foreign–Japan. 3.
Japan–Foreign economic relations. I. Title.
HG5772.B74 1994
332.6′73′0952–dc20   93-31921
CIP

To William F. Haworth: Who recognized
that knowledge came to different people in
different ways and had the wisdom to let each person
find their own path

CONTENTS

FOREWORD

This is a book written in terms of the foreign banking players in post-war Japan, overwhelmingly the American players. Since it is written in terms of the players, it necessarily deals in the nitty-gritty issues that the players faced. Sometimes in analyzing issues from an overall economic perspective we lose sight of the struggles on the ground. Brown recounts these struggles in colorful language. Thus we learn of the struggles for entry into the Japanese market, for additional branches, for undertaking trust activities, for advertising interest rates on deposits and so on. The story begins in the period when Japan isolated itself from the international financial community and continues into the period, post 1973, when Japan recognized that it was necessary to be part of this community.

Professor Brown sees the position of the foreign banks in Japan to be the product of not only their entrepreneurial imaginativeness in the face of restrictions but the support given by their governments. He sees foreign government pressure having its best chance of success where it joins positions already taken by Japanese domestic forces pressing for change.

Critics of Japan's behavior toward foreign financial institutions have often pointed to the insignificant position of foreign institutions in Japan by comparison with the scale of Japanese institutions abroad. One of Professor Brown's most astonishing statistics has to do with the difference between market share and profit. He comments: "Through the early 1960s, Citibank, with its four paltry branches, was more profitable than Fuji, Japan's largest bank."

Some would hold that only persons with Japanese-language capabilities are entitled to write about Japan. This would preclude many valuable observers, however, including Professor Brown.

Eleanor M. Hadley

ACKNOWLEDGMENTS

This book took more than two years to write. Even with the considerable time and effort, I could not have succeeded without the enormous help of a handful of people – in Europe, the United States and Japan – who took a personal interest in this project. A list of all the interviews is included at the end of the book but some deserve particular mention.

I am particularly indebted to John F. (Jack) Loughran, who worked in Japan for J.P. Morgan and had personal contact with, or knew about, almost every major development that occurred from the 1960s through the mid-1980s. He devoted countless hours in conversations about activities in Japan and was often able to put me in touch with the individual or individuals in the middle of particular developments, enabling me to get the necessary first hand accounts.

Tristan Beplat, who played a critical role in determining banking policy during the occupation and then went on to a lengthy career with Manufacturers Hanover, also gave considerable time to the project. In particular, he provided a great deal of information on the thinking behind the decisions of occupation officials on financial reform. Louis F. Dempsey, currently at Brown Brothers Harriman & Co., also deserves special mention. He took an active interest in the project from the very beginning. In addition to providing help with and reading relevant portions of the manuscript, he went out of his way to make contacts for me in Japan. Some of my most successful Japanese interviews were because of his intervention.

Francis X. Stankard from Chase Manhattan gave liberally of his time, providing additional contacts and reading a draft of the manuscript. Raymond A. Kathe also proved to be a fountain of information, with the additional advantage of perspective, having worked with the Japanese financial markets for much of his 30 year career at Citibank. Jackson Huddleston, from Chemical and American Express, also brought long years of experience to the manuscript. He read drafts and expunged a number of errors.

To name a few others, I spoke at length with Leo de Grijs from Continental Bank, Tom B. Coughran from Bank of America, Frank W. Gooding from First Chicago, A.S.I. (Butch) Ahmad from National Bank of North America, Olof D. Linstedt from First Chicago, Richard W. Wheeler from Citibank, Robert J. Wynn from J. P. Morgan, Roger Christiansen from Citibank and Seafirst, and Paul Draughn from United California, the precursor to First Interstate.

Citibank played a central role in activities in Japan and a central role in the book. I received considerable cooperation from individuals at the bank, including quick responses to various requests for documentation. In particular, Masamoto Yashiro, who oversees activities in Japan, and James Weadock, the Personnel Director in the country, made time and people available. In New York, John Skelly and Joan Silverman responded to incessant requests for documentary materials. Peter Howell also provided considerable insight into the government relations process.

A number of officials from the Department of the Treasury also provided assistance. I found the past members of the yen–dollar team to be accessible and informative although in some cases unwilling to talk about some matters not yet in the public record. In particular, Margot Machol, a former member of the team, and John Abbott, a former Treasury attaché in Japan, provided some of the most helpful information and colorful vignettes. Beryl Sprinkel also gave considerable time to the effort.

On the Japanese side, I found doors thrown open with little hesitancy, whether in the private sector or the government. In general, I found people receptive and willing to talk once they determined the seriousness of the project. I spoke with officials in the Ministry of Finance, the Bank of Japan, the banking industry, and a number of industry organizations, including the Japan Center for International Finance and the Federation of Bankers Associations. Contacts at the Bank of Tokyo, the Industrial Bank of Japan and Mitsubishi Bank were extremely helpful.

In particular, Takeshi Watanabe and Gengo Suzuki provided considerable insight into the occupation period, Hideo Suzuki and Yusuke Kashiwagi on the 1950s and 1960s, and Tomomitsu Oba and Makoto Utsumi on more modern events, including the yen–dollar process. Shirjuro Ogata represented an invaluable source about the activities of the Bank of Japan over much of this period. Tadashi Nunami, representative in Washington DC, also provided valuable contacts at the Central Bank. Finally, I am indebted to Yoshiaki Koyama at the Ministry of Finance, an author in his own right, who not only provided information but gave me access to a number of well informed officials in the banking community.

Michio Umegaki, a former professor of mine at Georgetown and now at Keio University, provided the inspiration for the interest in Japan. Danny Unger, currently a professor at Georgetown, provided helpful comments on drafts of the manuscript and insisted that I not lose sight of the political dimensions of the reform process in Japan. But for his comments, I doubt that

I would have included as much about the domestic process within Japan, most of which is included in Chapter 9.

Much of the research was conducted at various archives. David Giordano at the Suitland branch of the National Archives provided considerable help and, often more important, his pleasant nature made the hours of tedium easier to withstand. Bank of America, Chase Manhattan, and American Express let me examine a number of internal documents mostly dating from the 1940s and 1950s. Mary Hedge at American Express was particularly helpful.

I also received assistance from Denver Investment Advisor, a fund manager with operations in Japan. In particular, Frederick Herman helped me better understand the pension markets and provided me with a number of extremely valuable contacts in Japan and the United States.

I obtained generous financial support for the project from the Hughes Research and Development Fund at the University of Denver College of Law. The members who reviewed and agreed to fund the efforts included Robert Yegge, Richard D. Schwartz, Victor Rosenblum, and Millard Ruud. I used a portion of the funding to hire a series of excellent research assistants, including Stephanie Watson and Maureen Juran, both of whom did early work on the project. Deborah Zalesne, Stacey Bowers, and Susan Richardson carried the laboring oar through the most trying period, all doing outstanding jobs. Finally, Hideki Maedomari, also a student at the Law School, acted as both a sounding board and a translator for the project.

Holland & Hart, a Denver based law firm, provided considerable support. The firm has developed strong ties with Japan and was able to provide assistance on how to approach the Japanese side of the research. The firm also gave considerable logistical support, with the word processing center doing a yeoman's job typing (and retyping) the manuscript – no small task given my incessant revisions.

It goes without saying that, while many gave considerable time and effort, this does not suggest complete agreement with the contents. Indeed, some disagreed strongly with portions of the book. The conclusions and any inconsistencies or errors, therefore, remain my responsibility.

J. Robert Brown, Jr

1

A QUESTION OF BALANCE

A great deal of misinformation exists over the lack of success of foreign enterprises in Japan. The tendency has been to brand the Japanese as the most significant, if not the exclusive, cause of the problem. Books on the topic range from the relatively insightful to the hyperbolic to the conspiratorial.

In *Unequal Equities*, the authors asserted that "[t]he primary reason for the insolubility of the trade issue can be traced to the structure of share ownership" in Japan.[1] Clyde Prestowitz, in *Trading Places*, took the position that the Japanese succeeded by using "the international system without conforming to it or accepting its burdens."[2] Pat Choate, in *Agents of Influence* referred to "the manipulation of America's political and economic system by Japanese and other foreign interests . . . ."[3] Even the titles themselves illustrate the attitude, referring to the Japanese as everything from enigmas[4] to gnomes.[5]

Apportioning blame in this fashion has significant consequences. It lends itself to solutions essentially designed to punish the recalcitrant behavior of the Japanese. Not surprisingly, therefore, many of these same authors have favored the use of managed trade and other punitive measures to solve the trade imbalance.

The propensity to blame the Japanese for the problem amounts to a one-sided and oversimplified view. It almost completely ignores foreign complicity in the trade imbroglio. Foreign companies and governments share responsibility for the current state of affairs, suggesting that part of the solution entails changed behavior outside of Japan.

Explaining the difficulties piercing the Japanese markets must first account for the fact that, for all of the failures, a host of notable successes exist. The IBMs, Coca-Colas and Xeroxes have done famously well and demonstrated that the barriers to operations in Japan could be overcome. This suggests that company-specific behavior can determine the success or failure of a particular venture.

1

These successful companies had common attributes, including a quality product, a sophisticated understanding of the market, and a long-term commitment to Japan. More subtle, however, they were linked by a common attitude. Knowledgeable about the market, the companies with the best record of success took a less complacent approach toward government regulation, constantly testing boundaries to obtain competitive advantages.

These companies illustrated that foreign enterprises could succeed in Japan. To the extent that the Japanese government did restrict competition, however, it succeeded only because of the complicity of foreign firms and foreign governments. Although operating in the country for more than a century, foreign banks managed to obtain only a diminutive share of the country's domestic markets. By the early 1990s, the entire foreign banking community held only 1.5 percent of outstanding loans and profitability had plummeted.[6]

The dismal statistics have been cited to show the exclusionary behavior of Japan, Inc.[7] The true explanation, however, is considerably more complex. For one thing, they represent an inadequate basis for judging banking success or failure. They focus only on yen lending. By the mid-1980s, foreign banks in Japan began deliberately to eschew yen lending. They instead favored higher margin activities, particularly more lucrative off-balance-sheet activities such as foreign exchange and derivative products. In these areas, foreign banks in Japan have a far more commanding position.

Moreover, even when focusing on yen lending, the decline cannot be attributed solely to the policies of the Japanese. While the Japanese government, specifically the Ministry of Finance (MoF), did, for a time, discourage yen loans, foreign banks contributed to the problem. More profit focused and less relationship oriented, foreign banks remained marginal lenders in the Japanese market. They preferred to use periods of capital shortage to exact higher margins rather than obtain long-term clients.

An unwillingness to assume the responsibilities of a lead bank also exacerbated the difficulties penetrating the lending market. In Japan, the role of a primary lender entails obligations well beyond the occasional provision of funds. Primary lenders act as implicit guarantors for other lenders and play a role in the management of the borrower, particularly during periods of financial difficulty. In those circumstances, Japanese banks often provide the personnel and funds needed to surmount the difficulties and, in extreme cases, may arrange a merger of the failing company. The foreign banking community in Japan has generally not wanted this type of responsibility.

The decline in profitability of foreign banks also ignores the reality of the trade imbalance. Profitability fell not because of the policies of the government *per se*, but because of the change in the economic position of Japan. With Japan shifting from a debtor to a creditor nation, the country became awash in dollars. The historical and profitable role of foreign banks as purveyors of dollars disappeared. No change in the regulatory system of Japan will bring those halcyon days back.

2

That is not to say that the history of foreign penetration of the banking sector has been simple or problem free. Far from it. The Japanese financial community, in particular the MoF, deliberately limited foreign banking activity through most of the post-war era. Less a demonstration of anti-foreign bias, the approach arose out of the unique role played by the banking system in the country's economic recovery.[8]

The MoF used banks to implement industrial policy by funneling capital to designated industries. To function effectively, the system required a close relationship between regulator and regulated. Japanese banks accepted the Ministry's instructions in return for what amounted to guaranteed profits.

Foreign banks represented the Achilles heel of the system. Their unconstrained operations threatened to make the system of government control and, concomitantly, industrial policy impossible to sustain. Foreign financial institutions had overseas sources of funds. To the extent that foreign capital flooded into the country, Japanese companies would no longer be dependent upon Japanese banks and the MoF for funding. The tight system of industrial control through capital rationing threatened to become porous.

The MoF therefore went to great lengths to seal off the domestic market from foreign competition. The Ministry's goal was to promote Japanese economic recovery and protect the Japanese financial system. Excluding or limiting foreign banks amounted to an integral part of these protectionist policies.

Other than the dozen foreign banks that entered the country under the aegis of the occupation, the MoF refused to issue a new branch license to a bank from an industrial country until 1968.[9] In addition, those already in the country suffered from a series of constraints. Most noticeably, resident banks were denied an adequate supply of yen and subjected to prohibitions on expansion. Not until 1981 did the MoF for the first time allow a foreign bank to have more than four branches.

Foreign banks were limited to dollar loans to Japanese companies and banks, a small but lucrative area of operations. With Japanese banks lacking the credit standing and the regulatory authority to raise currency in international capital markets, foreign banks became the exclusive conduit for dollars.[10] Moreover, guaranteed by Japanese banks and, implicitly, the Japanese government, the loans were extraordinarily safe.

Consigning foreign banks to a prescribed niche in the financial markets was not unique, but consonant with the general approach toward financial regulation. The entire financial sector had been divided into compartments. Containing commercial, trust and long-term-credit banks as well as more specialized institutions, each category of financial institutions had a specific role in a highly regulated financial system. They were expected to perform their designated functions and remain within their prescribed operating parameters. Foreign banks were no different. They could monopolize dollar loans but not engage in ordinary commercial banking activities within Japan.

3

In general, foreign banks accepted the limitations, for obvious reasons. They retained a small but lucrative niche in the Japanese financial markets. For years Citibank's operations in Japan ranked second or third in profitability among its entire international network. Through the early 1960s, the US bank, with its four paltry branches, was more profitable than Fuji Bank, the country's largest.[11] Nor were the experiences limited to Citibank. Other foreign banks benefited from the monopoly over dollar loans.

Profitability bred complacency. Pressuring the Japanese government for additional authority or for additional branch licenses might have threatened the steady and lucrative stream of business. The foreign banking community therefore had little interest in disrupting the cozy state of affairs.

Through the 1970s, therefore, few foreign banks offered serious resistance to government imposed restraints. Employment policies showed the complacency. Consigned to foreign currency loans guaranteed by Japanese lenders, the banks had little need to understand the subtleties and intricacies of the Japanese market. They generally did not take the time to train adequately those stationed in the country. Few foreign employees spoke the language; few Japanese had positions in management, at least through the 1970s. Foreign staff also tended to rotate in and out of the country, often in an effort to minimize the time spent in a post far from the home office. The absence of continuity and the constant turnover meant that few banks had personnel with a sophisticated understanding of the Japanese financial markets.

Exceptions to the general rule did exist. Citibank, primarily under the tutelage of George Moore and Walter Wriston, gradually became less accepting of the constraints on operations. The bank was the first to dispense with loan guarantees by Japanese banks, to increase the number of branches in Japan, and to enter the securities industry. The bank also played a significant role in inducing the MoF to take the first steps toward the deregulation of interest rates and remains the only foreign bank in Japan aggressively pursuing a retail strategy.

Similarly, J. P. Morgan in a less public, but no less telling, fashion pushed against the regulatory boundaries. J. P. Morgan invested the time and resources to become the first US bank since 1953 to obtain a newly issued branch license. J. P. Morgan also became the first foreign bank to operate on a non-unionized basis and set in motion the process that culminated in the government granting nine foreign banks the authority to engage in trust activities, a nail in the coffin of compartmentalized banking in Japan.

Not coincidentally, both J. P. Morgan and Citibank ranked among the most successful foreign companies in Japan. They demonstrated that, contrary to conventional wisdom, a less deferential attitude toward government policies could yield benefits and would not necessarily arouse the hostility of Japanese regulators. Few other foreign financial institutions, however, shared these attitudes. When the monopoly on dollar loans evaporated in the

4

1970s as Japan's trade balance shifted into the black, the effect of the years of complacency became apparent. Most foreign banks found themselves with limited operations, declining profits, and few alternative sources of earnings.

In some respects, the ability of the J. P. Morgans and Citibanks to alter the status quo and succeed in Japan was remarkable, given the almost complete absence of support from their own government. For much of the post-war era, the United States had deliberately sanctioned the closed nature of the Japanese economy. The laws used by the Japanese to seal off various sectors of the economy were written during the occupation with the complete knowledge and approval of Allied personnel.[12]

Even afterwards, the geopolitical role of Japan as a bulwark of anti-communism in East Asia meant that the US Embassy had little interest in the pleas of businesses over economic concerns. The Treasury's attaché stationed in the Embassy in Japan had little regular contact with, or interest in, the banking sector. Insular policies and barriers to entry therefore remained in place at a time when Japan was weakest *vis-à-vis* the United States. Had efforts been made to open the markets, the Japanese government would have had a hard time resisting.

The US government only came out of its stupor after the trade imbalance became too large to ignore. Negotiations began over financial reform in 1983, although ironically the talks were driven less by the concerns of foreign financial institutions in Japan and more by a desire to redress the mis-valuation of the yen. The efforts led to the Yen/Dollar Accord, a comprehensive agreement committing the MoF to broad reform of the financial markets. Negotiated by officials within the Department of the Treasury, the agreement dealt with a range of issues and exacted commitments from the MoF on a variety of reforms, including specific timetables for implementation.

The talks leading to the Accord taught a number of lessons. They demonstrated the benefits of a united front between the private and public sectors. In advance of the discussions, negotiators in the Department of the Treasury consulted extensively with officials from financial institutions operating in Japan to understand better the Japanese markets and the barriers to operations. These contacts helped to refine the bargaining agenda and to facilitate the negotiation process. They also provided a psychological boost. Treasury entered the talks speaking for both Washington and the financial industry, making the calls for reform harder to ignore.

The talks also demonstrated that, if properly done, foreign influence could play an important and sometimes determinative role in the Japanese reform process. The Yen/Dollar Accord greatly accelerated the dismantling of the Japanese post-war financial system. The neat set of compartments that had existed since the occupation was permanently breached. Likewise interest rate deregulation eroded a critical source of government control of the Japanese financial markets.

The success did not occur because the United States commanded change. Instead, success resulted in large part because negotiators from the United States interjected themselves into an existing debate within Japan over financial reform. Sentiment for reform had already arisen in Japan but the requisite consensus remained stymied, within both the financial community and the MoF. US efforts helped break the impasse.

Negotiators in the yen/dollar process focused primarily on reforms supported by segments of the Japanese financial community. They also showed sensitivity to the Japanese policy making process by involving the entire upper echelon of the MoF in the negotiations and by involving high-ranking politicians from the Liberal Democratic Party in the process. Success could be seen from the subtle but unmistakable reaction within Japan. Foreign pressure became part of the process. Interest groups in the private sector and the Japanese bureaucracy recognized the potential of the foreign influence and effectively used it to achieve their own agenda.

The lessons learned and influence obtained, however, did not last. Following execution of the Yen/Dollar Accord in 1984, officials from the Department of the Treasury continued to meet, at least annually, with their counterparts in the MoF to discuss the ongoing process of reform. The efforts reflected little understanding of the domestic reform process within Japan. Unfocused, they tended to emphasize symptoms rather than causes. Time and time again, negotiators discovered that, even after the Japanese had removed an offending provision, little in fact had changed. Rather than illustrate the recalcitrant nature of the Japanese government, the scenario demonstrated weaknesses in the bargaining approach of the United States.

This could be seen most clearly from the emphasis on greater "transparency." Treasury negotiators insisted that the MoF reduce policies to writing as a way of making the markets more open. The approach, however, reflected a fundamental misunderstanding of the MoF's role in the financial markets. As long as bureaucrats retained their interventionist approach toward financial regulation, banks would continue to accept Ministry "advice" no matter how much was "written down."

Effectiveness also fell as bureaucratic turf wars erupted in Washington. Highly territorial, the Department of the Treasury went to great lengths to prevent other agencies, particularly the Office of the United States Trade Representative (USTR), from having any role in the process. Preserving territory sometimes became more important than achieving results. Maintenance of the monopoly also had a psychological effect. By excluding other agencies, Treasury officials could not, in the talks, represent that they spoke for a united executive branch.

Nor could they represent that they spoke for the banking community. By the late 1980s, industry support for the efforts had slipped. Calls for more open markets lost appeal. Competition in Japan was already difficult; free markets would simply make matters worse. Moreover, Treasury officials emphasized macroeconomic issues and had little interest in the specific concerns or problems of particular banks. With the interests of the private sector and government diverging, relations between Treasury officials and bankers in Japan suffered.

An analysis of the history of post-war banking operations in Japan, therefore, demonstrates that the foreign financial community – both governments and banks – bears much of the responsibility for the present state of affairs in Japan. This conclusion has significant implications. Facilitating foreign banking operations requires more than pressure on, and changes by, the Japanese. Much must also change within the foreign financial community.

Foreign banks do continue to suffer constraints on operations. The remaining barriers are subtle, however. The most obvious have long since been eliminated. Foreign banks now have access to the government bond syndicate and an adequate supply of yen. They can operate trust banks and, if Citibank is any indication, can open additional branches with little difficulty. Acquiring a Japanese bank is no longer sacrosanct. The MoF in the late 1980s even tried to induce a foreign financial institution to buy a bank.

The primary problem today concerns the system of regulation. The MoF continues to implement policy decisions through informal guidance. The system of guidance itself is not the concern. Most sophisticated foreign banks in Japan have long ago learned to tap into the Ministry's network. Indeed, those with the right contacts consider the Japanese financial system more open and information more accessible than in the United States. Instead, the principal problem arises out of the MoF's continued insistence that anything new or innovative go through what amounts to a lengthy and sometimes difficult vetting process.

The need for preclearance applies to all banks in Japan, domestic and foreign. The approach, however, disproportionately affects foreign banks. Lacking the relationships with most of corporate Japan, they compete primarily by offering services not otherwise available. Having to clear new practices or products through the Ministry, innovative financial institutions incur delay and lost opportunity. Moreover, MoF officials often obtain the opinion of other bankers (particularly Japanese but sometimes foreign bankers) before approving a practice. This effectively telegraphs the innovation to the entire market, sometimes even before regulatory approval occurs.

Changing an entire regulatory approach represents a seemingly intractable task. Bureaucracies everywhere do not readily give up authority. Yet opportunities exist. The MoF has recently been undergoing an identity crisis of sorts. For most of the post-war era, the MoF's interventionist policies were supported by a broad consensus within Japan. Banks benefited through guaranteed profits. Consumers benefitted indirectly through double-digit economic growth.

The fall off in economic growth, the collapse of the stock markets, the growing financial problems of Japanese banks, and the recent scandals involving compensation paid by Japanese securities companies to certain corporate clients for losses in the stock market, have all raised questions within Japan about the existing system of regulation. The scandals in particular illustrate how the system has been contorted to help the largest companies at the expense of small investors.

With the fracturing of the historical consensus over the MoF's role in the financial markets, a new consensus will gradually emerge. Political upheavals, particularly the ousting of the Liberal Democratic Party in the summer of 1993, will hasten the process. The opportunity therefore exists to influence financial reform and to encourage a more market oriented, less interventionist, approach toward regulation.

Yet before this can occur, changes must take place outside of Japan: changes in the attitudes of both the banking community and government officials. The banking community needs to adopt a less accepting stance toward limitations imposed by the Japanese government. Opposing even small barriers can have a disproportionate impact on the regulatory system. Citibank's decision in the late 1980s to break ranks and advertise rates paid on deposits conflicted with existing rules and Ministry guidance. A seemingly small matter, greater freedom to advertise particularly benefited innovative (read foreign) banks.

Standing alone, a more aggressive attitude by the banking community will not be enough. The banks must also devote far greater effort to training, especially language, and to continuity. They also need to know that their efforts will be supported. Foreign governments, particularly the US government, can only succeed if they act in conjunction with the private sector. Both groups must develop a consensus on the direction of reform. Within that consensus, the efforts of the foreign banking community needs to know that efforts to cast off Ministry interference must be promoted by active, aggressive government policies.

Government negotiators also need to have greater understanding of the domestic reform process within Japan. The efforts have the best chance of succeeding when they weigh in on issues already supported by Japanese constituencies. Historically, that has meant a segment of the banking community. Increasingly, however, reform proposals will also appeal to consumers, whether corporate or individual.

To bring these interest groups into the equation requires a restructuring of the negotiation process between the United States and Japan. Talks over financial reform currently take place between officials of the MoF and the Department of the Treasury. Concerned primarily with the financial community, the MoF has little incentive to adopt pro-consumer policies antagonistic toward interest groups within its regulatory bailiwick. The talks, therefore, need to be expanded in a way that ensures broader representation of interest groups within Japan.

Achieving this goal, however, requires resolution of the bureaucratic squabbles within the US government. Treasury has jealously maintained a monopoly over international financial talks. By eliminating the monopoly and giving other agencies a role – particularly the USTR – US negotiators would obtain a strengthened bargaining posture and would ensure comparable expansion on the Japanese side. That would almost certainly involve the entry of the Ministry of International Trade and Industry into the process, the closest thing to a corporate/consumer oriented ministry in Japan.

All of this suggests some level of foreign responsibility for the trade row with Japan and the need for the United States to get its own house in order. These represent more productive avenues rather than focusing exclusively on perceived Japanese recalcitrance and the need for punitive trade measures.

2

ENTRY AND OCCUPATION

Foreign banks have a long but limited history in Japan. Before the Second World War, a few British and Dutch banks, as well as a French colonial bank, had pre-war outposts. From the United States, only Citibank, with offices in four cities, had significant operations in the country.

Typical of the times, pre-war activities were limited affairs. The banks did little more than engage in trade finance, with minimal involvement in the local economy. Citibank specifically counseled employees against competing with local banks in the apparent hope that good relations would lead to a steady stream of business referrals.

The staid existence came to an end with the Second World War. From 1945 through 1952, Japan was obliged to cede authority over the financial system to allied officials. The Supreme Commander of the Allied Powers (SCAP) allowed a dozen foreign banks into the country, including four from the United States: Citibank, Bank of America, Chase, and American Express. By the end of the occupation, the US banks had displaced their British counterparts as the dominant foreign financial institutions in the country.

The influx of banks represented an exception to SCAP's usual approach toward foreign investment. In general, occupation officials kept the country hermetically sealed and foreign business interests out, with businessmen not even allowed into the country until July 1947. Foreign banks were treated differently largely for reasons of administrative convenience. They were needed for a variety of occupation related functions, including the handling of SCAP funds, the selling of military script, and the conversion of yen to dollars. In the early years, therefore, foreign banks amounted to little more than supplicants of the military, performing necessary banking functions for occupation officials.

The role, however, quickly evolved. The banks agitated for increased authority and, to a limited degree, SCAP complied. As the occupation progressed, SCAP officials realized the importance of trade to economic recovery. Foreign, particularly US, banks became the source of credit that allowed Japanese companies to finance trade. The banks, therefore, played a critical role in the economic revival of the country.

Foreign banks, however, never received complete freedom to operate in the domestic economy. Occupation officials carefully kept the banks from competing directly with Japanese banks. SCAP did so by issuing licenses that limited the ability of the foreign banking community to accept yen deposits and make yen loans. When the Ministry of Finance (MoF) regained control over the financial system, the restrictions were largely retained. The limitations, however, received little criticism from the US banking community. They were content with their lucrative but limited lot.

HISTORICAL OVERVIEW

Foreign banks had a long history in Japan. The British established a foothold before the turn of the century. The Hong Kong & Shanghai Bank sent agents to Yokohama in 1865 and opened a full fledged branch a year later. The bank expanded to Kobe and Nagasaki and finally, in 1924, to Tokyo. Chartered Bank became the second British bank to open in Japan, with a Yokohama branch in 1880.

US banks took longer to realize the importance of international operations in general and Japan in particular. Although a US bank opened an overseas branch in 1887, widespread international expansion did not occur until shortly after the turn of the century. The International Banking Corporation (IBC) opened a number of branches throughout Asia, including one in Yokohama in October 1902, the first US branch in Japan. Citibank acquired the IBC in 1915, providing an immediate network of Asian branches. By 1926, Citibank had branches in four Japanese cities: Yokohama, Kobe, Tokyo, and Osaka.[1] Operations were lucrative. In 1929, loan volume in Japan ranked fourth among all of Citibank's foreign branches, exceeded only by Cuba, China, and the United Kingdom.

Citibank represented the only US bank with a significant presence in the country. American Express opened a travel agency in Yokohama in 1917 and, for a brief time, used the office for banking operations. The office was destroyed in 1923 following the Great Earthquake. Although reopened as a travel office two years later, banking operations ceased. Other banks also temporarily opened in Japan, with only Citibank retaining a permanent presence.

In general, foreign branches had little involvement in Japan's domestic economy, although Citibank's office in Osaka did an extensive business with local textile companies.[2] Instead, the offices primarily serviced the needs of foreign corporations. Branches in commercial cities such as Yokohama and Kobe were heavily involved in import–export financing and foreign exchange activity.

Competition in the local economy was specifically discouraged, a policy designed to avoid the enmity of the indigenous banking community.

11

Once a branch manager has the local bankers against him it would be far better for him to close up shop and go home, and by doing so he would probably save money for his bank. For, if he is unable to get the friendly advice of the local bankers and that of the members of the local business community who know the field far better than he does, he becomes useless as a source of information for his head-office and clients at home, and, by reason of being out of touch, he is almost certain to cause this institution actual loss.[3]

Citibank specifically emphasized that the policy "of cooperating instead of competing with the large [local] banks will, of course, be strictly adhered to . . . ."[4] The absence of domestic activity meant that foreign and Japanese financial institutions had little need to interact and largely operated in separate domains.

Not all of the limitations on domestic business were self induced. Some emanated from government policies. By Imperial Ordinance, foreign banks were made to acquire and hold a certain amount of government bonds. They were prohibited, however, from acquiring debentures issued by Japanese corporations.[5]

The domestic limitations did not prevent fierce competition for business from foreign companies operating in the country. Citibank actively tried to lure clients away from the two British banks in Japan, the Hong Kong & Shanghai Bank and Chartered Bank, causing one official of a British bank to observe: "I don't like their methods. They are always ready to poach or spoil their neighbors but when left with the body they are too scared to handle it."[6]

While foreign operations proved profitable, they could not withstand the growing political instability in the region. By the late 1930s, the Japanese government had imposed restrictions on foreign banks in an effort to force them out of the country. In April 1941, Citibank's Osaka branch closed. Three months later, Japan froze all US assets, essentially eliminating Citibank's business. Operations in Yokohama and Kobe ceased shortly afterwards.

The Tokyo branch, however, remained open, prepared to do business if the difficulties between the two countries receded. In early December, the US Ambassador to Japan advised remaining personnel to leave the country. The manager of the Japanese offices, Jack Curtis, left the country on December 3, with only a skeletal crew remaining. The bombing of Pearl Harbor five days later effectively put an end to all operations.

THE OCCUPATION

With the onset of the war, everything changed. The pre-war foreign banking community had essentially been evicted, their operations halted.[7] When the conflict ended, opportunity existed for those with the foresight to see the advantages in returning to the country, something that required considerable

12

vision given the existing devastation. As hindsight subsequently made clear, the occupation represented a briefly opened window. As long as allied officials rather than the MoF controlled the financial system, foreign banks could get in. Once control reverted back, the door slammed shut.

The occupation descends

The war ended on August 15, 1945. Speaking for the first time on radio, the Emperor acknowledged that "the war situation [had] developed not necessarily to Japan's advantage" and agreed to an unconditional surrender. US forces under the command of SCAP entered the country shortly afterwards and the occupation began. They would not depart for seven years.

Military forces initially disclaimed responsibility for the economic recovery of Japan. As the difficult conditions became clear, however, that attitude began to change. Economically prostrate, Japan suffered from housing shortages and inadequate supplies of food and coal. Unemployment increased with the disbanding of the military, the closing of munitions plants, and the repatriation of persons from a defunct empire. In the economic sphere, ensuring a minimal level of sustenance became the order of the day.

Little was left of downtown Tokyo except the area bordering the Imperial Palace. One observer described the area as a sea of chimneys. Neighboring government buildings had been spared and were taken over by occupation officials. On September 11, officials requisitioned the MoF building in Kasumigaseki and gave Ministry officials three days to move out. SCAP officials moved in on September 15. The MoF had to find new space and ultimately settled for Yotsuya Primary School, a rickety wooden building.

Oversight of the financial sector fell to the Economic and Scientific Section (ESS) of SCAP, specifically the Finance Division. Within the Finance Division, the Money and Banking Branch carried the laboring oar, although others participated. ESS had responsibility for oversight of economics, labor, finance, and science and included "[a]ll of industry, foreign trade, price control, rationing, antitrust activities, and economic statistics . . . . "[8]

With respect to banking, however, the ESS had relatively constrained authority. The ESS was instructed to "[c]lose all banks and other financial institutions whose paramount purpose has been financing of war production or control of financial resources of occupied territories."[9] Military officials could shut down other banks, but "only for purposes of introducing control, removing objectionable personnel or taking measures connected with blocking [the] program, . . . " and were instructed to "re-open these banks as promptly as possible . . . ." Otherwise, the Section was to take "no steps to maintain, strengthen, or operate Japanese financial structure except insofar as may be necessary for achievement of provisions of this directive."[10]

Officials quickly took control of the financial sector, with the effect felt almost immediately. By memorandum dated September 30, 1945, allied forces announced the closing of a raft of overseas and special banks with wartime functions.[11] The Japanese government received instructions to "immediately close and not allow to reopen" the designated institutions. The principal officers were to be "discharge[d] and summarily remove[d] from office . . . ."[12] The MoF had to "present at the earliest possible date proposals for the liquidation of all closed institutions,"[13] with the Bank of Japan ultimately overseeing the process.

The decision was dramatized by the method used to implement the closings. After the end of the business day, military personnel swiftly occupied 21 financial institutions in Japan, including the Bank of Taiwan, the Bank of Chosen (Korea), the Hypothec Bank, the Yokohama Specie Bank, and the only two foreign banks remaining in the country. The action occurred without warning; employees were ordered out of the building without time to clear their desks. The occupying forces also prohibited overseas communication absent approval, cutting off contact with correspondent banks and branches located abroad. With one swift act, international operations of Japanese banks ceased.

Citibank returns

Citibank began taking steps to regain entry to the country almost contemporaneously with the beginning of the occupation. In September, bank officials petitioned Washington for permission to reopen the closed Tokyo branch.[14] The response was indicative. While acknowledging that the Treasury and War Departments had no objections, a decision was "premature" pending consideration by General MacArthur. "It is contemplated that General MacArthur will be queried within the next month as to his views on the subject and further advice will be given to you at that time."[15] In other words, the reopening was up to the occupation officials in Japan. MacArthur apparently had no objection. SCAP cabled to Washington in October seeking permission for Citibank "to resume operations [in Tokyo] as soon as possible."[16]

Unwilling to wait for official approval, Leo Chamberlain, who had managed the Tokyo office before the war and had been interned during the early years of the conflict, managed to get back into the country in December of 1945; no small feat.[17] Civilians were generally barred from Japan and no commercial airline flights had yet begun service, although Northwest and Pan Am eventually would. Chamberlain used the need to repossess bank assets from the pre-war branch as the rationale for returning to Tokyo.

Once there, Chamberlain began to "renew old acquaintances and [keep] informed on the progress of the occupational program and the ultimate return of Japan to civil government and international trade."[18] With the assimilated rank of lieutenant general, Chamberlain had access to military officials and considerable latitude to operate. All of this allowed Citibank to

14

get an edge on the other US financial institutions and to hold it throughout the occupation.

Chamberlain was not the only Citibank official in the country. The bank's international expertise represented a rare and valuable commodity. Former Citibank officials held a host of sensitive positions in the finance and banking sections of SCAP, something that would raise eyebrows and even lead to allegations of favoritism. Charles F. Thomas, a former manager of Citibank's Tokyo branch, became the Chief of the Finance Division in the ESS of SCAP, the unit responsible for administrative oversight of financial institutions. A successor as head of the Finance Division, Walter LeCount, came from the bank's Far East Division. Richard Marlow, who served as the Chief of the Banking Operations Branch within ESS and eventually became the controller for SCAP, also had worked for the bank.[19]

The close connection between Citibank and SCAP would prove nettlesome. The relationship created at least the appearance of a conflict of interest. Allegations were in fact made of possible "collusion between Staff members of the Economic and Scientific Section and [Citibank] . . . as a result of past and possible future affiliations with the bank."[20] Nothing apparently came of the charges although the War Department recommended that, for certain actions, the Finance Division obtain "review by an expert not officially associated with SCAP."[21] SCAP officials remained concerned with the issue throughout the occupation.

Given these close connections and the perception of favoritism toward US banks, Citibank's efforts to obtain a branch license from SCAP took on a political tone.

> If the plan . . . to permit the opening of a branch of [Citibank] in Tokyo to perform certain special functions for the American Army of Occupation is carried into effect without granting similar permission to banks of others of the United Nations, it is certain that some of our Allies, particularly Britain, will be most suspicious of our motives and intentions. We should be open to the accusation that we are utilizing our occupation of Japan to promote our own financial and commercial interests, while denying similar opportunities to our Allies.[22]

To address these concerns, SCAP agreed to grant Citibank a license but expressly invited other banks to apply for similar status.[23]

Granting the license also forced SCAP to come to terms with the operating authority of foreign banks within Japan. Occupation officials were concerned with the reaction of the Japanese to the sudden influx of foreign competition. Entry could also stunt the development of domestic banks. The license issued to Citibank, therefore, reflected these concerns.

The license prohibited any activity that might bring the bank into competition with Japanese financial institutions. Specifically, the bank could not "engage in any ordinary commercial banking activities . . . . " Operations were limited "solely to services related to . . . occupation needs . . . . " They included currency conversions, safekeeping services, and operation as a depository for funds of the United States, for dollars held by military personnel, and for yen arising from "[a]n official nature" or from non-profit organizations "such as those of [the] American Council of Churches."[24]

SCAP's decision to approve the Citibank license had nothing to do with liberalization of the financial system or an opening of the market to foreign penetration. Quite the contrary. The decision was a response to administrative expediency. SCAP received operating funds from the United States and needed a depository in Japan. Soldiers had to convert dollars into yen, and vice versa, cash checks, and make deposits. Someone had to sell, accept, and count military and trader script. Citibank did all of this, acting as a depository and remitting funds back to the United States. Having the bank physically on hand in Japan simply made things easier.

With SCAP's approval given, Citibank's Board of Directors adopted the appropriate resolution authorizing the opening of the branch and the bank began operating in July 1946. To mark the occasion, Douglas MacArthur and his wife opened the first account.[25] The branch had a staff of four US and 70 Japanese employees, many of whom worked for the bank prior to the war.[26]

Bank of America and Chase

Unlike the pre-war days, however, Citibank no longer retained a monopoly on US operations in Japan. The bank's re-entry piqued the curiosity of two other banking giants, Bank of America and Chase. Neither had the Far East experience of Citibank. Chase had pre-war offices in Asia, including China and Hong Kong, but none in Japan. Bank of America had no Asian offices before the war. Nonetheless, they took a hard look at overseas banking opportunities, particularly those provided by military occupation, and liked what they saw. By late 1947, both were operating branches in Japan.

SCAP favored entry of other banks, something occasionally misconstrued as an invitation. Additional banks could provide additional administrative services. More importantly, however, SCAP had become increasingly aware of the need of banks to facilitate trade finance. A larger number of banks meant more sources of credit, something Japan desperately needed. Foreign banks, therefore, were poised to play a role in the revival of the Japanese economy.

Bank of America became the second foreign bank to enter Japan. Officials at the bank wrote to the Assistant Secretary of War in May 1947 requesting the authority to open a Tokyo branch. The bank was told to apply directly to the relevant theater commanders, although the request would be forwarded to the Far East Command with a request for "an early decision."[27]

The request, however, languished. The circumstances surrounding issuance of the license illustrated the importance of being on location. Those in the country found opportunities not otherwise apparent. That occurred in connection with the Bank of America license.

The bank had sent Tom Coughran to Manila to open a branch in that city. Before he left, headquarters in San Francisco had begun negotiating a loan to the Japanese government to be secured by gold in the vault of the Bank of Japan.[28] Coughran was told to go to Tokyo to complete the transaction. Once in Tokyo, he realized that the bank had an opportunity to acquire branch licenses, an opportunity that might disappear if the propitious moment passed. Seizing the moment and without authority from headquarters, Coughran applied for branch licenses for Tokyo, Yokohama, Kobe, and Osaka on a borrowed typewriter from SCAP. The Finance Division approved the applications "in a few days without any capital requirements."[29]

Contemporaneously, Chase began to agitate for a license. The bank received a license on July 31, nine days after Bank of America. The bank dispatched James Duddy to set up and manage the Tokyo branch. Arriving in Yokohama in September, he was greeted with a typhoon that, among other things, cut off communications with headquarters in New York.

Having received licenses almost simultaneously, Bank of America and Chase raced to be the next US bank to open in Japan. Coughran's efforts made the difference. Bank of America won the race by a mere 10 days, opening the office in November 1947. Success, however, came at a price. The California bank had rented an extremely cramped office from Mitsubishi Bank. Chase opened the following month, on December 1, with a staff of 17.[30]

All three of the banks now had branches in Japan. Chamberlain, with pre-war experience in Japan, oversaw Citibank's operations. Joseph Johnson, a former Citibank employee who had worked in Asia, managed Bank of America's facilities. James Duddy ran the Chase offices. Duddy was the only one without Citibank or pre-war Asian experience.

Logistical nightmares

Assignment to Tokyo represented no soft post. A war-torn country offered few amenities. Initially, "[b]illets and messing facilities . . ." were furnished by the military.[31] Those entering the country were searched for goods that could be sold on the black market. Saccharin, insulin, and similar products were often confiscated.[32]

US businessmen had to use dollar denominated script, rather than yen. Military script was blue and could be used in the post exchange. Trade script was white and could be used in special stores and hotels. The British had comparable script in pounds. Bank officials did a rousing business trading the currency. Access to script in pounds would buy a lamb dinner at the Marunouchi Hotel; dollars would provide hamburgers at the Teito.

The debilitated nature of the country presented US banks with immense

17

logistical problems. Post-war Japan had no system of public transportation, usually requiring the banks to buy managers a car. The country also suffered from an energy shortage. While trains ran, they conserved precious supplies of coal by forgoing heat. As one occupation official described, it was "miserable to travel."

Finding sufficient commercial space for a branch was usually the first hurdle. Much of Tokyo had been leveled and SCAP occupied most of what remained. Citibank's pre-war office in Tokyo survived intact, but fell into the hands of occupation officials. The situation was complicated by the inability of the foreign banks, at least initially, to hold title to property. In some cases, they acquired facilities but put title in the hands of a Japanese bank.[33]

The shortage of adequate space inevitably meant cramped quarters, often in less than ideal locations. As the first one in, Citibank received the best accommodation. The bank occupied facilities previously held by the Bank of Chosen (Korea), one of the financial institutions closed by the military during the first month of the occupation.[34] A five-storey concrete building located in the Marunouchi District and close to the Bank of Japan, the facilities were "well located in spacious premises . . . ."[35]

Nevertheless, space remained at a premium. The bank had to share the building with the Army Finance Office, and was primarily limited to one floor. To provide extra room, Citibank dispensed with the luxury of a two-storey open lobby and put in extra flooring.

Chase and Bank of America also wanted space in Marunouchi, the financial district.[36] As latecomers, they had a more difficult time. To open before Chase, Bank of America obtained well located but extremely compacted office space – a "splinter" that had been occupied by Mitsubishi Bank. The office was so small that the manager had to put his desk in the vault.

Efforts by American Express to open an office toward the end of the occupation almost foundered on the inability to locate adequate space. The first employee to arrive borrowed a desk at the Bank of America's Tokyo office. A tedious search turned up nothing. Only the intervention of the Industrial Bank of Japan resulted in location of an appropriate office for the bank. American Express, however, almost lost the space and the license following nitpicking from the home office over the terms of the lease.

Obtaining adequate staff, particularly with sufficient understanding of English, also proved difficult. As one bank official wrote: "Japanese girl typists of any English are scarce and any Japanese stenographer is almost out of question. I am trying to get the services of a dependent wife, part-time if necessary. Time must hang heavy on the hands of some of them who would like to do something useful and make a few extra dollars . . . ."[37] Only Citibank among the US banks had a cadre of trained personnel from the pre-war days, although many had died in the conflict. The other banks had to make do, often with employees borrowed from Japanese banks.

Hiring was also impaired by the prevailing and horrendous economic

18

conditions in the early years of the occupation. As one observer from a US bank described:

> [L]iving quarters of so many of the Japanese have been wiped out and they must travel great distances – some two hours or more each way to and from home and their trains are crowded at all hours worse than any subway you could imagine – their food is expensive and scarce, so that absences are frequent – they faint and have weak spells in the office. All electricity is turned off in some Japanese sections of the city every night at 8:00 p.m. so that they must be home, fed and in bed by that time. Even some of the Japanese bank officers to whom I talked lived in these circumstances with several families and crowded quarters.[38]

The banks could not ignore the conditions. Employees would often buy sugar or soap at SCAP facilities for bargaining with farmers in the countryside. They would return with fresh vegetables and give them to the Japanese staff.

The problems did not end with the location of office space and adequate personnel. The mundane but necessary accoutrements – office furniture for one – presented headaches. With no manufacturers in Japan, materials sometimes had to be borrowed from Japanese banks. What could not be purchased or borrowed had to be imported. Everything from erasers to paper clips to automobiles were shipped in, literally, from the United States.

The difficulties seemed never-ending. Communications were another problem area. Mail took more than a week.[39] The early branches had no phones. They would contact headquarters in the United States primarily by mail or military cable.[40] Although phone lines existed, they were cumbersome and hard to use. Bank officials had to make an appointment for an overseas call, typically for the following day. Invariably the time periods would slip, forcing bank officials to spend a significant portion of the day waiting. Phones were not, therefore, a primary means of communicating with home offices in the United States.

The difficulties in communicating sometimes worked to the advantage of those in Japan. Meddling from headquarters was correspondingly harder, resulting in greater autonomy for the branches. In his swing through Japan in 1947, Tom Coughran of Bank of America used communication problems as the excuse for not first asking permission from San Francisco before applying for branch licenses. Had he done so, an answer may not have been forthcoming until the opportunity to obtain the licenses had passed.

Finally, the banks needed housing for employees. In general, civilians stayed at the "trader hotels," the Teito and the Tokyo, both converted office buildings. They had begun operation in July 1947 and were designed to accommodate visiting businessmen. With space in short supply, single travelers often had to share rooms. Civilians paid $10 per night, including meals.

The hotels were operated by the military, and SCAP limited stay to 60 days.

Employees therefore needed a more permanent abode. In renting or buying houses, the US banks again confronted a shortage of adequate space. Houses had been either destroyed or appropriated by SCAP. During those early days, Joseph Johnson, the branch manager of Bank of America, slept in the branch office. All three of the banks eventually acquired property in Tokyo, something that would prove to be an outstanding long-term investment.[41] A house purchased during the occupation by the Bank of America would net the financial institution an enormous cash infusion during its deep financial crisis in the 1980s.[42]

Bank expansion

After establishing footholds, the three banks gradually expanded their branch network. Next to Tokyo, Osaka was the most popular destination. The old commercial center of Japan, the city remained the spiritual if not the physical center of a number of companies and banks. Citibank opened a branch in Osaka in October 1947, Chase in March 1949.[43] Bank of America ultimately did the same, completing the hat-trick in 1952.

Citibank also opened offices in Yokohama and Nagoya; Bank of America in Yokohama and Kobe.[44] These cities were shipping centers, natural locations for branches specializing in trade finance. Yokohama had been the most active and profitable pre-war branch in Japan. With the advent of air cargo, however, the cities did not regain their primacy as centers for Japanese trade. Still, they seemed an important source of business and an attractive place for additional offices.

Citibank had equivocated over the branches in Kobe and Yokohama, obtaining approval from the Federal Reserve Board to open but letting the authority lapse after determining that the country's economic development had not advanced sufficiently. The bank reversed course when it learned that Bank of America intended to open in the two cities. Citibank was not about to cede those markets to a competitor.[45]

Other than these three banks, American Express was the only other US financial institution to show serious interest in opening a branch in Japan. Early efforts, however, were discouraged. Military officials considered the market saturated; overbanked.[46] SCAP encouraged an American Express travel office but not a bank branch. American Express eventually received a license from the military to operate a banking facility at Misawa Air Base in February 1952, becoming the fourth US bank to open an office in Japan. The company obtained a domestic banking license from the MoF the following year, after the occupation ended.

US banks were not the only ones to open branches in Japan. A number of foreign banks also received licenses from SCAP, a decision of sufficient importance to require concurrence from Washington. In addition to those from the United States, SCAP authorized entry of banks from Great Britain,

France, Holland, and China.[47] Moreover, to avoid the appearance of preferential treatment, SCAP maintained accounts at all of them.

The relationship between SCAP and the banks generally remained harmonious, although conflicts occasionally arose. SCAP regulation was sometimes burdensome. To control foreign exchange, allied officials required daily reports on the foreign exchange position of the banks. The banks did not receive paperwork requirements happily and internal SCAP documents indicate problems with compliance.[48]

EVOLVING ROLE OF FOREIGN BANKS

Bank officials initially spent a great deal of time performing administrative functions for, and working closely with, the military. Citibank, for example, stationed employees at the trader hotels to sell script, otherwise known as military payment certificates (MPCs). Handling the MPCs entailed the mind numbing task of counting and sorting the script for hours. The bank also had responsibility for disposing of used script, which had to be burned in the presence of two bank officials. In at least one instance, employees falsified the cremation certificate without destroying the currency. Bank staff learned of the incident when military police arrived to make arrests.

The banks played a critical role in SCAP's control of foreign currency transactions. Occupation officials had the authority "to establish and maintain 'effective controls with respect to all foreign exchange transactions.'"[49] Japanese citizens and companies, including banks, could not hold foreign currency. To control the exchange, SCAP relied on foreign banks as depositories for foreign funds. This enabled SCAP to exercise control without any involvement from the Japanese government, yet to do so consonant with Japanese law.[50]

Banks also assisted in monitoring foreign trade. Trade from each country had to balance at the end of the fiscal year, although in practice it rarely did. To facilitate administration, SCAP would run all imports and exports for a given country through one or a small number of foreign banks. In doing so, SCAP could readily determine the status of the trade balance at any given time.[51]

Proceeds from foreign trade were deposited in SCAP accounts at each bank. The Trust Fund account contained dollars earned through trade with the United States. The Commercial Account contained foreign exchange earned from exports, although not limited to dollars from the United States. SCAP opened account #1 at Citibank on July 31, 1947, and deposited proceeds from Australia for the purchase of raw silk.[52] It also opened accounts at other banks in an effort to share the business on a non-discriminatory basis.

In the early years of the occupation, therefore, foreign financial institutions seemed more like government post offices than private banks. They did little except perform administrative functions for SCAP. While the banks accepted deposits, their business was primarily limited to occupation and military officials. A small quantity of dollar loans were made but only to officers and other foreign personnel.

Unsatisfied with remaining an adjunct of the military, foreign banks constantly agitated for expanded authority. In June 1948, SCAP authorized foreign banks to act as agents for foreign nationals in the recovery and administration of assets owned before the war. The banks could also make yen loans to business organizations licensed by SCAP, engage in certain foreign currency transactions, and invest yen deposits in short-term government obligations. The following year, SCAP expanded the lending power of the US banks to include *dollar* loans to "private commercial" companies.[53]

The most significant expansion, however, concerned trade finance. By 1947, SCAP realized that the economy would not recover unless exports increased. The country needed other sources of dollars to pay for the raw materials required to manufacture finished goods. The US government had made clear that Japan could not expect increased aid. Lacking the funds to pay for the imports, the economy stagnated. Foreign banks could help by financing imports, but doing this required a broader license. By 1947, an internal SCAP authored report recommended the expansion of banking authority into trade finance, concluding that:

> foreign banks with recognized experience in foreign banking and with demonstrated ability to handle world-wide accounts, should be allowed to establish or re-establish branches in Japan for the purpose of providing banking services in connection with Japanese foreign trade; . . . SCAP should be authorized to license such banks to perform normal commercial and export–import banking services, subject only to limitations imposed by the availability of physical facilities and other relevant factors.[54]

The report also recommended that "authority be delegated SCAP to provide additional banking facilities as events and attending circumstances required, and to amend licenses to permit expanding functions to meet economic developments as will be effected in expanding foreign trade."[55] The new powers, however, came with limits. Banks still could not compete in the domestic economy and all trade related transactions remained subject to exchange controls.

Following issuance of the report, foreign banks received the authority to provide export related services in 1947; authority broadened the following year. Thereafter, foreign banks began to provide credits for trade finance. This sometimes took the form of a letter of credit backing up one provided by the Japanese bank (back to back letters) or a confirmation of the Japanese letter on the face of the document. In either case, exporters knew that US banks stood behind the Japanese letters of credit.

Under the system, a Japanese exporter provided the necessary documents to the authorized Japanese bank for payment. The Japanese bank forwarded the materials to the relevant foreign bank. Once the foreign bank received and credited the export proceeds to a SCAP Commercial Account, "the Japanese bank paid the yen equivalent to the seller."[56] Foreign banks, therefore, had a role in all exchange transactions and gave SCAP a mechanism for enforcing controls.

Occasionally, the financing was for specific projects. In June 1948, Chase, Citibank, and Bank of America provided a $60 million advance to finance the importation of low grade cotton to be used for manufacturing textiles. The three banks secured the loan against the finished goods. Congress subsequently created the Natural Fibers Revolving Fund to facilitate the importation of the cotton. The US banks issued the appropriate letters of credit for payment, with reimbursement coming from the Fund.[57]

For all of the authority, however, the banks still operated under considerable limitations. They were not permitted to compete head-to-head with Japanese banks or otherwise operate in the domestic economy. This was no big surprise. The SCAP licenses restricted deposit taking and yen loans. Unable to tap Japanese sources, the only significant source of yen deposits was foreign companies operating in Japan.

The Motion Picture Exchange Association constituted a major source of deposits for foreign banks. SCAP had licensed the Association to distribute films throughout Japan. The license provided that all payments would be in yen but the currency could not be used for investment or be converted into foreign exchange "for an indefinite period . . . . "[58] With few other leisure activities, the Association did an impressive business.

Unable to repatriate the profits, the Association had little choice but to leave the funds on deposit. This gave the banks a substantial and captive quantity of yen. Through most of the occupation, however, the banks could not make loans to domestic companies. Instead, they would typically sell the yen to the Bank of Japan for dollars, although after the occupation the funds were available for loans to foreign corporations doing business in Japan.

As the occupation started to wind down, SCAP began to contemplate the return of foreign exchange back to the Japanese government. Currency transactions were transferred in July 1951 to the newly created Foreign Exchange Control Board (FECB) which operated "under the general supervision of SCAP." The transfer reflected the gradual process of shifting responsibility to the Japanese government for financial and commercial matters. The government abolished the Board after the occupation ended, with the MoF absorbing the functions.

Following formation of the FECB, foreign banks continued to dominate the foreign trade area. Japanese financial institutions with foreign exchange had to deposit the funds in a foreign bank, only receiving the authority to hold US dollars in June 1952. With sizable SCAP deposits, foreign banks

23

could use the funds to provide credit to Japanese banks, much to their irritation.[59] The preeminent position, however, lasted only as long as MoF permitted. By the end of the occupation, the role of foreign banks had begun to evolve.

FOREIGN BANKS AND THE MINISTRY OF FINANCE

Efforts to further expand the licenses of foreign banks generated controversy. Washington was concerned about the impact of foreign competition on Japanese banks. Broader lending authority also threatened to expand credit, increasing inflation.[60] SCAP officials, in contrast, took the position that foreign banks were unlikely to compete effectively for deposits, a prescient observation. Corporate deposits went to Japanese banks providing loans while retail deposits were considered unattractive.[61]

Expansion of banking authority posed a jurisdictional problem. SCAP officials had taken the position that foreign banks performing occupation and trade functions were subject only to SCAP oversight. As activities expanded, however, that ceased to be the case. With the winding down of the occupation, SCAP began to consider returning supervisory responsibility to the Japanese government.

Foreign banks had maintained contact with the Japanese government since entering the country. Although licensed by the occupation, the banks almost from the beginning took a solicitous attitude toward the Bank of Japan and the MoF. Doing so was politic. Eventually the occupation would end and control would revert back to the Japanese government. The meetings, however, could not escape reminders of the ubiquitous presence of the military. Visits with the Finance Minister or Governor of the Bank of Japan had to have a SCAP official present.[62]

By the summer of 1949, SCAP decided to bring foreign banks "fully within the purview of Japanese laws and regulations."[63] That meant returning control to the MoF. Doing so, however, caused some concern. Occupation officials knew full well that the MoF exercised broad discretion over the financial system. As the Edwards Mission in 1946 had described:

> Japanese financial laws follow a common pattern. They prescribe certain general standards with respect to the institutions they purport to regulate and vest absolute power in the Minister of Finance to define, alter, and enforce the standards. In reality, they place no serious limitations upon the Minister's power.[64]

The high level of discretion concerned occupation officials and reform proposals designed to limit the authority surfaced. A SCAP inspired effort called for the removal of banking oversight from the MoF, giving it to a newly created Board of Banking and Finance.[65] The proposals also sought to minimize government discretion through the adoption of more explicit standards, an increase in capital requirements, and heightened shareholder control.

The radical proposal was not well received. Japanese officials objected, particularly the MoF. The Ministry rightfully saw the reforms as limitations on its authority.[66] Officials at the Bank of Japan also reacted negatively, viewing the proposals as impractical. Ironically, however, the proposals died mostly as a result of opposition from the United States. Officials in Washington expressed hesitancy about the apparent attempt to transfer the Federal Reserve System in the United States to Japan without "adequate consideration of the many fundamental differences which exist between the two countries and with little regard to Japanese customs and psychology."[67] Questions were also raised over the country's ability to supply the capital contemplated by the proposed legislation.

With the mixed support from US officials, opposition within the Japanese government, and the distractions of inducing economic recovery, the reform effort went nowhere. At the same time, SCAP became embroiled in the battle against inflation and seemed to lose interest in comprehensive reform of the financial system. A 1949 amendment to the Bank of Japan Law did create a Policy Board. Intended to weaken the Central Bank, the Board received some control over credit policy, including the authority to determine interest rates for loans from the central bank and maximum interest rates to be charged by financial institutions.

Somewhat of a disappointment,[68] the Policy Board was intended to be only "an interim measure," until a more favorable atmosphere for comprehensive reform could develop.[69] Occupation officials therefore continued to favor legislation designed to restrict the discretion of the Japanese government over banks.[70] More general reform, however, was never implemented, despite representations that legislation would be completed "within the near future, and made ready for presentation to the Diet at the appropriate time."[71]

Without reform, the MoF would emerge from the occupation with considerable discretion over the financial system. As foreign banks came under Japanese oversight, they suddenly found themselves subject to the broad administrative discretion of the MoF. In transferring authority, SCAP officials naively anticipated that foreign and domestic banks in Japan would receive "as near comparable and non-discriminatory" treatment as possible.[72] The licenses issued by the MoF suggested equal treatment, simply stating that the branch could "operate a banking business by observing the banking law, relative procedure of the banking law . . . and other laws, ordinances and regulations."[73] Once the occupation ended, however, foreign banks would be subjected to very different treatment.

US officials did retain exclusive control over banks on military facilities. Under the Administrative Agreement between the two countries, the Treasury reserved the right to designate banks on military bases without MoF approval. Banks with a military license were not subject to foreign exchange controls or other Japanese domestic requirements.[74] The result was a two-tiered banking system, with domestic branches subject to the oversight of the MoF and military facilities subject to SCAP and later the Treasury, to some degree creating regulatory duplication.[75]

With licenses to operate in the domestic market, foreign banks became subject to the almost daily oversight of the central bank. Overseeing foreign exchange trading, the Bank of Japan had to pre-approve any loan that required conversion of dollars into yen. The foreign banks also confronted limits on volume and trading in foreign exchange.

Early oversight caused some unexpected problems. The personnel within the liaison office at the MoF were chosen in part because of linguistic ability: they could speak English. They were not, however, the same people devising rules and policies applicable to foreign banks. The result was often confusion. Instructions in Japanese were conveyed to the liaison personnel who would translate them into English. Questions and queries in English in turn had to be translated into Japanese and told to the policy people. Information was often lost in translation.

Foreign banks entering the country during the occupation never received freedom of action comparable with that held by their Japanese counterparts. Some did use the window provided during the occupation to establish a more pronounced foothold in Japan. Although gradually expanding their role in the country, they largely remained outside the conventional banking functions of deposit taking and yen lending to Japanese companies. Moreover, with the end of the occupation, the MoF had little interest in seeing an expanded role for these banks. The limited role and the small number of foreign entrants remained the rule for the next 20 years.

3

BEHIND THE SHOJI CURTAIN

With the end of the occupation, the United States was at its zenith. The country had the world's largest financial institutions and dominated international capital markets. Japan, in contrast, remained in a trough. The banks were weak, with little stature abroad.

Despite the pronounced imbalance, the Ministry of Finance (MoF) managed to marginalize the operations of foreign banks and limit their penetration into the domestic economy. It did so with hardly a protest from either the US government or the foreign banking community. At a time when the United States had the greatest latitude to pry open the markets and the Japanese government had the least ability to resist, nothing was done. The explanation is to be found in the method the MoF used to limit banking operations and the attitude of the US government toward economic issues.

Restrictions on bank operations took two forms. First, banks not already in the country were barred from entry. Once the MoF regained control of the financial system, a "shoji" or "rice paper" curtain descended. Only banks arriving under the auspices of the Supreme Commander of the Allied Powers (SCAP), many of which had been in the country before the war, were able to operate in Japan. A few anomalous situations aside, no foreign bank from an industrial country obtained a new license to enter the country until 1968.

Second, those lucky enough to have gained entry had little freedom to maneuver. Consistent with the highly compartmentalized system of banking, foreign banks were largely walled off from other categories of financial institutions. They could not sell securities, engage in trust activities, or issue debentures. To some degree, these were the same constraints imposed on most Japanese commercial banks. Foreign banks, however, were singled out for additional, unique treatment that made broad based activity in the Japanese market all but impossible.

The primary limitation was the deliberate denial of yen funding. To compete with Japanese banks for loans in the domestic economy, foreign banks needed a supply of yen. Practical or legal restraints effectively made accumulation of the necessary funds impossible.

The MoF compensated for these limitations by ceding to foreign banks a small but highly lucrative niche in the financial markets. Unable to raise sufficient funds in the country, corporate Japan had a desperate need for additional capital. Funds from abroad seemed an obvious source. Japanese banks, however, lacked the branch network and the creditworthiness to tap international capital markets. Foreign banks filled the breach. They provided funds and credit initially to Japanese banks and, eventually, to Japanese companies.

In bringing in the funds, foreign banks obtained essentially risk free, highly profitable business. Dollar loans and letters of credit carried attractive margins. They were also safe. Japanese banks guaranteed repayment, a promise implicitly backed by the government. With the guarantee, foreign banks had no need to assess or worry about the creditworthiness of a Japanese borrower.

The benefits of a monopoly on dollar loans therefore outweighed the costs of the restrictions on operations in the domestic financial markets. Foreign banks accepted the situation. Content with their prescribed niche, earning monopoly profits, the banks had little incentive to upset the status quo. Moreover, much of the business came through Japanese banks, placing a premium on the relationships. Competing directly for yen loans arguably would have made the relationships more difficult to maintain.

Involvement in the domestic markets also would have meant considerable change in the manner of doing business. Unlike the United States, stock markets in the immediate post-war period played an insignificant role in the capital raising process in Japan. With most of the funds coming from banks, this evolved into a system of lead banks, with each large company having a primary lender.[1] The lead bank relationship, however, carried considerable responsibility. In times of financial difficulty, banks were expected to provide additional loans and even management. US banks had little interest in these obligations. In general, they wanted the business but not the responsibilities.

At the most propitious time for foreign banks to become entrenched in the domestic market, therefore, they chose to sit comfortably on the sidelines, fat and happy. Even Citibank, at least through the early 1960s, saw its primary role as a banker's bank. As a long-term strategy for maintaining operations in Japan, the approach proved disastrous.

A NECESSARY EVIL

The MoF saw the foreign banking community as a mixed blessing. Unhindered operations within Japan represented a threat. The financial system resembled a Japanese garden, rigorously tended and artfully arranged, with each component contributing to a harmonious whole. Banks had been neatly divided both by source of funding and geography, something encouraged by SCAP during the occupation.[2]

Commercial (city and regional) banks could not raise long-term funds through the sale of debentures. Funds came almost entirely from deposits, with loans from other financial institutions and the Bank of Japan playing an important role. In contrast, the three long-term-credit banks received the authority to issue debentures and provided corporate Japan with financing for a more significant duration.[3] They were not, however, allowed to accept retail deposits.

Trust banks represented a third class of banks.[4] They raised funds neither through debentures nor, in significant amounts, through retail deposits.[5] Instead, the primary mechanism was the loan trust certificate, funds left with the bank for a term of three years at fixed interest rates. Only one city bank and seven trust banks had the power to manage and invest client funds, eliminating a source of profits for other institutions.

In addition to funding sources, geography played a role in the compartmentalization of the banking sector. Commercial banks were subdivided into city and regional (or "local") banks. Roughly equivalent to money center banks in the United States, city banks had the lion's share of deposits and loans. Operating primarily in the large urban centers, they represented the bank of choice for the largest Japanese companies. Regional banks, typically smaller, tended to operate in a single prefecture.[6] Often unable to find sufficient corporate borrowers, regional banks through most of the post-war era lent excess funds to cash starved city banks.

Finally, Article 65 of the Securities and Exchange Law prohibited commercial banks from selling securities, a function left to the emerging class of Japanese brokers. With origins traceable directly to comparable provisions in the United States, the ban meant that banks could not sell stocks or bonds for corporate clients.[7] The loss of this potential source of profits made the banks more dependent upon commercial lending and more susceptible to government control.

The operation and structure of the financial sector had one critical purpose: economic recovery. This meant raising and controlling the direction of capital. The MoF rationed funds and directed lending. Funds were funneled through banks to designated industries such as steel, fertilizer and shipbuilding. For funds to be properly directed, the MoF had to retain a tight grip over the financial system, with bank activities made consistent with the government's overall goal of managed growth. No step could be taken, no office opened, no significant policy adopted, without Ministry assent.

Foreign banks were no different. They also had their niche, their prescribed role in the compartmentalized financial system. With local supplies of capital inadequate, additional funds had to come from abroad. The level of economic growth depended in large part upon the amount of capital that could be raised overseas. Foreign banks provided the funds.

Foreign financial institutions, however, raised concerns not presented by Japanese banks. Less susceptible to government control, they constituted a huge exception to the tightly regulated financial sector. The same devices used to make Japanese banks conform to government policies were far less effective. With funds available from abroad, foreign banks were not dependent upon the discount window at the Bank of Japan. Uninterested in retail operations, the MoF's authority to approve or deny additional branch licenses caused little concern.[8]

Foreign banks, therefore, could not be counted upon to conform to government inspired policies. Moreover, dwarfing their Japanese counterparts, they represented formidable competitors and had the capacity to affect the continued growth and recovery of domestic financial institutions. For a government on a mission to protect and promote the fledgling financial system, unrestricted access was anathema.

Excluding foreign banks completely from Japan was not possible. For one thing, that would have generated a diplomatic donnybrook. Foreign suspicion of the Japanese had already delayed the country's entry into the General Agreement on Tariffs and Trade (GATT).[9] For another, they were necessary. Foreign banks provided much needed access to overseas capital. Domestic banks from a war-torn, defeated country lacked the capital and the creditworthiness to tap international markets. With Japanese industry starved for funds, foreign banks became a conduit for overseas financing.

To make the system work, the MoF wanted foreign banks to remain but with limited discretion. The Ministry succeeded by controlling access to yen funding. Denied an adequate supply of the currency, foreign banks could not compete directly with Japanese financial institutions for corporate loans and other conventional banking business. The government did this by restricting new branches, limiting on interbank borrowing, closing the discount window, and imposing swap ceilings.

Retail deposits, the most obvious source of funds, represented a non-starter. Foreign banks had an insufficient presence to access the market. Those with the most extensive network – Bank of America, Citibank, Chartered and Hong Kong & Shanghai – had only four branches each. No other foreign bank had more than two and the MoF was not about to allow further expansion. The denial not only affected the ability to raise yen but, with interest rate controls on deposits, foreclosed the cheapest source of funding.

Foreign banks did obtain deposits through compensating balances. In return for dollar loans, Japanese borrowers often had to keep a designated percentage of a loan in yen on deposit.[10] Because the deposits received little or no interest, they could be lent at great profit. Bank clients – particularly the small number of foreign companies operating in the country – also provided yen deposits. Neither source, however, proved sufficient to sustain a significant yen-based business.

30

Absent unusual circumstances foreign banks also could not borrow from the Bank of Japan. No law expressly barred the banks from taking advantage of the discount window; the government simply refused to make it available. To some degree, this put foreign banks on a par with most Japanese financial institutions. In the early post-occupation period, the Bank of Japan made extensive loans only to city banks; regional and other banks had limited access. The effect, however, was disproportionate. With no retail operations, closing of the discount window deprived foreign banks of the remaining source of low cost yen funds.

Limitations existed in the interbank market, although of a more subtle nature. Banks with a surplus of funds could make short-term secured loans to those with an inadequate supply. As a practical matter, regional, agricultural, and other banks located in non-urban areas tended to have an oversupply of deposits and were therefore net lenders in the market. City banks, in contrast, suffered a continuous shortage of funds and were net borrowers.

Loans were arranged by a small group of brokers, known as Tanshi brokers. They remained in contact with, and were susceptible to influence by, the Bank of Japan. The relationship was further solidified by the practice of former officials of the central bank routinely obtaining positions with the brokers upon retirement. The close relationship meant that the Bank of Japan could influence the availability of funds and the interest rates charged. Foreign branches seeking funds in the market often found them unavailable.

The interbank market had other limitations. The loans required collateral. With few assets in the country, foreign banks could borrow only relatively small amounts even if funds had been available. The market also represented a relatively expensive and short-term source of yen. Funds in the market carried the closest thing in Japan to a market rate, with brokerage fees added on top, and had a short maturity.

Given all of these limits, the most obvious source of funding was from offices outside the country. That avenue, however, was also severely constrained. Under the currency restrictions in place, the conversion of foreign currency into yen required government approval.[11] The MoF used the authority to impose limits on funds brought in from abroad. Known as "swap ceilings," each foreign bank received a limit on the amount that could be converted into yen.[12]

The situation with the Motion Picture Exchange Association illustrated the degree to which the Japanese government would go to dry up sources of yen for foreign banks. The Association had generated prodigious amounts of yen on movies shown during the occupation, a popular form of entertainment. SCAP, however, had prohibited conversion of profits into dollars. The Association therefore left the yen profits on deposit with US banks, which in turn lent the funds into the domestic economy.

When Japan regained control of the financial system, the MoF allowed the

31

Motion Picture Exchange Association to convert the profits into dollars and repatriate them to the United States. This was done despite the strain the conversion placed on the country's reserves. The MoF agreed to do so at least in part to eliminate supplies of yen and exercise "tighter control" over funding sources for foreign banks.

Without a sufficient supply of funds, foreign banks were in no position to make yen loans to Japanese companies, at least on a significant scale. The inability occurred at a time when Japanese companies were capital starved and probably would have overcome any hesitancy in dealing with foreign lenders. US banks therefore lost an opportunity to gain permanent relationships with Japanese companies, something that would subsequently loom in importance.

CAPITAL IMPORTERS

Foreign banks, like all Japanese banks, had a carefully prescribed niche in the financial system. They emerged as purveyors of dollars to a currency starved country. Japanese industry was desperate for capital. Factories had to be rebuilt and retooled, raw materials imported. The country needed dollars to pay for goods from abroad. These funds largely came into the country in the form of loans from foreign banks, although other institutions such as the World Bank also acted as an early source of loans.

The banks did more than lend and finance trade, however. They trained Japanese bankers, often bringing them to New York and rotating them through their operating departments. They also provided what amounted to emergency financing to the Japanese government when reserves fell to unacceptably low levels. In at least one very celebrated instance, the three largest US banks provided standby credits at a time when the country's reserves seemed about to disappear, a very public transaction that sent an important message to the international community about the viability and creditworthiness of Japan.

With the end of the occupation, Japanese banks began to open overseas offices, with the Bank of Tokyo leading the way. In September 1952, the Bank of Tokyo opened offices in Great Britain and the United States, with branches following in Hong Kong, Karachi, Bombay, and Calcutta.[13] Other large Japanese banks were also allowed to open international offices although on a much reduced scale.[14]

The banks, however, lacked the credit standing to raise the necessary quantity of dollars.[15] Even as late as the mid-1960s, the banks had little name recognition and limited credit. One Japanese banker remembered that, in order to obtain a line of credit from Chase in 1964, Mitsubishi had to provide deposits of equal amount.

Foreign banks, in contrast, had access to dollars. The decision to lend them to the Japanese, however, did not occur without controversy. The abnormal conditions caused by the occupation had created important and profitable sources of business for foreign banks. Troops needed servicing. SCAP deposited large sums with the foreign branches as, eventually, did the Foreign Exchange Control Board. The military controlled all trade and would run transactions through foreign banks.

With the end of the occupation, however, most of these activities disappeared. Moreover, as the MoF regained control over the financial sector, Japanese banks were allowed back into trade finance, ending a foreign monopoly. Foreign banks therefore had to make a transition from occupation to post-occupation banking. This meant looking to the Japanese market for business. As one US bank official noted:

[T]he return to normalcy of the Japanese business scene is going to materially reduce the earnings of our Japan branches. It is imperative that we develop new sources of business – both new clients and new sources. Competition will be severe. Japan is overbanked – there are 12 foreign banks there now as compared to four pre-war. It is extremely doubtful that there will be enough business for all. [The Bank] will have to devise sources of new business if it is to be one of the three or four to remain on the scene. It will have to take a place for itself in Japan, and to do so, it will have to conform to the banking standards accepted by the Japanese banks.[16]

They ultimately found an effective role providing international credit to Japanese banks and companies.

The role did not come easily, however. Banking officials in the home office had to be educated about the "unique" circumstances prevalent in Japan. Usual "sound" banking criteria were of little value. Japanese banks uniformly had unattractive balance sheets. Capital – the cushion that would ensure repayment of a bad loan – hardly existed. Loans to the banks, therefore, looked to be high risk affairs. Reliance upon conventional indices of financial health – capital ratios, profits, etc. – ignored the particular characteristics of Japanese companies and banks. Loans instead had to depend upon such factors as payment record, past experience, reputation, and size. Finally, the role of the government as ultimate guarantor had to be considered.

In addition the banks had to overcome the hesitancy to provide long-term funds. Until the late 1960s, banks saw themselves as purveyors of short-term funds, usually no more than six months. Japanese businesses, however, had to rebuild factories and make other capital investments. They needed the funds for more extended periods of time. With the advent of impact loans in the late 1950s, foreign banks overcame their resistance and began making loans with durations of more than one year.

The foreign banks with branches in Japan were the first to realize that the numbers did not tell the full story; recovery was under way. Nevertheless, bankers in Japan still had to do a sales job on loan committees back home to induce acceptance of the "unique" lending criteria. Only the most sophisticated banks were initially willing to accept the arguments. To limit risk, they usually set ceilings on the aggregate amount of exposure to all borrowers in Japan. Those banks in the country tended to have the greatest familiarity with the system and the highest exposure limits.

Foreign banks initially provided credit to Japanese financial institutions, particularly in the form of trade finance. Payment for goods was typically guaranteed by a letter of credit. Exporters to Japan had little faith in a letter of credit issued by a little known, financially weak Japanese bank. To provide sufficient assurance of payment, US banks would add their "chop" to the instrument, thereby confirming the letter and guaranteeing its repayment. This often involved notation on the surface of the document. The banks sometimes issued a back to back letter of credit, guaranteeing repayment in the event that funds were not provided under the initial letter.

Banker's acceptances represented another active area. Prevalent in trade finance, an acceptance amounted to a short-term loan to pay for imports. The bank would receive payment from the importer when the instrument matured, typically in 30–180 days. Exporters, however, often wanted immediate payment. US banks would honor the acceptance, discount it and resell the instruments. To facilitate negotiability in New York, US banks added their name to the document, for a fee.

As with other developments, the MoF's footprints were evident all over the area. Only approved companies could engage in trade finance. While theoretically negotiated by banks and companies, the Ministry controlled the terms of the banker's acceptances. This was particularly obvious in the mid-1960s when the MoF decreed that the duration of acceptances should increase from 90 to 120 days. Thereafter, Japanese banks uniformly sought acceptances from US banks of four months.

Foreign banks incurred little real risk for providing these services. Only if the Japanese importer and the Japanese bank failed would they not be repaid, unlikely events. Moreover, even in those circumstances, the Japanese government was expected to make good on the loans. As time progressed, Japanese banks obtained name recognition abroad and no longer needed the guarantees.

By the latter part of the 1950s, the activities of foreign banks began to change. First, competition for business developed. While foreign banks remained critical, those with offices in Japan no longer had a complete monopoly. Japanese banks began opening offices abroad, albeit slowly, with the Bank of Tokyo leading the way. The banks were able to create relationships with financial institutions in other locations, particularly New York.

Foreign banks within Japan provided the largest quantity of credit. Japanese banks, however, constantly sought other sources. After opening offices in the United States, they aggressively solicited other banks for business. By the late 1950s, banks such as J. P. Morgan, Chemical, Manufacturers, Bankers Trust, First Chicago, Wells Fargo, and Continental Illinois were extending credit to Japan. So were smaller financial institutions in the New York area such as the National Bank of North America.

Second, credit was no longer supplied solely to Japanese banks. Foreign financial institutions began making dollar loans *directly* to Japanese companies. Labeled "impact" loans, these transactions typically involved loans for general, rather than specific, purposes, usually with a duration of one to five years. Japanese banks made the introductions and guaranteed the loans. Although dollar denominated, the loans were typically converted into yen and used for expansion within Japan. The introduction of impact loans meant that foreign financial institutions dealt directly with corporate Japan.

The government could and did regulate the volume of impact loans as well as the terms. They could not be less than one year. Volume was strictly controlled, primarily through limits on the amount of dollars that could be converted into yen. The Bank of Japan also limited volume by restricting the amount that Japanese banks could guarantee. The limits allowed the government to ensure that a minimum supply of reserves was maintained.

Some of the funds for the loans, ironically, came from the Japanese government. The Bank of Japan used foreign financial institutions as depositories for dollar denominated reserves. Banks used the funds as collateral for letters of credit and other forms of credit extended to Japanese banks. In return for the deposits, however, foreign banks were expected to lend a multiple of the amount to Japanese banks and companies. When British banks failed to extend sufficient credit, the reserves were withdrawn and moved to more accommodating US banks.

Impact loans were essentially risk free. A Japanese bank always guaranteed the loan and, perforce, the company's creditworthiness. The guarantees were not accidental; the MoF required them. The guarantees ensured that Japan retained an impeccable credit rating. Moreover, a default on a non-guaranteed loan would have left the foreign bank in possession of the assets of a Japanese company. By requiring Japanese banks to make good on the loan, this was avoided. The MoF strictly controlled those eligible to borrow dollars, limiting them to a short list of companies.

The guarantees made lending by foreign banks a relatively painless affair. Foreign banks had no need to research extensively the company's financial condition, although a few did. They could count on Japanese banks guaranteeing repayment to perform the task. In the event of default, those banks had to step in and make good the loan.

The failure of Sanyo Special Steel in 1965 illustrated the safety of the loans. When the company defaulted on $11 million to Chartered Bank and Banque Bruxelles Lambert, the loans were repaid by the Japanese guarantors within 24 hours, well before they were legally required. This was not lost on the foreign banking community. Swift repayment reassured the international capital markets of the safety of lending to the Japanese, ensuring a continued flow of foreign bank loans.

Japanese banks solicited impact loans for their corporate clients, particularly during periods of tight money. Whenever reserves came under pressure, the Bank of Japan engaged in *hikishime*, or squeezing. This entailed the use of window guidance to constrict lending by Japanese banks. With continuing obligations to their corporate clients, the banks actively sought alternative sources. To the extent that foreign banks had lending capacity available, Japanese banks beseeched them to lend to their clients. Indeed, foreign banks suffered from an overabundance of business. With impact loans published, their major task was explaining to Japanese banks why they would not accept a particular piece of business.

The value of foreign banks as purveyors of international credit was perhaps most clearly illustrated in 1961. The Japanese economy had undergone a downturn. After two straight years of current account surpluses, Japan experienced a substantial reversal. Through July 1961, the country ran a deficit of more than $700 million.[17] Reserves dipped below $1 billion, a paltry level creating a serious financial crisis.

At a meeting of the International Monetary Fund (IMF) in Vienna, Ministry officials approached three US banks for a short-term balance of payments loan. In general, banks were hesitant to make these types of loans. In this case, however, the banks agreed to provide the credits, ensuring that the government had the reserves necessary to get past the crisis. The three resident banks participated in the rescue operation: Citibank, Bank of America, and Chase, each providing credits of Japan $200 million.

Although the Ministry received the commitment in Vienna, the details were subsequently ironed out in New York, with Bank of Japan officials carrying the laboring oar. Hideo Suzuki oversaw the process for the MoF, a task aided considerably by his strong relations with the BoJ officials in the United States. A second group including J. P. Morgan, Manufacturers Hanover, and Chemical provided additional credits. Ultimately, the balance of payment problem receded, the crisis passed. This emergency assistance was not forgotten, however. When the MoF opened the market to foreign branches in the late 1960s and early 1970s, the banks participating in the bailout were among the first to receive licenses.

COMPLACENCY

Despite all of the limitations on operations in Japan, foreign banks by and large did not complain. A few exceptions aside, foreign banks had no serious designs on the domestic market. The carefully controlled system made life easy. Operations were lucrative. Credit enhancement for Japanese banks, trade finance, and the monopoly over impact loans all provided a steady stream of profitable business. The foreign banks lucky enough to be in the country therefore had little incentive to disrupt the status quo. This bred a non-confrontational attitude with the MoF over additional operating authority. In other words, foreign banks accepted their lot.

When foreign banks did obtain yen funds, they did not typically take the time to build relationships with Japanese companies. The interbank market provided a ready, lucrative and safe place to lend. The loans were typically overnight (although often renewed) at attractive interest rates. Foreign banks, therefore, were net lenders rather than borrowers in the market. To the extent that loans were made to businesses, they typically went to foreign multinationals operating in Japan. There was no need to engage in riskier behavior such as seeking out domestic borrowers.

Lending to Japanese companies involved a more difficult affair. Companies already employing a lead bank provided few opportunities. Many small companies, however, lacked the relationships and desperately needed capital. The economy was full of Sonys and Hondas that had not yet emerged as world class competitors. A prescient foreign bank that had sought out these companies would have developed a stronger position in the domestic market. This, however, rarely occurred. Foreign banks had little need or incentive to develop a system for assessing the creditworthiness of Japanese companies.

The failure to aggressively seek domestic business flowed from an inability to obtain sufficient yen and an unwillingness to upset the status quo. Most of the foreign banks accepted that continued business depended upon maintaining good relations with Japanese banks. Attempts to win over large Japanese companies threatened to incur the ire of these banks. To the extent that a foreign bank approached a Japanese company directly, referrals for impact loans might cease. The system therefore bred complacency.

To avoid losing clients, Japanese banks tried to keep tight control over the impact loan process. They provided the introduction between corporate borrower and foreign lender, obtained the requisite governmental approvals for the loans, and guaranteed repayment, almost eliminating the Japanese company from the process. The banks also conducted investigations into the financial health of the corporate borrower and vouched for creditworthiness. That meant that, while loans went to companies, foreign banks dealt almost exclusively with Japanese banks.

Foreign banks accepted the situation, opting to get along by going along. They eschewed direct competition with their Japanese counterparts.[18] They did compete among themselves for business from Japanese banks, assi- duously maintaining and strengthening relationships, but not for business from Japanese companies. While understandable given the high profitability of the operations during the period, this attitude of complacency would have long-term harmful consequences on the competitive position of US banks. The unwillingness to disrupt the status quo caused some to suggest that resident employees treated country rather than the bank as the client.

37

EXPANSION

One of the more remarkable things about foreign banking presence in Japan through the late 1960s was how little things changed. Operations were limited but profitable.[19] The small number of foreign banks represented a cozy club that benefited from the government's decision to prevent others from entering. With hindsight, however, the period proved damaging. The financial institutions had nothing but wasting assets, areas of business that were destined to decline.

The state of affairs could not last. A chasm opened in 1968 when J. P. Morgan obtained a license to open a branch. The following decade would see a flood of entrants, with the number of foreign participants going from less than 20 to more than 80. As the numbers grew, fierce competition developed for the relatively small amount of business assigned to foreign banks. Some of the niches disappeared altogether. Japanese banks gradually ceased to need credit enhancement. Similarly, by the mid-1970s, impact loans declined in importance. As circumstances deteriorated, foreign banks found that they had no firm base in the Japanese domestic market. That, however, came later. Through the 1960s a Japanese outpost was a source of continual and easy profits.

Through the 1960s

At the end of the occupation, three US banks had licenses to operate branches in Japan: Citibank, Bank of America, and Chase. Although other foreign banks had a presence in the country, the troika dominated the market. Two other US banks had toe-holds. American Express operated an office on one of the US military bases and the Manufacturers Bank had a representative office.

A representative office amounted to little more than a listening post. The office could engage in few activities; deposit taking and lending were prohibited. Although having a less prominent presence in Japan, Manufacturers had a distinct advantage: Tristan Beplat. Beplat had been the chief of the Money and Banking Branch in the Economic and Scientific Section within SCAP through 1947. He had come into contact with large numbers of Japanese bankers and government officials. That alone would have given him stature.

In the eyes of the Japanese, however, Beplat had done much more. He was known in Japan as the man who had saved the trust banks. He succeeded in inducing the MoF to give them banking powers and blocked their absorption by the large city banks. He also intervened to soften relatively harsh occupation policies towards the banks. Japanese bankers remembered those efforts, providing Beplat with access others did not have.

Manufacturers, therefore, had a unique position. With only a representative office, the bank did not compete in the domestic economy. Nevertheless, Manufacturers received dollar deposits from the Bank of Japan and actively participated in impact loans to Japanese companies.[20]

American Express also had a Japanese presence. Almost immediately after the occupation, the company prevailed upon the MoF to issue a branch license, the last US bank to obtain a *new* branch license until 1968. The decision to apply for a branch came only after substantial soul searching. During the occupation, officials traveled to Japan to assess the viability of an office but concluded that restraints on banking activities made profitability an iffy proposition. Business seemed limited, with plenty of foreign banks fighting over what was there. Nor did SCAP support the efforts. Officials felt that Japan already had a sufficiently large foreign banking presence, and actively discouraged American Express from opening a branch.[21]

By the early 1950s, however, American Express changed its mind. With foreign banks allowed to engage in domestic activities, the company concluded that the prospects for profit had increased and decided to enter the market. First obtaining approval from SCAP to open a military facility,[22] American Express sought a license the following year from the MoF to open a Tokyo branch. The MoF granted the license, but not without some hesitancy.[23]

Even then, the license proved no simple affair. Among other things, the MoF refused to issue the license until American Express had a representative permanently stationed in the country and office facilities secured. Moreover, the Ministry subsequently informed the company that it had intended to issue a limited license, restricting the company's banking powers within the country. Officials therefore had to negotiate intensively with the Ministry to retain general banking authority.

The MoF's decision with respect to American Express had little to do with a liberal attitude toward a foreign banking presence in the country. Instead, the license seemed almost a housekeeping measure. With American Express already conducting banking activities on military bases and in Okinawa, the MoF simply provided comparable powers to operate in the Japanese domestic market. The license therefore completed the symmetry; all four US banks now had both military and commercial banking facilities. In that way, the Ministry had control over all foreign banks operating in the country.

The early operations of American Express illustrated the economics of, and source of profitability for, foreign branches in Japan. A relatively small office with 16 employees, the branch initially fell into the red. Shortly after opening, the office was losing ¥1.5 million a month. Profitable operations, however, did not require long-term, time-intensive business strategies. Obtaining and lending yen to Japanese banks provided fat margins. As one American Express official noted, the market gave yen working funds an "extraordinarily high earning capacity . . . . "[24]

Although the opportunities were obvious, so were the difficulties.

39

American Express could not obtain sufficient quantities of yen to lend into the interbank market. The company needed only a relatively small quantity (¥250 million or about $700,000 at prevailing exchange rates), but obtaining it was "the problem." The most company officials could venture was that doing so "should not be impossible."[25] The problem with obtaining sufficient quantities of low cost yen would continue to plague foreign banks through the 1980s.

American Express represented the last foreign bank to enter on the coat-tails of the occupation. With the anomalous exception of Continental Illinois in 1964, no other bank from an industrial country obtained a branch license until 1968.[26] Through 1969, a handful of foreign banks did obtain access. These were generally from other Asian countries, however, and typically under special circumstances, usually a quid pro quo for Japanese access. Licenses were awarded to banks from South Korea (Korea Exchange Bank, 1967; Hanil Bank, 1968), Thailand (Bangkok Bank, 1955), Singapore (Overseas Union Bank, 1963), and Indonesia (Bank Negara Indonesia, 1969).

The lack of expansion was particularly apparent given the rapid overseas activity of US banks. With the removal of most government controls on foreign exchange in Europe in 1958, international expansion accelerated. Approximately 12 US banks had emerged as active overseas participants, with the number of international branches increasing from 117 in 1957 to 180 in 1965 to 460 in 1970.[27] The Far East in particular represented an area of dynamic growth. From 21 branches in 1955 to 40 in 1965, US banks had 77 branches in the region by the end of 1970. Almost none of that expansion took place in Japan.

This was no accident. The MoF used the Banking Law of 1927 to restrict entry. Opening a branch required the Ministry's approval, a potent weapon. The MoF did not have to do anything affirmative to keep banks out. Rather than deny an application, something that might create a diplomatic fracas, the Ministry could simply let it languish and die from inaction. The effect was the same.

The MoF's motivations during the period were clear. Additional foreign competitors, particularly from the United States, were unwanted. The attitude in part flowed from the fear that foreign banks would interfere with government control of the financial system. Japanese officials also feared that the financial system could not withstand the onslaught of powerful overseas banks. To some degree, therefore, the policies arose out of efforts to protect the fledgling Japanese banks.

The "shoji curtain" could not, however, be blamed entirely on the MoF. Certainly, the almost complete absence of expansion by banks from industrial countries was no accident. The matter was more complex than parochial Japanese behavior, however. The government in fact enforced comparable policies against Japanese banks. During the post-war period, the

MoF rarely, if ever, granted licenses for the formation of new Japanese banks. The few noticeable exceptions were exactly that: new trust banks formed out of the severed operations of city banks and two additional long-term-credit banks with highly specialized functions.

Equally important, US banks had limited interest in the market, at least until the mid-1960s. Few international banks not already present in the country wanted a branch in Tokyo.[28] The three US banks with the most extensive overseas networks were there and few others were overtly agitating for entry. In some ways, the attitude flowed from hubris. In the eyes of most foreign banks, Japan amounted to a third world country still buried under the debris of a devastating war. This was not the optimal environment for conducting banking business.

A handful of banks, however, did have an early inclination that something in Japan was going on. J. P. Morgan was the first foreign bank both to get the message and to do something about it. The bank opened a representative office in 1961. A flood of foreign banks followed. Commerzbank from West Germany and Wells Fargo opened the same year, with two Canadian banks and First National Bank of Chicago following in 1962.[29] As the decade progressed, other foreign banks placed agents in Japan, including representatives from Switzerland and France.[30]

The opening of representative offices posed few regulatory hurdles. Superficially, the MoF had no role in the process. The Banking Law required only notification as a precondition to opening the office.[31] As a practical matter, however, no foreign bank opened an office without first obtaining the Ministry's assent. Foreign banks had to complete questionnaires and provide other information. One banker described the process as a "mini-branch application."

The MoF, however, welcomed the offices. They promised additional sources of foreign capital with little additional interference in the domestic market. Bank regulators did not, however, take such a benign view toward branch licenses. Approving a branch meant domestic competition, with the foreign bank able to accept deposits and make yen loans. As the decade progressed, though, the MoF's adamant opposition to branch licenses was forced to give way.

The first brick in the wall: Continental Illinois

By 1964, attitudes of foreign banks toward Japan had shifted from curiosity to active interest. With the 1964 Olympics, an event televised worldwide, the industrial world began to wake up to the transformation that had occurred in Japan. The country had shifted from a war-torn, devastated nation to a bustling, vibrant economy. The same year, Japan hosted the World Bank and the IMF. The meetings had a comparable effect but on a more select and potent audience. Officials from the most prominent and high powered banks

41

worldwide experienced first hand the economic energy of Japan. Enthusiasm swelled; banks wanted in. Foreign banks not already in Japan began to see the advantages of a branch license.

Some noticed the Japanese market even earlier. The first major inroad to the MoF's exclusionary approach occurred in March 1964 when Continental Illinois received approval to operate two branches in Japan. The circumstances were, to say the least, unique. Continental Illinois obtained the branches from a departing Dutch bank. In that way, the MoF did not have to approve the issuance of new licenses but simply the transfer of existing ones. This avoided any precedent that would encourage other foreign banks to seek entry. Still, the Continental Illinois situation was important. For the first time since 1953, the MoF seriously confronted and authorized the entry of a bank from an industrial country into Japan.

SCAP, during the occupation, had authorized two Dutch colonial banks to reopen branches in Japan: Nederlandsche Handel Maatschappij and Nationale Handelsbank. They had operations throughout Asia with an emphasis on Indonesia, a Dutch colony at the time. As the Dutch empire disappeared, however, Nationale Handelsbank began to contemplate withdrawal from Asia. During the 1950s, the bank sold branches in India, Pakistan, and the Philippines. Purchased by the Rotterdamsche Bank in the early 1960s, Handelsbank moved to sell the remaining Asian branches, including the ones in Tokyo and Osaka.

Chase had particular interest in the Hong Kong branch. Having operated in the city since before the war, Chase had closed its Hong Kong branch during the Korean War. The acquisition of the Handelsbank branch provided a neat mechanism for getting back in. To a lesser extent, Chase also wanted access to Singapore and Thailand. With two branches already in Japan, however, the bank had no interest in additional offices in Osaka and Tokyo.

Handelsbank would sell the remaining branches only as a package. Chase, therefore, had to find a bank interested in acquiring the two Japanese branches. While any number of banks had an interest in entering the Japanese market, the successful candidate had to be acceptable to both Chase and the MoF. Presumably neither wanted another money center bank from the United States. Continental Illinois seemed a perfect choice.

Not a New York bank, Continental Illinois would be less likely to compete directly with Chase. From the MoF's perspective, the bank had shown commitment to the market by lending increasing amounts to Japanese banks and companies. The bank's location also helped. Chicago was a desirable destination for Japanese banks. Illinois law, however, foreclosed foreign entry. Efforts by Continental Illinois to get into Japan were therefore conditioned upon reciprocal efforts of the Bank of Tokyo to gain entry into Chicago.

Continental Illinois had already been exploring possible entry into Japan.

The MoF had made clear that a new license was too big a shift in policy and would not be forthcoming. Buying the branches of a departing bank, however, was a more acceptable alternative. Continental Illinois therefore viewed the acquisition of the Handelsbank branches as a once in a lifetime opportunity and jumped at the invitation.[32]

Desire was not enough. Continental Illinois still had to obtain assurances from the MoF that transfer of the branch licenses would be approved. The issue presented the MoF with something never addressed seriously in the post-war era: access by a bank from an industrial country. Predictably, fissures emerged. Some within the Ministry opposed the effort by a major foreign bank to enter the country. Others were concerned with the uncomfortable precedent created by approval. The last thing they wanted was an avalanche of branch applications from other foreign banks.

Approval required hard negotiations and they started at the top. The Chairman of Continental Illinois and future Secretary of the Treasury, David Kennedy, flew to Tokyo and met with the Minister of Finance, Kakuei Tanaka, and the Governor of the Bank of Japan, Masamichi Yamagiwa. In addition to the usual pleasantries, Kennedy stressed the "opportunity" presented by allowing a midwestern bank from an important city into the country. He also educated officials about the important role played by Continental Illinois in the development of the Japanese economy.

While acceptance by the higher-ups accelerated the process, approval still did not become automatic. Lower level officials within the MoF, particularly Yusuke Kashiwagi, who subsequently became Vice Minister for International Affairs, also had to be brought on board. Again, the process involved intense negotiations. Ultimately, Continental Illinois prevailed.

The Chicago financial institution succeeded in part by limiting opposition from Japanese banks. The Bank of Tokyo, with obvious incentive, actively supported the efforts. Kennedy and Shigeo Horie, the Bank of Tokyo's Chairman, had a long-standing, close relationship. While the position of the other Japanese banks was not as clear, they presented no active opposition to the purchase. The MoF, therefore, did not have to confront a rebellion within the financial community. In a country emphasizing consensus, this represented no small factor.

Even with approval, Continental Illinois had to go through some hoops. Never so blunt as to require, MoF officials informally conveyed to the bank orally, often at informal settings such as a cocktail party or meal, a number of conditions. The MoF was concerned with appearances. It looked better to have Continental Illinois upgrade an existing office than to open a new one. Continental Illinois therefore had to open a representative office. The bank did so in late 1963. That meant finding space and sending over personnel even though the facilities would be redundant once Continental Illinois acquired the Handelsbank branches.

Continental Illinois also had to acquire both branches. The Chicago bank

43

would have been happy to purchase only the office in Tokyo. Chase, however, did not want a second office in Osaka and lobbied the MoF to approve transfer of both branches, which ultimately occurred. With an understanding that the MoF supported the purchase, Continental Illinois finalized the deal with Chase. Chase bought all five Handelsbank outposts and immediately sold the branches in Osaka and Tokyo to Continental Illinois.[33]

In the end, the MoF approved the transfer for a number of reasons. The transfer had domestic advantages. Keeping the branches open avoided layoffs, something important in a country that prized lifetime employment. More importantly, the MoF obtained access to Chicago for the Bank of Tokyo. Although Dai-Ichi had opened a representative office in 1957, state law prohibited foreign branches. The Bank of Tokyo was anxious to get into the city and Continental Illinois was willing to help. The same year that the MoF approved the acquisition of the Handelsbank branches, the Bank of Tokyo obtained a presence in the city through a minority interest in the Chicago–Tokyo Bank.[34]

Approval also represented a shift in thinking within the Ministry. A faction inside the bureaucracy had become increasingly aware of the country's role in international capital markets. To the extent that their own market remained closed, Japanese banks would have a difficult time gaining access to foreign markets. They also began to realize the growing prominence of the country's financial markets. The changed role meant that the attitude toward an increased foreign banking presence had to evolve.

Approval of the purchase by Continental Illinois did not, however, portend a more liberal attitude toward access by foreign branches, at least in the short term. Other banks continued to have a difficult time obtaining offices in Japan. Shortly after the MoF approved Continental Illinois' acquisition of the Handelsbank branches, J. P. Morgan launched the arduous process of obtaining a new branch license from the government. The process would take years, involve innumerable meetings, and require the expenditure of immense energy.

On the other hand, the Continental Illinois situation amounted to a critical milestone. The issue of foreign access to Japan had become lodged within the Ministry. For the first time since the immediate post-occupation period, a US bank had been allowed to operate a branch in the country. Knowing other banks were interested in entering, the MoF clearly wanted to avoid the appearance of any kind of precedent. For those banks, circumstances provided little room for optimism over the prospects for entry. Nonetheless, the MoF was wrestling with the issue, with the consensus development process under way. In a country inculcated with a step-by-step approach toward reform, this represented the first step. Greater strides would occur later.

Through the looking glass: J. P. Morgan

Evidence of a more complete shift in Ministry policy became apparent in 1968 when the MoF relented and granted a license to J. P. Morgan to open a branch. This represented the first *new* license given to a US bank since 1953. The success, however, came only after enormous effort and intractable resistance. The story of the branch license illustrated both the parochial attitude of the MoF, the benefits of tenacity, and what foreign banks could accomplish even without assistance from their own government.

J. P. Morgan had a long history in Japan. During the 1920s, J. P. Morgan & Co. acted as underwriter for the Japanese government. In 1924, J. P. Morgan, Citibank, and others syndicated $150 million in "Earthquake Bonds" to help rebuild Tokyo and Yokohama following the devastation that struck the cities the year before. Through 1931, J. P. Morgan acted as underwriter for seven bond issues, including the Toho Electric Company in 1930.[35] The activity only ground to a halt with the invasion of Manchuria and investor resistance in the United States to the sale of the bonds.

Guaranty Trust Company of New York, which eventually merged with J. P. Morgan, also had long-standing involvement in the Japanese market. The company entered into a correspondent banking relationship with the Yokohama Specie Bank at the turn of the century. Guaranty Trust acted as the underwriter for Tokyo Dento [Electric Light] Company in 1925 and 1928, the first offering by a private Japanese company in the United States.

J. P. Morgan's early involvement had more than historical significance. Japanese companies had long institutional memories. J. P. Morgan was remembered at the financial institution that provided financing during periods of great difficulty. Both the Japanese government and Japanese businesses would remember this when J. P. Morgan returned to Japan in the 1960s.

J. P. Morgan decided to open a representative office in October 1961, although not without some deliberation. It saw the need for a regional office in Asia to better service existing clients. The choice came down to Hong Kong or Japan. The bank opted for Tokyo because of the level of business done in that country. Like other US banks, J. P. Morgan had gradually increased the loans made to Japan, typically in the form of lines of credit for trade finance. With J. P. Morgan's exposure climbing to the $50 million range, the bank decided it was time to have a presence in the country. Robert Wynn traveled to Japan to open an office in Tokyo.

A presence in Japan had a number of immediate effects. Trusting the advice of agents in the country, J. P. Morgan began lifting the exposure limits for Japan, permitting increased lending to Japanese companies and banks. In addition, the bank uncovered a little known fact: operations in the country were extraordinarily lucrative. The Bank of Japan published reports on the earnings of foreign banks in Japan. The publications showed that Citibank, the largest of the foreign banks, made enormous profits.

45

Still, the decision by J. P. Morgan to upgrade from a representative office to a branch was not automatic. The bank had offices only in financial centers such as Brussels, London, and Paris.[36] Tokyo in the early 1960s did not fit into that category. On the other hand, the moneymaking opportunity could not be ignored. After much study and teeth gnashing, J. P. Morgan decided to seek a branch license.

J. P. Morgan in some respects represented an ideal candidate to pierce the shoji curtain. The bank had a long-standing commitment to the Japanese market, pre-dating the war. J. P. Morgan's approach to business also helped. Ministry officials remained concerned about competition from foreign banks in Japan. They wanted to protect underdeveloped sectors in the financial markets, particularly consumer finance.

Foreign banks had a far more developed system of consumer lending. In contrast, the area had atrophied in Japan, with most of the available capital directed toward large companies. An aggressive consumer bank might have locked up that segment of the market before the Japanese banks even sought access. J. P. Morgan, however, was a wholesale bank. It posed few potential threats to the retail sector.

The MoF had other concerns. With some cause, the Ministry remained suspicious of the permanency of the commitment of foreign banks to the Japanese market. The government was vitally concerned with its credit rating in international markets. Funds from abroad were still critical to the continued economic recovery of the country. A foreign bank with a branch in Japan that withdrew or otherwise cut off credit could cause a domino effect that might deprive the country of access to the international financial markets.

This was no idle concern. In 1965, First Chicago had decided to reduce short-term credit lines extended to Japanese banks and companies. The economy had softened and First Chicago, alone of all major US banks, had significant concerns about repayment. The bank's Vice Chairman, Gaylord Freeman, favored the reduction in credit and, despite opposition at the bank, gained approval for the shift. The Ministry was horrified and went to great lengths to lessen the impact of the decision. Ministry officials let First Chicago know that this was a bad idea and would be remembered.

First Chicago did it anyway, but decided to pull only half of the credit lines. To lessen the impact of the decision, Olaf Lindstedt, First Chicago's representative in Tokyo, was advised by officials at the Ministry to ask Japanese clients to use only half of their existing lines. This avoided the need actually to pull them. The clients agreed, apparently having been contacted by the government before Lindstedt got to them. Damage control completed, the MoF would long remember the slight by First Chicago. When other banks received branch licenses to enter Japan in 1971, First Chicago had to wait.[37]

J. P. Morgan's efforts to upgrade the office to a branch required MoF approval. Wynn, who headed the office, had already sounded out officials about a possible license. He was constantly told that the matter was under

46

consideration, code for "don't hold your breath." With little progress, J. P. Morgan upped the ante.

At an IMF meeting in Washington in 1965, Thomas S. Gates, the Chairman of J. P. Morgan, raised the issue with the Minister of Finance, Mikio Mizuta. Gates was polite but blunt. In a no nonsense fashion, he asked point blank whether the MoF wanted J. P. Morgan in the country. Although receiving a noncommittal response, Gates was promised an answer in six months, when John Meyer, the president of the bank, would be traveling to Japan. On cue, the MoF gave the answer: in principle, J. P. Morgan could have the license.

Rather than an end, however, the commitment represented the beginning of a long, almost interminable negotiation process. Approval simply meant that the issue was transferred to the appropriate people within the MoF to iron out the details. That initially meant Yusuke Kashiwagi, who had responsibility in the MoF for international matters. Having spent his childhood in the United States, Kashiwagi spoke flawless English. During the 1960s, he participated in most major decisions affecting foreign banks. J. P. Morgan's license was no exception.

In 1966, Kashiwagi had risen to the post of Director General of the International Finance Bureau, then the highest ranking international post within the Ministry. Although he had nominal authority over all international matters within the Ministry, the license still needed to be approved by the Banking Bureau. Officials in that bureau had primary responsibility for the negotiations with J. P. Morgan. Primary responsibility devolved to Michio Ochi, deputy section chief of the commercial banking section within the Banking Bureau.[38]

Responsibility for obtaining the license on the J. P. Morgan side fell to John Loughran. Loughran had been stationed in Japan after the war and had studied Japanese at both Yale and Keio University, one of the most prominent private universities in Japan. J. P. Morgan hired him, rushed him through the training program, and shipped him off to Tokyo.

Officials within the Banking Bureau imposed ground rules on the talks. J. P. Morgan could not apprise the US Embassy of the progress of the talks and could not discuss the matter with a lawyer. The limitation on conversations with the Embassy reflected an early concern with *gaiatsu*, or foreign pressure. The Japanese had already been criticized by the United States over the sale of textiles, providing the MoF with considerable incentive to minimize the role of the US government in the process.

This was an easy condition, since J. P. Morgan officials had little incentive to approach the Embassy. In general, bankers at the time had no affection for the US Embassy. State Department officials had shown little interest in promoting the economic interests of US banks. Japan was viewed primarily in political rather than economic terms, a democratic bastion against the communist tides in Asia. Only in the 1970s would Japan obtain ambassadors that had a more pronounced pro-business perspective.

The other condition, the prohibition on legal consultation, proved a different matter. Loughran regularly consulted J. P. Morgan's attorney in Japan, Richard W. Rabinowitz. Rabinowitz was one of a small cadre of Western attorneys who had obtained the right to practice in Japan following the war. In 1954, the window closed and no new lawyers were allowed in. The exclusionary practices remained in place until the 1980s, heightening the importance of those already there. Rabinowitz and his firm, Anderson, Mori and Rabinowitz, played an active role advising the foreign business community.

Advice about J. P. Morgan's application amounted to educated guess-work. The MoF had never granted a license under these circumstances, rendering the process a mystery to all of the participants. The two conditions made clear that the MoF wanted to deliberate over the license with minimal outside interference. While that might have reflected an imperious attitude by an imperious bureaucracy, the truth seemed to be less nefarious. The MoF needed to achieve an internal consensus on how best to handle the license application. The Ministry wanted the discretion to guide the process and achieve a consensus without foreign government intrusion.

For the first six months of the negotiations, Loughran relied upon David S. Phillips as his translator. Raised in the United States but born in Japan, Phillips provided a subtle but invaluable commodity: Japanese citizenship. "Because of my Japanese face, the Japanese press would never question why I was going into the Ministry of Finance all the time."[39] By avoiding unwanted attention, he could discuss matters with Ministry officials without the accursed glare of public exposure. He also provided a back door channel to MoF thinking. An informal meeting, a drink at the Ginza, a chance encounter, all helped Phillips learn the prevalent attitudes within the Ministry and get a feel for what issues should or should not be raised.

Negotiations ultimately took two years. Sessions were held four and five times a week. After the first six months, the MoF barred Phillips from participating. Loughran attended all of the meetings, was on perpetual call, and, during the period, never left the country. Negotiating sessions did not involve give and take discussions. Instead, each side stated and restated issues, like two ships passing in the night. MoF officials also requested reams of information about J. P. Morgan, down to the identity of the bank's shareholders.

The only serious issue centered on the scope of the license. Reflecting the protective attitude toward the retail sector, the Ministry wanted to give J. P. Morgan a license comparable with that held by the long-term-credit banks. Those banks could only accept client and government deposits, not retail deposits. J. P. Morgan adamantly refused to accept the condition and the Ministry ultimately gave up the demand. The concern would come up again, however, in connection with branch applications by other foreign banks.

The MoF finally granted the license in 1968. J. P. Morgan received the word informally on July 4 but was told not to hire employees or rent space. Once again, Loughran ignored half of the mandate. He held off hiring employees but found space. The Ministry formally issued the license on December 8. The delay apparently gave officials in the Banking Bureau extra time to determine whether the license would engender opposition within the MoF or the financial community.

The timing of the license resulted at least in part from dynamics within the Ministry. MoF officials changed every year or two. As officials retired from the Ministry, they would engage in an *amakudari*, or descent from heaven. Typically in their mid-50s, with a relatively small pension, the retiring officials sought a lucrative position in the private sector, often with a bank or trade association. A retiring official could provide a new employer with a number of advantages, most notably access and insight into the views of the MoF. To the extent that a departing official left behind difficult or embarrassing issues for his successor within the Ministry, however, accessibility might also disappear.

In practice, therefore, retiring MoF officials tried to eliminate all remaining issues that might discomfort their successor. J. P. Morgan's branch license amounted to such an issue. Officials working on the matter decided that the issue could not be left for their successors. As their retirement approached, they finally granted the long sought after license.

The MoF knew that the license would set a precedent. Other banks would lobby for access. The MoF therefore made clear that approval came with limits. A license would be granted for only a single branch. Banks were to have no expectation that, once in, they could expand freely. J. P. Morgan only wanted a Tokyo presence, and so the limitation was of little moment.

Two years would transpire before the MoF granted another license, an observation period to see how the new entrant fared. Thereafter, the flood gates opened. Manufacturers Hanover became the second to be promised a branch license, largely due to the sway of and reverence for Tristan Beplat. Kashiwagi even took the unprecedented step of contacting Beplat and asking him if his bank wanted the next license. As he put it, "I don't think we could have refused him."[40] Chemical, Bankers Trust, Wells Fargo, Security Pacific, and United California followed in 1971 and 1972, as did a handful of European and Latin American banks.

The decision to allow an increased number of foreign banks into Japan did not arise out of altruism. The government had become increasingly conscious of problems of reciprocity. Concern had arisen that, because of the closed nature of the market, Japanese banks would have difficulty expanding overseas. Thus, the opening of the market coincided with rapid expansion of Japanese branches abroad.

Nor was the liberalization across the board. While attempts by foreign banks to open offices in the country received the bulk of the attention, less publicized were efforts by existing foreign banks to expand the number of branches.[41] Citibank had been agitating for additional branches, to no avail. As a practical matter, foreign banks were allowed only a single branch. By definition, this limited access both to lending markets and deposits.

THE BEGINNING OF THE AWAKENING

The late 1960s started a dynamic process that would ultimately result in dramatic change in the Japanese financial markets and almost continual intervention by foreign governments. The quiescent period through the late 1960s contained the seeds of change. With Japan resuming a position among the community of nations, membership brought responsibilities. Both the GATT and the IMF took a dim view of the closed nature of the Japanese economy. Slowly and grudgingly, the Japanese government began to realize that the hermetically sealed financial economy could not remain intact.

The MoF began to improve access to the financial markets, most noticeably by allowing growing numbers of foreign banks into the country. Access alone was sufficient as long as the new foreign entrants had adequate amounts of business and profit opportunities. That, however, could not last. The economic upheavals of the 1970s, particularly the first oil crisis, kicked the legs out from under the foreign banks. In 1974, the economy went into an uncharacteristic tailspin. Business vanished. Suddenly profits were no longer guaranteed and the gaggle of foreign banks had to scramble for business. This caused them to refocus on their limited operating latitude in Japan and on the impediments imposed by the government.

As this sunk in, the banks became less complacent. By the end of the next decade, the MoF could no longer act in quite the same imperious manner. The ability to allow Citibank branch applications to sit for more than a decade without action ended. Suddenly financial matters became topics of discussion at the highest levels of government. Only then did foreign banks start to edge out of their prescribed compartment within the financial system.

In the financial sector, the implicit quid pro quo with foreign banks began to erode. Banks had accepted limits on operations in return for guaranteed profitability. The foreign bank monopoly over certain functions, however, ceased. With the erosion went assured profitability; by the late 1970s red ink became common. As compensation, foreign banks increasingly sought expanded powers, in particular greater access to the domestic economy.

The decade also saw the stirring of activity in Washington as the complacent approach toward barriers in the financial sector began to change. By 1970, trade friction between the United States and Japan had begun. Concerns arose over both Japanese protectionism and the effect of imports on certain US industries. Textiles and agricultural products received considerable attention. The country also came under pressure to do away with restrictions on foreign exchange. Eventually, calls would arise for systematic changes in the financial system.

4

FOREIGN PENETRATION IN THE 1970s

J. P. Morgan shattered the barriers to foreign entry into Japan. After a two-year observation period, the Ministry of Finance (MoF) viewed the experiment as successful and allowed a spate of other foreign banks into the country. Beginning with Manufacturers Hanover in 1971, the largest banks in Europe and the United States obtained licenses, ending the tight-fisted monopoly of the occupation banks. This was not to suggest that the process was always smooth. The MoF occasionally said no to a putative entrant, as United California, the predecessor to First Interstate, discovered.

For foreign banks, the decade had a Doctor Jekyll and Mr Hyde character. Until 1975, operations were highly lucrative. Profits soared, particularly when the Bank of Japan clamped down on lending following the first oil crisis in 1973, causing Japanese companies to flock to foreign banks. The favorable circumstances were short-lived. The second half of the decade saw earnings begin a steep decline.

The fall was inevitable. Dollar loans, the core of the foreign banking business, no longer had the same allure. With the trade balance growing, Japan went from a net importer to a net exporter of dollars. Moreover, the creditworthiness of Japanese banks was firmly established, their position in New York and London secure. The need for foreign banks as conduits to the international capital markets abruptly ended.

With lending to blue chip companies in terminal decline, the banks embarked on a mad scramble for alternative sources of business. Banks went "down market," sometimes at the encouragement of the MoF. Some energetically pursued consumer loans, others went after companies lacking established reputations. These activities shattered the veneer of riskless lending in Japan. By the latter half of the decade, the implicit understanding that the government would rescue foreign banks from any lending mishaps evaporated.

With profitability no longer guaranteed and market share shrinking, foreign banks began to awake from their stupor. The prescribed market niche was no

51

longer enough. Pressure built for change. Although initially tentative, the banks had become more confrontational by the end of the decade and, for the first time, began calling on home governments for assistance.

The 1970s therefore represented a transitional decade. As the number of foreign banks continued to grow, the MoF had to adjust to the new reality of a sizable – and less controllable – foreign presence. The Ministry also had to get used to increasing foreign government intrusion into its bailiwick. Gradually, financial developments became matters of bilateral concern. The days when the MoF could insist that foreign banks keep embassies and outside lawyers uninformed were gone.

CONTINUED EXPANSION

The J. P. Morgan license represented an epochal event. A new consensus within the Ministry concerning foreign banking access had emerged. International banks could now enter, although only in an orderly procession. A queue formed. Banks had to wait their turn, with those that had already demonstrated their commitment to Japan first in line. They also had to accept restrictions, including a limit of one branch and a ban on retail operations.

The MoF granted the first post-J. P. Morgan branch license to Manufacturers Hanover, a bank with a representative office in Japan since 1949. It then swung the door ajar even wider, approving branches by Wells Fargo, Chemical, Bankers, Deutsche Bank, Swiss Bank, and Banco Do Brasil. The first wave of US branch licenses coincidentally included the banks that had provided the crucial balance of payment loans in 1961. Memories in Japan were long; the contribution had not been forgotten.

The mechanics

Even after J. P. Morgan, branch licenses required careful orchestration. Requirements still had to be met; proper steps taken. A representative office became the initial step in opening a branch.[1] Although no law required foreign banks to obtain Ministry approval for the office, the reality was quite different. The opening of a representative office, if done properly, amounted to provisional approval of a branch license. Foreign banks, therefore, did not dare set up an office without first discussing the matter with, and obtaining consent from, the appropriate officials within the MoF.

A representative office provided an observation period, a form of dues payment. The MoF could get to know the bank and see its commitment to the country's economic recovery. Rather than accept brash promises about increased credit for Japanese companies, the MoF wanted to see the commitment in practice. Once the office was opened and the commitment demonstrated, the MoF would signal the bank at the propitious moment to submit a branch application, a formality typically approved upon filing.

Commitment foremost meant increased lending activity. In the early 1970s, Japan still needed capital and depended on foreign banks for necessary credit. The MoF also wanted to see that the relevant bank took operations in the country seriously. The top people in the bank were expected to visit the country a few times to show that the branch had support at the highest levels. United California, the predecessor of First Interstate, scored points when it flew in the Chairman of the Board and threw a huge gala to open the representative office. The bank stunned the prominent guests by getting oranges past customs for use as gifts.

In allowing access, the MoF continued to take a protective attitude toward the consumer sector. The efforts had begun with J. P. Morgan. Despite strong pressure, J. P. Morgan refused to accept a license that barred retail deposits. The MoF, however, did not give up. As a condition of obtaining a branch license, foreign banks after J. P. Morgan had to promise not to engage in retail banking. Some even execute a letter to that effect. The letter – a draft of which came from the MoF but was retyped on bank stationery – had to contain representations that the foreign bank would not seek additional branches or retail deposits and a commitment to hire a Japanese employee who would speak for the bank.

To avoid any appearance of retail operations, banks took a variety of steps, including the imposition of high minimum account balances and the placement of tellers in the bowels of the branch. All were designed to minimize accessibility to ordinary Japanese. With foreign banks having little interest in the retail market, the restrictions meant little.

The MoF further insulated the retail sector by making clear that foreign banks could open only a single branch. In some instances, the MoF included the restriction in the license. A blunt approach, the limitation represented an obvious and flagrant example of discrimination. As the decade progressed, the MoF deleted the offending provision from licenses. More form than substance, a *de facto* prohibition continued on additional branches until 1981 when Citibank was allowed to expand.

The limitations ended any thought of expansion by an entering bank. Some of the new entrants came in with grandiose schemes, including branches in other cities. United California thought about buying a bank in Okinawa and opening branches in far-flung cities like Sapporo. The plans evaporated when, during the application process, MoF attitudes about expansion became clear.

As part of the branch application process, foreign banks had to show adequate sophistication about the local market. This required the appointment of an "advisor" to help the bank better understand the system. Always a senior Japanese official, the advisor inevitably amounted to a retiring employee from a city bank, the Bank of Japan or the MoF. The advisor acted primarily as liaison with the government.

The requirement may have originated out of parochialism; the MoF felt more comfortable dealing with its own kind. On the other hand, foreign banks entering the country often had little understanding of the arcane financial system. An advisor therefore had a basic utility. He could facilitate, explain and otherwise provide necessary guidance about how the system functioned.

The Ministry also expected foreign banks to have the employees necessary to operate effectively. Finding sufficient and qualified Japanese employees was an eternal headache. Working for a foreign bank lacked status, making entry level hiring difficult. Moreover, raiding Japanese banks, the most obvious source of experienced personnel, was not a viable option. With lifetime employment and strong group loyalties, employees generally would not leave. Finally, raiding risked the impairment of relationships with Japanese banks, something still to be avoided.

Foreign banks typically had access only to employees nearing retirement age or to "loaners" from Japanese banks. With retirement at around 55, senior officials were often willing to consider a second career at a foreign bank. Qualified junior employees, however, were a different matter. Some could be hired from Japanese banks, but typically only those whose career had foundered.[2] Japanese banks that wanted to establish (or had already established) close relations with a particular foreign bank might lend employees. At the end of the two- or three-year period, many returned. During the stay, foreign bankers often noticed phone lines lighting up at the end of each day as intelligence about the bank's operations went back to Japanese employers.

To sidestep these sources, J. P. Morgan in the 1970s began to recruit entry level employees actively from Japanese universities. Even then, the bank had considerable difficulty obtaining candidates from the best schools, particularly the University of Tokyo. The bank targeted universities like Sophia, a Jesuit-run school in Tokyo. Sophia tended to have Japanese students who either had not done as well on standardized tests or had been abroad too long to qualify for the Japanese school system. Students emerged from Sophia with an unusually international perspective. The Bank developed close relations with particular professors, such as Father Robert J. Ballon, a Belgian priest teaching at the university since the war, and counted on them to funnel employees to J. P. Morgan.

J. P. Morgan also sent shock waves through the Japanese banking community in 1970 when Loughran convinced Osamu Toba to leave the Bank of Tokyo. Toba, a Wharton graduate and son-in-law of a former vice chairman of the Yokohama Specie Bank, was a rising star. High level officials at the Bank of Tokyo approached J. P. Morgan to try to get the event undone, to no avail. Although the switch earned the ire of the Bank of Tokyo, Toba went on to have a lengthy and successful career, ultimately becoming head of J. P. Morgan's Tokyo branch and chairman of its trust bank.

Employment practices also had to confront rampant labor unrest. In

Japan, unions were typically company, rather than industry, based. The foreign banking union, however, was an exception. A single union – Gai Gin Ro – operated in all of the banks. The largest foreign banks in the country, Chase, Citibank, Continental Illinois, and Bank of America, were all unionized. Generally viewed as militant and leftist, the union frequently resorted to nasty strikes and demonstrations to terrorize foreign banks.

Predictably, the resident banks had various run-ins with the union. Protests could take the form of simple arm bands or refusal to work overtime. Protracted demonstrations were also common. Chase seemed to get the worst of it. When the bank laid off a handful of Japanese employees following staff reductions at military banking facilities, the union demanded that they be rehired at the Tokyo branch. Insisting that the two facilities were entirely separate, Chase refused. The result was a strike and, more unusual, a lawsuit seeking reinstatement of the employees. Chase chose to fight.

During the protracted legal wrangle, former employees would hang red banners outside the bank as a weekly protest, causing Chase to be referred to as the "red flag" bank. Employees at the bank contributed a portion of their salary to a fund used for the maintenance of the displaced workers. Eventually, the court ordered the bank to rehire half the employees and compensate the union. With other issues unresolved, Chase capitulated and rehired the suing employees.

With the new influx of foreign banks, something had to be done about Gai Gin Ro. The task fell to J. P. Morgan. In advance of the branch opening, bank officials decided to resist unionization. Doing so, however, required both deliberation and resolve. J. P. Morgan consulted corporate clients in Japan and received some basic but critically important advice on how to approach the matter. The bank was advised to form groups within the branch to encourage collective activity, all under the J. P. Morgan banner. The bank also needed to foster a strong relationship with Japanese employees. J. P. Morgan became the first foreign bank to extend a profit sharing plan to all employees and to designate Japanese employees as officers of the New York bank, with their names listed in the back of the annual report.

This did not go down lightly with Gai Gin Ro. For six months after the branch opened, the union engaged in angry demonstrations in front of the offices. In some instances, the police had to remove demonstrators forcibly from buildings where J. P. Morgan had its offices. As J. P. Morgan's resolute attitude became clear, the demonstrations died down and ultimately disappeared. The battle had been fought and won. No foreign bank entering after J. P. Morgan accepted unionization.

The difficult cases

Not all of the branch applications went smoothly, however, something discovered by United California. The predecessor to First Interstate, the bank

55

had followed all of the necessary procedures, including the opening of a representative office and visits by ranking officials. Paul Draughn, the bank's representative in Tokyo, began to agitate for a license. Things progressed smoothly until suddenly overtaken by events.

At about the same time, an officer of a Swiss subsidiary of United California tried to corner the market on cocoa, ultimately generating huge losses for the bank as well as unsavory publicity.[3] As the problem surfaced but before it became public, bank officials met with a Ministry representative visiting the United States and informed him of the problem.[4] With that, the prospect of a branch license evaporated.

Draughn found himself summoned to an unheard of 7:00 a.m. meeting at the MoF. He was told bluntly that the scandal and resulting loss of face in the international capital markets meant that United California should not expect a license anytime soon. Draughn conveyed the information to the home office in California.

Officials at United California were angered by the decision. The denial occurred at the same time that other big California banks such as Security Pacific and Wells Fargo were getting into Japan. Essentially, the MoF had relegated United California to a back seat position. The bank would not take this slight lying down.

Officials approached California's Superintendent of Banking, expressing disappointment with what had happened. The Superintendent took the complaints seriously. A number of Japanese banks, including Tokai Bank, had applied for a license to open branches in Los Angeles.[5] The Banking Superintendent let it be known that denial of United California's license would result in reciprocal treatment for Japanese banks. In other words, they could forget about expansion in the state as long as United California was excluded from Japan.

The Japanese took the threat seriously. A raft of Japanese bank officials descended on United California asking for help in getting a license from the Superintendent. They were politely told that United California had a comparable problem and would appreciate any help they could give with the MoF. The MoF even became directly involved. One high ranking official reputedly met with John McCone, a member of the United California Board, to see if a solution could be devised.

In the end, however, neither United California nor the Banking Superintendent would back down. Within weeks, the MoF relented. Draughn was again summoned to the Ministry and told that the license would be granted. The controversy seemed settled. Draughn's ability to function in the country, however, had been permanently compromised. As a face saving gesture, the MoF made clear that it would not be pleased if he remained to head the branch. Draughn, therefore, left the country.

Other banks also had trouble getting licenses. The Ministry applied a policy of strict reciprocity to foreign branches. To the extent that a country or state did not allow entry by Japanese banks, the MoF did likewise. Texas banks found themselves subject to this policy. With Texas prohibiting foreign branches, Japanese banks could not get access to boom towns like Houston and Dallas. The MoF reacted accordingly.

Four Texas banks opened representative offices in the 1970s, each eagerly wanting a branch license. The sunbelt had become an economic hotbed, with Texas banks growing exponentially and spreading internationally. MoF officials always responded to the requests by indicating that the matter was under study. At the same time, they would ask about the likelihood of Texas allowing Japanese banks to open branches. The linkage was clear; only after Texas law changed would the MoF become more amenable to applications from Texas banks. When that eventually occurred, the sunbelt had become an economic wasteland, with Lone Star banks no longer in a position to expand overseas.

Texas was not the only example. With Canada restricting access to the Japanese, their banks could not get branch licenses, instead having to settle for representative offices.[6] The MoF also used reciprocity against the Swiss. Until 1984, banks from the European country could enter Japan on a one for one basis. A Swiss bank received a license only when a Japanese bank gained access to Switzerland.

Swiss Bank became the first to receive a license to operate a branch in Tokyo. The financial institution had opened a representative office in 1965, a year before any other Swiss bank. Date of entry had its advantages. When the Bank of Tokyo sought access to Zurich in 1971, Ministry officials approached Swiss Bank and indicated a willingness to issue a license for a branch in Tokyo.

Union Bank, the second Swiss bank to open an office in Japan, learned of the efforts and sought comparable treatment.[7] The MoF, however, refused. Applying the one for one approach, Union Bank had to wait until another Japanese bank gained access to Switzerland. When Fuji Bank obtained approval in 1972, Union Bank received a license to operate in Tokyo. Credit Suisse became the third Swiss bank to open in 1977, but only after Dai Ichi Bank opened in Zurich.[8]

The routine

In general, however, the licensing process seldom involved such controversy. Banks taking the proper steps, acting in a politically astute manner, and waiting their turn generally got in. The experience of Irving Trust seemed typical. Wanting a Japanese branch, Irving approached the Bank of Tokyo for advice. The New York bank had a long-standing relationship with the Bank of Tokyo, going back to the days of its predecessor, the Yokohama Specie Bank. During the war, Irving hired some Yokohama Specie Bank personnel who returned to the Japanese bank once the conflict ended. Irving also helped the Bank of Tokyo set up an agency in New York following the war.

Consistent with Ministry policy, Irving had to hire a senior Japanese advisor. The Bank set its sights on an employee nearing retirement at the Bank of Tokyo and succeeded in landing the official after a protracted pirouette. Irving had to provide certain assurances, particularly about title and length of employment. After some mulling, Bank of Tokyo officials advised the US bank at an informal gathering in Australia that the hiring could go forward.

As with other banks, Irving had to open a representative office. Thereafter, officials from the bank met regularly and informally with the MoF's International Finance Bureau. The Japanese advisor assisted in setting up the meetings and preparing agendas. After the proper amount of time, the deputy director general, the number two person in the Bureau, indicated that the time was right for a branch application, tantamount to a promise that the license would be forthcoming.

As the decade progressed, the number of foreign banks in Japan grew dramatically. From 18 in 1970 to 22 by the end of 1971, 41 foreign banks had branches in Japan by March 1974.[9] Following a freeze on new licenses in 1975, the numbers resumed their climb. An additional 12 banks entered the country during the next four years. By the end of 1978, 61 foreign banks had branches in Japan.[10]

With the MoF's looser policy toward the issuance of branch licenses, a Tokyo outpost no longer fell within the exclusive purview of the biggest and best. By the end of the decade, modest sized banks were obtaining access. Almost lemming like, Tokyo seemed to be at the top of everyone's list of international offices. This was true even as business declined.

The Ministry even let First Chicago have a branch. Infamous since the 1965 decision to reduce credit to Japan, the bank had been relegated to the bottom of the MoF's list of possible entrants. Nor did things seem any better by the early 1970s. When bank officials met over lunch with Yusuke Kashiwagi, Vice Minister for International Affairs, he reminded them of the credit line issue and indicated that they would not receive a branch license while he remained Vice Minister.

Only after Kashiwagi stepped down in 1971 did Wallace Anker, the bank's representative in Tokyo, succeed in obtaining a license. The process, however, also saw an unusual meeting between the Japanese consulate general stationed in Chicago, Yasuhiko Nara, and Gaylord Freeman, Chairman of First Chicago. In an unusually blunt fashion, Nara made very clear to Freeman that the pulling of the credit lines had caused a loss of face and could not be repeated.

As the numbers grew, the tortuous application process became more routine. Foreign lawyers had seen numerous examples and were highly proficient at the application process. The MoF continued to take a hard look at the operational capacity of banks but ceased to insist on the employment of a Japanese advisor. The change reflected the MoF's increased comfort with the foreign banking community. Translated, this meant that the MoF no longer saw them as a significant threat to the domestic financial system or as a source of novel and difficult issues.

By the 1970s, therefore, a fundamental shift had occurred at the Ministry with respect to access by foreign banks. The days of exclusion were over; foreign banks wanting access to Tokyo could get it. The shift reflected the MoF's heightened sensitivity toward international sentiment. Japanese banks had begun concerted expansion abroad, something that threatened to cause a backlash. Others in the Ministry realized that Japan's role in the international markets necessitated increased opening to foreign banks.

None of that newfound attitude, however, transferred to activities within Japan. The Ministry had little sympathy with plans to expand existing branch networks. Letting foreign banks in was one thing; allowing them to compete aggressively in domestic markets was an entirely different matter. Citibank through the 1970s tried to open additional branches, as did Chase. Neither succeeded.

GOVERNMENT CONTROL OF FOREIGN BANKS

The influx of foreign banks brought new challenges to the prevailing system of government control. In the early years, government control of foreign banks was straightforward and complete. Through limits on yen funding, the banks had little access to the domestic economy. They primarily dispensed dollars in the form of bankers acceptances and impact loans. Administrative guidance or *gyosei shido* gave the Bank of Japan and the MoF full control over their activities.

All banks, not just foreign, were subjected to close oversight. The primary source of control arose out of the vagaries of the Banking Law of 1927. It gave the Ministry almost unlimited discretion over banking activities, particularly branch openings. Those wanting to expand had to remain on good terms with MoF.

Foreign exchange activities represented another source of control. Banks had a monopoly over currency transactions; securities firms were excluded. To engage in the activity, they needed to be licensed as an Authorized Foreign Exchange Bank. Getting the license did not end control. Each individual transaction also had to be approved. Even after foreign currency transactions were essentially deregulated, the Ministry continued to require pre-notification. The MoF would not accept a notification whenever the deal was unfamiliar or inconsistent with its wishes.

Ministry approval for a particular transaction required one-on-one negotiations with the relevant official in the relevant bureau. In the case of foreign banks, this usually meant the International Finance Bureau.[11]

Approval therefore amounted to an intensely personal affair. With edicts rarely reduced to writing, government officials could ultimately avoid blame by disavowing responsibility when things went wrong.

The MoF used guidance to exercise tight control over the banking system. Administrative guidance involved "advice" on the appropriate course of activity. Informal and generally oral, the advice could be distributed on the phone, at social occasions, or in face-to-face meetings at the Ministry. Guidance affected all banks and all practices. Financial institutions did not take any significant step without first informing the Ministry. Banks learned to pre-clear all important developments, whether or not legally required. There would be "no surprises."

To express displeasure, the MoF rarely actually had to say no. A simple statement that the time was not right for an application or activity was ordinarily sufficient. Banks did not dare submit an application or otherwise go forward in the face of such bureaucratic disapprobation. Once the MoF agreed to accept the application, however, official approval amounted to a rote formality, a final ritual.

Every aspect of the financial market fell under the MoF's watchful eye. The most potent manifestation of Ministry authority, however, was rarely seen. This came from the ability to alter or eradicate practices before they became public. Asking Japanese bankers for examples of MoF influence often generated blank stares. The authority was ubiquitous. Banks simply did not take steps of any significance without giving the MoF an opportunity to shape and alter them.

Foreign expansion in the 1970s, however, caused leaks in the highly regulated financial system. The banks stood ready to circumvent central bank policy, particularly tight money policies, at a moment's notice. They eagerly lent funds any time that the Bank of Japan clamped down on Japanese banks. They therefore posed a potential challenge to government control. As one official noted, "foreign banks in Japan have grown to the stage of having an influence on the nation's economy."[12]

The government, unsurprisingly, began to tighten its grip over foreign banks. For one thing, this meant day-to-day contact with the government, particularly the central bank. "Regular meetings" were scheduled with officials from foreign branches and representative offices. Banks had to report yen loans to the central bank every day by 3:00 p.m. and could expect a dunning phone call for reports even a few minutes late. Foreign exchange dealings also had to be reported on a daily basis. Like their Japanese counterparts, foreign banks filed quarterly forecasts of lending activity.

During the early 1970s, the Bank of Japan made clear that foreign banks had no permanent immunity from window guidance, the system used to control lending volume by Japanese banks. The Bank of Japan wanted to curtail lending in an effort to control inflation following the first oil crisis in 1973. The clamp-down was extended to the handful of large US banks in the country, bringing them within the system of window guidance for the first time. After about 18 months the restrictions were lifted.[13]

Failure to follow guidance could result in any number of nasty consequences. Financial regulators had the ability to dry up supplies of yen. Recalcitrant foreign banks might discover their swap limits cut or at least not increased in the same proportion. The Bank of Japan also controlled funds in the interbank market. An offending bank trying to arrange a loan through a Tanshi broker might find its calls not returned.

The growing role of foreign banks in exchange trading also caused concern. The MoF limited the trades to real use, prohibiting speculation. Daily reporting requirements carried the implicit threat that anything smacking of speculation would be penalized. Following allegations of "currency speculation" in 1977, the central bank threatened to impose reserve requirements on all foreign exchange holdings.

The Ministry initiated more frequent inspections of foreign bank branches, with examinations taking place every two or three years. To show that no foreign bank fell beyond the pale, the government inspected the Bank of America in 1977, followed by the other large US banks, including Chase, J. P. Morgan, Citibank, and Manufacturers Hanover. The government also required the banks to make additional financial disclosure.

Even if uniformly applied, administrative guidance often had a disproportionate impact on foreign banks.[14] In an effort to control inflation in the early 1970s, the government prohibited banks borrowing funds in the yen call market from making new loans. Because foreign branches relied extensively on this market, they were severely impacted by the policy.

The informal unwritten system also caused considerable confusion. Foreign banks did not always know whether they were being treated equally. Unorganized, the banks were also susceptible to a strategy of divide and conquer. When officials from the Tax Bureau at the MoF tried to impose a standardized method of determining the cost of funds from overseas, they got a handful of banks to agree first, despite the increased costs. Other banks were forced to follow suit.

Whatever the precise parameters, foreign bankers felt the ubiquitous presence of the government. As one bank official commented: "I have the feeling that every time I flush the toilet, a red light goes on in the Bank of Japan."[15] The failure to follow the government's wishes could result in a meeting at the MoF. As Walter Wriston put it: "If that didn't work, a second meeting would be held, and this time there was no tea served."[16]

THE DREAM ERA: 1970–1974

Despite the flood of new entrants and the high level of government control, Japan during the first half of the decade represented a banker's dream: plenty of business, fat margins, and, best of all, no risk. The growing number of

61

banks initially had little impact on profitability. Japan in the beginning of the 1970s still suffered from a capital shortage, although the country's global balance of trade was already shifting to the black, and foreign banks provided corporations with much of the necessary funding. Business was bountiful and lucrative.

Foreign banking activities in Japan largely fell into four categories: dollar loans, yen loans, trade finance, and foreign exchange, with military banking an additional source of revenue for American Express and the three largest US banks.[17] Impact loans in particular continued to play an important role in the Japanese financial system, although ominous signs loomed. Japanese companies still needed foreign capital. In 1970, Japanese banks raised 12 percent of all lending funds from external sources, down only slightly from 16 percent in 1951.[18] They also remained more or less risk free. Japanese banks guaranteed the loans, receiving in return a fee of 0.5 percent of the loan amount.

Foreign banks continued to have a monopoly on the loans, something that ended temporarily in 1974. With the country in need of dollars to pay increased oil bills, the MoF expanded the categories of banks that could bring in the funds. The entry of Japanese banks caused the market share of foreign banks to plummet. The loss of the loans also had collateral consequences. Foreign banks still required a portion of any impact loan converted to yen to be left on deposit with the bank. The decline in impact loans saw a concomitant decline in these compensating balances. The MoF, however, withdrew the authority from Japanese banks, reinstating the foreign monopoly. While dollar loans by foreign banks returned to normal, compensating balances did not recover.

In contrast to impact loans, yen dominated loans were not guaranteed. Still, as a practical matter, they remained essentially risk free, at least for loans made to the right companies. To protect the country's credit rating, the Japanese government was not about to allow foreign banks to suffer. The collapse of Ataka & Co. made this clear.

The failure of a Canadian oil refinery drove the Japanese trading company into bankruptcy. Foreign banks found themselves with outstanding loans, creating the prospect of large losses. Robert Wynn called headquarters in New York to let them know that the bank was about to have the ignominious distinction of becoming the first foreign bank to incur significant loan losses in Japan. The call, however, proved premature.

Later the same day, officials from the Bank of Japan called to assure J. P. Morgan about the losses. The bank was told to expect a visit from Sumitomo Bank. On cue, an official arrived with the news that the loans would be assumed by the Japanese bank and full payment made. The next call was back to New York to explain that, despite the absence of any legal obligation, J. P. Morgan would not be held accountable for the bad loans.

The loan assumption was part of a government sponsored bailout. The

Banking Bureau had instructed Sumitomo, the lead bank for Ataka, to come up with a solution to the trading company's financial problems. C. Itoh & Co. acquired a significant portion of Ataka's assets but refused to accept all of the liabilities. Pushed by the Bank of Japan, Sumitomo and Kyowa agreed to absorb the lion's share of the company's bad debts, including those from the foreign banks.[19] In addition to J. P. Morgan, Continental Illinois and Citibank also apparently benefited from the bailout.

The system of loan guarantees and government inspired rescue operations had a critical purpose. They helped the country maintain an impeccable credit rating. For a country dependent upon foreign funds, the perceived safety of lending activities facilitated the capital raising process. Things would change as the country began to show a consistent trade surplus, dramatically reducing the need to import dollars. The shift would become clear by mid-decade.

Exchange trading represented another area of foreign banking activity. Banks had a monopoly over exchange trading; securities firms had no comparable authority. Foreign banks were all licensed under the Foreign Exchange Control Law. Through the early 1970s, foreign exchange trading remained relatively straightforward. Until Nixon ended the system of fixed exchange rates, transactions involved little risk. Guidance ensured that fees were fat and fixed. For each dollar exchanged, a bank typically made one yen, a high margin in a no risk transaction. With guidance used to set the margin, foreign banks had little opportunity to compete on price.

Japanese banks had most of the exchange business. Companies typically assigned the business in proportion to the amount borrowed from each bank. Responsible for a paltry percentage of lending, foreign banks received only a small share. They would, however, obtain half of the exchange business on any impact loan converted into yen and vice versa.[20] Inclusion of exchange trading could transform a marginal loan into a profitable transaction. Only in the 1980s, when the MoF eliminated much of the guidance in the area, did the foreign exchange volume of non-Japanese banks jump.

The early 1970s did witness the first serious efforts of foreign banks to break out of their post-war niche in the financial markets. The first breakthrough occurred when the MoF allowed them to engage in management consulting and leasing ventures with Japanese banks. Citibank was the first, forming a consulting firm with Fuji Bank. The venture was intended to provide advice to foreign companies entering the country and Japanese companies going abroad. The joint ventures proved popular. Following the efforts by Citibank and Fuji, other ventures surfaced, including Chase/ Mitsubishi and Bank of America/Sumitomo.

Citibank also became the first to enter into a leasing venture, contributing capital to Fuyo, a subsidiary of Fuji Bank.[21] Leasing companies amounted to a more significant commitment. The companies would acquire property, typically with borrowed funds, and lease it to the relevant business. Capital starved companies did not have to come up with the entire purchase price. Margins on the business were higher but so were the risks. Leasing companies also fell outside the MoF's oversight authority; they were the primary responsibility of the Ministry of International Trade and Industry. Foreign banks would learn that, in the absence of the paternalistic protection of the MoF, successful operations became far more problematic.

Foreign banks in general found the leasing ventures limiting. To provide additional expertise, the MoF insisted that the ventures include a Japanese partner. Foreign banks therefore did not have the flexibility to act in a unilateral fashion. The extent of foreign ownership was also capped. Finally, the expanded authority had an air of reciprocity. Not coincidentally, joint ventures received approval at a time when Japanese companies were attempting to engage in similar activities in the United States.[22]

In the greater scheme of things, the new activities did not amount to much. The requirement of a Japanese partner constrained the operating flexibility of US banks. By the early 1980s, the leasing and consulting ventures had either ended or become relatively insignificant portions of foreign banking operations. Still, in the early 1970s, they had psychological significance. They represented the first major foray out of the MoF prescribed market niche for foreign banks. Over time, agitation would grow for even greater operational latitude.

The first half of the decade, therefore, generally went well for foreign banks. Activities expanded; more banks were allowed in; profits remained high. Even the oil crisis in 1973, an economic disaster for Japan, proved to be a boon to foreign banks. With growth rates declining and Japan undergoing a rare brush with high inflation, the Bank of Japan imposed a harsh, tight money policy. Not for the first time, the use of *hikishime* dried up funds for Japanese business. Once again starved for capital, Japanese industry flocked to foreign banks, with earnings hitting an all time high. Ship building and oil refiners in particular had high demand. Foreign banks saw a return to the days of yore when business was plentiful and margins fat. By September 1975, foreign banks had increased their share of total bank loans to 3.2 percent.[23]

Clouds, however, loomed. Increases in lending did not mean an improvement in deposits, with the percentage hovering around 1 percent. The practice of compensating balances had ended. Moreover, the increase in lending activity occurred as a result of unusual economic conditions and government intervention. Neither would last.

THE DECLINE: 1975–1979

As the decade progressed, the position of foreign banks in Japan changed or, more accurately, deteriorated. Additional banks continued to pour into the market; the MoF no longer seemed to invoke licensing procedures to restrict entry. Limitations on access to the domestic market, however, remained. Increasing numbers of banks were therefore fighting over a shrinking amount of business. When the inevitable occurred and profits fell, the complacent attitude of most foreign banks changed. A cacophony of voices calling for reform developed, something increasingly heard by foreign governments. The era of foreign pressure had arrived.

Through the middle of the decade, foreign banking in Japan remained dull but profitable, with four US banks leading the pack.[24] That ended abruptly in 1975. With a positive trade balance, Japan was awash in dollars. Moreover, the fall-off in growth following the oil crisis sharply reduced corporate Japan's need for loans. As a result, the volume of impact loans – the bread and butter of the foreign banking community – began to fall. What business remained no longer had the same allure. Decreased demand and increased competition squeezed margins.

To add insult to injury, Japanese companies began to repay existing loans. As the Bank of Japan loosened controls on lending by Japanese banks, interest rates fell. At the same time, the value of the yen strengthened. Both made it financially advantageous to repay earlier dollar loans, which Japanese companies did in earnest. Overdependent upon impact loans, repayment had a disproportionate effect upon foreign banking activities.

Even worse, by decade's end, foreign banks permanently lost their monopoly. In the late 1970s, the Ministry relaxed rules on foreign currency loans to Japanese borrowers in an effort to support the yen. This included authorization to make impact loans. Within two years, the volume held by foreign banks fell below 50 percent.

Impact loans were not the only problem area; yen loans also declined. Foreign banks remained higher cost, marginal lenders. As the government eased tight money policies, Japanese companies went back to their preferred domestic lenders. Moreover, as economic growth in Japan slowed from blistering to only torrid, Japanese companies simply did not have the same need for bank loans, causing a sluggish lending market.

The numbers told the story. By the end of 1977, lending by foreign banks had gone into steep decline. With the fall-off in lending went profitability. Between 1976 and 1979, return on assets fell from 0.93 percent to 0.29 percent.[25] By mid-year 1978, total foreign banking assets in Japan ranked below those in Bulgaria, Liberia, and Bermuda.

The inability of foreign banks to obtain substantial market share was in part a result of the difficulty in obtaining yen funding.[26] That was not the only explanation, however. Difficulties flowed from conceptual differences over the role of banks. Foreign banks wanted the business but not the responsibility. Japanese companies operated under a system of primary or lead banks. Lead banks had responsibilities well beyond occasional loans. The bank was expected to be informed of, and involved in, the operations of

65

the company. Typically this meant share ownership, indirect representation on the board of directors, and loans during times of trouble.[27] The bank might even engineer a bailout, with bank officials transferred to key positions at the company until it was nursed back to health.

Companies accepted the relationship – including the resulting control – for one critical reason: supply. With essentially no public market for corporate debt, Japanese businesses remained dependent on bank funds for financing. The lead bank ensured that the company had sufficient supplies of capital. This did not comport with accepted notions of banking. To the extent offered a position as lead bank for a Japanese company, most foreign financial institutions would have refused. Foreign banks wanted the business but not the obligations that went along, even had Japanese companies been willing. This necessarily constrained competitiveness.

Relying on a foreign bank as a primary lender had other implications. With foreign financial institutions less susceptible to government control, companies using them would be subject to reduced influence, something that no doubt caused shudders within the Japanese bureaucracy. Banks and bank loans represented the critical vehicle for implementing industrial policy. Foreign banks could not be counted upon to be as solicitous toward government policies.

All of this was clear from the only significant exception to the unwillingness of foreign banks to play the role of lead bank to a Japanese company. Bank of America acted as chief lender for Idemitsu, a Japanese oil refinery. Known as a maverick, the company had a fractious relationship with the government. When financial problems developed, Bank of America found itself having to provide the company with additional funds. While the loans were ultimately repaid, the circumstances demonstrated once and for all to foreign banks the risks associated with a primary banking relationship.

The decline in conventional sources of business – particularly impact loans – set off a mad scramble for alternatives. Blue-chip companies offered few prospects. Companies had reduced funding needs, with much of the necessary capital coming from earnings. For the first time to any significant degree foreign banks began to move "down market." This meant high risk areas like consumer lending or commercial loans to less well established companies. With the shift, the nature and risk of banking in Japan increased dramatically.

Consumer finance demonstrated the opportunities and costs of the new environment. Consumer finance had been the stepchild of the Japanese banking system. The MoF wanted scarce capital to flow to corporate Japan to build factories for exports, not to individuals to buy refrigerators. In the 1950s, the MoF had imposed a priority system for all bank loans, with consumer loans at the bottom. Individuals wanting a loan to buy a stereo or take a vacation found banks unresponsive. To get a loan meant resorting to the sarakin.

Sarakin were Japanese finance companies, many with alleged ties to organized crime. They lent funds at exorbitant rates, often over 100 percent. Requiring little paperwork or evidence of credit standing, sarakin instead relied upon questionable, even violent, methods of ensuring repayment. Regulated by municipal governments, the finance companies fell outside the oversight of the MoF. As long as the companies had only a fringe presence, they escaped much official notice or concern.

In the mid-1970s, however, things changed. The finance companies began aggressively marketing their services. Salarymen were encouraged to take out loans for pocket money or vacations. Borrowers often had trouble repaying the loans at the exorbitant rates. Examples of personal tragedy surfaced, as some lost their homes and others committed suicide. The Ministry decided to rein in the companies, and used foreign banks as the vehicle for doing so.

The MoF authorized banks to enter the consumer sector and they did with vigor. Citibank, Security Pacific, and Bank of America created consumer finance companies. US banks actively sought business through competitively priced loans, charging a maximum interest of 48 percent. They also offered more straightforward collection methods or, as one banker put it: "We won't break your kneecaps if you don't pay."[28] Their presence was quickly felt. Consumer loans went from ¥3.1 billion in 1970 to ¥38.6 billion in 1977.

The MoF also helped reduce the competition from sarakin through a dose of administrative guidance. Japanese banks were told not to lend to the finance companies. The guidance had a double edge, however. Many Japanese banks ceased lending to the entire consumer finance industry, making it harder for the foreign finance companies to raise funds.

Foreign banks did not find the consumer market easy going. The MoF still imposed administrative barriers. More importantly, the market proved unprofitable. The country had no credit bureaus, making it difficult to obtain background information on prospective borrowers. The credit standing of each borrower had to be analyzed separately, generating a large rejection rate. Even when loans were made, a high default rate caused red ink to swell. Those in hock to the sarakin often borrowed from foreign finance companies to repay the loans.[29] With the less harsh collection methods, Japanese borrowers preferred to owe foreign banks rather than the sarakin.

As the banks branched into these areas, the safety of the market declined. Japanese banks did not guarantee repayment of lower quality loans. By the summer of 1977, guarantees were no longer common. Foreign banks had to determine creditworthiness and absorb more risk.

In the search for alternative sources of business, lines of business quickly appeared and disappeared, with the advantages going to the quick and nimble. Wells Fargo discovered a Japanese traveler's penchant for dollars rather than travelers' checks. The bank did a rousing business by converting yen into greenbacks. The vault was stacked high with dollars.

Aircraft leasing represented another example. The leases arose from a short-term effort to reduce the trade surplus with the United States. Leasing companies acquired the planes and leased them to airlines that lacked the credit standing to purchase them outright. Dubbed Samurai leases, the planes were purchased with funds borrowed from the Export–Import Bank at attractive interest rates.[30] The aircraft did not enter Japan but went directly to the country of the airline executing the lease.

The MoF never shared much enthusiasm for the leases, maintaining a stony silence. A few US banks, however, including Chase, did a number of quick deals. Ultimately, the MoF put an end to them. The Ministry of Foreign Affairs became less enamored with the transactions once it became apparent that they did little to improve the trade imbalance. The Ex–Im Bank stopped the cheap loans used to buy the planes. After more than $700 million worth of aircraft sales, the program vanished.

The late 1970s also saw the first participation by foreign banks in a yen currency syndication to a foreign borrower. A consortium put together by Tokai Bank for a loan to an Algerian bank included nine foreign financial institutions. The effort by foreign banks to become managers of yen loan syndicates proved harder to engineer. For obvious reasons, Japanese banks opposed the step.

PRESSURE ON JAPAN

As the financial system continued to evolve, a new, less predictable source of reform emerged. For the first time, foreign governments began to respond to the complaints of their banks about restrictions on operations in Japan and started doing something about it. The United States was the laggard, arriving late to the bargaining table. Clearly, however, stirrings were even beginning back in Washington.

Through most of the post-occupation period, the US government, particularly the State Department, had little interest in banking issues. The political and military role of Japan in the containment of the Soviet Union predominated. More preoccupied with geopolitical issues, trade in general and the financial services sector in particular hardly broke the surface. Bankers talked about the role of the Embassy during the period with disdain, claiming that help rarely emerged.

The first significant public use of foreign government pressure by banks occurred in 1976 and came not from the United States but from Europe. The Tax Bureau of the Ministry attempted to impose additional assessments on foreign banks. The bureau accused the banks of overstating interest costs in an effort to reduce tax revenues in the country. Foreign banks collectively confronted an additional $100 million in taxes. This caused an outcry in the foreign banking community.

The banks approached both the MoF and their respective governments.

68

The controversy showed the different attitudes of foreign officials. While some embassies intervened, US bankers complained that theirs did little. The furor ultimately died without assessment of additional taxes. The efforts showed that foreign government intervention at a minimum would cause the MoF to act more cautiously.

Two years later, Christopher Tugendhat, a member of the European Commission, traveled to Japan to discuss the treatment of foreign banks. He raised a number of complaints, including the inability to obtain an adequate supply of yen. A few modest reforms followed from the talks. Tugendhat was assured that, to the extent that Japanese banks received the authority to issue certificates of deposit, the same power would be extended to foreign banks. The government also agreed that the establishment of branches by foreign banks would be "flexibly handled." Nonetheless, the promises were vaguely worded and entailed little change in practice. The visit had one immediate, positive effect, however. After Tugendhat departed, the Japanese government raised the swap limits for foreign banks.

The trip seemed to embolden foreign banks. Almost contemporaneously, foreign banks began to go public with complaints about regulation in Japan. By 1978, words such as "demanded" were being used to describe the position of the foreign banking community on liberalization. Citibank as usual led the pack. The bank weighed in on the debate over the right to issue certificates of deposit. Participation occurred in league with Japanese city banks. Working through the Federation of Bankers Associations, Citibank and others agreed to publicly push reforms sought by the large Japanese banks. Following this initial foray, city banks followed with public support of the positions. This represented an early example of the deliberate use of foreign pressure or *gaiatsu* by a domestic constituency in Japan.

As the complaints of foreign banks grew louder, the MoF invited representatives to talk to the Financial System Research Council about reforms of the banking system. The Council, an advisory group of the Banking Bureau, had been considering revisions of the 1927 Banking Law. In November 1978, four foreign banks testified: Bank of America, Deutsche Bank, J. P. Morgan, and National Westminster. Among other things, the banks contended, in an unusual display of outspokenness, that they were disadvantaged by the existing regulatory scheme. They called for increased liberalization of the capital markets, emphasizing the difficulty confronted by foreign financial institutions in raising yen funds.

The reaction of the complaints was defensive and surreal. The central bank took the position that "foreign banks operating in Japan have not been subject to any discriminatory treatment."[31] When confronted with allegations that foreign banks could not borrow from the Bank of Japan and had been subject to limits on loans from home offices, the bank gave half-hearted explanations. The central bank claimed that foreign banks could borrow in the interbank market. When told that Japanese banks declined to do so

69

because of "window guidance," the central bank claimed that the situation was unique.[32]

The report ultimately issued by the Council did little to address the problems of foreign banks. The report essentially found the complaints to be without basis.

> Criticisms that there are differences in the treatment meted out to foreign banks in Japan and to Japanese banks have been raised in certain quarters. However, in actuality, foreign banks are treated equally in all fields, including branch office administration, transactions with the Bank of Japan, and foreign exchange control matters. No substantial differences exist in the treatment of the two types of banks. At the root of such criticism lies the fact that profits made by foreign banks have recently fallen.[33]

The report did make a handful of recommendations concerning the treatment of foreign banks, although none that would fundamentally alter their position in the financial sector.

Nor did the government seem to appreciate the more outspoken position of the foreign banks. To some, the displeasure seemed clear. As part of the reform process, Japanese banks were permitted to make impact loans, something that had historically been a monopoly of foreign banks. Some viewed the act as a penalty imposed on foreign banks for having been outspoken about reforms in the late 1970s.[34]

These developments represented a watershed. For the last time, US banks attempted to induce reform without any significant assistance, implicit or explicit, from Washington. The US government was awakening slowly to the difficulties of banks in Japan. The Tugendhat trip was followed by a visit to Japan by a senior officer of the Federal Reserve Bank of San Francisco. Banks took the opportunity to once again issue complaints about discriminatory treatment in the Japanese market. These were discussed informally with the Ministry.

The real impetus for the shifting attitude, however, came from Congress. As part of the International Banking Act of 1978, Congress ordered the Department of the Treasury to draft a report examining the treatment of US banks in certain designated countries, including Japan. To write the report, the Treasury sent a fact finding mission to Japan. The Treasury attaché in the US Embassy in Japan began to develop information on foreign banking problems. The results appeared in the first National Treatment Study issued in 1979. Although noting some progress, the study concluded that there was still a "substantial lack of national treatment in equality of competitive opportunity" in Japan.[35] Treasury was becoming accuated and would eventually take the lead in negotiating the opening of the Japanese financial markets.

The same period also saw the beginning of growing congressional concern with Japanese financial matters. In addition to requiring the National Treatment Study, Congressman James Jones from Oklahoma, the Chairman of the House Budget Committee, had previously visited Japan on a fact finding mission. In 1978, he returned and issued a report criticizing a variety of trade practices, particularly procurement and barriers to merchandise imports. Almost as an afterthought, the report included charges of discrimination against foreign banks.

The report drew a visceral reaction from Japanese officials, who labeled it unfair. The response, however, seemed disingenuous. For example, in refuting allegations that the MoF discriminated against foreign banks in the opening of branches, the director general of the Banking Bureau of the MoF noted that 61 foreign banks had branches, 13 of which had more than two. While the statistics demonstrated a willingness to let the banks in, they likewise demonstrated an unwillingness to permit them to expand into the domestic economy.

Still, the early efforts to obtain reform had some positive impact. Complaints about yen funding got the attention of the Ministry. Swap ceilings were lifted. The decision to authorize certificates of deposit also occurred at least in part from foreign pressure. The Jones report therefore became one of the first concrete examples of how foreign pressure could be used to induce change. Irrespective of the merits, Japanese government officials preferred to address some of the complaints rather than risk a return trip and further public criticism.

5

BREAKDOWN OF CONSENSUS
Reform of the Japanese financial markets

Foreign banks were not the only financial institutions chafing under the system of regulation in Japan. Pressure was also building within the Japanese financial community for reform. By the end of the 1970s, Japanese banks confronted a system still highly regulated and rigidly compartmentalized. Divided into segments – trust banks, regional banks, long-term-credit banks, trust banks, city banks, and sogo banks – each had a particular role in the process of funneling funds to Japanese industry.[1] In many respects, foreign banks were no different. They amounted to purveyors of international capital to corporate Japan.

That was not to say that the financial system had remained immutable since the end of the war. The banking system actually seemed to be in a continuous state of change. Whether the addition of reserve requirements, laws facilitating mergers, or a deposit insurance scheme, the financial sector had been subject to periodic revision. In general, however, the reforms did not alter the basic symmetry or the underlying approach toward regulation.

The usual state of affairs came to an abrupt end in the 1970s. The decade experienced a series of upheavals that could not be ignored. No matter how effective the Japanese financial system had been in contributing to the country's economic recovery, matters could not remain the same following the floating of exchange rates and the first oil crisis. The highly compartmentalized, tightly controlled system of regulation began to show strain.

The increase in oil prices wreaked havoc, with economic growth falling from double to single digits.[2] The system of credit rationing started to unravel. In coping with the effects of more restrained growth, corporate Japan began to borrow less and to search for alternative sources of funding. Companies looked increasingly to the Euromarkets for financing, although pressure also began to build for more liquid debt markets in Japan. The historically close relationship between corporate Japan and banks began to weaken.

Japanese companies also became increasingly dissatisfied with the low rate of return on deposits inside the country. With interest rates still controlled, deposits began to trickle, then flow, away from the banks. As the percentage of deposits spiraled downward, city banks agitated for reforms designed to attract back the lost funds. That meant offering instruments with market rates. The end of the decade therefore saw the introduction of certificates of deposit, the first major inroad into the system of controlled interest rates.

These developments effectively ended the consensus within the financial community over the shape of the post-war regulatory system. City banks, in particular, became increasingly unhappy with their prescribed niche. Unable to raise long-term funds, they learned the consequences of the limitation first hand when short-term deposits vanished during the oil crisis in 1973, forcing the banks to borrow at premium rates.

Of greater moment, however, city banks began to clamor for the authority to sell securities. Whether dealing in government bonds or underwriting corporate debentures, banks wanted a role in the burgeoning debt markets. The authority ran directly into the occupation-imposed wall separating banking and securities functions. Brokers adamantly opposed the intrusion, not without reason. Banks could use their sizable branch networks and close corporate relationships to make serious inroads into the securities business.

The Ministry of Finance (MoF) rested at the center of the storm, confronting a seemingly impossible task. Notwithstanding immense authority and often imperious attitudes, the Ministry remained incapable of dictating the evolution of the financial market in the face of intractable opposition. As the need for reform became increasingly clear, divisions within the financial community over the direction and contours of change made any effort to obtain a consensus almost insurmountable. The compartmentalization that had contributed so heavily to the development of the financial system had now become a source of paralysis.

The early efforts at casting off post-war vestiges, however, remained almost imperceptible or tentative. While deregulation of interest rates had started, reforms were incremental and, by decade's end, had stopped. Similarly, the conflicts between banks and securities firms were papered over, with amendments to the Banking Law essentially acceding to banks small inroads into the securities area. It would take involvement by the United States before the reform process would become more dynamic.

THE REFORM PROCESS

Reform of the Japanese financial markets during the post-war era amounted to a relatively complex affair. Despite all of the MoF's apparent authority, the bureaucracy had little ability to command when it came to changes in the financial sector. Instead, change entailed an intense process of negotiation, involving a host of interest groups, including politicians, industry, and the bureaucracy.[3]

Reform required a consensus among those affected. The need for industry acceptance caused the MoF to adopt a number of expedient practices in administering the financial markets. The top tier of Japanese city banks, for example, was treated in an essentially identical fashion. Within that tier, international expansion and increases in lending tended to be uniform. The Ministry knew that any disparity would generate a revolt.

Consensus building meant that reform was a long-term process. Reform also tended to be incremental. While changes in the financial system occurred with some frequency through the 1970s, they generally did not involve alterations in the fundamental approach toward regulation. Indeed, the primary source of regulatory authority – the Banking Law of 1927 – remained unchanged in any significant respect for more than 50 years.

Efforts at comprehensive reform did surface during the occupation. The changes inspired by the Supreme Commander of the Allied Powers (SCAP) died as a result of opposition in Washington and lack of interest in Japan.[4] Proposals in 1950 by the Banking Bureau would have increased Ministry control over the financial system.[5] Japanese banks opposed the changes and when occupation officials declined to promote the reforms, they quickly disappeared. Thereafter, no serious attempts were made at comprehensive reform.

In the mid-1950s, the Bank of Japan received the authority to set reserve requirements. Designed primarily as a mechanism to increase government control over banks, the reforms engendered resistance in the financial community. Banks had little interest in placing scarce funds that could be lent to corporate borrowers in reserve accounts. The eventual decision to set reserves at extremely low levels no doubt contributed to ultimate acceptance by the banking community.

The 1960s saw the adoption of provisions designed to facilitate bank mergers. The changes were implemented under the guiding hand of Satoshi Sumita, who became director general of the Banking Bureau in 1966 and later served both as administrative vice minister, the highest career position within the Ministry, and Governor of the Bank of Japan.[6] The changes were intended to encourage consolidation among smaller banks by, among other things, permitting commercial and sogo banks to merge.[7]

In the early 1970s, the MoF continued to tinker mildly with, and modestly refine, the financial system, most noticeably through the addition of a long overdue system of deposit insurance. The system guaranteed depositors repayment of funds up to a designated limit in the event of a bank failure. The system had a small staff and low initial capitalization.[8] The small staff necessarily meant that the system had to rely primarily upon the Bank of Japan for assistance in the implementation of policies. Indeed, the deputy governor of the central bank headed the deposit insurance corporation.

Financial reforms had therefore been under almost continuous consideration since the 1950s. They resembled refinements, however, rather than substantive revisions. Financial institutions were still rigidly compartmentalized, interest rates still governed by government fiat. The principal elements of the post-war system remained unchanged.

The approach came to an abrupt end in the early 1970s when the Japanese economy suffered a series of externally administered blows. On August 15, 1971, President Nixon prohibited the conversion of dollars into gold, imposed a 10 percent surtax on imports, and allowed the dollar to float. With the destabilizing of exchange rates, the international capital markets for the first time significantly intruded into the domestic regulatory system. Japanese companies suddenly found themselves subject to unaccustomed exchange risks; the MoF suddenly found itself having to defend the yen in international capital markets.[9]

Disconcerting though the Nixon shocks proved to be, the Japanese financial sector was even more convulsed by the first oil crisis. OPEC's announcement of a substantial increase in the price of oil hit Japan, a country with no known reserves, hard. The country's economy temporarily seized, with gross national product (GNP) actually falling. The crisis effectively divided eras. Double digit growth in GNP from 1950 to 1973 halved. In 1974, economic growth actually fell. Thereafter, economic expansion hovered around 4 percent.

The change in the economic growth rate caused corporate Japan to become more cost sensitive. Losing patience with the paltry return paid on bank deposits and in search of alternatives, they began to move funds out of low yield deposits to higher paying investments. Volume in the *gensaki* market, a short-term market for secured loans and dominated by securities firms, jumped.[10]

Companies also became more sensitive about the cost of capital. The days were gone when corporate Japan would pay almost any price to obtain the funds necessary to expand. Companies searched for alternatives to yen loans from Japanese banks. Initial sights were set on the Euromarket as a source of cheaper funds.

The oil crisis did more than encourage companies to move away from banks, however. It highlighted weaknesses in the Japanese regulatory scheme. The crisis caught Japanese banks in the Euromarket flat footed, demonstrating the risks associated with the compartmentalized banking system. Limited to short-term sources of funding, city banks had nonetheless made long-term loans in the Euromarket. With the sharp increase in petroleum prices, the imbalance wreaked havoc.[11]

Short-term dollar deposits in the Euromarket, a primary source of funding for Japanese city banks, disappeared. To obtain the funds necessary to satisfy existing loan obligations, the banks had to borrow. Exacerbating the problem, the Bank of Japan withdrew foreign currency on deposit with Japanese banks and began borrowing heavily in the market to pay the increased oil bills. The spike in demand for dollars forced Japanese banks to

75

pay premium rates, reflecting the collective decision of the market about the declining creditworthiness of these borrowers.

The debacle illustrated the consequences of the MoF's tight rein over Japanese banking activities as well as its interventionist approach toward crisis management. The MoF reacted by overreacting, essentially shutting down overseas lending activities by Japanese banks. A handful of representative offices aside, Japanese banks were prohibited from opening new overseas outposts. Long- and medium-term lending was banned and limits were imposed on the percentage of syndicated loans held by Japanese banks. Overseas lending came to a screeching halt.[12] Only in the latter half of the decade would the MoF finally remove the restrictions.

THE EFFECTS

The oil crisis started a chain of events that challenged some of the fundamental tenets of the Japanese financial system. Interest rate regulation and compartmentalization represented the core of the system. Developments in the 1970s made each increasingly less sustainable.

Interest rate deregulation

The government obtained control over interest rates during the occupation. Before the war, interest rates had been set by agreement among banks. The first case brought by the Japanese Fair Trade Commission under the SCAP-inspired Anti-Monopoly Law, however, ordered 27 financial institutions in the Tokyo area to abolish agreements on interest rates. The authority to set rates was transferred to the government with the adoption of the Temporary Interest Rate Law, a direct response to the case.

Intended, as the title indicated, to be "temporary," the controls ultimately became permanent. They emerged as a principal source of government control over the financial system. By keeping interest rates on deposits low, banks essentially received cheap funds. They could lend to companies at reasonable rates, while maintaining an attractive spread.

During the 1970s, pressure to end controlled interest rates came from two disparate quarters. City banks needed a vehicle to attract back corporate deposits and pressed for the authority to issue certificates of deposit with market interest rates. Simultaneously, deficit spending by the government led to the development of a secondary bond market at something resembling market rates.

Government bond sales

The oil crisis resulted in the first substantial government deficit, shattering the placid and mundane realm of government bond sales. Deficit spending represented a recent phenomenon in Japan. During the occupation, Joseph

76

Dodge had mandated balanced budgets.[13] Only in 1964 did the government abandon the requirement, with a small deficit occurring a year later. Bonds issued in the mid-1960s went for public works and other infrastructure projects.

The sale of government bonds presented a number of problems. Attracting willing purchasers seemed to dictate a market interest rate on the debt instruments. That, however, would have made other investments subject to government controls less attractive. Purchasers also presumably would want the right to resell the bonds. A secondary market, however, threatened to introduce an uncontrolled interest rate into the financial sector.

The MoF avoided these problems by forming a syndicate containing a cross section of the financial sector and obliging it to purchase the bonds.[14] Unlike the "auction" system used to sell bonds in the United States, the MoF, through the Finance Bureau, negotiated interest rates with the syndicate, usually a single city bank acting as the managing underwriter. Discussions would occur annually over total volume and monthly over specific levels of sales and interest rates.

With a judicious use of administrative guidance, the MoF could dictate the terms of the bonds, including an unattractive, below market interest rate. Syndicate members purchased the bonds to help maintain positive relations with the government or, more crassly, to avoid the enmity of the MoF. As long as the quantity remained small, the banks viewed the purchases as a cost of doing business.

The MoF also devised a creative solution to the problem of a secondary market. Had banks been able to resell the bonds to investors, they likely would have traded at market interest rates. This would have generated losses for the selling banks, making initial sales more difficult. The Ministry also would have had to address the divisive issue of the right of banks to sell the bonds.

The problem was overcome when the Bank of Japan agreed to repurchase the bonds after a one year holding period. In that way, syndicate members could sell the bonds for their face amount rather than at a discount in the secondary market. In addition, they only had to tie up capital for a relatively pain-free 12 month period. The guarantee proved popular; banks generally resold the bonds after expiration of the holding period.[15]

Foreign banks and securities firms were initially excluded from the syndicate, an early example of reverse discrimination. With the bonds carrying below market interest rates, they had no desire to participate in the money losing proposition. That ultimately changed, as sale of the bonds became a profitable business.

The contrived system of sales represented a bald attempt to manipulate the financial system to finance the deficit at below market rates.[16] The system, however, began to fall apart as bond sales jumped in response to the first oil crisis. The resulting slowdown in growth meant lower tax revenues. Prime

77

Minister Kakuei Tanaka not only refused to reduce spending, he took the opposite approach. In an effort to expand demand and reinflate the economy, Tanaka proposed dramatic increases in government expenditures, particularly through improvements to the country's infrastructure.

The money had to come from somewhere and the answer was to be deficit financing. The government embarked on massive sales not seen since the war. By the mid-1970s, deficit spending and, concomitantly, bond sales, ballooned.[17]

As the volume jumped, banks and other syndicate members became increasingly resistant to the below market interest rates set by the government. To address the concerns while keeping interest rates low, the MoF instituted a number of reforms, such as the sale of shorter-term bonds. They did not satisfy syndicate members, however. As the MoF resolutely refused to increase interest rates, the syndicate began to take uncharacteristically direct action.

The first serious dispute arose in January 1979. Unable to obtain an increase in interest rates, the syndicate settled for a reduction in the monthly volume. Not a permanent solution, the unhappiness with below market rates continued to fester. In March, talks broke down completely. Only after intervention by the Prime Minister did the MoF ultimately increase the interest rate. Talks would again break down over the issue, with the result that bonds were not issued.

In the short term, the government could sidestep the syndicate's refusal to buy by selling the bonds to captive audiences such as the Trust Fund Bureau. The government, however, could only absorb so much. As long as resistance continued, the only solution was to reduce the amount of debt or raise interest rates. The MoF chose the latter. Inevitably, these changes resulted in government bonds paying market driven interest rates.

The increase in volume also damaged beyond repair the guarantee by the Bank of Japan to repurchase the bonds. Banks were effectively stuck with large volumes of government debt. A volatile and unhealthy situation, holdings of long-term government debt increased while lending remained primarily a short-term affair. Pressure grew for the introduction of a secondary market in the bonds, something that would be introduced by the decade's end.

These seemingly technical and esoteric changes in the government bond area contained the seeds of dramatic, long-term change in the Japanese financial system. The government was forced to relinquish some of its rigid control over interest rates, a step toward complete deregulation. Other deregulated, market-driven instruments, particularly jumbo certificates of deposit, would emerge by the decade's end. The development of a secondary market for bonds also edged banks and securities companies closer together, contributing to a titanic struggle that would occupy much of the next decade.

78

Certificates of deposit

The oil crisis also generated pressure to decontrol interest rates on bank deposits. Still highly regulated, Japanese banks already had experience abroad with market rate instruments. They had issued certificates of deposit in the United States in the 1960s and in the Euromarket in the early 1970s.[18] Paying market rates, certificates of deposit were attractive vehicles for attracting deposits. Japanese banks could not issue the instruments in Japan, however.

As the decade progressed, agitation for authority to issue the instruments increased. Pressure came from a host of sources. Companies, city banks, and, significantly, for the first time, foreign banks, all had incentive to push for the reform. Companies wanted a higher return; foreign banks, with their insignificant branch network, wanted decontrolled rates as a means of competing for deposits. City banks wanted to stop the erosion of their position in the Japanese financial markets.

The relative share of the financial markets held by city banks continued to shrink. Holding 50.5 percent of the assets in 1953, the percentage fell to 41.8 percent in 1963 and 36.1 percent in 1973.[19] In contrast, the percentage for most other categories increased.[20] The decline had a number of explanations. Through the 1970s, the MoF took a penurious attitude toward the opening of new branches by city banks. Other classes, including regional banks, received approval more readily and, as a result, were better able to attract deposits, particularly at the retail level. More ominously, by the 1970s, corporate depositors were moving away in the search for higher returns.

City banks lobbied for the authority to pay higher interest rates. The right to issue certificates of deposit had been "under study" for more than 10 years. Opposition successfully bottled up the reform efforts until the late 1970s. Long-term-credit, regional and trust banks resisted the reforms as did securities firms.[21] Long-term-credit banks were concerned with competition for their five year debentures; certificates of deposit in London had a duration of up to three years. Regional banks had an adequate source of deposits and saw the reform as a no-win proposition designed to help city banks. Securities firms viewed the instruments as a threat to the *gensaki* market.

Only in May 1979 after government bond sales increased and a secondary market emerged did the Ministry finally relent and allow the introduction of certificates of deposit. Foreign banks played an important, if not decisive, role in breaking the log jam. Still wanting additional sources of yen, they lobbied hard for the authority, coordinating efforts with city banks. The Ministry's growing sensitivity about the diplomatic repercussions associated with issues of concern to foreign banks helped.

In agreeing to the reforms, however, the MoF devised a typical Japanese compromise. By keeping the minimum amount of the certificates of deposit to ¥500 million, the Ministry appeased corporations and other large investors while ensuring that rates for small depositors remained controlled. City banks would therefore not use the instrument to take retail deposits away from smaller banks. With the duration limited to six months, certificates of deposit did not directly compete with the debentures issued by long-term-credit banks.

The initial efforts at interest rate deregulation proved successful. The MoF handled the situation in a way that appeased everyone. Future efforts, however, ran into a maelstrom of criticism, appreciably slowing the rate of reform.

Decompartmentalization

The external shocks that occurred in the 1970s also began the erosion of the prevailing system of compartmentalization. The financial system consisted of rigid and segmented compartments, with each category having its own particular role and business function. Through the post-war era, classes of banks vociferously and vigorously defended their particular turf. Trust banks wanted no additional competition with pension plan management or the sale of loan trust certificates, long-term-credit banks with the sale of debentures. Regional banks had a monopoly over loans to mid-sized companies located in their prefecture and resisted any efforts by other banks to intrude. The Bank of Tokyo had the most extensive international network and looked suspiciously at other banks expanding abroad.

These banks were most concerned with encroachment into their bailiwick by the city banks, the largest private financial institutions in Japan.[22] Trust, long-term-credit and regional banks therefore opposed anything that would give city banks an additional weapon in their competitive arsenal. They fought the introduction of certificates of deposits and could not agree on a unified position on the right to sell government bonds because city banks would have benefited most from the authority.

Despite the efforts, some encroachment did occur, blurring compartmentalization at the edges. Although international operations had been dominated by the Bank of Tokyo and, to a lesser extent, city banks, regional and trust banks in the 1970s began opening offices abroad. City banks in turn began to poach individual deposits, an area dominated by regional and smaller banks.

Conflicts within the banking community represented small change, however, compared with the pitched battle developing between banks and securities firms. Brokers had been the stepchildren of the financial system, bit players at best. The stock market had a limited role in the post-war recovery. Banks, not brokers, were the financial saviors of Japanese industry. Dominated by four companies, one of them – Yamaichi – had barely avoided collapse in 1965 following a government engineered bailout.

Even underwriting, an area left to securities firms, was indirectly controlled by banks, particularly the Industrial Bank of Japan. Through the lead commission bank system, banks, not brokers, determined the terms of corporate bond issues. Banks also acted as trustee for the bondholders, which were often banks, entitling them to continuous fees from the offering process.

By the 1970s, however, securities firms had grown in economic power and stature. Led by Nomura, they began to rival banks in profitability and political influence. This partly reflected the growing importance of the stock markets. As trading volume increased, fixed commissions guaranteed enormous profits. With the newfound wealth, securities firms became large contributors to Japanese politicians, solidifying ties that could be invoked to overcome bureaucratic intransigence.

Equally important, however, securities firms had emerged as conduits for MoF-inspired policies. To the extent that problems developed in the stock market, securities firms could help. Following the dramatic fall in share prices in October 1987, the Big Four, Nomura, Daiwa, Nikko, and Yamaichi, embarked on a purchase program designed to reinflate the market, apparently at the government's request.[23]

Securities firms also played a role in bailouts of Japanese industry. If requested by the Ministry, the securities firms could be counted on to sell the corporate debt or stock needed to rescue a failing company. As a result, the securities firms, particularly the Big Four, had become important players in the financial system. Flexing their newfound strength, they were in no mood to give a piece of their monopoly to banks.

In the mid-1970s, the relationship between banks and securities firms deteriorated. As corporate Japan searched for financial alternatives, they moved away from banks. Companies turned to public debt markets, particularly in the Euromarket. Banks wanted to stay involved in the capital raising process by underwriting or selling the bonds, earning fees in the process. This, however, ran headlong into the post-war separation of banking and securities activities. Banks needed Ministry authorization; securities firms resisted.

The first battle erupted in the Euromarket. Brokers succeeded in getting the MoF to impose controls on the underwriting of Eurobonds by Japanese banks. The Three Bureaus Agreement executed between the Securities, Banking, and International Finance Bureaus in 1975 restricted the ability of Japanese banks to manage syndicates selling Eurobonds. They could co-manage but only if a Japanese securities firm also managed the offering and had a higher position in the syndicate. Implicitly, securities firms also had to receive a larger allotment.

In imposing the restraints, the MoF emphasized prudential concerns. The Ministry did not invoke Article 65, the domestic prohibition on securities activities by banks. This meant that the restriction would remain in effect until the MoF concluded that the banks had the requisite expertise. Initially,

Japanese banks viewed the agreement as a nuisance, of little concern as long as only a small number of Japanese companies issued bonds in the Euromarket. Little did they realize that the restraints would remain in place for almost 25 years.[24] As the quantity of bonds increased, the restraints caused increasing irritation.

Nor was the conflict between banks and securities firms limited to the Euromarket. Banks sought the authority to buy and sell government bonds in the domestic markets. With the Bank of Japan no longer repurchasing the bonds, banks had to look for alternative ways to unload them. Efforts to establish a secondary market in government bonds began almost immediately after the government gave up the guaranteed repurchases. In 1977, the MoF permitted the resale of bonds after a one year holding period, a period gradually shortened and ultimately eliminated.

Banks, however, found themselves locked out. They were prohibited from engaging in securities activities, including the sale of bonds.[25] Even worse, they had to sell the bonds through their arch rivals, the securities firms. City banks in particular remained unhappy with the situation.

The dispute almost came to amicable resolution in 1976. The government decided to issue five year discount bonds. Banks opposed the efforts, viewing the bonds as a source of competition for deposits and debentures. In return for an end to opposition, the Banking Bureau indicated a willingness to permit banks to sell government bonds in the secondary market.

The offer, however, proved wanting. In a pattern that would recur, banks were incapable of responding in a unified fashion. With city banks likely to get the lion's share of the business, other classes of financial institutions saw little benefit from the expanded authority. The MoF therefore went ahead and introduced the five year bonds unaccompanied by the authority to sell government debt in the secondary market.

By the late 1970s, commercial banks began to lobby vigorously for the authority to sell the bonds. The issue moved to the forefront just as the MoF sought closure on the first comprehensive revisions of the Banking Law since 1927. Characteristically, efforts to revise the Banking Law took years of study. The MoF had convened the Financial System Research Council in 1975 to consider the issue of reform. A report issued four years later called for further consolidation of the banking sector, higher capital ratios, expanded disclosure requirements, and a handful of other changes. All of this seemed fairly straightforward and unlikely to generate much controversy.

Translating the report into law, however, almost foundered on the controversy over bank involvement in the sale of government securities. The issue continued to divide banks and securities firms. In an attempt to resolve the matter, the Banking, Finance, and Securities Bureaus came up with the "three principles." They provided for amendments to the Banking Law that would allow banks to deal in government bonds but only after obtaining approval from the MoF under the Securities and Exchange Law. Even worse, the Ministry indicated that approval would not be granted in the near future.

Predictably, the approach drew heated opposition from the banks. Moreover, to the annoyance of the banks, the principles had been leaked to securities companies much earlier. In a rare display of public disfavor, the banks lobbied supporters in the Diet to overturn the principles.[26]

The efforts, however, went nowhere. The banks apparently hoped for a sympathetic ear from Prime Minister Masayoshi Ohira, a former Ministry official.[27] His sudden death dashed those expectations. In a face saving gesture, a slightly altered version of the three principles found its way into the final reforms.[28]

Financial institutions were allowed to deal in government and municipal bonds as well as commercial paper. Even this limited authority, however, did not come unencumbered. The legislation made Ministry approval a pre-condition to selling the bonds. The broader issue of the right of banks to engage in securities activities was nowhere addressed.

THE WISDOM OF HINDSIGHT

By the early 1980s, the Japanese finance markets were under considerable pressure. The compartmentalized system which had functioned so well in funneling funds to industry seemed to be unraveling. Yet no consensus existed on the direction of reform. Moreover, the internecine conflict between banks and securities firms seemed to paralyze the reform process.

This was the situation that existed when the United States started to pressure Japan to reform the financial markets in 1983. The Department of the Treasury agitated for the removal of restraints both in Japan and in the Euromarket. Although the Treasury was not exactly pushing against an open door, considerable sentiment existed within segments of the banking community and the MoF for change. When the negotiation process began, the results were unexpectedly rapid.

6

THE YEN/DOLLAR ACCORD

Through the early 1980s, reform of the Japanese financial system amounted to an entirely Japanese affair. When changes seemed necessary, the Ministry of Finance (MoF) developed a consensus within the Japanese financial community over the appropriate revisions. The process took place with little outside interference. The presence of foreign banks did sometimes affect the reform process, although in general the influence was modest.

In 1983, all of that changed. The US government, particularly the Department of the Treasury, became directly involved in the reform of the Japanese financial markets. In May of 1984, the two sides executed the Yen/Dollar Accord, a comprehensive agreement committing the Japanese government to substantial reform of the financial markets.

The importance of the United States to Japan meant that the views of the Department were entitled to some deference. That, however, did not explain the degree or nature of changes obtained in the Yen/Dollar Accord. The Treasury could not simply compel reform. Instead, success in large part resulted from its ability to enter and influence an ongoing debate within Japan. With reform efforts within Japan stymied, primarily over divisions within the Japanese financial community, including the bureaucracy, the Treasury acted as a catalyst that overcame domestic inertia.

THE END OF IMMUNITY

Whatever immunity remained for the Japanese financial system from foreign intervention came to an abrupt end in the 1980s. During the early 1970s, the United States generally ran a trade surplus with the rest of the world. By the end of the decade, the situation had undergone dramatic reversal. The country went from the largest creditor to the largest debtor. Much of the red ink flowed from the burgeoning imbalance with Japan. With a sharp spike upward, the merchandise trade deficit with Japan spiraled forward until 1987, peaking at $59.9 billion, 34.5 percent of the total US trade deficit.

Attempting to stem the hemorrhage, US trade negotiators engaged in almost continual talks with the Japanese. In general, they stressed trade in merchandise and agriculture. Beef, oranges, and baseball bats captured public attention; financial services did not. That, however, changed as the decade progressed.

Services had become undeniably important to the US economy. More than half of all jobs and most new growth came from the services sector. In the midst of the doom and gloom over the trade deficit, services also represented one area where the country remained competitive. An imprecise category, services included transportation, finance, and travel. Through the 1980s, the United States consistently ran a surplus in service exports to the Japanese. The surplus peaked at $13.6 billion in 1981, although still a healthy $4.9 billion five years later. The statistics were not lost on politicians and others interested in the trade problem. Moreover, with the merchandise imbalance seeming intractable, services represented an area where removal of barriers could generate palpable results.

The US government therefore began to pressure the Japanese to eliminate service barriers. Early efforts focused on a hodgepodge of issues, including overnight mail, lawyers, insurance, and construction. Financial services, however, quickly became the most protracted and comprehensive area of discussion.

A single reason explained the initial prominence of financial reform, a reason that ironically had little to do with the plight of US financial institutions in Japan. The talks were undertaken in an effort to rectify the perceived misvaluation of the yen. The weak yen made the sale of US manufactured goods difficult. Personalities and ideological persuasions within the Treasury during the early 1980s meant that conventional methods of redressing the misvaluation, particularly government intervention in the currency markets, were unavailable. Negotiations represented an acceptable alternative. By seeking reform of the Japanese financial markets, the Treasury hoped to see the yen rise to its appropriate value, making US exports easier to sell. With the Treasury the hot bed of free market ideology during the Reagan Administration, negotiations with the Japanese promised to provide the double benefit of improving the trade balance while deregulating capital markets.

The talks, however, had another potential benefit. The Treasury had become increasingly aware of, and receptive to, the complaints of US banks in Japan. With an attaché in the US Embassy in Tokyo, the Department received a steady flow of information about the concerns. Efforts to induce reforms amounted to a mechanism for addressing the complaints and improving the competitive position of US banks.

In 1983, President Reagan and Prime Minister Nakasone signed a communiqué committing the Japanese to financial reform. For the next six months, negotiators hammered out a comprehensive, written blueprint for reform. Known as the Yen/Dollar Accord, the document constituted the most comprehensive trade agreement ever reached with the Japanese.[1] The Accord contained commitments for reform of the domestic banking system and for the internationalization of the yen. More than platitudes and promises, the agreement specified issues and time frames for implementation.

Negotiating the Accord took a herculean effort, with a number of standouts. On the US side, the team from the Department of the Treasury, headed by Beryl W. Sprinkel and David Mulford, expended huge energy and resources on the effort. Negotiators managed to convince and cajole assorted levels of the MoF into accepting reforms. Not completely congenial, the US side also assiduously relied on political intervention at the highest levels and implicit threats to break log jams and keep the negotiations moving forward.

On the Japanese side, the commitment of Tomomitsu Oba, the Vice Minister of International Affairs, provided a powerful proponent within the MoF. Oba skillfully used foreign pressure or *gaiatsu* to force the various bureaus within the MoF to reach consensus on reforms acceptable to the United States. He was able to discard antiquated remnants of the planned economy days and to ensure the MoF's hegemony over the reform process by blocking out other ministries from participation. Makoto Utsumi, the MoF's highest ranking agent in the Japanese embassy in Washington, also played an indispensable role as facilitator and go between. As a result of his contribution to the process, he was resurrected from a moribund career path and ultimately promoted to the highest levels of the Ministry.

THE PRESSURE BUILDS

In the 1970s and early 1980s, merchandise and agriculture received most of the attention from US trade negotiators. Financial services amounted to an unwanted stepchild. Suddenly, almost without warning, bilateral talks on financial reform swept to the forefront. Following a simple communiqué in November 1983, a comprehensive, sector-wide agreement emerged a mere six months later. The whirlwind seemed totally unexpected.

Appearances, however, were deceiving. Beneath the surface, matters had been percolating. A variety of disparate interest groups favored reform. Banks and securities firms wanted greater access to the Japanese markets. Manufacturers wanted changes designed to increase the value of the yen. The Administration very badly wanted to reduce the trade deficit but in a manner consistent with a free market approach. Once these groups coalesced, rapid reform became possible. All that was needed was a catalyst. The deciding event turned out to be a presidential summit that lacked an agenda. Financial services filled the gap.

Services and manufacturing

The most immediate impetus for the Yen/Dollar Accord was the perceived misalignment in the value of the yen. During the early 1980s, the value of the dollar had surged, with US exports becoming more expensive in foreign markets. Imports into the United States ballooned. The Japanese in particular seized an increasingly large share of the market. The auto industry represented an obvious, but not the only, example. The Japanese challenge was here to stay.

Manufacturers having trouble competing abroad argued that Japan was manipulating the value of the yen. The case was made most forcefully in a 1982 paper written by the Caterpillar Tractor Company. The paper contended that the Japanese government had deliberately undervalued the yen in order to facilitate exports. To prevent such nefarious behavior, the report called for liberalization of the capital markets in Japan.

The Treasury reacted viscerally to these claims of intentional mani- pulation, denying that they had any validity.[2] A second Caterpillar paper deleted references to intentional manipulation but continued to call for reform of the capital markets.[3] Lee Morgan, the company's chairman, presented the work to the White House and other officials.[4]

On a first name basis with the Secretary of the Treasury, Donald Regan, and the Under Secretary for Monetary Affairs, Beryl Sprinkel, Morgan's voice was respected and listened to. His message appealed in part because it eschewed quotas and other protectionist attitudes. Indeed, Morgan took the position that many trade problems would disappear with free and open financial markets.

His was not, however, the only voice. A steady stream of industrialists wanted the problem addressed. With growing pressure from the White House, the Treasury could not just ignore the complaints. The entreaties also fanned protectionist fervor on the Hill. A consensus was growing within the Department that something would have to be done to strengthen the yen. What and when remained the difficult questions.

US banking fortunes (or misfortunes) in Japan

At the same time, the Treasury became increasingly aware of the difficulties encountered by US banks in Japan. Brokers, commercial banks, and investment banks complained to the Treasury about barriers to operations in Japan. The firms found sympathetic ears. At the same time, the Treasury needed little convincing. The magnitude of the problem had become clear as a juxtaposition of performance in the two countries demonstrated.

Japanese banks had made immense inroads into the US market. Concentrated in New York and California, the Japanese presence provided bountiful statistics demonstrating the onslaught. They owned four of the top

15 largest banks in California and held a growing percentage of the banking assets in New York. The statistics were incendiary and dangerously incomplete.[5] Still, they were also handy and powerful.

In contrast, the early 1980s proved a disaster for foreign banks in Japan. Despite modest reforms of the financial system, their position continued to deteriorate. The loss of the monopoly on impact loans in 1979 hurt. With Japanese banks competing aggressively on price, foreign banks watched market share quickly erode. Profits had to be found elsewhere.

Yen lending within Japan proved equally dismal. With competition for corporate borrowers fierce and the system of lead banks firmly entrenched, foreign banks moved "down-market." Other banks simply got out of the lending business. Unable to compete for the blue-chip business, unwilling to accept the down-market risk, they decided to reduce the asset side. By the mid-1980s, foreign banks would brag about how quickly they had run down their loan book.

The numbers told the story. Except for brief respites during periods of tight money, earnings kept a downward trajectory while the number of foreign banks in Japan continued to increase.[6] Average profits shrank from 7.8 percent in 1977 to 2.4 percent in 1987. The number of banks actually losing money jumped from two to 17.[7] Marginal lenders, the market share for foreign banks improved only when the Bank of Japan used window guidance to restrict lending by Japanese banks. Once the restrictions were eased, however, the market share of foreign banks slipped back to more normal and dismal levels.

In some respects, the ability to grow during tight money periods actually demonstrated the *weak* competitive position of foreign banks. Not subject to window guidance, the banks could pick up the slack created by the reduced lending capacity of Japanese financial institutions. Indeed, city banks often directed clients to foreign banks. Unlike the more aggressive regional banks, foreign banks were not seen as serious threats to permanently win over corporate customers.

With lending activities and profits falling, foreign banks began to reassess activities in Japan. Some opted to retrench. In 1985, the Bank of America closed offices in Yokohama and Kobe, both of which had opened during the occupation. American Express, another occupation entrant, gave up the branch license obtained in 1953 in return for a securities license. To some degree, these banks had unique problems. Nonetheless, they represented harbingers. By the beginning of the 1990s, the rush out of Japan would go from a trickle to a stampede. In the words of Walter Wriston, US banks were "eating their seed corn."[8]

The problems in Japan came more clearly into focus when compared with foreign expansion elsewhere. From the mid-1970s through the mid-1980s the number of Federal Reserve member banks with branches abroad had jumped to 159 and $343.5 billion in assets, with the fastest growth occurring in Asia.[9] The growth came in Hong Kong and Singapore, not Japan.[10] Operations in Japan stagnated. This suggested problems with access to the Japanese market rather than lack of effort or interest in expansion by US banks.

The gripes

Banks had poured into the country in a lemming-like fashion, each thinking it had a special niche. Companies from a bank's home state were expected to flock to the newly opened branch. This source of business, of course, often failed to materialize. Without the hoped for business and with the disappearance of impact loans, foreign banks found the expected pot of gold replaced by a stocking full of coal.

Although the difficulties resulted in part from ineptitude by the banks, the MoF left in place a handful of largely unnecessary restrictions, remnants of earlier days. Among other things, foreign banks remained entirely shut out of the trust area and the government bond syndicate. These provided obvious targets for those claiming that the Japanese discriminated against foreign banks.

Access to the government bond syndicate had become a real irritant. Since its formation in the 1960s, foreign banks had been excluded. At one time, exclusion had been an asset. Japanese participants were required to purchase a designated percentage of government bonds at below market interest rates. No foreign bank wanted part of that money-losing proposition.

As the MoF began to issue bonds at something approaching market rates, however, exclusion from the syndicate deprived the banks of a source of fees and threatened to be a barrier to trading in the secondary market. The inability of foreign banks to participate in the government bond syndicate became a growing embarrassment, particularly as Japanese banks became increasingly involved in the sale of US Treasury bonds.

Scrapping the syndicate in favor of an auction was one possible solution. With a competitive allocation of the bonds, US banks would have had an equal opportunity to participate. The proposition, however, engendered bureaucratic resistance. An auction market drew considerable opposition from the Finance Bureau, the bureau within the MoF responsible for selling the debt instruments. The method would have reduced government control over placement and increased the expense of selling the bonds. The alternative was to give foreign banks and brokers a piece of action by bringing them into the syndicate. That meant squeezing out or reducing the share of Japanese participants, engendering domestic resistance.

Limitations on trust activities represented another area of concern. With demographics showing a rapidly aging Japanese population, management of pension fund assets loomed as a high growth industry. Once again, however, foreign banks found themselves foreclosed. The insurance companies, the seven trust banks, and Daiwa Bank monopolized pension plan management.

Foreign banks were not excluded from the market by any express legal prohibition. Indeed, legislation adopted in the 1940s authorized commercial banks to engage in trust activities. In practice, however, the MoF used administrative guidance to enforce a strict barrier between commercial and trust banking, with Daiwa Bank the only significant exception. Treating foreign banks no differently, the Ministry refused to allow them access to the trust bank monopoly.

The status quo came under frontal assault in 1982, with J. P. Morgan unexpectedly in the eye of the storm. J. P. Morgan recognized that standard banking activities in Japan were declining and began to search for alternatives. Corporate clients in the country, particularly foreign companies, complained about anemic returns on pension plan assets managed by the trust banks. J. P. Morgan did a study and determined that, with the aging of the Japanese population, a substantial need would arise for additional expertise in pension plan management.

At about the same time, Nomura, the largest Japanese securities firm, approached J. P. Morgan about setting up a trust subsidiary. The joint venture was to be structured not as a trust bank but as a trust company, a type of entity that had disappeared during the occupation. Nomura asked J. P. Morgan to participate in part because of the hallowed name and in part because of expertise. Nomura also knew, however, that a foreign participant would make it harder for the MoF to say no, an example of efforts by Japanese banks to manipulate *gaiatsu*, or foreign pressure.

Officials at J. P. Morgan gave the proposal considerable thought, including the difficulty of mixing the disparate corporate cultures. The obvious need in the pension area of Nomura's marketing strength caused J. P. Morgan to agree to the arrangement.

The license required MoF approval, an extremely sensitive matter. Negotiations with the MoF were viewed as a Japanese matter to be handled primarily by Nomura. The largest Japanese securities firm, Nomura had a unique relationship with the Ministry and did not opt for the usual method of obtaining approval. Most matters required negotiations from the bottom up. This meant careful negotiations with the relevant bureau, in this case the Banking Bureau. Nomura, however, decided to start at the top and bring the matter directly to the attention of the Finance Minister, Noboru Takeshita. A meeting was dutifully arranged. The purpose was disclosed only a few days before the scheduled event, to the irritation and discomfort of MoF officials.

Lewis T. Preston, chairman of J. P. Morgan, and Munetada Murata, chairman of Nomura, attended the meeting with Takeshita. MoF officials were also present, including the director general of the Banking Bureau. Takeshita asked numerous questions but remained noncommittal. The approach, however, won the enmity of the MoF and, in the aftermath of the meeting, the officials informally indicated that the proposal should not proceed.

The whole thing seemed destined to disappear, to the relief of J. P. Morgan, which was now having second thoughts, and of the MoF, which had little interest in the inevitable fall out that would have followed. Details of the proposal, however, were leaked to the press, apparently by Nomura. When the efforts became public, pandemonium broke out. Not only did the joint venture intrude into the unwritten monopoly of the trust banks, it also directly challenged the highly compartmentalized financial system by allowing a securities firm to cross the invisible line separating brokers and banks. While Japanese financial institutions might have accepted some additional authority for foreign banks, they would not accept the entry of securities firms into their territory.

Disclosure also caused the damage to spread. Other Japanese securities companies and foreign banks announced plans to form joint trust companies, including Citicorp and Daiwa Securities. Not about to sit on the sidelines, Japanese city banks demanded comparable authority, with Fuji, Sumitomo, Mitsubishi, and Sanwa seeking trust authority. MoF approval of the Nomura–J. P. Morgan venture threatened to cause a deluge.

The proposal predictably drew virulent opposition from trust banks and, to the extent that it involved securities firms, Japanese commercial banks. The uncompromising and unified posture of the banking sector doomed the efforts. Already disinclined, MoF officials were not about to approve a change that antagonized such large segments of the financial community.

The MoF ultimately denied the application, information conveyed to J. P. Morgan a day before Nomura and the public. The Ministry took the position that the joint venture violated the separation of securities and banking activities. The reasoning was critical and showed the MoF's concern with Nomura's role. The same rationale did not apply to a bank seeking a trust bank license alone rather than in a joint venture with a securities firm. The significance would become clearer when the US government began agitating for trust powers for foreign banks.

The J. P. Morgan application did illustrate the now prominent role of foreign pressure. In the past, the Ministry could have avoided the difficult issue by simply allowing the application to languish. When Citibank sought additional branch licenses in the 1960s, the MoF largely reacted by not reacting. The inquiries and entreaties simply gathered dust. Times, however, had changed. Inaction would raise a hue and cry in Washington.

The MoF could not ignore the possibility of retaliation. Japanese banks were expanding exponentially in the United States. In 1983, four of the top 15 banks in California were Japanese, with California First, the Bank of Tokyo subsidiary, ranked seventh. Moreover, California and New York ceased to be the only places with a sizable Japanese presence. By 1980, Atlanta had nine Japanese branches or agencies, Miami sixteen. Numbers were also up in Seattle and a host of other cities.[11] The MoF knew that obduration over the trust banking issue would have left Japan open to criticism and, possibly, retaliation.

THE ACCORD

The impetus

By the early 1980s, the complaints of US banks were being heard increasingly in the Department of the Treasury. As an institution, the Treasury, through most of the 1970s, had little interest in financial reform in Japan. Although the Embassy in Tokyo had had a financial attaché since the occupation, when William H. (Duke) Diehl served in the post, relations with the banking community were not particularly close. As one Treasury attaché explained, he did not see his role as "shagging little issues for banks."

While matters gradually improved, the real shift occurred in connection with the drafting of the first National Treatment Study in 1979. Mandated by Congress, the study examined trade barriers in banking in a number of countries, including Japan. The Treasury attaché had primary responsibility for writing the sections on Japan, necessitating systematic contact with the foreign banking community. Contact increased; embassy officials began to attend the monthly meetings of the financial institutions subsection of the American Chamber of Commerce.

The heightened activity in Japan coincided with increased interest in financial services in Washington. The Reagan Administration had come to power in 1981 with a pronounced bias against excessive government regulation. The Treasury was full of free market ideologues. Although the Department had historically favored more open international financial markets, the view unquestionably intensified during the Reagan Administration.

Treasury Secretary Donald Regan had grown up with a healthy respect for markets and a healthy disrespect for government intervention. With Regan, the winning argument was always to free the markets further. Appointees underneath Regan held comparable views.

Beryl Sprinkel in particular was a fervent open marketeer. The Under Secretary for Monetary Affairs, he had worked most of his career at Harris Trust & Savings Bank in Chicago. Sprinkel believed that government intervention rarely worked, particularly in matters such as exchange rates. The way to ensure accurate rates was to tear down regulatory barriers. Sprinkel applied this reasoning with vigor in talks with the Japanese.

Not surprisingly, therefore, the cauldrons of Treasury were bubbling with those predisposed towards Japanese financial reform. In particular, Deputy Secretary R. Timothy McNamar and Assistant Secretary for International Affairs Marc Leland played an early, aggressive role. Both received a steady stream of bankers complaining about restrictions in Japan. The complaints were relayed to the Japanese in a variety of forums. Bilateral discussions between Treasury and Ministry officials often followed G7, World Bank or IMF meetings, or visits by the President or Prime Minister. From the US side, however, the process lacked cohesion and seemed to generate little progress.

With the number of issues mounting, McNamar began to realize that they were too numerous to raise in a hodgepodge fashion. Comprehensive talks were necessary. Moreover, pressure in Washington was mounting, and if the Treasury did not act, others within the executive branch, particularly the State Department or the Office of the United States Trade Representative, were ready to pick up the cudgel. Congressional involvement also could not be ruled out.

An advancing summit between Prime Minister Nakasone and President Reagan scheduled for November 1983 proved to be the spark that both brought financial services to center stage and solidified the Treasury's ascendancy over the area. With only a few months before the meeting, the summit lacked a clear agenda. On short notice, McNamar called his counterpart in the MoF, Tomomitsu Oba. Both had a relationship that went back to 1982 when the two countries had become embroiled in the Mexican debt crisis. McNamar suggested the inclusion of financial services on the agenda and offered to fly to Tokyo to discuss the matter.

The trip to Tokyo seemed a failure. McNamar remembers arriving in Tokyo, having a quick shave at the Okura Hotel, attending a short meeting at the Ministry, and returning on a flight the same day. The Japanese reaction was not positive. Ministry officials indicated that these types of reforms would be "very difficult."[12]

Still, something had to go on the agenda. After a few days, Oba called McNamar and suggested a second meeting. A team from the Treasury descended on Hawaii, this time with a discussion paper that included a number of reform proposals. Over two days, Oba and his group again spent a great deal of time explaining why things could not get done. By the end of the meeting nothing had been finalized. Even worse, the summit was only a week away.

With McNamar back in Washington, the two sides agreed to a final meeting in San Francisco. A team from the Treasury and the MoF convened the day before the President's scheduled departure at Jacks, a seafood restaurant in the Bay area. The location had the advantage of small private rooms upstairs and the distinction of having once been a brothel, something the Japanese negotiators found highly amusing. By the end of the dinner, the two sides had hammered out the language that would launch the yen/dollar process.

The statement was initially intended to be signed by Treasury Secretary Regan and Finance Minister Takeshita. On short notice, the Japanese side suggested that it be elevated to a communiqué for execution by Nakasone and Reagan. Regan and Takeshita did, however, issue a joint statement calling for future talks and identifying eight specific areas for liberalization. Implementation was left to a working group of officials from the MoF and the Treasury.[13]

The negotiating teams

Signing the communiqué and drafting a comprehensive agreement represented two different things. Negotiators confronted the inevitable difficulties in transforming general pronouncements into specific proscriptions. Commitments by high level Japanese politicians were simply not enough. The bureaucracy within the Ministry had to be convinced, no easy task. An agreement liberalizing the financial markets essentially meant a reduction in the MoF's authority, something that would not be accepted without a fight.

The talks also started with very different goals. The US side wanted sharp, radical revisions, including firm commitments and specific timetables for implementation. Broad, vague promises would not suffice. While the MoF accepted the process with reasonable goodwill, broad reform was an anathema. The entire history of financial reform in Japan had been one of consensus building and incremental change. Under the MoF's guidance, the financial system had been carefully shaped, thoughtfully pruned. The Treasury, however, wanted something far more grand: an agreement that would provide for fundamental restructuring of the financial markets.

From the US perspective, success of the talks required a more sophisticated understanding of the Japanese financial markets and the decision-making process within the Ministry. International financial matters were the primary responsibility of the Vice Minister of International Affairs, or the *zaimukan*. One of two vice ministers, the *zaimukan* represented the highest ranking international officer within the Ministry and reported directly to the Finance Minister.[14]

The place in the MoF hierarchy, however, overstated the influence of the position. Effective power within the Ministry rested with the relevant bureaus. While international vice ministers could influence, they could not impose. Absent assent of the relevant bureau, shifts in policy represented a non-starter.

Policy decisions within the bureaus tended to flow from the bottom up. Beneath the vice ministers were seven primary bureaus and the secretariat, each run by a director general.[15] Policy initiatives and ideas came from the director/deputy director of the various divisions within a bureau. Divisions had front-line responsibility for specified areas and were expected to provide policy initiatives for matters under their control.

Despite residing under one roof, the bureaus amounted to separate fiefdoms. Sometimes described as balkanized, they competed with each other for power and influence. The only time the bureaus truly acted in a united fashion was over the budget. All of this meant that the MoF was no monolith. The Ministry seemed more a collection of individuals than a single voice. As one private sector official described: "There are no Ministry opinions, just individual opinions."[16]

Decisions required a consensus. *Nemawashi* or consensus building skills, therefore, were critical. In most instances, consensus entailed acceptance within both the relevant bureau and the affected industry. If banks vehemently disagreed with a particular policy, the Ministry had little ability to force through the changes. Attempts to do so would have damaged credibility and the likelihood of compliance. To the extent that other bureaus or ministries were affected, they too had to assent. Consensus, however, meant that decisions were often slow in coming and involved incremental shifts, with a step-by-step approach guiding the process. This worked well in ordinary times and less well during periods of crisis.

Convincing the various bureaus to accept reform, especially broad reform, represented a formidable task. The International Finance, Banking, and Securities Bureaus played critical roles in an agreement to reform the financial system. The Tax, Finance, and Budget Bureaus, however, were also entitled to a voice in the process, particularly over matters within their bailiwick. The Tax Bureau needed to sign off on any changes affecting revenues such as withholdings on interest and dividends paid to non-residents; the Finance Bureau had to approve changes in the bond syndicate. These bureaus had a particularly domestic, almost parochial, outlook on matters. Rapid internationalization held little interest. Nevertheless, they had to be brought aboard.[17]

Agreement of the bureaus was therefore essential, and the Vice Minister for International Affairs represented a critical figure in achieving the necessary consensus. The position constituted a relatively recent addition to the Ministry. The post had existed before the war, with the designated individual responsible for raising capital abroad. Primarily stationed in London, the *zaimukan* operated out of the local office of the Yokohama Specie Bank. The position was redesignated *zaimu sanjikan*, or financial commissioner, after the war. The commissioner still had responsibility for international finance but was ranked below director general of a bureau.

In 1968, the MoF reinstated the position of *zaimukan*. The post had become necessary, particularly for purposes of international parity. The United States typically had an Under Secretary of the Treasury attend all international meetings. The Director General of the International Finance Bureau would attend for Japan. He, however, had lower rank, reporting to the Vice Minister of Administrative Affairs. By resurrecting the position of *zaimukan*, the Ministry created an officer who reported directly to the Finance Minister.

The position also had a more personal explanation. The creation of the post enabled Yusuke Kashiwagi, the preeminent internationalist within the Ministry, to obtain a promotion from Director General of the International Finance Bureau and stave off mandatory retirement for a few more years. He was still in the Ministry when the Nixon shock occurred in 1971 and played an active role in the formulating MoF's response, eclipsing his successor.

In general, the *zaimukan* remained concerned with international policy.

95

By and large, he did not become actively involved in purely domestic matters. He was seen primarily as a figurehead who represented the interests of the Ministry in international forums. Thus, widely known abroad, the *zaimukan* often had little say or input in the pace of domestic financial reform. As one Vice Minister of International Affairs noted in proverbial fashion, the position was like a nail in a board: if it stuck out too far, it would either be hammered in or pulled out.

The success of the talks required a vice minister who would lead rather than simply mimic the views of the bureaus. The individual also had to be a sophisticated player in bureaucratic politics. The vice minister could influence and cajole but not require. That person arrived on the scene with the promotion of Tomomitsu Oba as *zaimukan*.

Oba was sometimes called the first true *zaimukan*. Until his appointment, the position usually went to a runner-up to the administrative vice minister. Oba, in contrast, seemed a true internationalist. He was not the first to recognize that domestic matters could have international consequences but was the first to do something about it. Oba entered the office with an agenda. The position was never the same after he retired.

Oba was committed to reform and willing to take a forthright role. He had risen through the Ministry hierarchy in the conventional fashion, giving no real sign that he would emerge as a critical proponent of internationalization. Wealthy and aristocratic, Oba was adept at *nemawashi* and the critical task of building relations within the Ministry. He was therefore respected by his peers and able to influence.

Oba saw the need to modernize and internationalize the financial system. He also saw foreign pressure as a mechanism for achieving reform and maximizing the influence of the *zaimukan*. With no domestic power base, the Vice Minister for International Affairs had little leverage over the bureaus. By emerging as the key negotiator with the United States, he vastly increased the influence of the *zaimukan* within the Ministry.

Oba also brought some important intangibles to the negotiation table. He had worked with a number of people from the Treasury. Treasury and MoF officials cooperated closely during the Mexican debt crisis, creating a sense of mutual trust and respect. He also had a close relationship with Finance Minister Takeshita and access to Prime Minister Nakasone.

To achieve his agenda, Oba relied on the US side for a supporting role. Fully aware of the institutional layout of the Ministry, Oba suggested that Sprinkel invite officials from the relevant bureaus, particularly the directors general, to attend personally and participate in the negotiating sessions. Sprinkel agreed. The resulting convocation represented a Ministry first. No one could remember a time when the entire hierarchy of the MoF had met over a single issue.

Oba also insisted on simultaneous translation, another first. Directors general with little or no fluency in English could now both attend and actively participate. They heard everything first hand rather than through the filter of lower ranked officials. Finally, with personal attendance, the reputation or face of the directors general became inextricably tied to the outcome of the talks.

Oba was not alone in his efforts, however. The Japanese side produced a number of other unsung heroes, particularly Makoto Utsumi. A University of Tokyo graduate, he joined the Ministry in 1957. Utsumi advanced in lock step with his class until his career struck shoals. While in the Tax Bureau, he became responsible for implementation of the green card system, an attempt to end tax evasion on deposits with the Postal Savings System. When the efforts proved a political embarrassment, Utsumi's career in the Ministry seemed over. As one official described, he had "blotted his copy book." Assigned a post in Nagoya, his future prospects were dim. He even seriously considered resigning from the Ministry.

Oba travelled to Nagoya to personally ask Utsumi to go to Washington. Things were clearly heating up in the United States, and Oba wanted someone there that he could both trust and count on to maintain good relations with those in the Treasury. Urbane and fluent in English (as well as French), Utsumi seemed designed for the role. After some wavering, he agreed to go, though recognizing that a post in Washington usually amounted to a ticket to oblivion.

The post, however, rehabilitated his career. He became a confidant of Oba's, talking to him early each morning in Tokyo. Utsumi jokingly asserted that he was forced to call in the morning because the Vice Minister's heavy social life made evening conversations unlikely to succeed. The talks became so regular that even after returning to Tokyo, Utsumi remembered having the urge to pick up the phone at the designated time to call Oba.

Utsumi also developed a close relationship with officials on the US side. In some respects, he could more easily communicate with Sprinkel and others on the US team. As one MoF official noted during the early days of the negotiations: "Oba thought Beryl Sprinkel was hard to communicate with. He hated to make direct contact, when all Sprinkel would say was just to free the market. So Oba relied on Utsumi to make contact." That would evolve, however, as Oba and Sprinkel forged a close relationship.

Although Utsumi attended most of the negotiating sessions, his real value was as a critical pipeline from Washington to Tokyo, particularly in between meetings. In addition to a 14 hour time difference, the talks occurred before the advent of fax machines, making informal communications logistically difficult. Treasury officials therefore relied on Utsumi as a conduit. They would communicate views and positions to Utsumi, knowing full well that they would be sent back to Tokyo.

Utsumi also acted as a translator, both linguistically and diplomatically. Respected on both sides, he was in a position to prod both the Japanese and the Americans to ensure continued progress. He would smooth over

97

messages from Japan that might irritate the US side. He suggested to the Treasury ways to present a position that would attract the most support within the MoF. Constantly in and out of the Treasury building, he assiduously moved the two sides closer together.

As a result of his role in the talks, Utsumi went through a stunning rehabilitation in Japan. Washington proved not to be an exit position after all, but a stepping stone. He returned to Japan as the Director General of the International Finance Bureau. During the annual rotation of Ministry jobs in 1989, he became *zaimukan*.

On the US side, Beryl Sprinkel and David Mulford headed up the negotiating team. Both brought different strengths to the process. Sprinkel was the theoretician and commercial banker, Mulford the international financier and tough negotiator. With a doctorate from Oxford, Mulford had immense practical experience, particularly in the Euroyen markets. He acted as the senior investment advisor for the Saudi Arabian Monetary Agency and had responsibility for investing much of the country's newfound oil wealth. He also worked for White Weld & Co., an investment banking firm with early experience in the Euromarkets.

Mulford's experience proved particularly useful. MoF officials tended not to be steeped in theory but instead versed in the practical. In a number of instances during the negotiations, usually in connection with Euromarket issues, Mulford could represent that he had more experience than anyone else in the room, perhaps in the world. In the face of these assertions, Japanese opposition often evaporated.

Less concerned with the theoretical and economic causes for the mis-valued yen, he took the position that, once restrictions in the Euromarket ended, supply and demand would take over. These changes, in turn, would eventually impact the domestic economy. Mulford also viewed the negotiation process as adversarial, favoring hard bargaining and minimal fraternization. He tended not to attend social events arranged by the Japanese side.

Sprinkel, in contrast, was more of the theoretician. With a PhD from the University of Chicago, he spent much of his career with Harris Trust. His negotiating style was just as dogged but without the hard edge. He provided most of the color at the negotiating sessions, often illustrating points with scenes out of his days on the farm. When Utsumi threw a cocktail party before the first meeting, Mulford refused to go while Sprinkel not only attended but put his tenor voice to good use through robust singing.

The US side also put together a strong team of assistants and devoted the time and energy necessary to make it work. Junior members remember leaving Sprinkel's or Mulford's offices with clusters of higher ranked officials waiting to enter. This reflected the Treasury's priorities. Other things would have to wait. Opening Japanese financial markets came first.

Finally, the team devoted immense effort to studying and understanding the markets in Japan. Officials prepared by exploring matters extensively with banks and securities firms to learn how things really operated. Even after the negotiations were under way, members of the team remained in constant contact with US officials familiar with the operations of the Japanese markets. They could quickly and accurately verify most representations made by the Japanese at the sessions.

A seemingly self-evident point, the high level of preparation represented an appreciation of the formidable negotiating skill of the Japanese. Ministry officials involved in the negotiations had devoted a lifetime to financial issues. They understood the smallest details of the markets, minutiae that could be used to slow negotiations. The heavy preparation on the US side provided some degree of parity and facilitated the negotiation process.

The negotiations

Six negotiating sessions took place before the Accord emerged.[18] The formal meetings, however, represented only a fraction of the communications. In addition to informal exchanges of information, high ranking officials from the two negotiating teams continued to meet at various international and G7 meetings. The discussion process was therefore continual, marked by episodic convocations of the yen/dollar teams.

The US side was always outnumbered, typically sending to the meetings seven or eight negotiators with the Treasury attaché attending convocations held in Tokyo. With directors general and deputy directors general in attendance, the Japanese team was two or three times larger. Even that understated the true differential. Sprinkel remembered a quick trip to the bathroom where he noticed a temporary wall separating the negotiators from a raft of additional MoF officials attentively listening to the talks. It seemed as if the entire Ministry wanted to attend.

The first two meetings were held in Tokyo. A great deal of time was spent discussing how markets operated, with the US side trying to inform their counterparts and, more subtly, highlighting the limitations of the Japanese system. US negotiators stayed at the Okura Hotel across from the US Embassy. Following a breakfast meeting at the Embassy and a briefing of the Ambassador, the team traveled to the Ministry for meetings that lasted until 6:00 or 6:30 p.m. No picnic, the MoF's building was drab, the days long. Translation devices habitually remained in each person's ear. Evenings were spent in more congenial settings, often a Japanese restaurant chosen by the host delegation.

Simultaneous translation provided some amusing moments. One of the directors general commented that foreign banks should form an association in Japan. The word "association" was translated as church, leading the US side to believe that they were being asked to breach the separation of church and state.[19] On another occasion, an official provided an articulate refutation of one of the positions on the US side. Sprinkel described the speech as "formidable." The Japanese staff thought this a tremendous compliment and for a long time beamed at the high regard paid their director general by Dr Sprinkel.

Much of the meeting was spent articulating views and listening to responses. On the US side, each committee member received an issue or issues to discuss at a negotiating session. Some had areas of expertise and repeatedly handled the same matters. Mulford was interested in Euroyen issues, Sprinkel in banking issues within Japan, particularly interest rate deregulation.

The individual designated to address an issue could be used as a signaling device. As the head of the delegation, Sprinkel was viewed by the Japanese as the most important spokesperson on the US side. His statements therefore carried added weight. Aware of the heightened Japanese sensitivity, Sprinkel would typically articulate the issues most in need of resolution, aware that they would receive a more serious reception.

In response to issues raised on the US side, a Japanese official typically gave a reply that included an exegesis on the origins of the policy, often going back to the days of the occupation. Few, if any, concessions were forthcoming at the sessions. Despite the lack of apparent progress, the Japanese team clearly listened. After the negotiations, officials returned to the Ministry and hammered out a new consensus. Signs of progress would surface some time afterward.

The meetings initially did not go smoothly. In Tokyo, Sprinkel pressed for immediate concessions.[20] After listing areas for reform, he insisted that the Japanese come up with a specific timetable for implementation. Sprinkel also wanted dramatic rather than marginal changes in the financial markets. The Japanese asserted that the US side simply did not understand the domestic situation. Internal opposition made broad reform impossible to implement. Instead, Japanese officials favored a more gradualist, "step-by-step" approach.

The step-by-step approach was no surprise. Prime Minister Nakasone had indicated in the communiqué launching the talks "that the parties concerned should spare no effort in taking step by step measures" to arrive at a settlement.[21] The go slow approach arose out of the Japanese aversion to sharp, radical change. That in turn seemed to flow from the need to form a domestic consensus before reforms could be implemented.

The US side, however, had little patience with the incremental approach. Sprinkel would exhort the Japanese to abandon the step-by-step approach. At one meeting while engaging in a particularly impassioned defense of broader reforms, he leapt up from a table and began walking toward the wall. He started with small steps but then switched to strides. "Not step by step, but strides," he said. Japanese negotiators were convinced that he would continue until he thudded into the wall. Sprinkel stopped just short but had gotten their attention and made his point.

At another meeting, Sprinkel again grew frustrated with the step-by-step approach. Harking back to his upbringing and days on a midwestern farm, he explained that when you cut off a dog's tail, you did it all at once, not step by step. The example drew laughter from the American side and startled looks from the Japanese.

Colorful yarns and antics were clearly not going to be enough to exact the type of agreement sought by the United States. Sprinkel and his team, therefore, had to turn to a variety of weapons to keep the talks moving. High level political pressure represented one device.

Finance ministers and even prime ministers in Japan rarely interfered in the bureaucratic process. Ministry officials resented the intrusion. Takeshita, the Finance Minister, respected the views of the Ministry and tended not to intervene unless absolutely necessary. Prime Minister Nakasone, in contrast, was more willing to pressure a recalcitrant bureaucracy. To induce Japanese politicians to apply the necessary pressure, the team rolled out its primary weapon: Treasury Secretary Donald Regan.

Regan shared the fervent free market attitudes of his subordinates involved in the yen/dollar talks. He was amenable to playing good cop, bad cop, and intervening to make sure the Japanese knew the seriousness of the US side. In a significant role reversal, however, Regan had no problem playing bad cop eschewing the role of conciliator. Regan's use had to be managed with care. Too heavy handed an approach might render him ineffective. Too much intervention might alienate the MoF's potent bureaucracy. Regan became a scalpel, used to make deliberate and precise incisions.

The Treasury Secretary had access to his counterpart, Takeshita. He also had an indirect line to the Prime Minister. While at Merrill Lynch, Regan had gotten to know Yukio Aida, an official from Nomura. Aida had spent time in a training program at the US securities firm. Aida knew Nakasone. Regan made it a point to keep Aida informed of his concerns over the yen/dollar process, confident they would be conveyed back to the Prime Minister.[22]

The Secretary did not attend the meetings but instead operated outside the yen/dollar framework. He occasionally wrote letters to, and made personal calls on, the Finance Minister. At one meeting in Tokyo in March, Regan got so angry he pounded his fists on the table at the press conference, calling the lack of progress "intolerable." Particularly concerned about the slow movement on the Tokyo Stock Exchange issue, he indicated in harsh terms that the failure to come to agreement could lead to protectionism in the United States.[23] Following the Regan visit, Nakasone told Oba to come up with a list of reforms in the Euromarket.

Political intervention was not the only method used to unblock stalled negotiations. The US side also brandished a "big stick." During the negotiations, David Mulford learned that Regan was about to give a speech placing the US imprimatur on Japan's ascension to the number two position at the World Bank. For matters of international prestige and face, Japan vitally wanted the increase.

Mulford's view was that you never gave away something for nothing. With the speech by Regan only a short time away, members of the yen/dollar team sent the Secretary a note asking him not to announce approval of the increase. Although they essentially gave no reason for the requested delay, Regan complied and did not make the expected announcement. Through the remainder of the talks, Regan repeatedly indicated that the change in voting power would not be approved until an agreement on financial reform had been reached.

The shift in policy angered the Japanese. For one thing, the decision to increase Japan's share had been approved the year before. Oba threatened to reduce the country's contribution to the World Bank, eliminating funds for loans to poorer countries. The approach also irritated allies who saw World Bank funding degenerating into a bilateral trade fracas. Still, the United States refused to budge until completion of the Accord. As Regan explained to Congress, Japan should only become number two at the Bank when it began to act like a world power and liberalized capital markets.

Despite support from Oba, a critical back door role by Utsumi and selective use of political pressure, the talks went through a number of rough spots, particularly at the last two meetings. At the penultimate scheduled convocation, the talks in Honolulu hit a brick wall. The usual US negotiation team showed up for another session of hard bargaining, primarily to draft specific language for the Accord. While Oba attended as head of the Japanese side, he came without most of the directors general of the various bureaus. Those present had no real authority to negotiate specific language changes. The meeting seemed destined to accomplish little.

Sprinkel hit the roof. He called Washington and told Regan that they could either close up shop and come home, perhaps irreconcilably damaging the negotiation process, or pack their bags and take the show to Tokyo. Regan's response was immediate: go to Tokyo. At the same time, Vice President Bush had traveled to Tokyo. Regan wanted Sprinkel to leave the same day in order to arrive in Tokyo in time to brief the Vice President. All of the commercial airline flights, however, had already departed from Hawaii. Undaunted, Charles H. Dallara, a member of the negotiating team, contacted the local naval base and talked them into holding a cargo plane destined for Tokyo for several hours. Sprinkel remembers overhearing a Navy officer exclaim: "If you are pulling my leg and an Under Secretary of the Treasury does not show up, there will be hell to pay."

Sprinkel in fact made it to Tokyo in time for the briefing. The rest of the delegation arrived the following day – some without passports. They essentially descended on the doorstep of the Ministry and insisted upon continuing the talks. To the US side, the arrival had pronounced psychological effect. The act demonstrated once and for all that the Treasury would accept nothing short of a substantial, comprehensive set of reforms and was prepared to do whatever it took to succeed. If the MoF thought the US side would settle for less, it was now disabused.[24]

The last meeting of the Committee was scheduled for the G10 meeting in Rome and proved to be one of the most difficult. The two sides had agreed in advance to use the opportunity to finalize the Accord. As the day advanced, however, progress slowed. By late in the afternoon, Oba told Sprinkel that his people would be leaving in the morning. With the agreement unfinished, Sprinkel was furious. He felt Oba had reneged on the commitment to finalize the Accord and insisted that the two sides work all night if necessary to complete the agreement. Oba agreed to stay at the bargaining table until morning.

Oba's announcement that his team would depart was motivated in part by commitments back in Tokyo. He also used the threat to induce greater movement from the US side. In particular, the two teams had come to an impasse over language in the Accord concerning the expected change in the value of the yen. By threatening to leave, both sides had an incentive to reach closure. Oba's gambit worked.

As talks dragged on through the night, discussions became heated and tempers flared. At one point, Toyoo Gyohten, Oba's successor as Vice Minister for International Affairs, asked whether Mulford was characterizing him as dishonest. Mulford responded: "Not dishonest, but intellectually dishonest." Momentarily, the process stopped as everyone in the room focused on the combatants. In the end, however, the two sides somehow persevered and by 7:00 a.m. had an agreement more or less ready to sign.[25]

The signing of the Accord represented a milestone. Unlike past agreements, the two sides executed a comprehensive written agreement with specific timetables for reform. The yen/dollar team from the very beginning wanted a document long on specifics. Full of people out of the financial community or with economic backgrounds, the team wanted to provide the market with specific information about the areas and pace of reform.

The agreement called for concrete steps toward internationalization of the yen. In general, internationalization meant an end to restrictions on yen transactions in the Euromarket. This required an increase in the entities that could tap the market and an increase in the authority of non-Japanese banks and brokers to sell yen denominated bonds. Japan also agreed to reform domestic capital markets, most critically by removing interest rate ceilings from large denomination deposits and removing a number of regulatory constraints on foreign banks. The Accord, however, represented a high water mark. US efforts to influence reform in Japan would, in the future, play a greatly reduced role.

7

REFORM AND FOREIGN PRESSURE

Banking in Japan changed considerably between the beginning and the end of the 1980s. The Yen/Dollar Accord explained much of the shift. Foreign banks saw their permissible range of activities undergo immense expansion, both in Tokyo and in the Euromarkets, with the elimination of a host of restrictions that had remained in place since the occupation.

The Accord provided for deregulation of interest rates; access by foreign securities firms to the Tokyo Stock Exchange; liberalization of the government bond syndicate; elimination of the real demand rule on foreign exchange transactions; and the right to operate trust bank subsidiaries. In the Euromarket, the Ministry of Finance (MoF) agreed to end all non-prudential limitations on yen lending. Side letters addressed other reforms such as the commitment by the Japanese to set up rating agencies for corporate debt.

Just as important, the Accord committed the Treasury and the MoF to follow up discussions over financial reform. The forum provided a ready mechanism for the Treasury to retain a role in the reform process in Japan. Early meetings centered upon the provisions of the Accord. In general, the MoF faithfully fulfilled the terms of the agreement. As time progressed, however, new issues arose and the agenda expanded.

By the latter half of the 1980s, the talks declined in effectiveness. The convocation became an annual slugfest, with the US side repeatedly accusing the Japanese of recalcitrance and bad faith. As the tone became more shrill, the influence of the United States on the reform process fell. In four short years, the role of the Department of the Treasury had gone from immensely influential to almost imperceptible.

THE PROCESS

Throughout the 1980s, the two sides held annual meetings to discuss the ongoing process of financial reform.[1] Much of the original negotiating group had disbanded after execution of the Accord and convocation of the first follow-up session. Only David Mulford remained, heading the US delegation until 1992.

The Japanese also experienced turnover. A director general typically served for one year; a Vice Minister of International Affairs no more than three. The personnel changes, however, masked both continuity and expertise on the Japanese side. For seven years after execution of the Accord, the Vice Minister for International Affairs was an official who had participated in the yen/dollar process. Oba was succeeded by Gyohten, Gyohten by Utsumi. Only when Tadao Chino became Vice Minister in 1991 did the head of the Japanese negotiating team have no involvement in the original Accord.

The meetings tended to follow a set pattern. The Treasury would use half of the meeting to state positions, the MoF the other half. In general, Ministry officials worked from prepared statements. The bureaus developed a consensus in advance on the position to be taken, providing the directors general with little room to deviate. As a result, actual negotiation rarely took place at the meetings. When those on the US side asked questions, the relevant Ministry official would often re-read a portion of the prepared text, as if replaying the same part of a record. Progress typically had to wait until the US side made its position clear and Japanese officials returned to the Ministry to develop a new consensus.

The follow-up fell into roughly two periods. From 1984 through 1986, the talks concentrated on implementation of the Accord. Some matters, such as interest rate deregulation, were unresolved in the Accord itself. Unwilling to accept a time limit for complete deregulation, the MoF simply agreed to remove controls "as expeditiously as circumstances warrant." Other issues required follow-up and pressure to ensure effective implementation. A trust bank license meant little if other subtle barriers impeded operations.

Having built a consensus around the issues discussed in the Accord, the MoF proved rigorous about implementation. A few disagreements arose over misunderstandings about language but they in no way amounted to bad faith or a retreat from agreed provisions. Not all matters progressed at an even speed, however, as domestic dissension in Japan mounted over some changes.

The last few years of the decade were less congenial, however. The Treasury sought to go beyond the Accord, with far more mixed results. The ability of banks to engage in securities activities represented an example of something not addressed in the Accord but an issue in the follow-up period. The period involved a hodgepodge of issues with no common thread and demonstrated a lack of understanding of the reform process within Japan and a US emphasis on symptoms rather than causes.

INTERNATIONALIZATION OF THE YEN

Internationalization of the yen represented a critical issue raised during the negotiation of the Accord. The MoF had deliberately stunted the use of the yen in overseas transactions, having only allowed Euroyen bonds for the first time in the late 1970s. The MoF kept the market small and tightly controlled. Restrictions were placed on the institutions eligible to issue bonds and the types of instruments that could be offered. By 1979, Euroyen bonds could only be issued by international organizations and governments, with private companies foreclosed.[2] Moreover, Japanese firms monopolized the sales, always heading the Euroyen bond syndicates.

In practice, these limitations meant that overseas investors did not have access to yen, stunting demand and, from the perspective of Washington, affecting the yen's value in international capital markets. Internationalization, it was hoped, would increase demand for the yen, causing the value to increase and, concomitantly, making American-made exports cheaper and more competitive. US negotiators recognized that this would not occur overnight. Indeed, in the immediate aftermath, the yen might actually fall in value. Over the long term, however, the impact of free capital markets was destined to be a substantial realignment in the value of the yen.

The Accord addressed the problem. The MoF agreed that the yen was to "play a role in international financial transactions that reflects Japan's importance as a great trading and financial world power."[3] The decision to permit greater internationalization did not come without some hesitancy. "[A] too rapid establishment of a free Euroyen market may have adverse effects on Japanese fiscal and monetary policies, exchange rates, and Japan's domestic financial systems."[4]

In general, internationalization meant an end to restrictions on yen transactions in the Euromarket. This required an increase in the entities that could tap the market and an increase in the authority of non-Japanese banks and brokers to sell the bonds.[5] The Accord mandated reforms in both areas.

Specifically, non-Japanese companies were permitted to issue unsecured, yen denominated bonds in the Euromarket beginning December 1, 1984. That month, a number of US companies issued bonds, with Sears edging out Dow Chemical to become the first to do so.[6] Foreign firms were also allowed to lead manage the offerings. Credit Suisse–First Boston headed a syndicate for an offering by Pacific Gas & Electric Co.[7] The MoF also agreed to expand gradually the foreign companies that could tap the market, a promise acted upon in 1986 when the eligible companies were increased to include those with a double A rating.

The more liberal attitude toward the Euromarket did not, at least initially, apply to foreign banks. The sale of long-term yen bonds threatened to provide an uncontrolled source of yen, giving foreign banks an expanded role in Japan. More importantly, however, sale of the bonds ran headlong into the compartmentalized system of banking. Barriers within Japan limited bond issuing authority to long-term-credit banks and the Bank of Tokyo. The Ministry knew that any new authority granted to foreign banks would lead to inexorable pressure from Japanese commercial banks for comparable powers.

Gaiatsu, however, intervened. At the December 1985 meeting of the Yen/Dollar Committee, Treasury negotiators forcefully raised the issue. As usual, no progress occurred immediately. Also as usual, Ministry officials listened and, after the meeting, developed a new consensus. Five months later, fully two years after execution of the Accord, the Ministry conceded the issue and permitted foreign banks to issue Euroyen bonds.[8] In order to preserve the compartmentalized system, however, the MoF refused to allow foreign banks to bring the funds back into Japan. Long-term-credit banks were therefore able to maintain their monopoly over this type of funding.

In addition to expanding the companies eligible, the MoF also disclaimed in the Accord any intention of restricting the size or number of Euroyen bonds. In general, the MoF took a hands off attitude to the development of the market, interfering little. The result was a creative surge in products. By 1985, a variety of instruments was introduced, including duel currency bonds, zero coupon bonds, deep discount bonds, and floating rate loans. The market's attractiveness largely gutted the samurai bond market in Japan.[9]

These changes led to an increased volume in Euroyen transactions. The principal source of growth in the market, however, flowed out of the Ministry's decision to abandon the "real" or "actual" demand rule for foreign exchange transactions. Real demand meant that foreign exchange trading was limited to the amount needed for actual transactions. This not only dampened speculation but limited hedging, swaps, and other techniques designed to minimize currency fluctuations. With foreign companies having little actual need for yen, the restraint promised to keep volume low. The MoF, however, agreed to abandon the restriction, announcing elimination more than a month before the signing of the Accord. The Accord did reiterate, however, that forward exchange transactions could occur for any purpose, "including investment, without limitation on amount."[10] The most immediate result would be a burgeoning swap market, with the MoF sitting on the sidelines largely as an observer.

Foreign companies selling Euroyen bonds had little need for the currency, although there were some exceptions. Instead, the funds were often swapped into dollars or other foreign currencies at advantageous terms. As the market developed, Japanese financial institutions in particular provided cheap dollars in return for a position as co-lead manager of the bond offering. The losses absorbed by the banks caused the transactions to be dubbed "harakiri" or suicide swaps.

Development of the market had a number of consequences. The daily volume of foreign exchange transactions in Tokyo exploded, going from $2 billion in 1979 to $48 billion by the end of 1986.[11] With banks in Japan having a monopoly over exchange trading, the increased volume provided additional opportunity for foreign financial institutions.

More significantly, swaps also created a mechanism for Japanese commercial banks to use to circumvent the restrictions on raising long-term funding. In Japan, only the Bank of Tokyo and the three long-term-credit banks had the authority to issue bonds. Without a source of long-term funding, other banks, particularly city banks, had a difficult time engaging in long-term lending.

The development of yen/yen swaps by 1986 gave the banks a way around the limitation. Banks would swap the interest obligations on short-term deposits for the obligations on Euroyen bonds issued by Japanese companies.[12] While expensive, at least the banks could be assured that the interest rates on the debt would remain unchanged for the life of the Euroyen bond. This further made clear the outmoded nature of the compartmentalized banking system in Japan.

As Mulford predicted, the Euroyen reforms in the Yen/Dollar Accord rippled back into Japan's financial system, forcing additional changes. Internationalization largely eliminated government controls over transactions outside of Japan, authority that would be difficult, if not impossible, to get back. While the MoF initially tried to retain control, insisting, for example, on pre-approval of yen swaps in the Euromarket, foreign banks ignored the requirement, forcing eventual abandonment.

Developments in the Euromarket put another nail in the coffin of the compartmentalized banking system. The distinction between long-term-credit and commercial banks had become increasingly illusory following the introduction of yen/yen swaps. Decompartmentalization would take another six years but by 1986 the reform already had an air of inevitability. Developments also spelled the death knell for window guidance. The ability to tap the more open markets in Europe made corporate Japan far less dependent upon banks. As Japanese companies increasingly turned to overseas capital markets, window guidance declined as an effective tool for controlling economic growth. When the reality dawned on the Bank of Japan, the longstanding practice of using guidance rather than interest rates to control lending suddenly had to be reconsidered.

Finally, the changes forced liberalization of the domestic bond markets. With controls lifted in the Euromarket, companies preferred the cheaper less regulated markets outside Japan. Absent reform, including an end to the need for Ministry pre-approval and a significant reduction in fees, the domestic bond market was destined to remain a place of last resort for companies unable to tap the Euromarket.

DOMESTIC REFORM

In addition to internationalization, the Accord also committed the Japanese government, specifically the MoF, to considerable domestic reform. While some reforms saw immediate implementation, others occurred in a halting fashion. Divisions within the MoF and among other ministries, particularly Posts and Telecommunications, slowed the process. More importantly, however, industry opposition intruded.

In the Accord, the MoF conceded ground on a number of issues. It accepted in principle the entry of foreign banks into the trust area, membership for foreign securities firms on the Tokyo Stock Exchange, the introduction of a banker's acceptance market, and liberalization of interest rates on deposits. By some measures, the reforms were puny. In general, they did little more than remove a number of blatantly discriminatory practices.

That was too narrow a view, however. First, they continued a practice of reverse discrimination – giving foreign banks unique advantages not shared by Japanese financial institutions. Foreign banks could engage in trust activities, ordinary Japanese commercial banks could not. Foreign banks could trade in securities trading, Japanese banks could not.

Second, they contained the seeds of broader change. The reforms destroyed the prevailing harmony within the financial sector by allowing foreign banks to surmount the barriers that had effectively segmented the financial system. The divide separating commercial and trust banks and, more significantly, the divide separating securities firms and banks were all breached by foreign banks.

Japanese financial institutions clamored for similar authority, something the Ministry could delay but hardly deny. Almost contemporaneously with execution of the Accord, the slow, laborious process of developing a consensus on systematic reform, particularly decompartmentalization, began, although completion would not occur until 1992.

Interest rate deregulation

Of all of the reforms, one of the most difficult but far reaching proved to be interest rate deregulation. Certainly, the Accord could not take complete credit. The process had begun in 1979 when the Japanese government authorized banks to issue large denomination certificates of deposit with market rates. These earlier efforts, however, illustrated the almost intractable difficulties of reform when serious domestic opposition surfaced.

For 10 years, city banks had argued for the authority to issue certificates of deposit. Opposition came from all other segments of the financial community. Only after a long struggle and after foreign banks jumped on the bandwagon did the MoF finally and grudgingly grant the authority. To appease domestic constituencies, however, the MoF kept the duration short and the minimum denomination large.

The advent of certificates of deposit in 1979 did not portend the beginning of the end on interest rate controls. In general, the banking community was satisfied by the compromise. City banks received an instrument designed to attract back corporate deposits. The large denomination, however, meant that smaller banks dependent upon retail deposits were unaffected. The short duration eliminated the instruments as competition for debentures issued by long-term-credit banks. No groundswell existed for complete deregulation. Only with the yen/dollar process did deregulation of interest rates recommence in earnest.

US negotiators aggressively sought further deregulation. Deregulated interest rates would allow foreign banks to compete effectively for deposits. More importantly, however, it eliminated a Japanese advantage. The low cost of deposits enabled Japanese banks to underprice foreign banks, permanently consigning them to the status of marginal lenders. With a lock on the domestic market, Japanese banks could pursue low margin activities abroad. A commitment in the Accord to further decontrol rates was therefore critical.

Interest rate deregulation, however, represented an area in which a domestic consensus within Japan had not yet evolved. Unsurprisingly, therefore, the Accord conceded only modest additional deregulation. The MoF agreed to a number of specific reforms, including a commitment to remove interest rate controls on large deposits within two to three years. Unlike other areas, the document left out firm dates for complete decontrol. The Ministry would only concede complete deregulation "as expeditiously as circumstances warrant without causing market instability."[13]

Following the Accord, the MoF permitted the introduction of money market certificates, instruments with a maturity of one to six months and an interest rate 0.75 percent of the rate on certificates of deposit. Although below market rates, the new instruments were more accessible to smaller depositors. The MoF set the minimum denomination at ¥50 million, well below the amount needed for ordinary certificates of deposit.

With that, progress became glacial. Decontrol generated considerable opposition within Japan. Smaller banks depended heavily upon controlled deposits for funding. They would be profoundly affected by deregulated interest rates, even to the point of impairing solvency. Opposition also came from the Postal Savings System. The largest financial institution in Japan, the Postal Savings System benefited through the ability to offer slightly higher interest rates. This advantage would be threatened by decontrol.

These constraints meant that there would be no sudden removal of controls, a continual irritant to the US side. Every meeting of the Yen/Dollar Committee after the signing of the Accord through 1992 involved a discussion of further interest rate deregulation. The Ministry gave ground, but only grudgingly. In the face of increasingly protracted domestic opposition, the reforms were designed to appease the United States rather than systematically change the financial system. This usually meant incremental steps such as reductions in the minimum ceilings for the accounts.[14]

Interest rate deregulation represented an area of reform strongly influenced by the yen/dollar talks. The impetus for further deregulation did not come from domestic sources. While city banks favored the changes, they had not yet developed a clear retail strategy. They were therefore content to compete primarily for large deposits, which had already been deregulated. Constant pressure from the United States, therefore, largely explained the changes.

Deregulation of interest rates more than any single reform fractured the system of financial regulation in Japan. Banks could now compete for funds without relying on the guiding hand of the Ministry. New branches – a key source of Ministry control during the post-war period – suddenly became less critical as deposits could be obtained through price competition rather than the location of the office.[15]

Moreover, decontrol caused some banks to edge closer to insolvency, forcing the MoF to react. The need for banks in different categories to step in and save failing financial institutions became the most immediate impetus for the introduction and passage of legislation designed to decompartmentalize the banking system.

Trust banking

With respect to trust activities, the MoF capitulated. The Accord called for a "new policy to license qualified foreign banks to participate in the same range of trust banking activities as is performed by Japanese banks."[16] The MoF did, however, reserve the right to determine the "precise form" that trust banking would take and the "criteria for selecting qualified banks . . . ."[17] Loose language, the Accord nevertheless contained a definite date for implementation, specifying that foreign banks would "be able to enter the trust banking business in 1985."[18]

Despite the commitment, the Yen/Dollar Committee had to engage in a short but sharp round of negotiations over the issue. Merely agreeing to grant the license was not enough. The licenses would mean little if the MoF imposed unacceptable capital requirements or limited the type of business that could be solicited. The goal, therefore, was effective implementation.

The initial dispute centered on numbers, something not addressed in the Accord. The MoF wanted to limit new licenses to eight. In the symmetrical world of Japanese banking, that would have left an identical number of foreign and Japanese banks with trust authority. The Treasury, however, took the position that a free market should reign, with any qualified financial institution entitled to a license.

The United States lost the round. At the first meeting of the Yen/Dollar Committee in November 1984, the Ministry announced that only eight foreign banks would receive licenses to engage in trust activities.[19] The Ministry also indicated that no future licenses would be issued until Japanese commercial banks received comparable authority.

111

The MoF did have to retreat a bit, however, in response to pressure from the Swiss. After the announcement, Union Bank of Switzerland, not part of the original group of eight, insisted on a license. Union Bank had been made to wait before, having received a Tokyo branch license in 1972, a year after Swiss Bank. There would be no repeat in connection with trust licenses. When the MoF initially resisted, hints were made of possible retaliation against Japanese activity in Switzerland. The MoF relented and agreed to issue a ninth trust license.

Approval of the trust licenses amounted to a door briefly opened and swiftly shut. Other foreign banks wanting a license were foreclosed. Even the ability of the fortunate nine to sell their franchise required Ministry approval.[20] The MoF could therefore control the process and impose conditions on any subsequent transfer. While a form of liberalization and a significant inroad into the system of compartmentalization, the changes were as narrow as the MoF could make them.

The nine licenses did finally put to rest the controversy caused by J. P. Morgan and Nomura in 1982 when they petitioned the MoF for approval to start a trust company. The licenses also demonstrated the growing importance of foreign pressure in the evolution of the financial system. In the old days, the MoF would have muttered that the time was not convenient for a trust application, expecting the issue promptly to disappear. Foreign pressure no longer made that approach realistic.

In granting the trust licenses, the MoF worked hard to appease foreign interests while limiting the domestic impact. It let a small number of foreign banks in but kept domestic securities firms out. This required subtle pressure on Nomura, which had started the whole controversy by seeking a trust company in conjunction with J. P. Morgan. The large securities firm dropped the matter when Ministry officials let it be known that if Nomura continued to make an issue of Trust Authority fixed commissions would become an issue at the yen/dollar talks. Smaller securities firms were in no hurry to give up fixed commissions, particularly for trust authority that would primarily benefit Nomura and the other large brokers. With all of the dissension within the industry, Nomura gave up.

The MoF also applied a significant dose of administrative guidance to the process. It insisted – without legal foundation – that foreign trust banks operate through subsidiaries incorporated in Japan. This allowed greater control over their activities. With trust banks managing Japanese pension plans, the MoF wanted to make sure that the funds remained under close scrutiny.

A seemingly innocuous requirement, the separation caused banks enormous headaches. The MoF insisted not only upon legal separation but also upon physical separation of the foreign branch and trust bank. That entailed considerable duplication, including the need for separate offices. With the high cost of land and office space, this added huge overheads to trust bank operations.[21]

Some banks resisted the guidance. When the Banking Bureau insisted that J. P. Morgan obtain a separate vault for trust bank assets, the bank had had enough. Officials approached higher-ups in the Ministry to protest. They indicated that the J. P. Morgan vault was apparently adequate to hold overflow from Japanese banks, including securities issued by the Japanese government, and was therefore adequate for trust assets. Irritated, officials within the Banking Bureau requested that J. P. Morgan cease providing Ministry officials with "irrelevant" details. When that did not work, J. P. Morgan officials took advantage of a back door channel to the Finance Minister. The approach eventually succeeded and the demand for the separate vault ended.

Entry into the trust area provided no magical cure for foreign banks. As was often the case, stripping away legal barriers did little to improve market share. Foreign banks confronted a host of practical difficulties in operating a trust bank, including substantial start-up costs and considerable difficulty obtaining business. While some did well initially, the overall results were in general disappointing.

As events unfurled, the early lack of success had explanations unrelated to ability or market sophistication. Although capable of bringing advanced skills to the fund management table, the foreign trust banks found Japanese clients more interested in guarantees of interest and principal. Subsequent scandals would show that Japanese brokers routinely provided the requisite guarantees despite their dubious legality.[22]

Securities activities

Securities activities represented another area addressed in the Accord, although the most significant changes occurred in the follow-up discussions. The Accord focused on one narrow facet: access to the Tokyo Stock Exchange. As things turned out, this proved surprisingly difficult to implement.

A contentious issue all along, access to the Stock Exchange was one of the last to be resolved. Foreign securities firms had been permitted to obtain seats since 1982, but only if they could acquire one from an existing member.[23] Given the limited turnover, this meant that foreign firms would be subject to an inordinate wait before gaining membership. To solve the problem more rapidly required expansion of the number of seats, with some assigned to foreign firms.

In the negotiations over the Accord, MoF officials took the position that the matter was outside their control. The Exchange amounted to a privately run organization not subject to government control. Theoretically true, the response ignored the MoF's pervasive influence throughout the financial system. Minions ran the organization. The head of the Tokyo Stock Exchange was usually a former vice minister from the Ministry, solidifying influence and lines of communication.

113

After tough negotiations, including a fist banging episode by Donald Regan, the Secretary of the Treasury, the MoF agreed to do something about the exclusion. Describing the Tokyo Stock Exchange as an "Autonomous Membership Organization," the Ministry promised to ask the Exchange to "study ways of providing opportunities" for foreign membership. The MoF also announced its willingness to "assist" any non-Japanese broker in applying.[24] The Tokyo Stock Exchange read the writing on the wall and agreed to expand the number of members to include foreign brokers. Still, matters moved slowly. In November 1985 six securities firms were told they would receive a seat on the Exchange.[25]

In general, the authority held little interest for foreign banks. Article 65 prohibited them from engaging in securities activities. The high-flying stock market of the 1980s, however, made the brokerage business increasingly attractive, particularly when compared with the decline in core banking functions. American Express even went so far as to close its bank branch – open since the early 1950s – in order to permit Shearson, a subsidiary, to begin brokerage activities.[26]

The first break, as usual, came from the maverick Citibank. The parent holding company, Citicorp, purchased Vickers da Costa Ltd, a British securities firm, in November 1983. With Vickers having a branch in Tokyo, the purchase suddenly breached the divide separating banks and brokers. The bank also violated an unwritten rule by failing to pre-clear the transaction with the MoF. Even worse, there was little the MoF could do. The purchase was by the holding company in New York rather than the bank in Japan.

The MoF could have ordered the Tokyo branch of Vickers to close. To head off that step, Citibank immediately began lobbying to retain the office. The bank also did everything it could to raise the profile of the purchase, including an announcement of the acquisition during a trip to Tokyo by President Reagan. The Ministry knew that efforts to close the office would generate a political fracas.

The MoF ultimately allowed the facility to remain open, unwilling to incur the political price of closing the office. Treating the acquisition as an "exception," the MoF agreed not to revoke the license, thereby approving Citibank's foray into the securities business.[27] The frontal assault demonstrated how aggressive policies were sometimes preferable. Had the bank discussed the acquisition in advance, the MoF almost certainly would have turned thumbs down.

Citicorp did make one significant concession. The MoF insisted that Vickers not be 100 percent owned. The holding company therefore acquired 75 percent, with the remaining 25 percent purchased by a management group. Later when the MoF prohibited other foreign banks from owning more than 50 percent of a securities company operating in Japan, Citicorp was asked but declined to comply with the requirement.

114

With Citibank in, others clamored for similar authority. The primary assault came from Europe, where Japanese banks were already allowed to engage in securities activities. The issue also gave the European Community an opportunity to establish a presence in the negotiation process. The European Commission had been concerned that the United States was using the yen/dollar process to cut its own deal and further its own agenda.

The Vickers transaction had involved the acquisition of an existing securities license. Few other licenses, however, were available. European banks wanted new licenses, a step the MoF had not yet taken. The MoF eventually agreed to issue new licenses and allow European banks to operate securities subsidiaries, but not without considerable pressure. The MoF got the word that, absent approval, Japanese banks would not get the regulatory approvals they were seeking in European countries. The MoF did impose limitations, however. A bank could not own more than 50 percent of a securities subsidiary.

Once European banks received the authority, Treasury officials used the yen/dollar process to pressure Japan for comparable powers for US banks. The issue came up at the September 1986 meeting. The MoF resisted, pointing out that Japanese banks could not engage in securities activities in the United States. The resistance caused one participant to describe the process as a "bloody battle." Waiving the concession to the Europeans like a big stick, Treasury officials invoked national treatment and insisted that all foreign banks receive identical benefits and authority.

Ultimately, the Japanese capitulated and allowed US banks to set up securities subsidiaries and obtain the necessary licenses. As with the Europeans, however, ownership had to be in the form of a separate subsidiary owned no more than 50 percent by the bank. In August 1987, J. P. Morgan received approval to open an office, the first US bank to do so through its own subsidiary rather than through the purchase of a securities firm. Chemical, Bankers Trust, and Manufacturers Hanover followed. As with the Europeans, the ownership limitation resulted in a number of odd pairings. Bankers Trust, for example, found itself in the venture with Exxon.[28]

Similar to the trust bank area, the MoF insisted that the securities firms and the bank branch be physically separated. The Ministry even required name changes to emphasize the separation. Chase, for example, could not use the name Laurie, Milbank & Co., its securities subsidiary, because the word "bank" appeared in the name. The bank opted to call the company LM Securities. J. P. Morgan, however, resisted the entreaties and insisted that the securities firm carry the J. P. Morgan name. The MoF relented but insisted that the initials JP be in Japanese script. Again J. P. Morgan refused and, after considerable time and effort, got the Ministry to drop the requirement.

The reforms represented an example of "reverse discrimination" and demonstrated the length the MoF would go to to satisfy foreign pressure. Japanese banks had been fighting since the 1970s for increased authority in the securities area, largely to no avail. In contrast, foreign banks received the authority and more after a brief but sharp set of negotiations. The step, however, also amounted to an acknowledgement by the MoF that foreign banks would pose no serious competitive threat to the banking system. Providing them with additional authority entailed little real change in the status quo.

Now that foreign banks had securities subsidiaries, the situation shifted back to the Tokyo Stock Exchange. The banks wanted seats on the Exchange. Only Vickers, the Citicorp subsidiary, had been part of the original group given membership in early 1986. The issue of increased membership, therefore, became as a topic of discussion at the yen/dollar meetings.

In 1987, additional seats were created, with a handful going to foreign banks. In June of that year, the Tokyo Stock Exchange invited 10 banks to apply, including Chemical, Bankers, J. P. Morgan, and Manufacturers. Not every bank seeking a license got one. Chase, through its securities subsidiary Laurie, Milbank & Co. (LM Securities), was turned down, as were four European firms. By the time the Exchange seemed ready to approve Chase, the US bank had lost interest and declined to apply.[29]

Government bond syndicate

The bond syndicate represented another area of protracted conflict. Addressed in the Accord, most of the progress occurred during the follow-up period and only after direct intervention by Congress. The issue posed broad domestic concerns. The MoF had resisted reforms during the negotiation of the Accord, grudgingly accepting them only toward the end of the process. Primary resistance came from the Finance Bureau, which had responsibility within the MoF for the bond sales.

Like the United States, the Japanese government ran deficits and sold bonds to cover the shortfall. The government did not, however, auction the bonds to those offering the lowest interest rates, as was done in the United States. Instead, the bonds were sold through a syndicate of Japanese brokers and banks. The applicable interest rates were determined through negotiation. The MoF had historically used the system to foist off on the syndicate bonds at below market interest rates.

Foreign participants had been excluded from the syndicate. Initially a benefit, they wanted no part of the money-losing proposition. By the 1980s, however, the government offered more competitive rates. A secondary market in the bonds also developed. Exclusion now became a disadvantage. Banks lost a potential source of profits and seemed likely to be kept out of the secondary market. They clamored for entry, with the topic arising in the yen/dollar talks. A seemingly technical and esoteric area, the bond syndicate issue unexpectedly became highly politicized.

Reform directly confronted the internal divisions within the MoF.

Responsibility for bond sales fell not to the Banking or International Finance Bureaus, the two offices with the most experienced relationship with the US side, but to the more parochial and domestic Finance Bureau. Responsible for raising non-tax revenues, the Bureau was suspicious of any change that might increase the cost of funds. The yen/dollar talks had to overcome this resistance.

Foreign banks and brokers had already begun to make inroads. Even before execution of the Accord, the MoF gave a number of foreign firms a place in the bond syndicate, but imposed significant limitations. Only those with a branch in the country for five years could participate. Foreign participants also initially received a paltry allotment. Treated on the same footing as regional banks, each received a quota of 0.032 percent of the bonds sold to the syndicate.

The Accord broadened the authority by conceding that foreign banks could purchase and resell the bonds, although subject to prudential limitations. In considering an application, the government would take into account the foreign bank's "experience in trading in government securities" in the home country.[30] At US insistence, the MoF agreed that membership in the syndicate was not a prerequisite to dealing in the bonds. In June 1984, banks received the authority to act as dealers, although only on bonds with a remaining maturity of less than two years.[31] The time limit would eventually be eliminated.

Foreign firms pushed for and received an increased share of the bonds sold to the syndicate, an issue repeatedly raised at yen/dollar meetings. Representing approximately 8 percent of the participants in the syndicate, foreign entities initially had only a small share, although it eventually increased. Membership restrictions were also eased. By 1987, the five year waiting period following the opening of a Japanese branch was eliminated as a precondition to foreign participation in the syndicate. A year later 30 additional foreign institutions were allowed in.

Generally unsatisfied with these modest improvements, the US side pushed for more radical change. The yen/dollar talks were used as a forum to urge the replacement of the syndicate with an auction process. Even here, the MoF made concessions. In advance of the 1987 yen/dollar meeting, the MoF agreed to "auction" 20 percent of all future issues of government bonds. The percentage doubled to 40 percent two years later.

The seemingly sharp break, however, represented another example of the MoF's approach to reform. Labeled an auction, the market did not function as one. Banks and brokers could "bid" for additional bonds, but the price was predetermined. The MoF put a ceiling of 1 percent of the total issue that each bidder could acquire and the syndicate continued to set the price of the securities. As one securities source described: "It's not an auction, it's a joke."[32]

Frustration with the pace of reform generated a response in Congress, the first instance of direct legislative intrusion into the process. The small share of the government bond market for foreign banks contrasted sharply with the growing Japanese presence in the United States. The Federal Reserve typically sold government debt in the United States through a small number of primary dealers. By the end of 1988, Japanese banks had seven primary dealerships. Legislative initiatives designed to restrict Japanese access to primary dealers began to appear, with one actually passing in 1988 as part of the Omnibus Trade Act. The government got the message. Reform of the bond syndicate accelerated.

Yen funding

Yen funding, the eternal problem, continued to be a headache for foreign banks. At the time of the Accord, they still operated under a number of pronounced disadvantages. Foreign banks lacked a sufficient retail network, were subject to swap limits, and were denied access to the discount window. While the interbank market represented a relatively available source of funding, the market was subject to collateral requirements and heavy handed control by the central bank.

The Accord addressed some of these issues, although not in a comprehensive fashion. The MoF agreed to create a banker's acceptance market, with one implemented in 1985. The market was intended to facilitate the financing of international trade.[33] The Banking Bureau and the Federation of Bankers Associations worked closely in establishing the parameters for the new market.[34]

Swap ceilings were also to be reformed. Immediately after the signing of the Accord, spot limits were eliminated. The change, however, illustrated the double edged nature of reform. Foreign banks had ceilings 10 times higher than Japanese banks. Disappearance of the limits created instant parity and provided Japanese banks with a greater opportunity to compete.

Other reforms in the availability of yen funding occurred, although not all as a result of the yen/dollar process. The MoF reformed the interbank market by eliminating the collateral requirement. Smaller foreign banks had often lacked sufficient collateral to support significant borrowing. When the uncollateralized market began in 1985, foreign banks had a dominant role. The favorable position, however, could not last. By the end of the 1980s, Japanese banks had entered with full vigor, causing the share of foreign financial institutions to fall to 12 percent and costs to rise.

More momentous, the Bank of Japan abandoned efforts to directly manipulate interest rates in the market. Although sometimes described as market driven, rates were closely controlled by the central bank.[35] When the Bank of Japan failed to keep rates at market levels, however, funds began to pour out.[36] The central bank realized that it was presiding over a shrinking market. As a result, interest rates were decontrolled and the terms of the commercial bill-buying operations were reduced.

118

By the end of the decade, one of the most flagrant remaining barriers to foreign access fell. Foreign banks finally received authority to borrow at the discount window. A quid pro quo, access came after the Bank of Japan allowed city banks to enter the uncollateralized call money market. The central bank did, however, impose tight limits on borrowing, with smaller banks limited to ¥1 billion.

THE DENOUEMENT

Despite continual reform, nothing in the talks substantially improved the prospect of foreign banks in Japan. Market share remained dismal. Some of the explanation rested with the banks, some with the Treasury. The Department took a macro-oriented perspective. The Yen/Dollar Committee emphasized structural change without any attendant focus on market share. Negotiators wanted barriers removed out of the philosophical belief that free financial markets operated more efficiently. A variation of the trickle down theory, the approach posited that all financial institutions, including those from the United States, would benefit from more liberal financial markets.

While perhaps intellectually justifiable, the approach was naive. Each negotiation victory removed an obvious barrier within the financial system but provided little additional opportunity for foreign banks. Their share of the traditional banking areas continued to decline or stagnate. Loans remained at 3 percent, deposits at 1 percent. One Treasury attaché remembered a Christmas party in the 1980s when US bankers bragged about how quickly they had wound down their loan portfolios.

As progress slowed, the tone of the yen/dollar talks changed. With the original agenda largely completed, the name of the group was symbolically altered. It became the "US–Japan Working Group on Financial Matters." As the US side pushed for additional reforms, the MoF developed a less compliant stance. The new aggressiveness emanated in part from the waning influence of the Treasury.

The first talks convened under the new appellation degenerated into an acrimonious slugfest. Although acknowledging some progress, Under Secretary Mulford expressed "concerns and some disappointments" over the pace of reform.[37] The talks also took place amidst a growing maelstrom in Congress.

By the end of the 1970s and beginning of the 1980s, Congress became increasingly frustrated with the lack of progress of US banks. The relatively mild view would gradually give way to more virulent approaches. As Japanese banks in the United States continued their exponential growth and US banks in Japan retained their intractably low market share, Congress increasingly sought to exact a pound of flesh from the Japanese. As Congress became increasingly involved, the dynamics of the yen/dollar process changed.

With all of the activity, one of the most significant developments of the decade hardly drew attention. In 1988, the Bank of Japan accepted the new international capital standards contained in the Basel Accord. The standards called for capital equal to 8 percent of assets by the end of 1992.[38] The capital standards did not have fair competition as a primary goal. Instead, they were motivated by an attempt to ensure the safety and soundness of international banking activity. One commentator described the Accord as "a modest, unpretentious document and, perhaps to the lawyer, unprepossessing."[39]

Capital of Japanese banks had always been low, averaging around 3 percent. Despite the called-for increase, Japanese banks viewed the new standards as a non-event. As a condition for agreeing to the new standards, the Bank of Japan succeeded in obtaining a provision that permitted a portion of unrealized appreciation on stock to be counted as capital. The Japanese banks had substantial holdings of stock acquired at very cheap prices. The holdings had appreciated significantly, particularly during the booming 1980s. The unrealized appreciation meant that Japanese banks could easily meet the standards.[40]

Certainly, had there been a crystal ball handy, the Japanese would have reconsidered acceptance of the standards. Unexpectedly, the stock market underwent swift and utter collapse. By mid-1992, the Nikkei average had fallen 60 percent from its December 1989 high of almost ¥40,000. The unrealized appreciation so heavily relied upon to meet the capital standards evaporated. Banks suddenly found themselves short of capital and desperately in need of additional funds. The fall in the stock market made the easiest source of raising capital – selling shares – impossible.

With funds difficult to raise, banks had to control or even reduce asset growth. Pell-mell expansion into low margin operations ended. By the early 1990s, expansion abroad essentially stopped. Banks began to take desperate, unheard of steps, including the sale of corporate loans. The compartmentalized banking system creaked even louder.

For the first time in decades, the Japanese tide eased. Foreign banks had an opportunity to regain lost ground. Unfortunately, by the beginning of the 1990s, many foreign banks, particularly those in the United States, had lost either the financial ability or the nerve to go on the offensive.

120

8

TREASURY VERSUS UNITED STATES TRADE REPRESENTATIVE

The 1984 Accord did more than designate areas ripe for reform. Less heralded but in some respects just as momentous, the agreement essentially resolved a bureaucratic dispute over control of the negotiation process. The Accord created a forum for future discussions of financial reform, the Yen/Dollar Committee. The Committee consisted of representatives of the Ministry of Finance (MoF) and the Department of the Treasury, although both would occasionally allow others to attend particular meetings. The Department of State and the Office of the United States Trade Representative (USTR) had no role in the process.

Designation of the MoF seemed reasonable enough. The Ministry had almost complete administrative control over the financial sector. Tax, budgetary, banking, insurance, and securities matters all came under the tight grip of the powerful Ministry. The Treasury, however, had no comparable claim. Aspects of the financial system fell within the bailiwick of the Federal Reserve Board and Securities and Exchange Commission. Similarly, the State Department had an inherent interest in anything involving international affairs, as did the USTR over anything involving international trade.

The result was effective bifurcation of trade talks with Japan. The Treasury controlled financial services; merchandise and agriculture were left to the USTR. The division of authority had a certain logic, given the Treasury's obvious expertise in the financial area. It also had a downside. The Treasury lacked the arsenal necessary to induce concessions by the Japanese. The Department could make demands but had little leverage when the MoF proved unaccommodating. This would become clear as the talks progressed through the latter half of the 1980s.

The set-up affected the negotiation process. As reform in Japan unfurled, the United States seemed increasingly less involved. The decline in influence had a number of explanations. To a large degree, support for the talks within the US banking community had waned. The decline also had a number of purely bureaucratic explanations. The talks did not receive the same level of government resources and commitment within the Department of the Treasury that had been so crucial to the original Accord. Interagency disputes within the executive branch also impeded progress. Squabbles over control of the talks sometimes became more important than the talks themselves.

JOCKEYING FOR POSITION

Until the Accord, any number of government agencies or departments had a claim to participation in the negotiation process. The two independent agencies with some jurisdiction over the area, the Federal Reserve Board and the Securities and Exchange Commission, had limited interest. Both were primarily concerned with supervision of domestic rather than international matters. Competition for negotiation primacy came from State, Treasury, and the USTR.

The Treasury edge

Particularly since the Second World War, the Department of the Treasury had emerged as the dominant force within the US government in international financial matters. Multilateral economic agreements had become fixtures, with Bretton Woods and GATT creating an international economic framework. Having the requisite expertise, the Treasury took the lead in negotiating these agreements. As economic matters increased in importance, the Treasury became a fixture in international forums, to some degree usurping the historical role of the Department of State. The attitude began to grow that international finance was somehow unique and needed to be kept apart from more politicized talks of the type spearheaded by State.

Interest in financial matters in Japan occurred almost inadvertently. The area suffered from bureaucratic benign neglect through most of the post-war period. The Treasury did have an attaché in Tokyo and officials occasionally traveled to Japan to meet with US bankers. Through the 1970s, however, little was done to address problems confronted by the banking community. The impetus for more systematic interest and contact came, ironically, from Congress.

The International Banking Act of 1978 required the Treasury to draft a National Treatment Study analyzing financial barriers in certain international markets, including those in Japan. To properly draft the study, Treasury officials had to become far more familiar with the problems confronted by foreign, particularly US, banks. That required systematic contact. For the first time, government officials began to canvass the banks and learn in a comprehensive fashion the difficulties they confronted.

The Treasury's role was facilitated by the presence of an attaché in Tokyo, a critical source of intelligence. The attaché had been in the country since the occupation, when William H. (Duke) Diehl received the post in 1946.[1] The attaché had primary responsibility for following financial matters and wrote a weekly report available to anyone in the executive branch.

The attaché, however, also had a more subtle role. His primary responsibility was to the Treasury. Although reporting to the Economic Minister within the Embassy – a State Department official – the attaché had lines of communication directly back to Washington. The Treasury could therefore learn first hand what was going on. Information might be conveyed by phone and, eventually, by fax. The same material did not necessarily appear in the weekly report.

In the early 1980s, little coordination occurred within the Embassy. The Treasury attaché maintained a physical and psychological distance from other Embassy officials. The economic section (State Department people supporting the USTR) and the commerce section (Department of Commerce people) shared a floor in the Embassy and had some overlapping responsibility. They also often belonged to what was euphemistically called the Chrysanthemum Club – those officials who saw Japan as an island of democracy, a bastion against Soviet expansionism, and were therefore unwilling to upset the apple-cart over economic issues.

The Treasury attaché, in contrast, had an office on a different floor. Carrying a sword rather than a chrysanthemum, the attaché viewed the relationship with Japan as almost adversarial. By the 1980s, financial reform had become a daily battle, hand-to-hand combat. With an assistant and two Japanese employees, the attaché found himself involved in a constant process of collecting information and cajoling the MoF over reform.

The informational advantage possessed by the Treasury meant more in the early 1980s. Learning about the Japanese system – particularly arcane areas like finance – was an impossible task. Articles in the press about Japan tended to focus on geishas and sushi. The attaché therefore provided information about the financial markets not otherwise available. This would eventually change, weakening the Treasury's informational monopoly, but not until later.

The Department of State

The Treasury therefore had the expertise and information necessary to play a dominant role in financial talks with Japan. Other agencies wanting to play a role had to affirmatively elbow their way into the process. The Department of State represented one possible claimant.

The international thrust of the talks gave State grounds for participation. State seemed to have interest. Secretary George Schultz met with Foreign Minister Shintaro Abe in September 1983 and proposed discussions between the two countries over exchange rate matters. In October, the US–Japan Advisory Committee, consisting of business and labor leaders from both countries, issued a report citing exchange rates as a significant priority.

123

To the Treasury, however, State involvement was anathema. Part of the reason was hubris. Only the Treasury could do the job. Placing immense emphasis on the geopolitical and military importance of Japan, State could not be counted upon to support financial reform with equal vigor. State also had little permanent interest in economic affairs, particularly those involving such esoteric and technical matters as financial markets.

Part of the reason was also bureaucratic turf. In the arcane world of government bureaucracy, no agency or department wanted to give up control of something already within its jurisdiction, irrespective of the wisdom. The Treasury was particularly territorial, with then Secretary Regan not about to share authority under his control with another department, least of all State.

Given the Treasury's obdurate opposition, participation by State in the yen/dollar process could only have been accomplished one way: by elevating the issue to a high level dispute within the executive branch, necessitating arbitration by the White House. That meant the President. The approach, however, required an expenditure of political capital for an uncertain outcome in an area that held minimal interest.

In the end, State did not try to force its way in. Personalities and relations between the two departments largely explained the failure. In State, Secretary Schultz and Under Secretary Allen Wallis were content to leave the matter to the Treasury. Both departments shared an almost messianic faith in free markets. With the fervent ideologues at the Treasury, State had little fear that the Administration's policies would not be followed.

Schultz also had a more specific reason for not intervening. Having previously served as Secretary of the Treasury, he had witnessed first hand meddling by State. He repeated on more than one occasion that he would not commit the same sin. Had the ideological compatibility not been so strong or the personalities at State been more confrontational, the Treasury's monopoly may not have been as easy to maintain.

Even had State tried to squeeze in, the Treasury had a trump card. It could rely on opposition by the MoF. Entry of State would have permitted participation by Japan's Ministry of Foreign Affairs, something the MoF opposed vigorously. MoF officials wanted nothing to do with their counterparts in Foreign Affairs. The Ministry, therefore, insisted that the talk be limited to the two financial regulations. Whether in fact the talks would have collapsed had State and the Ministry of Foreign Affairs participated, however, was never put to the test. Still, opposition in Japan gave the Treasury handy leverage.

State therefore remained outside the process. As talks proceeded over the communiqué and later the Accord, State was kept informed and given an opportunity to provide views. Secretaries Schultz and Regan and key staff members met at breakfast every Tuesday morning. Yen/dollar issues were often discussed. State's involvement, however, never became more direct.

The United States Trade Representative

The USTR also found itself excluded from the yen/dollar process, although more by default than intent. Created in 1962, the USTR (then known as the Special Trade Representative) initially had as a primary function the administration of agreements reached through the GATT process.[2] The Office obtained cabinet level status in 1974.[3] Renamed in 1980, the USTR was assigned responsibility for overall trade policy.[4] Congress wanted a trade oriented organization independent of the institutional interests of the departments in the executive branch.

The Office was headed by a trade representative and two deputies, all with ambassador rank.[5] Reflecting the low profile of international trade talks in earlier eras, the Office through the 1970s had a small staff. As the area grew in political prominence, however, the size underwent measurable increase, doubling to almost 80 professionals by 1980.

The professional staff brought to the negotiation process a number of advantages. Foremost, the USTR developed a type of trade negotiation expertise. Unlike the multi-faceted agencies and departments in the executive branch, the USTR had a single bailiwick: international trade. The Office could concentrate on process and results. For substantive expertise, the Office relied on the support of other agencies.

As a corollary, the USTR generally had good working relations with other departments. With a small staff, the Office lacked the wherewithal to engage in negotiations in a multitude of sectors involving a host of different matters without relying considerably on the substantive expertise of the other departments and agencies in the federal government. The Office had no interest in acquiring a permanent fiefdom over any other agency's turf. The USTR therefore generally avoided bureaucratic squabbles over control of particular programs. Had trade negotiations been assigned to an existing agency or department, other parts of the bureaucracy would have viewed the efforts with considerable suspicion.

The system of interagency cooperation was not, however, left to chance. The USTR chaired the Trade Policy Committee, a committee consisting of the heads of various executive offices and departments.[6] The Committee promoted coordination on trade issues. It also had two subcommittees, the Trade Policy Committee Review Group and the Trade Policy Staff Committee, both designed to resolve interagency disputes.[7] Negotiation instructions for any trade matter had to be approved by the Committee.

Cumbersome, the interagency committee process required considerable time and effort. The USTR had to engage in fierce bargaining and compromises to obtain approval of negotiating instructions. Objections often arose from bruised egos or bureaucratic positioning rather than true substantive differences. Despite the drawbacks, however, the process provided the practical advantage of forcing the USTR to defend and refine particular strategies and approaches. Moreover, the end result gave the Office an immense psychological advantage. The final positions represented not the exclusive view of the USTR but the unified position of the entire executive branch.[8]

The USTR brought other advantages to the trade negotiation process, particularly heightened visibility. Increasingly, both the White House and Congress looked to the USTR for answers to international trade problems. The Trade Act of 1974 specifically made the Office responsible to Congress for implementation of trade agreements. The trade representative became a fixture on the Hill, explaining the talks and assuaging congressional concerns.

A close relationship with Congress created impurities. The high profile could politicize the negotiation process. Both to appease Congress and to shield the White House from criticism, the Office emphasized results. The USTR paid lip service to the free market approach prevalent in the 1980s but in the end wanted to see concrete improvement. That meant better access for US companies and products. The USTR also had an objective benchmark for measuring success: a fall in the trade deficit.

A result oriented philosophy sometimes led to tactics antithetical to the then prevalent free trade philosophy, particularly at the Treasury. The USTR had an arsenal of retaliatory measures that could be brought to bear on recalcitrant negotiating partners. These included the threat to take away or deny benefits in other areas or to stand aside while Congress engaged in protectionist legislation. The USTR could and did incite Congress when necessary.

The result oriented philosophy had another side, however. Success or failure depended upon whether an agreement could be reached. This put immense pressure on the USTR to come to successful closure. The Office was sometimes accused of giving away issues in order to reach a final agreement.

Finally, the Office was highly responsive to industry. Consultation with the private sector represented a mandatory task. Result oriented, the USTR would almost certainly have maintained lines of communication with industry groups, even absent legal compulsion. Industry support created a legion of proponents that could lobby Congress.

Again, however, the process was not left to chance. Private sector advisory committees developed as a formal mechanism for soliciting industry views. The Trade Agreement Act of 1979 made the committees a permanent fixture. Among other things, the committees assisted in monitoring compliance with trade agreements and "provide[d] input and advice on the development of US trade policy."[9] Industry learned that trade gripes – no matter how small or ideologically impure – would at least get a sympathetic ear and often more direct action.

As the 1980s began, the USTR focused almost exclusively on agricultural and merchandise trade, with little involvement in services, particularly financial services. Interest in services failed to gel for a number of reasons. A small agency, the USTR had plenty of other things to do. Already taut, seizing a broad yet undeveloped area would stretch the Office even further. Moreover, given the politicized nature of the USTR, financial services had not really captured Washington's attention.

Over time, however, a handful of service-related issues percolated to the surface. Lawyers and construction firms wanted greater access to the Japanese market; so did overnight mail carriers. Financial services also began to attract attention. To some degree responding to congressional pressure, a 1982 report issued by the Office called for an increased need to promote US service exports.[10] Listing Japan as a country with restrictive laws, banking received specific mention. The following year, the USTR prepared the National Study on Trade in Services for the upcoming GATT meeting and included a discussion of banking and finance issues.[11]

US financial institutions also occasionally turned to the USTR for assistance in dealing with access problems in the Japanese markets. Particularly before bureaucratic demarcation, banks were prepared to talk to anyone that might help. Moreover, the USTR seemed more willing to play the role of industry spokesperson while the Treasury preferred to avoid smaller, nuts and bolts issues designed to assuage the problems of a particular bank.

THE PUTSCH AND THE CONSEQUENCES

By the early 1980s, the Treasury and the USTR both danced around the issue of financial services, with neither staking an unequivocal claim. The Yen/Dollar Accord, however, resolved the issue by giving the Treasury exclusive control. The document provided for regular talks between the Treasury and the MoF, with no required participation of other groups. Non-Treasury officials occasionally attended, but only at the Department's discretion.[12]

The net effect was that Treasury had exclusive control over the process.[13] Not subject to the interagency committee process, however, the Treasury had no regularized method for ensuring participation by other departments within the government. Negotiation instructions did not have to go through the Trade Policy Committee. Essentially boxed out, the USTR could obtain a role only through the tolerance of the Treasury, an unlikely event. As a consequence, however, the Department could not claim that it spoke for the entire executive branch.

By monopolizing the talks, the Treasury sacrificed leverage. To induce change in Japan, the Department had a limited arsenal. Recalcitrant Ministry negotiators might be threatened with adverse publicity, something officials from the MoF roundly disliked. That tended to be an idle threat, however. A technical area such as financial services did not capture the public's imagination and generate the necessary outcry. Nor could Treasury rely upon

127

retaliatory measures. The talks were intended to open markets. Threatening reprisals amounted to an oxymoron.

Treasury could raise the specter of an unleashed Congress, an increasingly worrisome problem for the Japanese. This, however, also ran into problems. The approach represented a blunt instrument that in general ran counter to the controlling open market philosophy. The free market Department had difficulty siding with an aroused, protectionist Congress threatening retaliation. The Treasury was therefore left with moral suasion and the expectation that the Japanese would not allow the talks to deteriorate to the point of significant interference with bilateral relations.

In addition to an absence of leverage, the Treasury suffered from a type of hubris that caused a de-emphasis on practical results. The Department approached the yen/dollar talks with visions of grandeur. Eschewing the role of industry lobbyists, the Department had as an ultimate goal open financial markets. A "trickle down" approach, the Treasury reasoned that liberalized financial markets would provide greater competitive opportunities for all banks. Although efforts were made to ascertain current grievances about treatment in Japan, banks had no guarantee that their problems would get on the agenda. With limited meeting time, the Yen/Dollar Committee had only modest patience with pleas to help particular banks. Ultimately, the interests of the Treasury and the banking industry began to diverge.

The problem of leverage and negotiating tactics was academic as long as the Treasury achieved results. With the Japanese committed to specific reforms in the Accord, progress continued for a time, although haltingly. When, toward the end of the decade, the talks moved into unchartered areas, forward movement slowed to a crawl.

The consequences were readily apparent. Congress became increasingly involved. Not imbued with the same attachment to open international capital markets, Congress focused on what the Treasury ignored. Whatever negotiating battles had been won, the United States seemed to be losing the war. Japanese market share in the United States continued to ratchet upward, the inverse to what was happening to foreign banks in Japan. Nor did Congress think a free market approach was the only solution. Increasingly, the body focused on more punitive measures to open the Japanese financial markets.

MAINTAINING CONTROL

Maintaining control over talks with Japan represented only part of the problem. Treasury also found itself expending considerable energy in an effort to retain its monopoly over financial reform in a variety of other forums. By the second half of the 1980s, banking issues seemed to spring up everywhere. GATT took up the broad question of services and the specific question of banking. The Free Trade Agreement with Canada contained banking provisions; so did the one with Mexico. GATT and the free trade agreements fell under the negotiating auspices of the USTR. The bureaucratic turf war was suddenly re-engaged.

Similarly, trade talks with Japan began to edge into gray areas involving both merchandise and financial services. The Structural Impediments Initiative focused on systemic barriers to foreign imports into Japan. Among other things, the talks addressed the system of keiretsu, the Japanese industrial groupings. With a bank at the center of the groups, the talks veered toward policies that impacted banks.

The Treasury would have preferred to have financial services removed from these various forums. The yen/dollar talks were more to their liking. They involved single sector negotiations conducted exclusively by the Treasury. Broader forums meant participation from other departments and agencies, the very thing that had been resisted so strenuously in connection with the yen/dollar process.

In participating in these other forums, the Treasury's early approach was to try to duplicate the single sector experience by running a closed shop. That meant gaining responsibility for financial negotiations and engaging in them as if no other agencies were involved. This was particularly true in connection with the negotiations over the Canadian Free Trade Agreement.[14] The financial sub-group contained only Treasury officials. Negotiators tended to work at their own pace and report primarily to the Department of the Treasury, with USTR officials learning of positions only in the final stages.

Efforts to chart an independent course created tension. In the context of the Canadian Free Trade Agreement, the separate track threatened to slow the entire negotiation process. For one thing, the Canadians were not particularly interested in changes in the financial area. For another, Treasury was attempting to exact concessions from Canada with little to give in return. The United States already had relatively open financial markets and could offer few incentives as a quid pro quo for Canadian reform. Finally, in preserving its monopoly, Treasury officials bargained hard for special treatment such as a dispute resolution process that allowed Treasury to arbitrate any problems.

When the lack of progress threatened the process, Treasury Secretary Baker apparently intervened, with an agreement ultimately emerging. Within the trade community, the Canadian Free Trade Agreement was described as the "beer for banks" agreement. This flowed from the appearance that the US side had induced the Canadians to agree to reform of their banking markets in return for more favorable treatment for the Canadian beer industry. In other words, cross-sectoral concessions were necessary to obtain banking concessions.

Similarly, tension arose between the USTR and the Treasury in the GATT talks. With a services accord having become part of the process, a banking annex had to be negotiated. Responsibility for the banking annex fell to the Treasury. In order to ensure that there be no repeat of the situation with

Canada, the USTR insisted on direct participation. The USTR wanted to be notified of any meetings and to have the option to send a representative.

This gave the USTR a presence but not substantive participation. The Treasury continued to decide all significant matters with little or no input from other departments or agencies. Perhaps tolerable in a bilateral context, this raised concerns in a multilateral forum. The USTR and the Treasury brought very different negotiation approaches to the Uruguay Round. The USTR had assiduously tried to allay fears of developing nations over a services accord. Draft language was circulated to GATT participants at very early stages, in part to avoid the appearance of a deal done by the United States and a small gaggle of industrial nations.

The Treasury, in contrast, tended to consult industrial countries, obtain a consensus, and then circulate a draft to other GATT members. This left little room for comment. The approach irritated some participants and in part explained why the banking annex remained a blank page attachment at what was expected to be the final GATT negotiation session in December 1990.

Inexperienced, the Treasury also seemed to seek too much. The Treasury wanted a provision that would make public all rules affecting trade in financial services and a procedure that would permit countries to challenge decisions deemed protectionist. More controversial, the Treasury wanted commitments for financial reform from other countries and to condition most favored nation status in the financial area on those concessions.

The jurisdictional tension between the USTR and the Treasury over financial negotiations resumed in connection with the Structural Impediments Initiative. The talks demonstrated the Treasury's growing difficulty maintaining complete control over international financial matters. They centered upon a fundamental restructuring of aspects of the Japanese economy, including reform of the anti-monopoly laws, the large-scale retail store laws, provisions governing corporate takeover bids, and tax rates for farm land in urban areas. In general, therefore, they focused on impediments to merchandise trade.

The talks also, however, targeted the keiretsu, the Japanese industrial groups. Banks were at the center of the groups and tended to be the largest shareholder in companies in the group. By making the keiretsu a trade issue, the Structural Impediments Initiative crossed the divide into banking. Although State and the USTR had taken the lead on formulating the talks, the Treasury insisted upon participation. This time, however, the Treasury found itself in the odd position of having to elbow its way in, with negotiations already under the control of other departments.

INTO THE 1990s

The Treasury, therefore, spent a good part of the 1980s protecting its jurisdiction over international financial matters. In some respects, the

Department seemed more willing to engage in turf wars than to do what was necessary to obtain the most effective agreement. This was particularly true in connection with the yen/dollar process.

By keeping the USTR and other government agencies out of the process, the Treasury sacrificed leverage. Momentum also slowed. As the yen/dollar process lost steam within the Treasury, no other participants existed to pick up the cudgel. Finally, when Treasury officials went to the talks, they could not go to the bargaining table and represent that they spoke for the entire executive branch. As time progressed, therefore, the talks became increasingly less effective.

9

BREAKING THE LOG JAM
The reform process and the Ministry of Finance

The yen/dollar talks succeeded in part because of the rare intercession of Japanese politicians into an area ordinarily left to the expertise of the Ministry of Finance (MoF). Through most of the post-war period, financial reform represented a bureaucratic affair. The Liberal Democratic Party (LDP) rarely interfered directly, instead relying upon the MoF to devise policy initiatives and obtain a consensus among competing interest groups.

The yen/dollar process was different, however. The talks saw involvement of US officials at the highest levels, particularly the President and the Secretary of the Treasury. Their presence elevated the importance of the talks and attracted the attention of Japanese politicians. The President and Prime Minister began the process with the execution of a communiqué. Prime Minister Nakasone also provided occasional boosts by exerting pressure on Ministry officials to reach an acceptable agreement.

The practical effect was that the MoF lost some of its usual discretion over the reform process. Although still having to assent to any specific change, the powerful bureaucracy could not ignore a direct command from top ranking politicians. An acceptable agreement, therefore, became a political necessity. When high level US involvement ended, however, pressure from Japanese politicians subsided and the progress of the talks slowed to a crawl.

The talks also succeeded because the US side became an integral factor in the domestic debate over financial reform. The negotiating team showed considerable sophistication about the dynamics of change within Japan. This included an awareness of the process of obtaining consensus within the MoF. Moreover, the Treasury's goals coincided with the interests of important constituencies within the Japanese financial markets. The US efforts, however, were not entirely a demonstration of acumen. Foreign pressure was deliberately manipulated by these groups to achieve the desired policy changes within Japan.

THE MINISTRY OF FINANCE AND THE PRIVATE SECTOR

Accurately characterizing the MoF's role in the reform process represents no easy matter. Some have stressed the omnipotence of the powerful Ministry, an understandable description given the MoF's central role in the financial system. The MoF has been directly involved in all major reform efforts, initiating the proposals and drafting the necessary legislation. Yet such a characterization lacks subtlety and misses the indispensable role played by the private sector in the process.

Indeed, the evidence can also support an opposite characterization. In many respects, the MoF remains beholden to the financial industry. No reform can advance until a consensus exists among the affected industries. The MoF therefore often amounts to little more than a spokesperson for banks and securities firms. In this sense, the supposedly powerful Ministry has minimal freedom to act and represents a supplicant of the private sector.

The reality lies in the middle. The MoF often acts as the voice for the collective wisdom of the financial community. Powerful though the MoF may be, it cannot impose policy changes without a consensus of all important segments of the financial sector. Moreover, while the MoF always initiated the reform process, the proposed policy goals often came from the private sector. The initiative for interest rate deregulation resulted from agitation by the city banks.

Moreover, the appearance of a strong Ministry sometimes was deceiving, understating the true balance of power between the private and public sector. The private sector benefited from the appearance and therefore did little to dispel the impression. Banks preferred that unpopular policies emanate from the MoF. The Ministry has taken the lead, for example, in organizing the bailout of unhealthy Japanese banks. While perhaps necessary, the banks involved in the rescue favored the active role. They could take the position that they had no choice in making the expenditures; they were subject to government compulsion.

Although limited by the need for a consensus, however, the MoF does play a proactive role in the financial reform process.[1] Achieving the necessary consensus often amounts to a complex affair. Reform has frequently not divided the financial community. Trust banks and long-term-credit banks have vigilantly opposed changes that would provide greater opportunity for city banks. Commercial banks and securities firms have remained at odds over the removal of the barriers separating the two industries. In those circumstances, the MoF has the task of forging the necessary consensus.

All of this suggests a symbiotic relationship between regulator and regulated. Neither side can be said to control the process fully. As one commentator put it, the bureaucracy and private sector are in a state of "permanent negotiation."[2]

Focusing only on the reform process, however, ignores another critical manifestation of the Ministry's authority. To a large degree, the MoF acts as enforcer of the reigning consensus. Once agreement has been reached on the appropriate regulatory approach, every bank must adhere or earn the ire of the Ministry. Financial institutions often claimed that the system operated through consent; that banks adhered to Ministry supervised policies voluntarily. This was at best a partial truth. The system also worked because of the implicit threat that non-compliance would have collateral consequences.

Japanese banks preferred not to learn first hand the consequences of an aroused MoF. For those needing a lesson, however, the heavy hand of the Ministry surfaced during the 1950s in one spectacular respect. This occurred in connection with efforts by Daiwa Bank to resist the separation of commercial and trust banks. During the war, banks had been authorized to engage in trust activities. Many had done so. The MoF, however, decreed that banks should cease all trust functions.[3]

The commercial banks did as instructed and divested or ceased trust activities. By 1959, the last of the city banks, with the exception of Daiwa Bank, had spun off their trust departments, forming a number of new banks including Toyo Trust[4] and Chuo Trust.[5] That left seven trust banks, a monopoly that remained intact until the efforts of a foreign bank, J. P. Morgan, almost 25 years later.

Daiwa's president, Terao, however, refused to give up the trust activities, apparently feeling that they were too critical to the bank's future. The validity of his reasoning aside, the practical effect was that he resisted the guidance of the Ministry. Daiwa's approach was not well received. Future branch applications received a cold shoulder, making Daiwa's rise out of the bottom tier of city banks all but impossible. The message was clear: ignore the Ministry's guidance at great peril.[6]

Japanese banks preferred not to duplicate the experience of Daiwa. They were generally unwilling to test the MoF's reaction by ignoring existing policies. In many respects, the task fell to foreign financial institutions. Japanese banks, particularly city banks, often encouraged foreign banks to take the lead on reform matters. This enabled the Japanese banks to avoid the MoF's ire and yet, to the extent that reform followed, to benefit from the changes.

Foreign pressure therefore represented a device used by segments of the Japanese financial system to advance reform. Moreover, by challenging the status quo, foreign banks upset the existing equilibrium, often requiring the formation of a new consensus. Efforts by foreign banks to enter the securities business accelerated the breakdown of compartmentalization; the decision to advertise rates paid on deposits led to significant changes in the rules governing bank advertisements.

Japanese banks were not the only ones that used foreign pressure to advance policy objectives; the MoF also made active use of the involvement.

Acceding additional powers to foreign banks invariably led to demands from Japanese financial institutions for comparable authority, generating pressure for systemic reform. Concessions to foreign banks, therefore, sometimes amounted to the first step in the process of comprehensive reform.

The most obvious example occurred in the 1970s in connection with the MoF's efforts to control the sarakin. A segment of the financial market not directly regulated by the Ministry, sarakin were finance companies that charged interest rates of more than 100 percent. To rein in the companies, the MoF allowed foreign banks to operate finance companies in competition with the sarakin.

More significant, the MoF's decision to let foreign banks into the trust and securities markets seemed a deliberate attempt to manipulate foreign pressure to encourage the formation of a new consensus on decompartmentalization. Banks were unhappy with the system of compartments and wanted reform, particularly an end to the ban on securities activities. Yet each effort to allow banks to inch into the securities area generated vociferous opposition from brokers.[7] By allowing foreign banks in, the MoF largely sidestepped the domestic conflict while at the same time permanently fracturing the compartmentalized financial system.[8] This both increased the need for and accelerated the process of achieving a new consensus on decompartmentalization.

The manipulation of foreign pressure did not indicate ineffectiveness; indeed, it suggested the reverse. By selecting issues of importance to constituencies within Japan, foreign pressure became a factor in the domestic debate. When the designated issues no longer appealed to Japanese interest groups, something that occurred in the period following the Yen/Dollar Accord, the manipulation largely stopped but so did the effectiveness of the talks.

THE MINISTRY OF FINANCE AND THE POLITICAL PROCESS

The private sector was not the only source of limits on the MoF's authority. Constraints also came from politicians, although they were not always obvious. Nor were Ministry officials willing to admit to the brooding omnipresence of the political process. Yet the constraints existed, imposing parameters on the MoF's ability to engineer changes in the financial markets and subtly affecting bureaucratic behavior.

In general, policy formulation in the financial area fell to the Japanese bureaucracy rather than politicians. The MoF, not the Diet or cabinet, originated and drafted legislative proposals for reform of the financial markets. The Ministry, not the politicians, arbitrated most of the disputes among competing interest groups and forged the consensus necessary to ensure adoption of any reforms. The addition of reserve requirements in the 1950s, provisions facilitating mergers in the 1960s, and the deposit insurance scheme in the 1970s, were all MoF inspired.

These determinations at first blush suggested that the MoF had an omnipotent role in policy formulation. Books that emphasized the importance of the bureaucracy like *MITI and the Japanese Miracle* contributed to this impression.[9] The reform process, however, was considerably more complex. Change occurred through the interaction of the MoF and industry, all within parameters approved by politicians. In other words, the MoF operated within a system full of constraints.

Drafting legislation illustrated the process and the central role played by the MoF in obtaining consensus. The impetus for reform typically came from the MoF, in consultation with affected industries. To the extent that legislation became necessary, the MoF controlled the formulation and drafting process from beginning to end. Moreover, with rare exceptions, the legislation was adopted without amendment.

The entire process involved a host of compromises and devices designed to achieve consensus among affected industry groups. Once the process had begun, views were solicited from industry. The relevant bureau absorbed the comments and attempted to draft a position likely to win widespread support. A draft would then be circulated. With the contours of the reform relatively clear, the Ministry would convene a council to take up the issues. The council included representatives of industry, academia, relevant associations, a member of mass media, and the Bank of Japan, with the list eventually expanded to include consumer representatives. The council therefore gave the appearance of broad based support.

Any appearance of true deliberation or independence, however, was misleading. Councils often included former officials of the MoF who could be counted on to accept the reigning bureaucratic position. Most others had little interest in bucking the powerful Ministry or lacked the technical expertise needed to disagree forcefully or offer alternatives. The representative of the Bank of Japan was an obvious exception although outright opposition to Ministry sponsored reforms rarely occurred.

Upon completion, councils issued reports. The Ministry, however, actually wrote the document. The draft would be circulated among council members who obtained comments from their respective interest groups. The report, therefore, reflected not so much the specific views of council members as an industry-wide consensus on the shape of future reform.

The council constituted a formality. Some within the Ministry saw the process as a needless expenditure of energy. Nevertheless, it was necessary. This allowed all groups at least an opportunity to articulate views. On rare occasions when someone vehemently opposed a policy, the views had to be reconciled in order to obtain a consensus.

Once the report was issued, drafting final legislation usually amounted to a straightforward process. Most interest groups had been consulted, most critical issues decided. That left the formality of transforming the report into specific proposals. Draft legislation did have to be reviewed and approved by other affected ministries, sometimes resulting in sharp conflict and compromise.

Significant opposition from another ministry could doom or compromise a reform proposal.[10] To avoid the possibility, the carefully structured system of inter-ministry review would sometimes be short circuited. Proposals occasionally surfaced directly in the Diet, sidestepping the whole ministry consultation process. Legislation to regulate leasing and financing companies occurred in this fashion. In general, however, this was unusual. The MoF did things by the numbers, usually getting its way.

Legislative proposals also had to be cleared by the politicians, particularly the Policy Affairs Research Council (PARC) of the LDP. The PARC consisted of seventeen divisions, including one responsible for finance. Typically dominated by former MoF officials, the division was kept informed by the Ministry throughout the drafting process. When the division formally met to consider legislation, therefore, little real deliberation occurred. Once accepted by the PARC, the bill usually went to the cabinet, and then the Diet, with passage typically occurring without amendment. Drafting legislation to prohibit insider trading illustrate the process.

Through the mid-1980s, the Securities Bureau had occasionally employed guidance to restrict the practice. Nonetheless, the activity seemed endemic, with some describing Japan as "insider heaven." Occasional proposals to toughen the prohibition on insider trading met with strong opposition, particularly from securities firms and public companies. Reform, therefore, seemed to be going nowhere. That changed with the scandal over Tateho Chemical in 1987. Just before announcing bad financial news, one of the company's banks, Hanshin Sogo, sold 337,000 shares. Although the bank was ultimately exonerated, public outcry and foreign pressure demanded reform.

The task fell to the Securities and Exchange Council, the advisory body for the Securities Bureau. More specifically, the matter was handled by the Unfair Trading Special Department, a committee of the Council. The Special Committee met once or twice a month. Additional interaction occurred between Ministry officials and a smaller group of committee members, usually academics. The process gave officials immediate feedback on their progress.

To understand the problem areas, officials from the Ministry engaged in extensive preparations. They spent 10 days translating and studying about 50 insider trading cases from the United States. They also asked various securities firms, insurance companies, and banks to provide fact patterns and examples of insider trading, receiving more than 500 examples. Each was discussed and additional hypotheticals were created, with the total number eventually reaching about 2,000. From the examples, officials formalized the type of behavior to be prohibited.

The Securities and Exchange Council issued a report on May 24, 1988, with draft legislation following shortly afterwards. The director general of the Securities Bureau read and signed off on the proposal. Consistent with the usual rituals, the legislation was also routed through the Vice Minister and Finance Minister, although neither provided significant input.

Legislative proposals were then circulated to other relevant ministries. The Ministry of International Trade and Industry had some interest in the implications for Japanese companies operating abroad. The Ministry of Posts and Telecommunications, which ran the post office, and Home Affairs, which was responsible for local government authorities, also expressed interest. In addition, protracted negotiations took place with the Ministry of Justice, particularly over the penalty provisions.

Enactment by the Diet represented the last but hardly the most exacting step. With the MoF having arbitrated all disputes and forged the necessary consensus among industry and other ministries, politicians had no incentive to disrupt the scheme. Diet members therefore had little direct role in the process of forging the legislation.

The absence of direct political involvement in devising reforms was no accident. The MoF jealously guarded its independence from outside intrusion. Indeed, resistance was ingrained into the Ministry's bureaucratic psyche. Officials saw themselves as controls on otherwise irresponsible and profligate politicians. Even by the early 1990s, Ministry officials still ruefully talked about their "failure" to control better the spending of Prime Minister Tanaka in the early 1970s.

Finance ministers, although political appointees, had little sway over those within the MoF. The ministers were expected to support the policies of the bureaucracy rather than impose their own. They did not, for example, interfere directly with personnel decisions. Career officials within the Ministry determined who became director general or vice minister. An effort by the Minister of International Trade and Industry to interfere in promotions in 1963 resulted in pandemonium and work stoppages. Less well known, Jiro Yoshikuni became the Administrative Vice Minister in the MoF only because the leading candidate, Osamu Hashiguchi, had become too closely identified with Fukuda, who had just lost a power struggle with Tanaka for Prime Minister. Such obvious politic-ization of promotions, however, was decidedly rare.

In a number of celebrated instances, politicians did succeed in forcing the MoF to change course. Hayato Ikeda, who served both as Finance Minister and Prime Minister, was able to convince the fiscally conservative MoF to adopt policies more consistent with economic growth. Similarly, after rejecting the budget submitted by the MoF in the early 1970s, Prime Minister Tanaka obtained one that contained far more expansionary provisions.

These were unusual cases, however. They also tended to center on one particular area: economic activity. Committed to a policy of rapid growth, the LDP was less willing to accept bureaucratic policies inconsistent with that goal. Other areas did not receive the same degree of political scrutiny.

138

Economic issues aside, the LDP intervened only when the MoF failed to obtain the requisite consensus, either among ministries or within the affected industries. The Diet had to arbitrate a number of inter-ministry conflicts between the MoF and the Ministry of Posts and Telecommunications, the ministry responsible for the Postal Savings System, and the Bank of Japan. In the 1960s, a Ministry inspired bill designed to cement the MoF's control over the Bank of Japan went nowhere following vociferous opposition from the central bank.

The MoF also occasionally went forward with legislation despite the absence of a consensus within the banking community. In those circumstances, banks sometimes appealed to the politicians. This occurred in connection with the amendments adopted in 1981 to the Banking Law. Similarly, the MoF drafted legislation designed to eliminate tax evasion on deposits in the Postal Savings System but agreed to repeal following a public outcry and loss of support within the banking community.

In general, however, financial reform was left to the MoF. As long as bank loans went to the proper industries and the economy continued to grow, the LDP had little reason to intervene directly. Moreover, banks profited by the system of tight ministry control and, in general, did not resort to the political process.

The absence of interference had a number of practical explanations. Through much of the post-war era, the Diet lacked the staff necessary to obtain independent expertise in areas such as banking and finance. Finance ministers also typically served for only a year or two, hardly enough time to gain control and impose policies.

More importantly, however, the hands off attitude served the interests of the politicians. The LDP let the MoF arbitrate contentious and controversial issues while staying above the fray. In the case of financial reform, the MoF had the task of achieving a consensus over the proper direction within the affected industries. This involved intensive discussions and lobbying. Once completed, the LDP had little interest in tampering with the final results.

Despite the relative freedom, however, MoF officials remained intensely aware of the political consequences of their actions. In the end, the MoF had relatively free rein only because it did a proficient job achieving consensus on the direction of reform without conflicting with the broad political goals of the LDP. To the extent that the MoF failed to operate within those constructs, political intervention was more likely.

Retaining independence, therefore, meant a sophisticated understanding of the reigning political goals. Political sensitivity, however, had other benefits. Large numbers of former Ministry officials went on to have successful political careers. Beginning with the second Yoshida cabinet, bureaucrats entered the political process in droves, with some rising to the highest levels. From 1948 through 1972, a former civil servant continuously served as Prime Minister, with only the relatively brief 27 month period from

December 1954 through February 1957 excepted. A substantial component of these bureaucrat politicians came out of the MoF, including many who served as Prime Minister.[11] Antagonizing politicians, therefore, could harm the prospects for a successful career in the Diet.

THE YEN/DOLLAR PROCESS

The reforms arising out of the yen/dollar process did not follow the usual pattern. Although within the MoF's bailiwick, the talks saw the dramatic and critical involvement of Japanese politicians. Foreign pressure explained the difference. Not part of the consensus building process and without equal access to the MoF, the US side appealed directly to its political counterparts. With the complaints hard to ignore, Japanese politicians reached into the bureaucratic process and influenced the direction of reform.

It was Prime Minister Nakasone who signed the communiqué in November 1983 committing the country to negotiating an agreement with the United States over financial reform. With the MoF unable to ignore a direct command from the head of state, some level of reform became inevitable, notwithstanding continued divisions over the issue within the Ministry. Nakasone also intervened when the process seemed to be breaking down and on at least one occasion summoned the head of the Japanese delegation to his office to get the talks moving.

On the US side, the Yen/Dollar Committee did its best to keep Japanese politicians involved in the process. The occasional use of Secretary Regan to apply pressure necessarily generated some type of response from his counterpart, Noboru Takeshita. While Takeshita in general was content to allow the bureaucracy to handle matters, he could not simply ignore high level pressure from the United States. Efforts were also made to employ back door channels in order to keep Nakasone informed.

MoF officials therefore knew that the progress of the talks was being closely watched by politicians, particularly the Prime Minister, and knew that some type of agreement had to be reached. Moreover, in the Byzantine world of the Japanese bureaucracy, some within the Ministry welcomed and even encouraged political intrusion. The MoF was divided on the need to liberalize the financial markets. Political intervention represented a mechanism for tipping the balance.

In negotiating the communiqué that started the yen/dollar process, US officials had expected to produce a document for signature by the Secretary of the Treasury and the Minister of Finance. At the last moment, however, the document was elevated to a communiqué between the President and Prime Minister. The change was made at the suggestion of the Japanese and was probably the work of the Vice Minister of International Affairs, Tomomitsu Oba.

Oba had decided that reform of the financial markets within Japan could no longer be delayed. The international vice minister, however, had little sway within the MoF. In general, he was expected to defend Ministry policies abroad but otherwise stay out of domestic policy formulation.

Responsible for negotiating the communiqué, Oba almost certainly was the one who decided to elevate the document to an edict from the Prime Minister and President. In doing so, Oba strengthened his position within the Ministry. Whatever opposition to reform existed, officials within the powerful bureaucracy had no choice but to negotiate an agreement with the United States once the communiqué was issued. Oba therefore used the edict as leverage within the Ministry to obtain an acceptable agreement and reform the Japanese financial markets.

In the post-Accord period, however, the dynamics changed. Foreign pressure had played an important role in breaking the domestic log jam over reform. But for high level US involvement, changes in the financial markets would probably have been more incremental and over a longer period of time. Gradually, however, the talks ceased to command the same level of support within the US government.

Baker, who replaced Regan as Secretary of the Treasury, seemed to have little interest in the area. Nor did financial reform again command the protracted attention of the President. In the absence of high level US pressure, Japanese politicians had little incentive to intervene. Regaining control over the process, the MoF was able to conduct the follow-up with little direct political interference. Reform returned to the step-by-step, consensus building approach favored by the MoF. The MoF only had to concede enough reform to stave off collapse of the talks. Collapse would have generated a diplomatic fracas and brought Japanese politicians back into the process.

10

PUSHING AGAINST THE ENVELOPE
Citibank in Japan

The difficulties operating in Japan were not abstract. Foreign banks had been in the country since the 1860s. In all that time, they remained on the periphery. Particularly in the post-war era, the Japanese government successfully prevented foreign banks from playing more than a small, albeit sometimes critical, role in the domestic financial markets.

The lack of success had a variety of explanations, including the stifling control exercised by the Ministry of Finance (MoF). Foreign banks, however, shared in the responsibility. In general, they grumbled and complained but did little to improve the situation.

There were a handful of exceptions. J. P. Morgan for one constantly tested the status quo. Whether battling over major issues, such as the right to open a branch or engage in trust activities, or small issues, such as the right to spell the name of its securities subsidiary in English rather than Japanese, J. P. Morgan did not simply accept pronouncements from the MoF.

The most notable exception to the reigning complacency, however, was Citibank. The first US financial institution into Japan and the first to reopen after the war, the bank also became the first to chafe under the limitations imposed by the government. A maverick, Citibank constantly sought to shake up the status quo, whether at home or abroad. The bank had less patience with the cultural norms that stymied others and was far more willing to go head-to-head with the MoF.

Citibank became responsible for a number of firsts. The bank was the first to abandon Japanese bank guarantees on impact loans, facilitating direct relationships with corporate Japan. The bank entered into the first 50–50 joint venture with a Japanese financial institution, became the first bank to operate a securities firm, and was the first to sell corporate loans. The bank was the first to seriously consider acquiring control of a Japanese bank and, when the price became prohibitive, increased the number of branches fivefold to almost 20.

Targeting retail services, Citibank became the only foreign bank to present a direct challenge to Japanese banks in their home market. The bank relied on product innovation, aggressive advertising, and customer segmentation to attract business. As part of the strategy, Citibank became the first foreign bank to tap into a Japanese automated teller machine (ATM) network, providing customers with access to 23,000 machines, and the first to have 24 hour ATM service.

These steps did not always come easily and sometimes required brinkmanship. The bank occasionally went forward with plans even in the face of an unfavorable reaction from the MoF. In the 1960s, Citibank did the unthinkable and directly confronted the MoF over the issue of additional branches, despite having been told that the time was not right. When Citicorp, the holding company, acquired a securities company in 1983, it crossed the barrier separating securities and banking activities in Japan, outraging the MoF.

Citibank's activities demonstrated that, while limitations existed, they could be circumvented through a combination of skill, nerve, and tenacity. Moreover, aggressive behavior, contrary to popular wisdom, was not necessarily punished. Despite the seemingly omnipotent nature of the MoF, Citibank time and time again engaged in unfavored activities without suffering the expected consequences.

The bank also showed that a single financial institution within the country could effect change. The bank's practices had implications well beyond its own immediate goals. Citibank often acted as a catalyst for more systematic reform. Once it obtained increased authority, the Ministry could hardly withhold it from other foreign and even Japanese banks.

OVERVIEW

By most measures, Citibank represents the preeminent bank in the United States. The bank leads in total assets and deposits. In the retail sector, Citibank tops the list of bank credit card issuers and is second in consumer loans and ATMs. The bank also leads in commercial real estate and leverage buyout loans.

Size alone, however, does not capture the bank's unique position in the US financial system. Citibank became the first US bank to truly see the need for a worldwide network of branches. Although others opened overseas offices earlier, Citibank alone devoted the energy and resources necessary to create a comprehensive international network. By the outbreak of the Second World War, the bank had branches throughout Europe, Latin America, and Asia. To describe the network as extensive was an understatement. The bank dwarfed all US competitors.

A quintessential corporate bank through much of its history, Citibank also became the first major financial institution to aggressively target consumer banking. This meant retail deposits and loans to individuals. The bank became active in the consumer loan market in the 1930s. With the end of the war, Citibank had the foresight to see the pent-up demand created by demobilization for all kinds of consumer goods such as cars and refrigerators and positioned itself to take advantage of the trend.

The bank's two strengths – retail and international banking – seemed unrelated. By the mid-1960s, however, Citibank began deliberately exporting domestic skills to overseas offices. It was only a matter of time before this would include retail banking. A retail bank strategy carried immense implications. Offices could no longer remain isolated outposts providing trade finance and commercial loans. Citibank had to integrate into the country's financial system. Nor would a handful of branches scattered through major urban centers be enough. Retail operations required a more substantial presence, including a network of offices. By weaving itself into the domestic banking system of targeted countries, Citibank became the first truly worldwide financial institution.

These attributes in large part explained Citibank's unique approach to Japan. Initially a wholesale bank, Citibank's operations in the 1970s began to evolve, with growing emphasis on retail operations. Early steps were tentative. By the following decade, however, the bank had developed a more unified and aggressive strategy, which included credit cards, access to the Japanese ATM network, and a dramatic increase in the number of branches. By 1993, Citibank had 19 branches, with no other foreign bank having more than four.

The aggressive attitude also had a more human dimension. First under George Moore, then Walter Wriston, the international division was exhorted to accomplish more. The search for additional sources of business and profits, the constant testing for competitive advantage, led to a corporate philosophy that had limited tolerance for convention and custom, an approach that strongly affected operations in Japan.

HISTORY

The early years

Incorporated in 1812, City Bank of New York had little to suggest future grandeur. Just one of a number of banks in the city, Citibank by 1836 had a paltry 3.1 percent of the combined assets of New York's 23 banks and almost did not survive the economic panic the following year. The bank continued to grow steadily, obtaining a national charter in 1865. True prominence, however, only emerged at the end of the nineteenth century with the ascendancy of James Stillman as president.

Under Stillman, the bank became the nation's largest and most prominent corporate lender. To service corporate America, Citibank expanded into underwriting, taking an active hand in the reorganization of Union Pacific

Railroad. Stillman also oversaw the initial foray abroad, creating an extensive network of correspondent banking relations.

When national banks received the authority to open branches abroad in 1913, Citibank wasted no time creating an international network. Early expansion tracked trade. Citibank opened its first branch in Buenos Aires in 1914 at the request of US companies in the country. Other South and Central American branches quickly followed.

Citibank expanded into Asia primarily through the purchase of the International Banking Corporation (IBC).[1] Commenced in 1901, the IBC received a special charter from Connecticut and concentrated on Asian and Latin American operations. The IBC took advantage of the sudden US interest in the Far East, particularly after the annexation of the Philippines in 1899 and the end of the Boxer Rebellion in 1900.[2] The bank opened offices in London in April 1902, Shanghai in May, Manila and Singapore in July, and Yokohama in October.[3] The IBC ultimately opened offices in more than a dozen countries, including Indonesia and India.[4]

The acquisition of the IBC in 1915 added 32 branches to the Citibank network, bringing the total to 69, a number that would increase to over 100 by 1930, or more than 75 percent of all overseas branches of US banks. Rapid expansion abroad did not come without costs. The revolution in Russia forced the closure of the three branches in that country, with Leo Shaw, the future head of the Overseas Division, barely escaping with the bank's gold reserves.[5] Cuba generated huge losses in 1921. These developments slowed but did not stop overseas expansion. The 1920s saw branches open in three additional countries, South Africa, Mexico, and Haiti.[6] International operations thrived, contributing about a quarter of the bank's profits and 20 percent of total assets.

The IBC tended to rely upon English and Scottish bankers for overseas assignments. In 1919, however, Citibank began a training program for US bankers. Focusing on college graduates primarily from well known east coast schools, the program involved training in London and included instructions on the relevant region. Citibank therefore obtained a cadre of highly trained, capable officials with considerable expertise on the local overseas market.

Those going overseas had to select a particular geographic area. In the Citibank network, that meant choosing among Asia, Europe, and Latin America. Selection was no small affair. Once the decision was made, employees remained in the same region for the remainder of their banking career. Even more confining, employees usually served the balance of their term in a single country. Bankers joked that the ideal Citibank prototype was a young bachelor who could easily move abroad. All of this was viewed as good for business.[7]

New personnel started at the bottom, perhaps as a clerk handling savings accounts. Promotion came with time and depended upon the vagaries of those running the office. Those in charge operated something resembling a fiefdom. Chief country officers were typically older and had been in the field for long periods of time. One official remembers marvelling that Red Newall succeeded in becoming manager of the Hong Kong branch at the "youthful" age of 50.

Overseas operations in Asia tended to involve a relatively small community dominated by a band of tough, colorful men. Red Reed in Shanghai, Alexander (Cal) Calhoun in the Philippines, and Jack Curtis in Japan were among the best known. Although they knew each other, the branches had little direct interaction. Lines of communication ran most easily back to New York rather than to other branches in the region.

International banking in those early days involved a rough and tumble existence. Activities entailed anything from delivering funds by oxcart or sedan chair to purchasing local silver coins for resale to the US government. Bank employees learned to become adept and accept opportunities where they arose.

Practical difficulty in communicating with New York gave the overseas branches immense autonomy. Headquarters could communicate by mail. An Asian branch, however, might receive overseas letters once every three weeks. More rapid communication could occur through cable, with the contents written in code to prevent leaks. Phone calls could sometimes get through, but they had to be carefully timed and were plagued by poor connections. Coincidentally, overseas static often seemed far worse when New York was conveying unwelcome instructions to the branch, far better when the news was good.

Although headquarters in New York fought the good fight, control of overseas operations represented a constant struggle. A foreign inspection team periodically visited the branches. After fully reviewing operations, the team would make recommendations in a report. New York and the branch then negotiated over implementation.[8] Still, the head office had only limited ability or will to compel changes, particularly when operations were so profitable.

Operations in Japan underwent significant expansion, particularly after the First World War. The branch in Yokohama was followed by ones in Kobe, Tokyo, and Osaka. Activities in Japan momentarily seized following the Great Earthquake of 1923. Most foreign banks in Yokohama closed, including the Hong Kong and Shanghai's busy branch. Although the quake leveled Citibank's Yokohama headquarters and killed more than 20 employees,[9] the bank continued to operate under cover of a tent, preventing any break in service.[10]

Operations in Japan also posed occasional cultural clashes. Citibank in the 1930s added the latest Burroughs adding machines to the branches, a technological innovation designed to facilitate operations. The Japanese staff, however, never trusted the machines. They would use the adding machines as expected but invariably recomputed the figures on an abacus.[11]

146

More ominous, however, were the looming signs of military conflict. In the 1930s, seven foreign banks had branches in Japan.[12] Political and military developments, however, began to make operations increasingly difficult. Citibank, with branches in the Philippines, a US possession, in China, a US ally, and in Hong Kong, a British protectorate, increasingly found itself on both sides of the conflict. As Japanese conquests accelerated, the bank confronted the difficult task of operating offices without appearing to favor either side.

Not surprisingly, Citibank suffered some anti-American sentiment in Japan, primarily as a result of US sympathy for China. Efforts by bank officials to photograph the Kobe branch in 1934 resulted in arrests and accusations of spying.[13] With the Japanese invasion of Manchuria, Citibank tilted to reality and placed the branches in the Japanese occupied territory under the auspices of the manager in Tokyo.

As the military/political situation continued to destabilize, the bank's business suffered. Operations in China grew increasingly tense. Citibank's Moukden branch closed in 1935, Hankow five years later. Harbin shut down in February 1941; Canton in August; Dairen in October; Peking, Tientsin, and Shanghai shortly after the bombing of Pearl Harbor.[14]

The four branches in Japan continued to function until 1941. Osaka shut down in April. Japan froze US assets in the country on July 27, 1941, essentially eliminating the bank's business. A few months later, operations in Yokohama and Kobe ceased. The Tokyo branch, however, remained open until the bombing of Pearl Harbor.

In the afternoon of December 8, 1941, officials from the MoF, along with armed guards, seized the Citibank branch in Tokyo. Three Citibank employees from the United States were arrested and interned: Leo Chamberlain, Tom Davis, and Gordon Thompson. Davis had been working for Citibank in Japan since the 1920s. Chamberlain, a foreign exchange trader in Shanghai, moved to Japan and became the manager first in Osaka and then in Tokyo. Rumors within the bank had it that exchange trading profits in China during Chamberlain's tenure funded the Citibank dividend for two years during the Depression.

The Yokohama Specie Bank handled the liquidation of the Citibank branch in Tokyo. On the date of the seizure, the branch had deposits of ¥17.6 million.[15] Outstanding loans were collected, deposits gradually withdrawn. By the war's end, deposits had fallen to ¥4.7 million, all belonging to foreign depositors.[16]

Citibank's other branches in the Far East also suffered as war enveloped the area. The branch in Manila operated for three weeks following Pearl Harbor. Bank officials knew that the city would be vulnerable to Japanese attack, although the speed of the country's collapse came as a surprise. They worked furiously to preserve records and remit funds to the United States. Bank documents were microfilmed and eventually transported to Corregidor and conveyed to the United States via submarine.[17]

147

Citibank personnel in Manila performed their task despite constant reminders of the surrounding conflict. Although declared an open city, Manila was continuously bombed by the Japanese. A bomb fell through the roof of the Treasury building while one official attempted to remit funds back to the United States. The Citibank office itself was bombed, damaging a vault and scattering money.[18]

The Japanese invaded Luzon at the end of December and Manila fell almost immediately. The branch closed on December 29. On New Year's Day, the Japanese arrested the employees of the bank, placing them in an internment camp at the University of Santo Tomas. All told, 13 bank officials were interned.[19] Some had just gotten out of China, only to find themselves captured in the Philippines.

One by one, the other Citibank offices in Asia closed. Rangoon and Singapore ceased operations in February 1942.[20] Some of the bank's employees embarked on daring escapes, with one official leaving Shanghai on horseback and making it to Rangoon six days before the branch closed. Most, however, were interned.

Internment in Japan was at best tolerable. Chamberlain remained in a two-storey school house for seven months. Food was inadequate and prisoners were not allowed to talk to each other. While interned, Chamberlain was befriended by his pre-war maid, who brought him food, at some risk. They were married after the war.

Davis had a rougher time. Fluent in Japanese, he seemed to raise greater suspicion among his captors. Following his arrest, he was placed in solitary confinement at the Yokohama prison in Gummyoji. While incarcerated, he was told not to make any noise, including "humming and whistling."[21] He remained confined without company for 122 days. Davis was mistreated in other respects. According to one account, he was threatened with execution by beheading and made to kneel on three iron bars with someone on his back.[22]

Chamberlain, Davis, and Thompson did not remain in Japan for the entire war but were freed in 1942 as part of the first *Gripsholm* exchange. The exchange amounted to a repatriation of citizens and diplomatic personnel trapped on the wrong side at the onset of the war. The two sides negotiated a swap, with an exchange to take place in a Portuguese possession in Africa.

Detainees in Japan were loaded onto the Asama Maru on June 17, 1942. Sailing to Shanghai, Hong Kong, and Saigon, the ship met up with the *Conte Verde* in Singapore, a second vessel containing repatriates from Shanghai. The two traveled to Lourenco Marques in Portuguese East Africa (Maputo, Mozambique), arriving on July 23. There, they met up with the *Gripsholm*, a Swedish ship that had taken aboard about 1,000 Japanese in New York and another 500 in Rio de Janeiro. Following the exchange, the *Gripsholm* sailed first to Rio and then to New York, docking in the city on August 25.

A second exchange occurred in 1943, with other bank officials, particularly those from China, returning home. Conditions aboard the ship were cramped but humane. Richard Henry of Citibank remembers an almost panglossian attitude among some of the passengers. When he tried to sit on a deck chair, he was told by a matronly woman that "those seats are reserved for first class passengers." He also overheard another passenger comment: "My dear, do you know that some of the steerage passengers come from really good families."[23]

Citibank employees in the Philippines were not so lucky. While some US civilians escaped from Manila on the *Gripsholm*, none were from the bank. As a result, they remained interned in the Philippines until liberated by paratroopers from the US 11th Airborne on February 23, 1945.

The return

The post-war period saw a tepid return by Citibank to Asia. Operations resumed in Manila first, with a branch reopening in June 1945. A Tokyo office reappeared in 1946, primarily to service the military.[24] A brief return to Shanghai and Tientsin abruptly ended as the reality of the country's civil war became clear. With the communist tide sweeping forward, the branches flickered and disappeared. Shanghai, the last Citibank office in the People's Republic of China, shut its doors in August 1950.[25] Only Hong Kong remained the only mainland outpost.

The situation in Europe proved little better. With a London branch still operating, Citibank opened an office in Paris, but under the appellation of the IBC.[26] The name reflected the hesitancy toward overseas expansion. With France politically unstable and possessing a vibrant communist party, the bank was concerned with a repeat of the events in China. Citibank allowed the license in Spain to expire, a franchise that would not be recovered until the 1970s.[27] Only in Latin America did the bank have an extensive, successful network of foreign branches.

In returning to Japan after the war, Citibank had a host of advantages over its US competitors. For one thing, the bank had experience. Both Chamberlain and Davis had been in the country before the war and spoke the language. They knew the market and had extensive contacts, particularly among Japanese banks. Citibank also had a reservoir of Japanese staff who had worked for the bank in the pre-conflict days.[28] This enabled the bank to jump back into the country with both feet, reopening the four branches and engaging in a high volume of business.[29]

Chamberlain oversaw the return. He had little to do with day-to-day operations, leaving the task of managing the Tokyo branch to Louis Cullings.[30] Chamberlain, who favored colorful attire, including red flannel shirts, plaid ties, and cowboy boots, spent most of his time making the rounds, visiting government offices and Japanese banks. Already, Citibank was building relationships and seeking to ensure a steady stream of business.[31]

Japan represented a fabulous money machine during the early days. Next to London and perhaps Manila, the office was the most profitable overseas outpost in the entire Citibank network. Margins were extraordinarily high. This did not go unnoticed at the MoF. Citibank had to report profits to the Ministry and officials still remember years when Citibank made more than Fuji Bank, at the time the largest financial institution in Japan.

In those halcyon days, business proved straightforward. With Japanese banks in desperate need for funding, attracting business literally meant waiting for it to come in the door. The problem was one of overabundance; the bank could not handle all of the volume available. Citibank extended lines of credit and confirmed letters of credit. The US financial institution viewed itself as a banker's bank, with most business coming directly from, or going through, Japanese financial institutions. During those early days, therefore, Citibank maintained harmonious relations with Japanese banks, eschewing direct competition.

The bank's business fell into three basic categories: trade finance, impact loans, and yen lending. Trade finance initially represented the largest component. This involved letter of credit relationships with Japanese banks and banker's acceptances. Impact loans or dollar loans directly to Japanese companies had developed, by the late 1950s, into another important source of profit.

Finally, Citibank also engaged in yen lending. The loans did not amount to much. A shortage of yen made this segment of the market permanently small. Moreover, the funds could effortlessly and profitably be placed in the interbank market or lent to multinational corporations. There was no need to find Japanese borrowers.

The 1960s

By the late 1950s, Citibank's international operations had stagnated. With only 61 foreign branches at the end of 1955, the bank's overseas presence was significantly below the size of its pre-war network. Reinvigoration was necessary and it came in 1956 with the elevation of George Moore as head of the Overseas Division.

Under Moore's leadership, a complete restructuring of overseas operations took place. Moore essentially installed a new generation of international bankers. With the average age of the chief country officers said to be 55, two-thirds were either induced to retire or called back to New York.[32] The process, however, was not without costs. Those replaced had years of training and understanding about local markets, something often lost in the abrupt changing of the guard.

Moore did more than replace people, however. He infused the international division with a new sense of elan. Known for his personal touches, another change from earlier eras, Moore kept his secretaries busy

150

writing letters to those in the field. Communications among branches also improved. Moore began an annual convocation of senior officers from each foreign country. While officers in a region often knew each other – from their days as a trainee or meetings in New York on home leave – they rarely interacted in the field. Moore's annual meeting amounted to the first systematic contact between these officials. Initially intended to educate branch personnel about the bank, the meetings began a process of cross-pollination.

Moore once and for all put an end to the practice of lifetime employment in a single country. Bank officials coming out of the military noted that, if the Air Force could train a pilot in a few years, surely Citibank did not need a decade or more to equip the head officer in a country. In some respects, the change was also designed to make life easier for Citibank personnel. Employees no longer had to make a permanent commitment to a particular foreign country. Instead, rotation became the norm. By moving employees, skills learned in one country or region could be transferred to another.

Finally, under Moore, the international branches were told to expand the franchise. Specifically, the bank turned to congeneric banking. Rather than just making loans and engaging in trade finance, congeneric banking involved the introduction of other types of financial services, including investment banking, finance companies, insurance, leasing, and perhaps travel. In other words, activities learned in the United States were to be transferred to overseas offices.

Moore's elevation to president also demonstrated that the Overseas Division could be a stepping stone to the highest positions within the bank. His replacement, Walter Wriston, continued and strengthened many of these programs. Wriston, however, brought a different kind of leadership to the Division. He was more cerebral than Moore, an attentive listener but exuding less warmth. Wriston was also more analytical. Where Moore operated by intuition, Wriston studied markets and used a more quantitative approach.

Wriston continued some of the personal touches begun by Moore. He often made a point of scheduling a one-on-one meeting with employees completing a tour abroad, with the conversation covering not only business but also family and friends. Still, there was a harsh side, at least with those who were not in Wriston's favor. Consistent with the bank's culture, mistakes – even small ones – were not tolerated, at least where the issue involved the extension of credit. A bad loan in Singapore demonstrates the attitude.

Following discovery, Carleton Stewart, head of the Far-Eastern District, dispatched a credit man to examine the situation. The memo back to Wriston stated that there was one bad loan and that the problem would not recur. If the senior country officer allowed the situation to happen again, early retirement would be the suggested course. The bad loan totaled a mere $33,000. While Wriston was not directly involved, he tolerated this kind of approach.[33]

Unsurprisingly, therefore, Wriston's tenure was not one of complete congeniality. Bad feelings were created by his continuing efforts to displace long-standing employees in the Asian theater. Moreover, while Moore tended to view international operations broadly, Wriston wanted to see profits at each individual branch. This caused considerable competition among the various branches, not always of the best kind.

Wriston early on placed his imprimatur on the bank's international operations. Rapid overseas expansion was the most noticeable. In Wriston's view, opportunities to enter a market had to be seized; the window might later close. Europe represented an early target. In the late 1950s, Citibank had only three offices on the continent: London, Paris, and Frankfurt. Wriston converted the representative office in Frankfurt to a branch in 1960. Offices followed in Brussels, Milan, Geneva, and Amsterdam. Wriston ensured that Citibank had a branch in all of the major countries in Western Europe by the middle of the 1960s.

Asia also received considerable attention. Offices opened in Kuala Lumpur in 1959,[34] Karachi in 1961, and Taipei in 1964, as well as additional branches in India, Hong Kong, and Singapore. The total numbers illustrated the level of activity. From 1960 to 1967, Citibank established 85 foreign branches, including 54 in Latin America and the Caribbean, 14 in the Far East, 15 in Europe, and two in the Middle East. That raised the total number of foreign branches to 148. By the 1970s, Citibank had branches in 103 countries. In 16 countries, the bank represented the only US presence.

Operations in Japan directly felt Wriston's influence. He remained unhappy with the complacent attitude of those in the country, viewing them as coopted by the Japanese system. Promoting a more aggressive approach, Wriston wanted to dispense with Japanese banks as intermediaries in favor of direct relationships with Japanese companies. Strengthened relations held out the promise of collateral business, including foreign exchange trading, consulting, trade finance, and other services.

Citibank employees from the pre-war days gradually gave way to a new breed. While the change brought a new energy to Citibank's operations, it also created some instability. Rapid turnover became the order of the day. Unlike earlier days, chief country officers seldom had experience in Japan before assuming the post and rarely stayed long enough to fully understand the market.

In the case of Japan, however, continuity remained in the form of Raymond Kathe. With the exception of three years in China, he devoted his entire 38 year career with Citibank to Japan. Sometimes known in banking circles as Mr Asia and sometimes known within the bank as the "Big Buddha", Kathe participated in almost every significant action taken by Citibank in Japan through the mid-1980s. He was a familiar face to the Japanese bureaucracy and made innumerable trips to the MoF and Bank of Japan.

152

Richard Wheeler, who later became head of the Asia-Pacific Division, represented the first of the new breed rotated through Japan. He went to Japan in 1965 after 10 years in Manila. With the bank's operations in the Philippines far more integrated into the country's domestic economy, he brought to the post a new variety of experiences – cross-pollination, in other words. Citibank gradually became more aggressive and, concomitantly, less trusted. Less trusted meant that the bank could not be counted on to stay away from a Japanese bank's clients or to abide by the status quo.

The difference in approach was palpable. Citibank began to promote a philosophy of flaunting convention, of acting first and asking for approval later. Slowly but tenaciously, the bank disrupted the myths prevailing in the foreign banking community. The requirement that loans had to be guaranteed by Japanese banks or that funds were unavailable in the interbank market and from the discount window where all put to the test.

Impact loans had always been guaranteed by a Japanese bank. The practice effectively severed the link between Japanese companies and foreign banks. As guarantors, Japanese banks were the ones that met company officials, assessed operations, and otherwise performed credit checks. Denied direct access, foreign banks had little opportunity to provide a full range of services to Japanese companies.

Citibank wanted to put an end to the guarantees and began lobbying the MoF.[35] The MoF was not pleased. Without the guarantee, Citibank would have the right to repossess a defaulting company's assets. They might be sold, perhaps to a foreign company wanting access to the country. Despite expressions of hesitancy, however, Citibank continued to push. The MoF ultimately capitulated, but with conditions. The guarantees could be eliminated but only if the loans were secured by shares in the company's portfolio, not its operating assets, and only if limited to a select group of the largest and healthiest companies. Citibank had to provide a list of eligible companies, with any changes having to be approved by the Ministry.

In dispensing with a guarantee, Citibank cost Japanese financial institutions a significant fee. More importantly, however, Citibank could now approach companies directly. No longer would a Japanese bank necessarily make the necessary introductions or determine credit worthiness. From the Citibank perspective, this raised the possibility of establishing direct relationships with corporate Japan. From a Japanese bank perspective, this meant direct competition.

Citibank tested other restrictions. A sufficient supply of yen represented a never ending problem. To obtain additional funding, the bank set its sights on the interbank market, something historically closed to foreign financial institutions. The Tanshi brokers represented the critical hurdle. Controlled by the Bank of Japan, they brokered all loans among banks. Foreign financial institutions seeking to borrow were typically told that funds were unavailable.

Citibank focused on a particular broker and began to hammer away for funds. The attempt took perseverance. Eventually, however, the Tanshi broker agreed and made the loan. Another barrier was gone. Obtaining a loan and obtaining complete access to the market were, of course, two different things. The government – particularly the Bank of Japan – still heavily regulated the market and limited access by foreign banks. Citibank could push the door open only so far. Without additional help, access to the domestic market was destined to remain limited.

The most significant confrontation over yen funding, however, came in connection with the bank's efforts to obtain rediscount privileges at the Bank of Japan. Headquarters in New York had been receiving complaints from US businesses in Japan about the lack of yen available for borrowing. Officials in Tokyo were instructed to obtain the right to borrow from the central bank, even if it meant preventing accounts from clearing so that the Bank of Japan would be forced to provide the loans.

The branch did exactly that. After briskly lending out all available yen, business closed one day without the accounts clearing. The expected call came in from the Bank of Japan, with Haruo Maekawa, a future governor of the bank, wanting to know how the bank intended to cure the imbalance. Officials at Citibank insisted that the problem could be cured through a loan from the central bank. After considerable wrangling, the Bank of Japan agreed to provide discount privileges, but only for two weeks. Thereafter, the deficit would have to be corrected through the conversion of dollars into yen. While Citibank did not receive permanent borrowing privileges from the Bank of Japan, it did receive increased authority to bring in funds from overseas.

Citibank also during the period began to make the first tentative steps toward consumer banking. As part of these efforts, the bank directly confronted the Ministry over the issue of additional branches.[36] The existing branch in Tokyo had an exalted business address: the Marunouchi District, near the Bank of Japan. It was not, however, a particularly good spot to attract individual deposits. Bank officials therefore approached the Ministry about a second Tokyo branch in Shinjuku.

Neither the MoF nor the Japanese banking community received the proposal warmly.[37] Suggestions that the license might be forthcoming if Citibank gave up one of its existing four branches were refused. MoF officials indicated hesitancy over the proposal, a strong hint that Citibank should drop the subject. For a Japanese bank, that would normally have been enough. Once again, however, Citibank refused to take the expected approach. The bank essentially responded to this disapprobation by dropping a six-inch thick request for a new branch on the MoF's doorstep.[38]

Actual submission of the document meant that the MoF could not simply allow the proposal to die from inaction. A response was now necessary. Moreover, with Richard Perkins, chairman of the bank's executive committee, scheduled to arrive in the country, Wheeler pressed for an answer. A promise was made that the response would come during Perkins' visit.

A meeting occurred with the Minister of Finance.[39] In addition to Perkins and Wheeler, MoF officials attended in force. The Finance Minister explained that, while sympathetic toward the branch application, there was a problem. Banks always wanted to be on the first floor of a building. Because there were no first floors available, that meant constructing a new office building in Shinjuku. With a ban on new construction, that would be impossible. The branch could therefore not be approved.

The first concerted effort to open additional branches had failed. It would begin an almost 20 year effort to obtain additional branches. When the MoF's views on expansion changed, however, Citibank was the first to benefit. In 1981, Citibank became the first foreign bank to have more than four branches, a number that would increase to 19 by 1993. Moreover, the approach also demonstrated that the MoF could be challenged without harmful consequences to the bank.

The 1970s

Operations through the 1960s could be described as dull but profitable. Impact loans and trade finance, particularly banker's acceptances, remained highly profitable. The activities involved a great deal of paper processing, requiring a large Japanese staff. The work was also routine.

Operations in Japan during the 1970s changed dramatically. Some of the shifts occurred because of policies in New York. Others occurred because of the changing banking environment in Japan, with the nature of operations evolving substantially by the latter part of the decade. Still others occurred because the bank continued constantly to test regulatory barriers.

Joint ventures were the first real change. Citibank had a close relationship with both Sumitomo and Mitsubishi. Neither, however, became Citibank's partner. Instead, the ebullient George Moore pushed the bank toward Fuji. The impetus came at a geisha party.

Moore had a long-standing relationship with Yoshizane Iwasa, the chairman of Fuji Bank. In 1968, Iwasa threw a party at a geisha house on Moore's behalf. Moore decided at the dinner to explore the possibility of the two banks working together and, in an unusual fashion, raised the matter that evening. Surprised but intrigued, Iwasa agreed to discuss the matter the next day. The meeting proved successful and the two decided to enter into jointly owned consulting and leasing firms in Japan and an investment banking firm outside the country. Not the first US–Japanese joint effort (some Japanese banks had already joined international investment banking firms in Europe), the venture was the first in Japan and the first structured as a 50–50 partnership.

The consulting company was intended to provide advice to foreign companies entering Japan and Japanese companies going abroad.[40] For foreign companies, the principal source of information was the small cadre of foreign lawyers that had entered the country shortly after the occupation. The consulting company represented an alternative. Moreover, with Fuji agreeing to make available economic research and other insight into the market, the venture promised to provide incoming companies with an inside perspective on the Japanese market.

Leasing, however, proved to be the more significant venture. Citibank acquired an interest in Fuyo General Lease, a Fuji subsidiary. In some respects, the company proved to be a difficult and eye opening experience for Citibank. The MoF did not regulate non-bank finance companies such as leasing companies. Although less regulated (and therefore less constrained), the companies also did not have the benefit of the MoF's protective wing. Risk was accordingly higher. Moreover, the company found itself subject to other regulators, particularly the Ministry of International Trade and Industry.

Asia Pacific Capital Corporation (APCO) was the third collaborative venture between Citibank and Fuji. An international investment banking firm, Fuji had only a minority share. APCO was intended to provide services to Japanese corporations operating abroad. Fuji provided contacts and funding. Based in Hong Kong, the operation also escaped the close oversight of the MoF.[41]

In entering the ventures, Fuji had to obtain the requisite approval of the MoF. The Banking Bureau's approach had all of the hallmarks of a conservative, hesitant bureaucracy. By allowing the ventures only on a joint basis, the MoF ensured that the larger foreign banks did not have free rein in the domestic economy. At the same time, Japanese banks had an opportunity to develop much needed expertise in an area where they had no experience.

Despite the expanded operations, Citibank entered the second half of the decade unprepared. The joint ventures notwithstanding, Citibank's operations differed little from operations in the late 1950s. Conventional business, however, had begun to decline. Trade finance and impact loans ceased to be lucrative, particularly as the trade balance shifted in favor of Japan. As the need fell for these routine, paper intensive transactions, the bank found itself with a bloated and inefficient staff.

Most employees had been with the bank since the 1950s and were in their mid-40s. The large numbers meant that the bank was in no position to hire additional, younger employees. Hiring in the first half of the 1970s therefore ground to a halt and little new blood circulated through the bank. One banker described the exchange trading desk as four old men sitting around a table with two rotary dial phones and a telex.

Branch operations needed to integrate better into the domestic market and reflect better the changing nature of Japan's financial activity. The first step was radical surgery on the bank's employment practices, a task that fell to Richard Huber. By the late 1970s, the pay system shifted away from seniority, the Japanese method, toward merit. Training also received increased emphasis, with the bank sending promising Japanese employees back to the United States for an advanced degree. The bank took a more aggressive stance toward Gai Gin Ro, the Japanese union, with a strike in the late 1970s hastening its downfall. Numbers fell steadily, going from 200 to about 10 by the early 1990s.

The most noticeable change, however, came in hiring. Existing staff were encouraged to leave through voluntary retirement programs. As retirements increased, a younger class of employees could be brought on board. Some came directly from Japanese universities.[42] The bank also began to target Japanese students studying for advanced degrees in the United States. They represented a self-selected group of people with the requisite knowledge of English and the energy to do the unusual.

During the same period, Citibank's dislike for restrictions on operations became more public. The bank took the lead in calling for the deregulation of interest rates, particularly the right to issue certificates of deposit. To some degree, this required intrusion into a domestic sparring match. Securities firms and some banks opposed the authority, while city banks were the primary proponents.

In pushing for reform, the bank worked closely with the Federation of Bankers Associations. Citibank and other foreign financial institutions publicly promoted reform, with the Federation and large Japanese commercial banks supporting the efforts. By favoring the reform, Citibank threw international attention and pressure on the side of the large commercial banks in their efforts to obtain the authority to issue certificates of deposit.[43]

The 1980s

In the 1980s, Citibank continued to press up against the envelope. The bank wanted still more access to the domestic market, now a matter of financial necessity. Withdrawing from APCO in 1983 and leasing in 1986, and with commercial lending in decline, other avenues were needed. During the decade, the bank became the first financial institution to operate a securities subsidiary. When the MoF issued nine trust licenses to foreign banks, one went to Citibank. Relentless expansion of the franchise continued.

The bank imported existing strengths from other markets. In the early 1980s, Citicorp set up Information Systems Inc., a company that, among other things, distributed foreign exchange information to Japanese clients. The company, however, ultimately proved unsuccessful, partly a result of increased competition and partly a result of policy decisions made in New York.[44]

Other areas confronted regulatory barriers. Expanding into securities activities involved brutal brinkmanship with the MoF. In 1983, Citicorp, the

157

holding company in New York, purchased a British broker, Vickers da Costa. The broker had an office in Tokyo. The purchase meant that Citicorp was now engaging in both securities and banking activities in Japan, crossing a barrier that had existed since the occupation.

The transaction infuriated the MoF; Citibank had not sought pre-approval, which almost certainly would not have been granted. More than anything else, the Ministry hated surprises, particularly those likely to cause controversy within the domestic financial system. Adding insult, the acquisition was announced during a visit to the country by President Reagan.

Although Citibank lobbied hard to keep the office, the MoF was initially not receptive. In some respects, however, the Ministry was trapped. Refusal would have caused a diplomatic donnybrook. With the trade deficit hitting new highs, this was no small matter. After much teeth gnashing, the MoF relented but with conditions. In deference to the Ministry, Citicorp acquired only 75 percent, with the remaining percentage sold to a management investment group.

Citibank also tested regulatory boundaries in connection with the sale of loans. The sales had a number of attractions. The bank could reduce assets, minimizing the need for capital. The sales also generated fees which amounted an immediate, positive addition to earnings. Until the 1980s, however, no bank in Japan had sold a loan. They were typically held until maturity. Relationships between banks and clients were sufficiently personal that a sale was viewed as unseemly. Once again, however, Citibank proved unwilling to accept the prevailing convention. The bank's attorneys in Japan indicated that no legal prohibition existed on the sale of loans. After much jawboning, the lawyers put the position in writing, although the letter advised disclosure of any sales to the Bank of Japan.

Confident a sale would violate no express legal proscriptions, the bank next sought approval of clients. Citibank knew that a Japanese company would not be happy to find its loan owned by an unknown third party. Bank officials, however, took the position that the sale of a loan had no effect on the bank's relationship and, in fact, amounted to a badge of prestige. The sale resembled commercial paper. Only the loans of the most respected companies could be sold.

With the opinion of counsel and the approval of clients, Citibank promptly disposed of some loans. Officials then met with the Bank of Japan and informed them of the transaction. They went prepared. Bank officials not only had the letter from counsel but also brought a great deal of information showing that the sales were a common practice in other countries. Officials at the central bank did little more than express interest and ask for periodic reports on the practice. With that, another seemingly intractable barrier had fallen.[45]

Citibank also became the first bank to operate a commodities fund. The bank operated the fund out of the leasing company, thereby avoiding MoF oversight. In addition to once again broadening the parameters for banking activities, Citibank also contributed to a jurisdictional dispute. Commodity funds fell under the regulatory auspices of the Ministry of International Trade and Industry rather than the MoF.

The more aggressive approach did not endear Citibank to the MoF. The bank was willing to push against the boundaries, doing things not otherwise expressly prohibited. In the end, however, combativeness rather than complacency was effective. Rather than earning the permanent ire of the Ministry, the bank in fact began to receive preferential treatment. This showed through most clearly in the area of retail banking.

RETAIL BANKING

Nowhere was Citibank's aggressive behavior more apparent than in retail banking. As a practical matter, retail banking in Japan did not exist through the 1970s. Japanese banks concentrated on corporate and other business clients, largely ignoring individuals.

In a country famed for an emphasis on services, individual depositors and borrowers had to deal with a host of inconveniences, some petty, some significant. Banks had limited service hours, including constrained access to ATMs.[46] Fees and charges remained high and uniform. Banks hesitated to, or were prohibited from, introducing innovative products designed to appeal to small depositors. They did not provide basic consumer services such as credit cards with a revolving line of credit or car loans. Nor did Japanese banks compete by breaking rank and offering better services; conformity was the basic rule. The sector therefore seemed ripe for an aggressive competitor – MoF permitting.

The MoF, however, had intentionally insulated the consumer sector from foreign competition. Foreign banks had not been able to expand their existing branch network in Japan. In the 1970s, banks coming into the country essentially had to agree to stay away from the consumer sector. The country also had no credit bureaus or rating agencies, making it difficult for foreign banks to assess risk. Cultural barriers also existed, including a Japanese aversion to borrowing.

Citibank challenged most of these barriers, leaping ahead of other financial institutions. The retail strategy reflected the guiding hand of Walter Wriston. He was the one who saw the huge potential of combining retail and international strengths and continuously flogged those abroad to get more out of the overseas franchise. It was only a matter of time before efforts focused on Japan.

Citibank took the first tentative steps in the 1960s, with the aborted effort to expand the number of branches. The bank also introduced consumer oriented services, including travelers' checks and the financing of car loans. Sold through Japanese banks, Citibank had the largest share of the market, despite competition from American Express and others. This dollar denominated travelers check occurred in part because of the commission offered, innovative marketing strategies, and because Citibank was the largest foreign lender to the banks.[47]

Early attempts to finance car loans also began in the 1960s. The Japanese bureaucracy did not look upon the efforts favorably, however. Loans to Ford dealers in Japan designed to fund car loans prompted a call from Haruo Maekawa, a future governor of the Bank of Japan. He essentially told bank officials to put a stop to the loans. Not in a position to ignore a direct command, Citibank complied.

Efforts at consumer banking sporadically continued. In the 1970s, specific consumer programs surfaced. Under the slogan of "Fly now and pay later," the bank financed plane tickets in a joint venture with airlines. The efforts, however, reflected only a limited commitment to the retail area, with most of the advertising originating with the participating airlines rather than Citibank having direct contact with consumers.

The bank also entered into a joint venture with Nippon Shinpan, a Japanese finance company. The Japanese company had an extensive data base, no small consideration in a country without credit agencies. The venture again, however, represented a limited entrée. Nippon Shinpan largely ran the operation, with Citibank relegated to a side role.[48] Nonetheless, with the MoF not allowing banks to go into consumer finance directly, this represented the only possible approach.

Citibank also tepidly began credit card operations. As part of a joint venture with Fuji and JTB, the bank began issuing Diners Club cards. The venture ran into an assortment of restrictions. The MoF did not allow credit cards with outstanding balances, only debit cards. Diners Club also could not issue a single, universal card that could be used in Japan and overseas. The cards therefore were limited to yen transactions within Japan, although a separate card with a short duration and credit limit could be issued for use outside the country.

By the late 1970s, therefore, retail operations were hardly noticeable. Operations concentrated on the wholesale side, with the bank not particularly accustomed to dealing with individual depositors. Greater emphasis on consumer banking, however, began to take shape in 1979 when Citicorp set up a consumer finance company, CCKK.[49] The MoF had finally relented in the wake of the sarakin loan scandals and granted a license. The operation was kept independent of the branch, avoiding some of the internecine conflicts within the bank. Emphasizing a more Japanese approach, Citicorp sent only one *gaijin* (foreign) employee to the company and otherwise decreed that all hires were to be Japanese.

In an effort to reflect local practices, CCKK offered a simplified application process and, for salarymen, did not require the spouse to co-sign. With wives often holding the purse strings, the loans provided husbands with an independent source of pocket money. The company also offered a variety of local products, including salary loans (loans deducted from the employee's bonus) and loans secured by a mishmash of items such as golf club memberships and cemetery plots. CCKK, however, never did particularly well or establish much of a retail presence.

The efforts confronted a central weakness. To have a true retail presence required more offices. As the 1980s began, Citibank had only four branches, the same four opened during the occupation, and no ATMs. In contrast, several Japanese banks had more than 100 branches in Tokyo alone and even more ATMs.

To expand, Citibank had either to open new branches or to acquire a local bank. The first break came in 1981 when the MoF granted Citibank the authority to open two additional branches.[50] Foreign pressure apparently played a critical role in the MoF's approval. The Ministry had adamantly refused to issue licenses for new branches. A replay of the 1960s, the process seemed to be going nowhere. The bank, however, made the branches a high profile issue and raised the ante by suggesting the possibility of unwanted foreign government intrusion. Continued obstinacy by the MoF threatened to become a matter of bilateral concern.

Critically, the White House apparently had a role in loosening the log jam. In a chance conversation, Walter Wriston mentioned the problem of obtaining approval of additional branch licenses to President Reagan. Within a matter of days, MoF officials contacted Citibank employees and indicated that the request for the branches would be approved forthwith. A high level phone call or two from the White House was apparently responsible.

The MoF's decision to approve the additional branches entailed no fundamental shift of opinion concerning foreign bank penetration of the retail market. Citibank would not obtain approval to open another branch until 1988. To get the necessary offices required a different strategy. Citibank decided to buy a Japanese bank.

Expansion through acquisition

Buying a bank was revolutionary. No foreign bank had ever tried to acquire a Japanese financial institution, much less succeed. The MoF had to approve any acquisition. A bureaucracy that had for much of the post-occupation period intentionally blocked foreign entry and foreign expansion was unlikely to view an acquisition favorably.

Unchartered territory, an acquisition also posed a host of unanswered questions. The average Japanese depositor might withdraw funds from a foreign owned bank. Replacing existing management and removing redundant personnel conflicted with the social norms of lifetime employment. Melding the corporate cultures of Citibank and a small Japanese financial institution posed daunting tasks.

161

Citibank decided that the risks were worth it. In some respects, the approach represented part of a global assault on restrictions on expansion. In the United States, Citibank was eyeing the purchase of savings and loans as a means of circumventing limits on interstate banking; in Australia, it was building societies. Buying a sogo (mutual) bank in Japan would further the same purpose.

Purchasing a bank had a number of advantages. The purchase circumvented the limitations on yen funding. Citibank would obtain an immediate presence in the market, including a steady source of low cost retail deposits. With sogo banks smaller and more localized, the deposit base would probably be working class and stable. Consumer products could be designed specifically for that market niche.

The possiblity of an acquisition had been discussed within the bank as early as the 1950s. During the occupation, Citibank officials seriously considered purchasing the Bank of Ryukyu in Okinawa but were deterred by the State Department. Although the matter was occasionally raised with Japanese officials, no specific steps were taken until the 1980s.

Efforts became more serious in the 1980s. Citibank officials in Tokyo received the green light to engage in a search for a viable acquisition candidate. The bank hired Sumio Hara, a former director general of the Tax Bureau and Chairman of the Bank of Tokyo, to assist in the search for a bank and make the requisite contacts. He also had the all important task of paving the way for MoF approval, something that had to be obtained or the entire activity would become a non-starter.

Early discussions with the Ministry were not favorable. The Banking Bureau had to be convinced that the acquisition would not in any way impair financial stability. Citibank also had to overcome the natural proclivity against foreign ownership. Conversations were met with repeated assurances that the matter was under consideration but was very difficult – the MoF's way of saying no.

The unwillingness of the MoF to affirmatively bless the acquisition strategy blocked the bank from moving forward. Citibank had located a potential acquisition candidate, a sogo bank in Yokohama. Meetings were held, with bank officers, Hara, and top officials from the Japanese bank in attendance. While officials from the bank expressed some interest, the effort wilted when Citibank proved unable to get the green light from the MoF.

As the search progressed, talks with the MoF continued. The process was personal and time consuming. Citibank officials met repeatedly with those in the Banking Bureau. The Ministry had a number of concerns, particularly the fear that a bank would enter, only to withdraw at the first sign of trouble. Citibank, therefore, had to essentially reconfirm its commitment to the market, a case made much easier given the bank's long history in the country and unique commitment to the retail sector. The bank also had on its side the MoF's almost desperate desire to appease US government officials and show that a foreign bank could succeed in the country.

As with any new idea, the MoF initially reacted with hesitancy and suspicion. Those within the Ministry were divided. Over time, however, views evolved and officials within the MoF grew more comfortable with the concept. The Ministry developed a consensus in favor of the acquisition and Citibank was told it could go forward. Citibank's willingness to push and persevere once again paid off.

The process of finding an appropriate candidate, however, proved slow. The likely bank had to be in Tokyo, be healthy and, preferably, have only a few large shareholders. The latter requirement would make the purchasing process easier. Relying on intermediaries, Citibank officials could only approach banks after proper introductions. A few banks were contacted, although the talks never advanced very far.[51] In essence, healthy banks had little interest in being bought. Other financial institutions ready to sell typically came with a fistful of bad loans, something of little interest to Citibank.

Although in motion since the early 1980s, the acquisition strategy surfaced publicly when Sumitomo took over Heiwa Sogo Bank in 1986. The sixth largest sogo in Japan, Heiwa had run into severe financial problems. The MoF embarked on a rescue operation, with Sumitomo designated as the putative purchaser. Heiwa had a much sought after asset – over 100 branches in Tokyo. The branches also had particularly favorable locations, often placed next to railway stations frequented by commuters, and had extended hours, typically open until 7:00 p.m.

Citibank heard about the negotiations and made inquiries. Published reports indicated that the bank wanted to buy the sogo but lost out to Sumitomo when the Ministry intervened.[52] Since Sumitomo had already been denominated as the putative rescuer, the MoF was unlikely to permit a foreign bank to interfere with the process. Moreover, the publicity over the matter was not something that would make the Ministry favorably disposed.

In the end, however, the MoF did not block the transaction. Citibank was simply unwilling to pay the price. Taking over Heiwa would have meant absorbing millions of dollars of bad loans. In fact, after Sumitomo completed the purchase, Ministry officials agreed to and did notify the bank of future acquisition candidates, although none fitted into Citibank's strategic plans.

The bank ultimately abandoned the acquisition strategy. For one thing, Citibank's retail strategy had evolved. Purchasing an existing bank meant no choice in the location of the branches. With Citibank deciding to target a specific market segment – upwardly mobile, high income customers – carefully placed branches became essential. Out of the way locations would not suffice. They needed branches near train stations, subways, and other highly visible spots.

The most important reason for shelving the acquisition strategy, however, was cost. From 1984 to 1988, the value of the yen had jumped from 260 to the dollar to 130, effectively doubling the price of any bank. This meant a huge investment for only marginally performing assets. The prohibitive cost caused the bank to abandon the acquisition approach but not the desire for a retail presence.

Abandonment did not mean that Citibank took the pressure off the Ministry. As late as 1990, the President of the United States broached the subject with Prime Minister Toshiki Kaifu. The effort had little immediate value; Citibank was not looking. The bank, however, might some day reconsider. It also served as a powerful reminder of the bank's political pull and the consequences of any regulatory resistance.

Consumer strategy

The aborted acquisition effort produced a sizable benefit. The MoF had become sensitized to, and educated about, Citibank's expansion strategy. The bank's problems obtaining approval for branch licenses suddenly disappeared. Citibank had a green light.

Equally important, the bank had the affirmative support of the MoF in obtaining its goal. As US negotiators continued to press the Japanese government for more open financial markets, the Ministry was desperate to show that a foreign bank could succeed. The only one really trying, at least at the retail level, Citibank suddenly found itself pushing against an open door.

The bank took advantage of the newfound latitude. The process began with a new branch in Tokyo in 1988, two more in 1989, and four more in 1990. That brought the total number to 13, by far the largest branching network of any foreign bank in Japan. Announcements indicated plans to open 50 branches by mid-decade, although the number was ultimately scaled back to around 20.[53]

Even with the additional branches, however, Citibank's network remained too small to compete effectively in the retail market. The average depositor was not likely to find the number convenient. To address the concern and more easily attract retail customers, Citibank set its sights on the network of 23,000 ATMs in Japan operated by the large Japanese commercial banks. No foreign bank had ever joined the system, forcing Citibank to move into uncharted territory.

Again, the process involved aggressive pursuit and perseverance. The first victory came when the bank successfully negotiated an agreement with Dai-Ichi to piggyback into its network of 1,500 machines. With that, Citibank depositors had access to ATMs all over Tokyo.

The bank continued, however, to seek access to the entire city bank system, BANCS. That proved a more intractable goal. The Japanese banks were in no hurry to let Citibank in. They wanted to limit membership to the original banks that had founded the system. The banks responsible for negotiating an agreement with the US bank over access to the system changed every six months. Each time an understanding appeared close, the parties changed.

Citibank did not take the response lying down. The bank made clear to the Banking Bureau and the Japanese city banks that it intended to make the exclusionary practices a matter of bilateral concern. Assiduously maintaining relations with US government officials, the bank passed on its concerns to the Treasury and the USTR.

The MoF responded by indicating that it had no jurisdiction over the matter, characterizing the activity as a private matter among banks. In contrast to its official stance, however, the MoF provided considerable behind the scenes help. Officials in the Banking Bureau twisted the arms of the commercial banks and Citibank gained access as an associate member. The process took 18 months and came at the cost of a hefty initiation fee. The bank also had to pay an additional fee each time customers used the system. Nor did Citibank receive identical rights. As an associate member, Citibank did not have access to the ATM network for regional banks. Still, membership in the city bank system represented a major victory.

Citibank, however, did not stop there. Attracting customers required innovation with Japanese banks typically allowing use of the machines only during limited hours, Citibank became the first financial institution in the country to offer 24 hour service and the first to offer bilingual ATMs.

The retail strategy involved more than opening branches and acquiring access to ATMs. The bank also by the mid-1980s had put together a more coherent approach. Citibank created the "Consumer Services Group," which included the retail branches, the finance company, and eventually credit card operations.

The 1980s also saw a more serious foray into the credit card arena, issuing MasterCard in March 1987 and Visa in 1988. The activity was hobbled by legal limitations, however. Credit cards generated income from fees charged to cardholders, interest rates imposed on card balances, and discounts from merchants. With revolving lines of credit prohibited, Citibank could only issue charge cards with balances that had to be repaid each month. Banks could therefore not earn interest on monthly balances. Citibank tried unsuccessfully to circumvent the limitation by attaching a loan application to every credit card bill.

The lost income had to come from somewhere. Citibank issued only premium "gold" cards, each with a significant fee. The operations generally remained small and were not particularly profitable. With only a small number of branches, Citibank had to resort to direct mail, an expensive and inefficient system in Japan. More importantly, the administration of the card program was handled by an outside company. With the company maintaining customer information, Citibank lacked sufficient data to segment the direct mail effort accurately.

Perhaps the most innovative aspect of Citibank's consumer strategy, however, was the focus on particular market segments. As a relatively small upstart, Citibank's success depended upon the ability to offer services or products not otherwise available. Somehow the bank had to find a way to break out of the pack.

It did, once again permanently altering the Japanese banking system in the process. Citibank developed a strategy oriented toward particular and underserviced segments of consumers. The bank had begun the process when it started a private bank, a vehicle for offering specialized services to the very wealthy. By the late 1980s, the focus shifted to particular consumer groups. With Japanese banks hardly seeing consumers as a group worth attracting and the Japanese government historically discouraging interaction, the idea of marketing to particular segments was a non-starter. In Japan, all customers were treated with equal inattention.

For a busy professional, domestic banks did not always meet their needs. Japanese banks were a pleasure to enter. They often had comfortable chairs, vaulted ceilings, and goldfish tanks. Tellers were fanatically accurate. These services, however, came at a cost. A bank transaction required a lengthy wait, even for the simplest of matters. Anything out of the ordinary moved at glacial speed. A check deposited in dollars could take a month to clear.

Citibank went after those well-off, younger professionals with liquid assets and little patience for the slow pace at Japanese banks. They were also the most likely to travel and to be in need of Citibank's international services. In addition, the bank focused on expatriates, upper level management, particularly those serving some time abroad, and women, who often managed the family's money and were highly return conscious.

For speed and convenience, the bank provided telephone services, including account statements and interest and foreign exchange rates, in the customer's choice of language. Customers could open an account, transfer funds, or perform various other transactions by phone. Phone service proved popular, with the bank processing 3,000 calls a day and plans to expand the availability of the services to 24 hours a day.[54]

Phone services were more than a convenience for customers. They allowed Citibank to reach a much broader geographic market by minimizing the importance of branches. The statistics illustrated the pattern. About half of all Citibank transactions were conducted by phone and one-third of all customers had not set foot in a Citibank branch during the previous 12 month period.[55]

Convenience was not the only goal; Citibank also offered a stream of innovative products. The bank created an international cash card that essentially permitted holders to access funds in Japan, the United States and, eventually, 14 other countries. With interest rate ceilings still existing on smaller deposits, the bank circumvented the problem by offering foreign currency accounts. Begun in the spring of 1988, the Multi-Currency Accounts allowed depositors to place funds in six different currencies plus gold, taking advantage of higher overseas rates.

166

Nor was Citibank about to hide these new strategies under a bushel. In another first, the bank employed aggressive advertising techniques. Advertising by Japanese banks had always been a staid affair, controlled by "voluntary" rules issued by the Federation of Bankers Associations.[56] Banks did not typically advertise rates or compare returns. Dispensing with the "voluntary" restrictions, Citibank began running advertisements emphasizing the high interest rates paid on dollar and other foreign currency deposits.[57] While indicating concern, the Ministry did nothing to stop the practice.

By the early 1990s, therefore, the bank had a substantial presence in Japan. The branch network employed 1,450 employees and included a securities company with a seat on the Tokyo Stock Exchange and a trust bank subsidiary. The bank was pursuing an aggressive and sophisticated retail strategy. The number of new customers seemed to grow exponentially.

By 1992, however, growth had cooled, particularly as interest rates in Japan rose and rates in the United States (and much of the rest of the world) fell, making investments in the Multi-Currency Account less attractive. The drop-off demonstrated a flaw in Citibank's overall approach. The bank spent much of the 1980s promoting international services. Multi-Currency Accounts, international cash cards, the panache of the Citibank name, all stressed innovative practices based on overseas expertise. The bank paid less attention to the mundane. To be a full service bank, however, required a fistful of domestic services.

The problems to some degree flowed from Citibank's philosophical approach to the Japanese market. Unable to compete head-to-head with domestic banks, Citibank disclaimed any desire to mimic Japanese financial institutions. Acting like a US bank in Japan, however, had little likelihood of success. Instead, the goal was to be an "international" bank operating in Japan. Citibank emphasized the worldwide conveniences of using its services and facilitated investments into foreign currencies. To some degree, therefore, the bank lost sight of domestic needs of the very class of consumers it sought to attract.

For one thing, Japanese rarely used checks. They often paid bills through automatic deductions from bank accounts. The largest Japanese banks had the ability to deduct automatically the bills from around 2,000 companies and creditors. Citibank in the 1980s had none. Similarly, employees usually had paychecks deposited directly into their bank account. Citibank lacked the computer interface to offer the service. Without these basic services, even many of the bank's own employees had accounts elsewhere.

The bank's strategy, therefore, needed to shift yet again. In addition to innovative international products, the bank had to be in better tune with the basic services desired by Japanese consumers. As the bank sought to become a bit more Japanese, it appointed a new chief country officer prepared for the task.

167

REORGANIZATION

While Citibank had made great strides in Japan, problems still existed. Many were self-inflicted. Management of the bank had left operations divided and facilities redundant. The principal problem arose out of the system of matrix management, an approach that, whatever its merits elsewhere, did not work in Japan.

Through the mid-1970s, Citibank had functioned through a relatively conventional geographic based chain of command. A senior officer in New York ran the International Division. Below him were various districts, including Far East North, which contained Japan. Each country was run by a resident vice president or, later, a senior officer in the field (Senoff). In the post-war era in Japan, Leo Chamberlain was the first to hold that title. Beneath the country head were branch managers.

In the 1970s, the bank radically revised the chain of command, moving to "matrix" management. This meant focusing less on geographic boundaries and more on industry categorizations.[58] Matrix management involved an industry based chain of command. The head of consumer banking in a country reported to a regional, then global, manager of consumer banking. The officer overseeing corporate or world banking would also report back to New York through a separate chain.

The approach had benefits. Issues went back to supervisors with expertise in the respective area. Problems, however, also existed. Officers in one area sometimes knew little about what others in the same country were doing. The senior country officer position remained, but more in form than substance. The position was necessary for purposes of hierarchy and reporting to government agencies, but ceased to have responsibility for all banking operations in the country. This caused duplication and made cooperation difficult.

The system had left curious legacies in Japan. For too long, operations lacked centralization and cohesiveness. Employees were scattered in more than 10 buildings and hardly communicated with each other. The separation of consumer and corporate banking created a decentralized system with overlapping functions. Both sides had personnel and marketing departments and technology systems, often incompatible with each other.

Matrix management remained in place until the appointment of Masamoto Yashiro, only the second Japanese national to run operations in Japan. The first, Tatsuo Umezono, had become chief country officer in 1981. With the bank since 1947, Umezono's promotion demonstrated the bank's increasing commitment to integrating operations into the local economy. Independent, entrepreneurial, Umezono had close contacts with a number of high level officials in the MoF and adroitly managed the bank's relationship with the Japanese bureaucracy. His advancement, however, was not without controversy. Umezono was from Osaka, or Kansai. Those from Tokyo, or

Kanto, viewed natives of Osaka as crassly commercial and uncultured, a particular problem in Citibank given that most Japanese employees were from Tokyo.

Although Umezono's replacement came from the United States, the bank remained committed to the appointment of a Japanese officer to run operations in the country. The approach was to be refined, however. The next Japanese senior country officer came from outside the bank and had considerable stature.

That person was Masamoto Yashiro. Formerly with Exxon, he brought to the position a wealth of experience and contacts. He also brought considerable administrative skills. Under his tutelage, the bank began to shift focus almost immediately. Yashiro was responsible for obtaining access to the massive ATM network of the Japanese city banks. He continued to stress market differentiation. He also decided to revamp credit card operations, an immensely profitable operation for Citibank in the United States but a money loser in Japan.[59]

His most pronounced change, however, came from the internal reorganization of the Japanese operations. The bank took two decisive steps to remedy the situation. First, the bank acquired Citicorp Center, a building that would house all of the bank's disparate segments.[60] Although outside of central Tokyo, a single building promised to unite employees and encourage cross-pollination of different groups.

Second, and more important, the bank decided to dispense with matrix management and combine all country-wide operations under a single bank officer. Japan became the first country in the Citibank international network to revert to the historical practice of operating under one person's control. This represented both an evolving vision of operations in Japan and an immense vote of confidence in Yashiro.

The end of matrix management promised a more cohesive approach to banking. Moreover, it gave operations in Japan a better chance to succeed. By eliminating redundant positions, Citibank could do away with the last vestiges of the bloated work force left over from the 1970s. Even as the bank's activities and branches grew, the number of employees held steady or fell.

THE FUTURE IN JAPAN

A history of Citibank's operations in Japan holds a number of lessons about the ability to pierce the seemingly closed Japanese markets. They show that one bank, acting aggressively but intelligently, can generate change. Time and time again Citibank did things that seemed to cross the line of acceptability. Yet the bank rarely suffered at the hands of irate regulators. More often, the bank discovered in crossing the line that the line really did not exist.

Equally apparent, however, the bank did not always exploit the advantages momentarily created. Citibank proved adept at sending officials to Japan who had little patience with the often stifling status quo. It was less adept at training a cadre of people who knew the markets intimately and could fully utilize shifts in the regulatory framework once that occurred.

The bank had done a 180° turn since the 1950s when bank officials spent their career in a single country and, as a consequence, became intimately familiar with the local market. Employees in the modern era tended to rotate in and out of a country every few years, hardly enough time to understand a market as difficult as Japan. Bank officials rarely wanted lengthy tours in such isolated outposts. Success and promotion meant getting back to headquarters in New York as fast as possible.

Another lesson was that the ability to succeed depended almost as much on New York as Tokyo. The 1990s in particular have been hard on Citibank, impacting operations in Japan. John Reed's rise to Chairman in 1984 began a roller coaster of huge peaks and steep valleys. The bank set a record for profits in 1988 and immediately stumbled. The purchase in 1986 of Quotron Systems resulted in large losses. Bad loans ballooned, first with the developing country debt crisis and later with the nationwide downturn in the real estate market.

The bank engaged in a frantic dash to raise funds to meet the new 8 percent international capital standards. Citibank sold assets and eliminated positions. Many of those eliminated came out of the money losing global finance unit and included positions in Japan and Europe. With all "non-essential" assets vulnerable, Citibank sold its Italian retail banking subsidiary to Banco Ambrosiano Veneto for about $273 million, and reduced it's interest in the Saudi American Bank. In late 1990, Citibank shut down its European stock brokerage and market-making activities.

In some respects, the problems were not unique but reflected economic conditions affecting all money center banks. This was particularly true with the LDC debt crisis and the collapse of commercial real estate prices. Moreover, by the early 1990s, the bank had shown its usual resiliency, with earnings and share prices recovering.

Nonetheless, operations in Japan felt the effects. The bank's "hard look" at overseas assets meant a change in expansion plans. The bank abandoned plans to open 50 branches, settling instead for 20. Lending activities stalled. With the bank focusing on meeting international capital standards, increases in assets were not favored.

All of this suggested that a foreign bank could succeed in Japan with commitment, a less accepting attitude about conventions and customs, and intelligently configured operations. To know the myths that could be dispelled also required an intimate understanding of the market, something that would not arrive overnight. Yet even these factors were not enough if policies of the home office lacked the requisite sophistication. Those sent to the country needed adequate training including competency in the language and the intention to remain long enough to learn the market and form relationships. Creating opportunities made little difference if the employees needed to take advantage were not in place.

11

THE OPPORTUNITIES

By the 1990s, many of the barriers that had plagued foreign banks were gone. They could engage in trust and securities activities, obtain adequate supplies of yen, and open additional branches. Despite the prodigious changes, however, few of the expected benefits had materialized. Market share remained small; profitability anemic.

In part this occurred because of unrealistic expectations. Open markets did not guarantee more profits, only more competition. When Japanese banks were allowed to make impact loans in the late 1970s, the market share of foreign banks plummeted. Moreover, open markets was a misnomer. Barriers to operations remained firmly in place. Innovative practices, a forte of foreign banks, confronted regulatory uncertainty and Ministry inertia. The brooding omnipresence of the Ministry of Finance (MoF) continued to restrict foreign banking operations.

The poor competitive position did not however, result solely, from unreasonable expectations or intractable Japanese practices. A series of self-inflicted wounds also explained the dismal showing. Barely recovered from a raft of bad loans to developing countries, money center banks confronted collapsing real estate prices. Losses sapped capital and minimized the ability to compete overseas. Even when the worst was over, foreign banks seemed to lack the will to compete aggressively.

The importance of these problems became clear as the decade opened. The 1990s saw a dramatic slowing of the Japanese juggernaut. Many of the advantages that fueled rapid growth dissipated, gone into temporary remission. Acceptance of the international capital standards and the precipitous fall of the stock market put an end to slapdash expansion and razor-thin margins by Japanese financial institutions.

Foreign banks, however, stood unwilling or unable to capitalize on the sudden shift in circumstances. At the very time when opportunities existed, they declined to fill the breach. They wanted the advantages but were unwilling to assume the risks.

171

The problems were not limited to banks. The early 1990s also provided the Department of the Treasury with unique opportunities to promote reform of the Japanese financial system. The falling stock market, the weakening economy and, most importantly, a wave of scandals, severely weakened the control of the MoF. Increasingly those within Japan and even the financial community began to question the value of the close relationship between regulator and regulated.

At the same time, the most significant reforms of the Japanese financial system in the post-war era proceeded apace, with legislation to decompartmentalize the financial sector finally passing the Diet. Yet, as events swirled, the Treasury sat on the sidelines, largely uninvolved. The inactivity demonstrated once and for all the need for considerable change in the negotiation process on the US side.

PROBLEMS IN PARADISE

The decade opened with a body blow to Japanese banks, demonstrating the growing weaknesses in the financial system. The need to conform with international capital standards coupled with collapse of the stock market brought expansion to a screeching halt. The piercing of the speculative bubble and resulting economic decline caused bad loans to hemorrhage. All of this dramatically affected banking operations and highlighted the consequences of a still unreformed financial system.

Japan's decision in the 1980s to adhere to the international capital standards seemed, at the time, a non-event. Although requiring capital equal to 8 percent of assets by 1992, the standard caused little consternation. Japan had prevailed upon the central banks devising the standards to count toward the total 45 percent of unrealized gain on stock holdings. The provision all but guaranteed compliance. Japanese banks possessed considerable quantities of stock, purchased in large part to solidify business relationships, at a time when prices were low. With the stock market seemingly on an inexorable trajectory upward, the value of the holdings made conformity with the capital standards a foregone conclusion.

In the first quarter of 1990, however, Japan's economic bubble burst. The bubble arose during the 1980s when the Bank of Japan dropped the discount rate to a post-war low.[1] Japan embarked on a period of cheap money and excessive liquidity. Funds were poured into the stock market and real estate, causing prices to explode. The value of the shares traded on the Tokyo Stock Exchange surpassed New York; the land values in Tokyo exceeded the book value of all property in the United States.[2]

All of that changed with the appointment of Yasushi Mieno in 1989 as Governor of the Bank of Japan. He quickly ratcheted up the discount rate, putting an end to the cheap money and speculative fever. The stock market

172

collapsed, land values fell, and Japan dipped into its most protracted recession since the occupation.

In the first quarter of 1990, share prices started downward and did not stop until the Nikkei average had fallen by 60 percent.[3] The hidden reserves that had been so heavily relied upon to meet international capital standards vanished. The consequences were immediate. Breakneck expansion ended. Suddenly asset sales, curtailment of unprofitable operations, and a frenetic search for additional capital became the order of the day.

The financial system was not up to the task. Banks needed to raise funds and cleave off assets. In both instances, limitations existed, depriving banks of the flexibility to respond to the changed circumstances. Pressure began to build to cast off the anachronistic restrictions.

The most obvious source of capital was the public offering of shares. Through the latter half of the 1980s, banks had tapped equity markets for immense quantities of cheap capital. The plummeting stock market, however, eliminated that option. To prevent further downward pressure on the market, the MoF decreed no new equity offerings.

Banks also could have raised capital by selling the shares they owned in other companies. Disposition, however, conflicted with accepted business practices. Ownership cemented business relationships, disposition weakened them. The sales therefore rarely occurred, and only after tactful negotiations with the company involved. The Long Term Credit Bank had to obtain the approval of Cosmos Oil Co. before selling "several percent" of the company's shares.[4]

Some tried to sidestep the problem through short-term expediencies. They sold shares, recognized the gain, and immediately repurchased them, actually losing money on the transactions.[5] As the capital crunch got worse, however, these forms of window dressing ceased to work. The MoF also used administrative guidance to limit the sales in order to prevent further downward pressure on the stock market.

Borrowing for extended periods represented another option. The source, however, ran directly into the compartmentalized banking system. Commercial banks had been barred from issuing debentures since the occupation, a monopoly left to, and vigorously protected by, the long-term-credit banks. Nonetheless, exigencies dictated change and the MoF devised a Solomon-like compromise.

Commercial banks were allowed to issue long-term debt to public investors overseas and to engage in private placements domestically to sophisticated investors such as insurance companies. This enabled commercial banks to obtain access to long-term debt markets while long-term-credit banks retained the appearance that they continued to monopolize the debenture issuing authority within Japan. The changes made a travesty out of the distinction between commercial and long-term-credit banks. Moreover, used to raising capital cheaply, commercial banks suddenly found themselves having to pay a stiff price through higher interest rates for the funds.

Meeting the capital standards also forced a re-examination of attitudes toward growth. Some banks wanted to downsize, both by shearing off assets and by toughening standards for new loans. The approach represented a dramatic reversal. Through most of the post-war era, size had been the determiner of profits and influence. One of the principal reasons for the merger between Dai-Ichi and Nippon Kangyo in 1971 was to reach a size sufficient to command additional attention and privilege from the MoF. The relationship of size and profitability ended with the capital crisis. Banks had to rationalize operations and cut back or get rid of marginally producing assets.

Again, the highly regulated financial system imposed barriers. Legal and practical restrictions existed on the sale of loans and asset backed securities. Securitization involved the disposition of interests in a pool of loans such as credit card receivables or car loans. Sale of the instruments ran directly into the conflict between brokers and banks. Treated as securities, banks could only sell the assets through brokers, their arch rivals, something they were loath to do. Legislation to clarify the area foundered when the MoF and the Ministry of International Trade and Industry could not agree on changes. The MoF was forced to cobble together a compromise, permitting banks to sell certain asset backed securities through trust banks.

The sale of loans also necessitated changes in the regulatory construct. The MoF had prohibited the transactions.[6] In March 1990, however, the Banking Bureau relented and authorized the sale of loans, although in a limited fashion. They could be sold only to other financial institutions and only with the consent of the borrower. The consent requirement was abandoned a year later.

The pressure on banks to meet the capital standards did more than force shifts in existing practices, however. They accelerated the erosion of the historically close relationship between banks and corporations. The bonds were fraying. Banks began to realize that more loans did not guarantee more profits, as a study by Mitsubishi Bank revealed.[7]

On the other hand, corporate Japan no longer obtained the same benefits from the close relationship with banks. The newfound authority to sell loans meant that a corporate borrower might find itself dealing with an unfamiliar, even foreign, lender. This irritated some Japanese companies. Mitsubishi refused to participate in any effort to sell loans while Fujitsu repaid them rather than allow a sale by Fuji Bank.

Companies also seemed less tolerant of the intrusion of banks into their business affairs. With funds in short supply, some had to accept a more aggressive approach by banks. When the Saison Group sought to refinance loans, the banks required assets of the Seibu Department Store as collateral and insisted that the group reduce indebtedness by selling other assets, including chunks of Intercontinental Hotels. Similarly, the decision of Isetan to expand into Yokohama was shelved when the company apparently had trouble obtaining bank financing.

174

This approach encouraged companies to seek financial alternatives. With continuing reform of the corporate debt markets, more companies could raise funds by selling bonds. Other avenues were also appearing. A nascent commercial paper market began in November 1987, although only a small number of companies were initially eligible and the instruments had a maturity of one to six months. All of these reforms further accelerated the trend away from banks.

The rush for capital, the curtailment in lending activities, the decline in the property market, all had the predictable effect on banks: profits fell and assets declined. Moreover, with the weakened stock market, the usual method of compensating for falling earnings – the sale of shares – evaporated.

All categories of banks saw profits decline. Regional banks were hard hit. In 1990, the drop was across the board, with even the largest affected. The top ten regional banks saw profits decline, ranging from 16.2 percent to 51.3 percent.[8] Nor did the city banks escape unscathed.[9] Pre-tax profits fell 23 percent, on the heels of a drop of 19.9 percent the year before.[10]

Trust banks, however, suffered the most. The fall averaged 45 percent, the first decline by all seven trust banks since 1979.[11] Overinvested in real estate loans, with a paltry network of domestic branches, the immediate future promised more of the same. Rumors swirled about the financial health of the banks, with some suspected of being in severe straits. The difficulties had collateral consequences. With concern about their financial health growing, trust banks saw their share of the pension management market decrease.

Overall, 1990 set a handful of dubious records. Deposits fell by 2.5 percent, the first such decline since 1948. The 5.1 percent increase in loans was the smallest ever. Finally, assets declined by 1.7 percent, the first fall since the Federation of Bankers Associations began accumulating the data.

Even the bad news was hopelessly optimistic. As the property market in Japan collapsed, leasing and other non-bank finance companies stood on the brink. Denied access to commercial paper and other sources of financing, the companies were in hock to lead banks. The MoF expected lead banks to stand by the suffering companies. In effect this meant continued financial support, requiring banks to throw good money after bad.

Accounting standards also minimized the true damage. Banks continued to book income from loans for a year after interest payments had ceased. The Tax Bureau had long insisted that banks minimize reserves and continue to report income on the non-performing loans in order to maximize revenues.[12] For a year, therefore, banks booked revenue but received no actual income.

Although originally designed to maximize tax revenues, the rule now had the affect of disguising the deteriorating financial condition of Japanese banks. As the volume of bad loans grew exponentially, they were not immediately reflected in earnings. Moreover, even when bad loans had to be reported, dodges existed. Banks would simply lend the failing companies the funds needed to keep interest payments current.

175

The problems generated increased pressure for further consolidation in the banking sector. For the first time in 20 years, city banks began to combine. Mitusi and Taiyo Kobe, the twelfth and twentieth largest banks worldwide, announced a merger in 1990. Renamed Sakura, the bank had approximately 600 branches, 200 more than the next largest Japanese bank.[13] Later the same year, Kyowa and Saitama Banks, the tenth and eleventh largest banks in Japan, combined, forming the eighth largest in Japan and the nineteenth largest in the world.[14] The merger created a retail powerhouse with an extensive network of branches.

Mergers of city banks had occurred before. Dai-Ichi combined with Nippon Kangyo in 1971; Taiyo and Kobe in 1973. The purpose, however, had changed. Earlier mergers amounted to a circumvention of the MoF-imposed restrictions on domestic expansion. Increases in size also brought greater notoriety and stature. The merged Dai-Ichi Kangyo became the largest bank in Japan and, concomitantly, found the MoF more willing to listen.

Mergers in the 1990s, however, seemed more directly driven by economics. With the cost of funds increasing, Japanese banks needed to improve profit margins. One way was to cut expenses. A merger might permit the reduction of redundant expenses such as overlapping branches and administrative functions. No bank needed two personnel offices or two computer systems. To the extent that the combined bank continued to produce the same loan volume but at lower cost, profits would increase.

Again, however, rigidity in the financial system made achievement of the necessary benefits difficult. The hoped for cost savings ran into a host of restraints. For one, the system of lifetime employment meant that mergers could not be followed by a raft of dismissals, forcing the combined entities to continue to carry redundant employees. No small matter, Mitsui Taiyo had a bloated work force. The bank employed 20 percent more people than Dai-Ichi Kangyo, the next largest.[15] Similarly, efforts to treat the two halves of a merger equally sometimes stood in the way of necessary cost savings.

Rather than result in a large, fierce competitor, therefore, the mergers threatened to create lumbering dinosaurs. Of all of the city banks, Sakura had the worst capitalization. To meet the standards, the bank had to prune assets vigorously, taking the lead in the very un-Japanese practice of selling loans.

These events created opportunities. With lending down, corporate Japan had trouble obtaining an adequate supply of capital. In particular, small businesses – the next generation of Sonys and Hondas – could not obtain the necessary loans. Foreign financial institutions had an open window and an opportunity to pierce the domestic markets, if they were willing to take it.

THE PRICE OF COMPARTMENTALIZATION

Japanese banks were not the only ones having trouble. The MoF suddenly found itself in the midst of a maelstrom. Economic difficulties seemed everywhere. With the financial system weakening, the MoF did what it could to contain the damage. Tried and true methods of controlling and limiting the harm no longer worked, however. Intervention was becoming counterproductive.

The financial system continued to suffer from the consequences of years of excessive government oversight. Compartmentalization proved to be a major culprit. With financial institutions divided into segments and each segment nurtured, the financial system led a sheltered existence, avoiding the rationalization incurred by most other sectors of Japanese industry. As the financial system continued to show strain, the inflexibility of the rigid structure became increasingly apparent.

The most critical problem concerned the growing risk of a major financial failure. The condition of banks and securities firms continued to weaken. With no banking failure having occurred in post-war Japan, the government was horrified at the prospect. Yet compartmentalization now stood in the way, preventing other classes of banks from assisting in the necessary rescue operations. The time had therefore arrived for the barriers to come down.

Since the occupation, an unwritten rule existed that no bank could fail. To avert a failure, the MoF counted on large, particularly city, banks to rescue failing financial institutions. That meant absorbing the entire bank, bad loans and all. In return for the rescue, the accommodating bank obtained additional branches and won the goodwill of the MoF, no small matter in a highly regulated financial system.[16] That explained the acquisition of Heiwa Sogo by Sumitomo in 1986 and Tokai's purchase of Sanwa Shinkin in 1991.

By the early 1990s, however, matters had deteriorated. As more and more banks edged toward the precipice, the MoF tried to "manage" the problem. Smaller banks were encouraged to amalgamate, in other words, to "restructure or die."[17] Pressure on the banks to merge, however, encountered unexpected problems. Small banks not yet on the edge of failure objected to MoF entreaties to combine. More dramatic, Japanese city banks – the putative rescuers – began to resist efforts to rescue the money losing financial institutions.

The MoF's capacity to dictate to banks that they absorb unhealthy financial institutions had declined. Even the prospect of branches in Tokyo was no longer enough to induce a merger, as the bailout of Taiheiyo Bank illustrated. Although Taiheiyo had offices in Tokyo, no city bank would agree to a complete takeover. Instead, Sakura and the other city banks sent staff to run the ailing financial institution, provided low interest loans, and gave up various claims against the bank.[18] City banks were simply not willing to pay any price to obtain Tokyo branches, particularly as their own economic difficulties increased.

177

Moreover, matters were only getting worse. As interest rate deregulation progressed, smaller banks continued to suffer. While city banks obtained most of their funds from market rate instruments, smaller banks still relied on retail deposits. As complete deregulation of interest rates loomed, they confronted sharply increased costs. Already operating on thin margins, many would not survive the transition to an unregulated market.

Problems were not limited to smaller banks. Trust banks as a class seemed vulnerable. Reform gradually opened up their most lucrative area – pension plan management – to increased competition. They were overinvested in property markets at a time when land prices were in free fall. Moreover, years of tight government control had left them without the branch network or the relationships with corporate Japan to make the transition to a deregulated environment easily.

The MoF's historical emphasis on consolidation made matters worse. By not letting in new competitors and inducing combinations, even small banks had grown large. Any bank failure would cause reverberations throughout the financial system. The MoF found itself in an increasingly hopeless position that it had created – the failure of the smallest bank would create considerable indigestion for the entire financial system.

The doctrine of no failures, therefore, continued to survive, but at growing cost. The precarious state of lower end financial institutions threatened to sap administrative energy and cause harm to the financial system. The MoF prevented failures and kept the relatively small deposit insurance system intact by essentially transferring the losses to healthier financial institutions at a time when they were already overburdened.

The bailout of Toyo Shinkin demonstrated the costs of the approach. The bank had suffered huge losses on loans to a stock speculator. While no one would acquire the credit cooperative outright, banks, particularly the Industrial Bank of Japan, engineered a rescue operation, with MoF pressure applied behind the scenes. The Industrial Bank of Japan had to absorb a significant percentage of the financial institution's bad loans. The bailout came at an inopportune time for the Industrial Bank of Japan. The premier long-term-credit bank had already seen its credit rating lowered the year before and was under close scrutiny. A few more incidents like Toyo Shinkin could drive the rating down and raise the Industrial Bank of Japan's cost of doing business.

Toyo Shinkin's problems also resulted in the crossing of another rubicon. For the first time, the Japanese government resorted to the deposit insurance system to facilitate a rescue. Put in place in the early 1970s, the insurance scheme had never been used. Instead, the MoF had successfully induced larger banks to absorb all of the failing bank's liabilities. In the case of Toyo Shinkin, however, the MoF had to subsidize the cost of the bailout through low interest loans from the insurance system.

As if all of this were not bad enough, the problems went beyond banks.

The early 1990s also saw a substantial weakening of the securities industry. The pirouette downward of the stock market following the initial collapse in 1990 sent investors scurrying for cover. Trading volume declined, the Nikkei average plummeted, and profits dipped into the red. Many smaller securities firms, particularly those outside the major metropolitan areas, seemed unlikely to survive.

Securities firms never had quite the same immunity from failure as banks.[19] In the economic slowdown during the early 1960s, a number had failed. The largest, however, were treated differently. In 1965, the government engineered a bailout of Yamaichi, then the largest securities firm. Failure of such a big broker could have destabilized the entire financial system.

While an occasional failure might be acceptable, large numbers were now at risk, some large. Until the early 1990s, the Ministry had counted on the Big Four (Nomura, Nikko, Daiwa, and Yamaichi) to step in and handle any destabilizing failure. As the MoF's relationship with the large securities firms soured, however, particularly in the aftermath of the compensation scandals, that ceased to be a viable option. Relying on other financial institutions, particularly city banks, however, also presented problems. The rescues ran headlong into the compartmentalized banking system. Banks still could not engage in securities activities.

One solution would have been simply to step back and let the market sort out who would survive and who would fail. That, however, would have meant a raft of insolvencies among banks and securities firms, an anathema to the government. The MoF lived in fear that, with the barrier broken, a torrent would be unleashed, causing a raft of failures. No bureaucrat wanted to have this happen on his watch. Better to have the financial system undergo incremental harm through additional rescues than to be responsible for a sharp and potentially damaging break with existing policies.

Allowing the market to function also represented a philosophical shift that the MoF was unable to make. The MoF had a history of managing the financial markets through periodic crises. During their entire career, officials had learned to solve problems through intervention; they had little or no experience in letting the market sort matters out. Despite a dramatically changed financial market, officials there were not prepared to abdicate control.

Yet the time-worn solution of managing the crisis by inducing large banks to acquire sick financial institutions conflicted with the compartmentalized banking system. Only a handful of commercial and long-term-credit banks had the wherewithal to bail out an ailing trust bank or significantly sized securities firm. Compartmentalization, however, prevented the very classes of banks capable of engaging in a rescue operation from doing so. For rescue operations to work, therefore, barriers separating classes of financial institutions had to come down.

All of this was the backdrop for the decision to finally bring closure to the efforts to decompartmentalize the financial system. The process had been in motion since the 1980s, with securities firms mounting almost intractable opposition. Matters, however, could no longer wait. In the early 1990s, pressure built up beyond containment, with the walls separating banking and securities activities finally coming down.

In June 1991, the Financial System Research Council issued a report laying out the final shape of the reforms, reforms enacted by the Diet a year later. The Council rejected universal banking, the European method, and instead called for changes that would allow financial institutions to engage in securities, banking, and trust activities through separate subsidiaries. By removing barriers, mergers and other takeovers became more likely. Indeed, the first bailout of a securities firm by a bank was under way even before the proposals became law.[20]

Uncomfortable with dramatic reforms, the MoF imposed limits. Securities subsidiaries of banks could only engage in underwriting, not brokerage activities. Newly formed trust subsidiaries would not be allowed to manage pension funds. Each subsidiary needed to have a relatively steep amount of capital and had to be wholly owned, a requirement imposed at the insistence of the Fair Trade Commission. Moreover, at least initially, MoF decreed that entry could not occur through acquisition of an existing trust bank or securities company.

The limits had a dual purpose. They assuaged the concern of securities firms and trust banks, the two categories most threatened by the reforms. More subtly, however, they also provided the MoF with additional leverage. A rescue of an unhealthy trust bank or securities firm could be induced through promises of expanded powers.[21]

The MoF's decision to push the reforms had a delicious irony. Financial reform had become necessary to manage the financial system. Over the short term, the changes helped solve existing problems by allowing different classes of banks and securities firms to combine. Moreover, the MoF intended to manage the process tightly. Even where banks gained new powers, the shadow of administrative guidance remained.[22]

Deregulation, therefore, at least momentarily, enhanced the Ministry's ability to shape the financial system. Over the long term, however, the reforms threatened to eliminate a critical source of government leverage. Banks would increasingly have funding sources and lines of business independent of the MoF, thereby becoming less susceptible to government influence.

THE SCANDAL: THE MINISTRY OF FINANCE IMPALED

As the MoF struggled to cope with the mounting difficulties, when things hardly seemed as if they could get any worse, an unexpected thunderclap broke. A financial scandal erupted that engulfed the Ministry, realigning the bureaucratic balance of power. The scandal demonstrated in clear terms the problems of the excessively cozy relationship between regulator and regulated. The result was a hue and cry for change and severe, perhaps permanent, damage to the MoF's reputation.

Isolated scandals within the financial system had arisen from time to time, but they tended to be firm-specific, not necessarily indicative of systematic problems, and easy to contain. Only a few years before, the markets had been rocked by blatant examples of insider trading. The MoF, however, engineered legislative changes that toughened restrictions on the practice and the furor died down.

By 1990, a scandal of unparalleled magnitude swept over securities firms, engulfing the MoF, tarring both and dramatically affecting their relationship. Dubbed the *tobashi* scandals, the four largest brokers stood accused of repaying business clients almost $1 billion as compensation for trading losses. The payments had been uncovered by the more independent National Tax Administration Agency, an arm of the Ministry, when securities firms tried to deduct them as entertainment expenses. Information about the scandals leaked to the press, although by whom remained unclear.

The revelation amounted to a Pandora's box. The scandal engendered a protracted public outcry that exceeded anything reasonably contemplated. Sharply criticized, the payments demonstrated that the brunt of the falling stock market fell on small investors who had no comparable ability to obtain compensation.

The compensation payments drew a harsh reaction from regulators. The MoF required the offending securities firms to "voluntarily" close their corporate sales divisions, assessed penalties, and induced resignations of top officers.[23] As additional practices came to light – such as stock manipulation or transactions linked to organized crime – the Ministry imposed a host of additional penalties.[24]

The Ministry's approach provoked an uncharacteristic outburst from Nomura's president, Yoshihisa Tabuchi. He indicated at a meeting of shareholders that the compensation payments had been made "in consultation with the MoF."[25] After Tabuchi resigned, the new president promptly apologized for the remarks, but the damage was done. The MoF was directly implicated.

The MoF often knew about, but overlooked, questionable practices. Officials almost never expressly approved them, but simply failed to object. This form of wink and nod allowed the bureaucracy to distance itself when things went wrong. Thus, while securities firms had been told in 1989 to stop making the compensation payments, the MoF took no affirmative steps to enforce the edict, particularly as the stock market started to collapse. Strict adherence would have caused clients to close accounts and sell shares, further weakening an already weakened stock market. The payments therefore continued.

By directly linking the MoF to the practices, the scandal suggested a conspiracy between regulator and regulated and highlighted problems with the informal system of administrative guidance. As one Japanese commentator noted:

> The uncovering of the clandestine compensations for stock investment losses this time has shown the nation that relations between the Finance Ministry and securities industry are dubious and questionable because they are not governed by law, but based largely on discretionary administrative power of which the legal foundation is uncertain.[26]

They also brought increased scrutiny to the hallowed practice of *amakudari*, or descent from heaven. Typically retiring in their mid-50s, MoF officials often obtained comfortable sinecures in banks and other financial institutions. While other Japanese ministries engaged in the practice, the MoF had "by far the most prominent positions in influential governmental organizations, affiliates, and big businesses."[27] A 1992 survey showed that 64 Ministry officials retired and obtained new positions. Maintaining good relations with industry facilitated the placement process, arguably discouraging aggressive enforcement.

The implication of the MoF drew an unusual and public *mea culpa*. Top officials took an unprecedented 10 percent pay cut. This time the act of *kejime*, or payment of a penalty followed by a fresh start, proved inadequate. Public pressure forced the Finance Minister, and leading contender for Prime Minister, Ryutaro Hashimoto, to resign.

Even these acts proved insufficient. The scandal generated calls for systemic reform, particularly the creation of an independent investigatory body to police the financial markets. The idea represented a throwback. Under the auspices of occupation forces, an independent Securities and Exchange Commission had been formed. Uninterested in the agency, the MoF absorbed the organization once the occupation ended. Public calls for a new independent agency now arose again and came from a host of prominent politicians including the then Prime Minister Kaifu and his successor, Kiichi Miyazawa.[28]

Unlike in the past, the MoF could not ignore the calls for change. At the request of the Prime Minister, the Provisional Council for the Promotion of Administrative Reform convened to examine the matter and issued a report in September 1991. Legislation followed in the spring of the following year. The legislation did not create an independent regulatory body as many had sought but did form a new investigatory body within the MoF.

Dubbed the Stock Trading Surveillance Commission and modeled somewhat after the National Tax Administration Agency, the Commission had the task of policing the securities markets. The new organization was to be run by a three-person committee appointed by the Finance Minister and approved by the Diet. The MoF disclaimed any intention of appointing officials from the bureaucracy and instead promised to look to academia, the legal profession, and the media. The reforms also changed the system for monitoring bank activities. Surveillance and inspection functions were stripped from the Banking and International Finance Bureaus and placed in a new Financial Inspection Unit within the Ministry's more independent Secretariat.

The reforms were criticized as paper tigers. Some viewed them as cosmetic efforts to placate the public, with little likelihood of any fundamental shift in behavior. After all, the Commission remained in the MoF and was subject to the full panoply of bureaucratic pressures. Moreover, the Commission could not impose penalties but only had the authority to make recommendations to the Minister of Finance. That, however, represented too sullen a view.

Given the government's predilection toward incremental reform, the formation of the Commission amounted to an uncharacteristically large step. Dynamics within the Ministry ensured that the Commission would receive real teeth. For one thing, by breaking the enforcement function out of the Securities Bureau, the MoF had an inspection unit less beholden to the industry. The unit also represented a vehicle for the Ministry as a whole to keep greater tabs on the securities industry and to learn in advance of potentially embarrassing practices.

The MoF, however, had another, more institutional reason for ensuring the success of the arrangement. For the first time in the post-occupation era, the MoF underwent significant internal reorganization as a result of scandal. The Ministry had come close to losing control over a segment of the financial system. While calls had arisen earlier to divide up the Ministry, they had never come so close.[29] The failure to use the enforcement authority to create the appearance of greater neutrality toward the financial industry would probably generate calls for the complete removal of the authority from the MoF. The next time, the Ministry might not be lucky enough to preserve regulatory oversight of the financial markets.

The MoF was losing its grip. Events were out of control. For the first time in the post-war era, the possibility that the MoF might begin to relinquish control over the financial system and take a less interventionist approach to regulation seemed possible.

12

THE OPPORTUNITIES FORGONE

The misfortune of Japanese banks created opportunities for foreign financial institutions. Close relationships between banks and companies were fraying. Japanese financial institutions could not provide the necessary services. With lending funds scarce and a less innovative approach to product development, Japanese banks could not meet all of the financial needs of corporate Japan. The opportunity therefore existed for foreign banks to fill the breach.

Despite the opportunities, foreign banks lacked the will and inclination to step in. Likewise, efforts by the US government to further open the markets had permanently stalled. The Treasury was flailing, with the negotiations becoming ineffective, even counterproductive. Opportunities were slipping past. The Treasury stood unprepared to take advantage of the Ministry of Finance's (MoF's) sudden fall from grace. The early years of the decade were therefore a period of opportunities forgone.

THE US BANKS

By the 1990s, foreign banks in Japan operated under a drastically altered financial system. The long-standing difficulty in acquiring yen had, to a large degree, been alleviated. Banks could bring in funds from home offices, largely without restraint. The interbank market became more accessible, particularly with the elimination of collateral requirements. Foreign banks were given access to the discount window, although some complained about the paltry amounts. Changes were even evident in the retail sector. The government agreed to complete deregulation of interest rates by 1994, reducing the advantage of retail deposits, and indicated a greater willingness to grant branch licenses to foreign banks.

The range of permissible activities had also expanded. Once limited to trade finance and impact loans, foreign banks had spread into the trust and securities business, finance companies, and investment advisory services.[1]

184

They were active in foreign exchange trading, swaps, and other esoteric instruments. The 1980s also saw one of the last great obstacles in the retail area recede with an end to restrictions on charge cards with a revolving line of credit.[2] Foreign banks even had advantages over their Japanese counterparts. They could set up trust or securities subsidiaries; Japanese city banks could not.[3] Even after Japanese banks received comparable rights, foreign trust banks and securities firms retained the authority to engage in a broader range of activities.[4]

That was the good news. The bad news was that, despite ongoing liberalization, foreign outposts in Japan remained weak. In 1990, half of the 82 foreign banks incurred losses, while the other half were mired in mediocrity. The depressing earnings led to ominous predictions that no more than 10 foreign banks would survive. US banks had a particularly dismal showing. Although Citibank was at the top of the profitability chart, a substantial reversal from the year before, only two other US banks ranked in the top 20. Instead, they dominated the bottom 10.

The vaunted trust banks that had cost so much diplomatic energy to acquire remained insignificant players in the pension management market. Moreover, hard as it was to believe, operations went from bad to worse. For the year ending March 1992, profits plunged, with five of the nine showing losses while only Bankers Trust had an increase in pre-tax profitability. One of the original nine even threw in the towel. In 1991, Manufacturers Hanover sold its trust subsidiary to State Street Boston Bank.

Trust banking was not the only area that failed to meet expectations. In general, bank entry into the securities area proved unsuccessful. While foreign brokers made money in the country, firms owned by banks generally did not.[5] Some of the early entrants shut or severely curtailed their Tokyo operations.

Commercial lending also remained low margin, with permanent improvement nowhere in sight. Foreign financial institutions continued to move away from conventional banking activities. Despite aberrational increases due to government policies, the trend was unmistakably in one direction, down. Some banks even sought to reduce their loan portfolio by asking clients to repay outstanding balances.

The same trend could be seen with deposits. Despite Citibank's efforts to attack the retail sector, total deposits held by foreign banks continued to fall. Yen deposits fell to ¥1.8 trillion in 1990, compared with ¥2.11 trillion in 1989 and ¥3 trillion in 1987.

As foreign banks searched for alternative sources of profit, Ministry oversight seemed increasingly pernicious. They continued to develop novel approaches to business but ran into bureaucratic recalcitrance. The MoF had never reacted well to innovation. The new and unexpected generated a hesitant response. The relevant official wanted reams of information and plenty of time to consider every aspect. As the usual source of innovation, foreign banks suffered disproportionately from the slow pace of approval.

185

Even where approval occurred, the process resembled a fish bowl. Officials at the Ministry routinely disclosed any new arrangement or product to other Japanese banks to get their reaction. Foreign banks therefore found their innovative approach transmitted to the marketplace even before the first deal occurred.

Options, futures, and other derivative products had a tortuously slow introduction in Japan, with the MoF relying on the usual step-by-step approach. Limits were initially placed on eligible investors, reducing the breadth of the market. Banks also ran into difficulty trying to market other types of products including collateralized mortgage obligations and some types of zero coupon bonds and mutual funds. Merrill Lynch was prohibited from selling US based asset-backed money market funds and approval was slow for Globex, Chicago Mercantile's 24 hour electronic commodity future system.

Moreover, the loosening of the regulatory reins did not always portend acceptance. Intervention could return and additional restrictions imposed anytime the bureaucracy felt necessary. The MoF treated the sale of derivative products as the principal scapegoat for the declining stock market. Despite earlier liberalization, therefore, the Ministry used administrative guidance to restrict their sale.

Securitization of assets represented a good example of the difficulties confronted by foreign banks in introducing new products. Banks would combine a large number of loans – credit card receipts, car loans, mortgages – and sell interests in the pools. This allowed the banks to reduce assets (and the need for capital) while earning fees from the sales. The Ministry, however, prohibited banks from selling the security-backed assets. The purported reasons were both prudential and legal.

The reasoning aside, the impediments to new products coincidentally benefited Japanese banks. Security-backed assets competed with bonds sold by long-term-credit banks. Restrictions also gave the banks time to catch up. With little experience in the relevant areas, Japanese financial institutions would have found themselves at a competitive disadvantage through rapid introduction of innovative products.

The confluence of these factors had the predictable effect. Foreign banks, particularly those from the United States, began to reduce or eliminate operations in Japan. Nor were those in the country the longest spared. Chase shut its Osaka branch, open since the occupation, and reduced the number of employees in Tokyo. Continental Illinois, in the country since 1963, drastically pared back operations in Tokyo. Wells Fargo and First Interstate, banks that had entered the country during the first wave of branch approvals in the early 1970s, sold their Tokyo offices. Mellon Bank went from 25 employees to single digits. Security Pacific announced a reduction in staff after losing $18.5 million on speculative trading.

Brokerage and foreign exchange activities suffered most from the reductions. Chemical Bank closed the Tokyo branch of Chemical Securities, Vickers reduced equity operations, and Bank of Boston dismissed all currency dealers. First Interstate moved foreign exchange and securities trading out of Tokyo before selling its entire operations. Even banks expanding overseas typically left Japan off the list. Everywhere, foreign, particularly US, banks were in retreat. As Walter Wriston described, the banks were "eating their seed corn."[6]

The problem was not limited to Japan. US banks seemed to be undergoing systematic withdrawal from overseas operations, particularly as red ink sprouted. First Interstate sold its international wholesale operations lock, stock, and barrel to Standard Chartered of Great Britain. Chase deliberately pared overseas assets, unloading retail operations in Spain and credit card operations in the United Kingdom. Security Pacific, Chemical, Bank of Boston, and Bank of America also reduced their international presence. Almost no US bank remained unscathed. Even Citibank had to slow growth, eliminate employees, and sell non-essential overseas operations.

Listing the retreating banks did not tell the full story. The US presence declined in markets that it had dominated since the end of the war. London in particular saw a dramatic drop-off. In 1990, First Bank System of Minneapolis became the twentieth US bank to withdraw from London since 1985, bringing the number of US banks operating in the city to 51, the lowest number since 1972. The lemming-like withdrawal also occurred in Canada and Australia.

The reasons for the departure were all too familiar. International capital standards played a role. To meet the standards, low margin areas had to be eliminated. For many banks, international operations were not sufficiently profitable to justify a significant presence. Japan in particular involved both high operating costs and low margins.

The US banking system, however, was another culprit. Until the early 1980s, banks could not operate in more than one state. When the restrictions were loosened, banks went on a buying binge, purchasing financial institutions in other states. Super-regional banks sprang out of whole cloth. An enormous amount of energy and capital went into domestic rather than international growth.

Even leviathans such as Bank of America concentrated on domestic expansion. Seeking to become the first nationwide bank in the United States, Bank of America engaged in a rapid series of domestic mergers, culminating in the acquisition of Security Pacific, the third largest bank in California. Unlike bygone days, the bank's preoccupation with domestic acquisitions left little inclination for international operations.

Perhaps more imponderable but nonetheless apparent, US banks seemed to lose interest in, and the will to develop, foreign operations, even when opportunities appeared. As one study noted:

US banks were perhaps becoming too myopic and inward looking in their strategic planning. As European banks continue to consolidate and grow bigger, and expand their provision of financial services throughout Western and Eastern Europe and the US and as the Japanese banks do the same in Japan and throughout the Pacific Rim, the US and Europe, these banks will become too big, too strong and too efficient for US banks to compete against effectively in the future.[7]

THE TREASURY'S TRIALS

Banks were not the only ones to see opportunities slip past. The sudden envelopment of the MoF in a financial maelstrom created unexpected openings for negotiators seeking further reform of the Japanese financial markets. Within Japan, criticism had erupted over the close relationship between the MoF and the financial sector, with the seemingly powerful Ministry having to pull out the stops just to prevent oversight of the securities markets from being legislatively exorcised.

The MoF was not happy with the public pillorying and the damage to its reputation. For the first time in Japan even some regulators were wondering if the close relationship between industry and government was worth it. Reducing intervention was one possible solution. Having less involvement meant less responsibility for what went wrong.

The opportunity therefore existed for foreign pressure to become a factor in Japan's domestic debate over the government's role in the financial markets. With matters in flux, the US Department of the Treasury, through the mechanism of the yen/dollar process, was in a position to influence the direction and speed of change. As the financial system underwent wrenching reorganization, however, the Treasury sat on the sidelines, increasingly marginal to the process.

Part of the decline was personal. The relationships that had played a fundamental role in the success of the yen/dollar process were gone. The government officials that had helped overcome the prevailing inertia within Japan had departed. In the annual reshuffling of Ministry positions in 1991, the popular Makoto Utsumi, who had risen to the rank of Vice Minister of International Affairs, was replaced by the Stanford-educated Tadao Chino, the first person to hold the position since 1983 with no direct role in the Yen/Dollar Accord.

So too significant personnel changes occurred on the US side. Sprinkel, Dallara, and Fauver from the pre-Accord days had moved on; Abbott, the particularly effective attaché, was gone. Only David Mulford remained, but he succeeded in irritating and alienating rather than building and compromising. When the two sides met, therefore, they were veritable strangers.

The problems, however, went well beyond personnel matters. The Treasury had also lost the unified support of US banks and securities firms operating in Japan. They had less and less interest in the increasingly shrill efforts of Treasury negotiators. Moreover, calls for open markets meant increased competition and reduced profits. Certain reforms such as abolishment of underwriting commissions and deregulation of brokerage fees actually drew opposition from the foreign financial community.

In part the difficulty arose out of the growing complexity of the remaining barriers. Few obvious ones remained. Reforms in the 1980s stripped away blatant and obvious discriminatory features in the Japanese financial system. Foreign banks had received access to the discount window, the right to open additional branches, and the authority to engage in trust banking, securities trading, and investment advisory services. The banks were allowed into the government bond syndicate, and to act as dealers in the secondary market.[8]

The remaining problems were more subtle. They arose less from specific legal barriers and more from the basic approach to regulation. Banks continued to chafe under the MoF's tight regulatory oversight. Yet the Treasury seemed to have little comprehension of the principal problems facing financial institutions and did little to facilitate resolution.

Unsurprisingly, therefore, progress in inducing further reform slowed. Japanese regulators also seemed to have less energy to meet US demands. Attentions were focused elsewhere. The MoF had its hands full with the raft of precariously perched financial institutions and the compensation scandals. US positions seemed increasingly unimportant compared with the current problems sweeping the financial system.

As progress fell off, the tone on the United States became sharper, even vitriolic. This could be seen from the National Treatment Study published at the end of 1990. The report castigated the Japanese, concluding that the banks still had "an unfair competitive advantage over foreign banks . . . . "[9] The advantage arose in part from the "slow pace of liberalization and deregulation . . . . "[10] Treasury heaped criticism on specific practices, including regulated interest rates, restrictive regulations, strong ties among related firms (the keiretsu problem), excessive compartmentalization, and lack of transparency.[11]

The shrill approach also became apparent in the negotiating process itself. The gloves came off. When the two sides met in the fall of 1991, Mulford was at his irritating and irascible best, engaging in what the press described as a "slashing attack" on the Japanese.[12] Mulford also began to play the "Congress" card. Complaining of the lack of "concrete progress," he noted in diplomatic doublespeak that, absent further liberalization, the process would undergo "substantial politicalization." With anti-Japanese legislation pending in Congress, Mulford's message was clear: a lack of progress would bring on congressional retaliation with the Treasury not standing in its way. The bastion of free market philosophy was suddenly prepared to jettison equal treatment in favor of punitive measures.

The Treasury was losing control, something increasingly apparent within

189

Congress. By the latter half of the 1980s, Congress had lost patience with "the tortoise pace of deregulation in Japan" and the "hare-like expansion of Japanese firms in the US" and moved off the sidelines. The Omnibus Trade and Competitiveness Act of 1988 gave the Federal Reserve Board the authority to deny licenses to securities firms from countries that did "not accord to US companies the same competitive opportunities in underwriting and distribution of government debt instruments."

The provision was a bald attempt to penalize Japan for failing to give foreign financial institutions access to the government bond syndicate. Japan got the word. Substantial reform followed swiftly. Foreign firms received a higher percentage of bonds allocated to the syndicate. The MoF also began auctioning an increased percentage of government bonds.

For the first time Congress had passed provisions designed to penalize Japanese financial institutions. The shift reflected growing frustration. Nonetheless, the step, while psychologically significant, was practically narrow. The legislation dealt with government bond sales, applied only to securities companies, not banks, and had a relatively broad grandfather clause. Moreover, the provisions amounted to a one-shot affair. Once the Federal Reserve Board made the requisite findings, the legislation ceased to have continuing validity. Future proposals would not be so limited.

The next efforts were much broader. Introduced by Senators Riegle and Garn, the Fair Trade in Financial Services Act authorized the Department of the Treasury to deny applications of foreign banks and securities firms from countries that did not afford US financial institutions "effective market access." Although using neutral language the legislation had one main target: Japan. The congressional record overflowed with statistics about the Japanese onslaught on the US market. The hearings on the legislation were also replete with references to Japan, some emotional.

While the legislation had not become law, it did pass one or both houses of Congress on more than one occasion. This indicated both strong support for the approach and considerable dissatisfaction with the Treasury's existing methods. It also made clear that Congress had decided on a common approach. Without greater progress, punitive measures would be the order of the day.[13]

FAILED EFFORTS

The failings of foreign banks and the Department of the Treasury did not exonerate the Japanese. Problems of access remained. Government policies still hindered operations. They did, however, highlight the critical complicity of banks and regulators outside of Japan. They also raised the question of continued reform and the benefits that would flow from it. Even with more open markets, it was unclear that foreign banks were prepared to take advantage of the opportunities presented.

13

SHARED RESPONSIBILITY

THE MYTHS

Review of the post-war history of foreign banking activity in Japan dispels a number of myths. *First*, the story has not been one of unmitigated disaster, as current statistics seem to indicate. Through the mid-1970s, foreign banking operations were lucrative. Thereafter, individual banks prospered, whether through product development and innovation or through risk taking and attention to market niches unattended (sometimes as a result of guidance by the MoF) by Japanese banks.

Moreover, even the current difficulties have not been spread evenly. Not all firms have suffered from the slumping financial markets. Foreign securities firms in particular have done famously well over the last several years, with Salomon Brothers and Goldman Sachs ranking among the most profitable securities firms in Japan.

Second, the historical review dispels the myth that banks had to conform to government expectations to succeed. Time and time again, Citibank, in an often vociferous fashion, and J. P. Morgan, in a more *sotto voce* manner, declined to accept the reigning restrictions. These banks did not suffer as a result and, indeed, often obtained at least temporary competitive advantages.

Third, the overview dispels the myth that the Ministry of Finance (MoF) somehow operated in a unique, even anti-foreign, fashion. Foreign banks, like all financial institutions, including Japanese, were limited to a prescribed niche in the market. When the system became outmoded, the MoF's behavior resembled that of most bureaucracies, including those in the United States. Conservative, entrenched, hesitant to relinquish authority, the MoF became responsive to change only when political or industry pressure was brought to bear or events made pre-existing policies completely unworkable.

The MoF's behavior was strongly influenced by a predilection toward stability. Stability rather than competition represented the fundamental premise underlying regulation. This made the bureaucracy hesitant toward

191

anything that disrupted the status quo. With foreign banks chafing most under the status quo and agitating for change, they incurred the brunt of the MoF's hesitancy and disapproval. Yet the Ministry would have responded in an even more unaccommodating fashion had the agitation emanated from a Japanese financial institution.

That did not, of course, mean that the complaints of foreign banks were unfounded. In conventional areas such as commercial yen lending and deposit taking, foreign banks never really penetrated the Japanese markets. While they generally did not build the close relationships with corporate Japan so prevalent within the banking system, the difficulties were exacerbated by government policies that impeded the operations of the foreign financial community.

Through the 1960s, the MoF limited the operations of foreign banks. Nonetheless, by the early 1990s all of the most obvious restrictions had been eliminated. The post-war ban on foreign entry into the country ended in 1968; the end of most swap limits by the mid-1980s; the restrictions on branch banking in the late 1980s and early 1990s. To the extent that restrictions continued to exist, they seemed to flow not from foreign bias but from a bureaucratic unwillingness to give up authority.

Fourth, the overview dispels the myth that the responsibility for the failure of foreign banks rested exclusively with Japan. The MoF's policies represented only part of the explanation. Responsibility existed outside Japan. Windows occasionally opened, providing the foreign banking community with opportunities to penetrate the domestic market. In general, most proved incapable or unwilling to take advantage of them. Rather than use the era of capital shortages to tighten relations with corporate Japan, many foreign banks chose to emphasize fat margins. The same thing occurred during periods of tight money. Once those aberrational periods expired, the short-term profit opportunity ended and most foreign banks found themselves with little permanent business base.

Part of the explanation was a lack of sophistication, part a lack of commitment. Foreign banking behavior resembled that of lemmings. They flooded into the country in the early 1970s without adequate preparation, driven by the awareness of the monopoly profits earned by the banks in the country since the occupation and by the desire for the adornment of a Tokyo branch, something that had become a necessity for any bank with the pretense of an international branch network.

The lemming-like behavior was apparent in a host of other areas, including foreign exchange and securities activities. Banks entered *en masse* when profits seemed easy and plentiful. When business ebbed, however, whether because of the flood of entrants or because of the inevitable end of the abnormal conditions that gave rise to the profitable behavior, the banks found themselves with expensive overheads and no permanent source of profitability. The result was a lemming-like withdrawal, with banks shutting down or cutting back operations.

Fifth, the overview demonstrates that foreign pressure can influence the reform process in Japan. In no circumstance did foreign pressure – whether exerted by foreign banks or foreign governments – represent a complete explanation for comprehensive revision of financial regulations. Yet foreign influence often became a factor in the domestic debate, sometimes tilting the balance and overcoming the prevailing inertia within the Japanese financial community.

Changes wrought by foreign influence disrupted the status quo, requiring a new consensus to form within the financial community, a consensus that usually entailed the jettisoning of previous restrictions. Foreign bank entry into the securities business in Japan accelerated the process of decompartmentalization. Citibank's success in aggressively publicizing financial products ultimately resulted in the elimination of rules restricting advertisements.[1]

Foreign pressure also became a factor in the domestic debate. City banks used it to advance interest rate deregulation. Brokers used it to try to breach the barriers to trust banking activities. MoF officials used it to advance the goal of updating the financial system.

Foreign pressure, however, was not always used effectively. For most of the post-war era, Washington practiced a policy of benign neglect toward economic issues in Japan. The government ignored blatant barriers to operations, unwilling to disrupt an important political and security relationship.

This was not lost on the Japanese regulators. Through the early 1980s, they knew that the failure to accede to requests from foreign banks for additional operating authority would generate almost no adverse reaction in Washington. This deprived US banks of an indispensable source of leverage. Thus, repeated calls for additional branches or access to additional yen funding were either refused or ignored.

In the handful of instances where foreign government intervention occurred, changes often followed. Whether the refusal of the California superintendent of banking to grant additional licenses to Japanese branches, the congressionally threatened prohibition on primary dealers, or a chance conversation at the White House over additional branches in Japan, the MoF averted the possible diplomatic donnybrooks by giving the banks what they wanted.

Even after turning toward financial matters, the Department of the Treasury did not manage matters in a particularly astute fashion. The Yen/ Dollar Accord aside, efforts to induce reform foundered, not for any mysterious reason. The decline resulted in part from bureaucratic squabbles in Washington over jurisdiction, with territory taking precedence over results. The Treasury also devoted less energy to the negotiation process, rarely getting top officials involved. Without high level involvement, Japanese politicians were less willing to intervene in the bureaucratic process to push for greater reform.

The lack of influence also flowed from the failure to understand the

193

process of change in Japan. The Treasury, like most foreign banks, did not devote the time and energy necessary to understand the domestic dynamics of reform and the places where pressure could be applied most effectively. Representing only one factor in a complex domestic debate, the Treasury emphasized a number of narrow issues that generated little interest within the Japanese financial community, marginalizing its role in the debate.

The Treasury also lost its domestic base of support. The partnership between the government and the financial community briefly flourished during the yen/dollar process, and then vanished. The Department of the Treasury disdainfully declined to act as a lobbyist for financial institutions. Instead, negotiators preferred the macroeconomic, stressing issues designed to facilitate international capital flows. That approach mistakenly assumed that issues raised by individual banks did not coincide with the broader goals pursued by the Treasury. With bank-specific problems attracting little interest, financial institutions continued to lack an effective representative capable of forcefully raising their concerns with the Japanese government.

The Treasury's problems were more than academic. Individual banks demonstrated that the MoF could be induced to change. Citibank showed this time and time again. Yet they could only accomplish so much. Without some additional leverage, the MoF had little incentive to address, in any significant respect, the remaining concerns of the foreign banking community. Effective foreign pressure would have provided the leverage.

Finally, the overview of the post-war operation of foreign banks in Japan dispels the myth of short-term solutions. Foreign influence can and has contributed to the reform process and the liberalization of the financial markets in Japan. Slow, the process requires deliberation and sophistication and an understanding of the reform process. To be most effective, the pressure must become a factor in the debate within Japan.

Short-term solutions do not work. Particularly as the trade imbalance continues to worsen, solutions such as managed trade seem increasingly attractive. This assumes, however, that the fault for the imbalance rests exclusively with the Japanese, an incorrect premise. Equally important, the approach plays into the hands of those within Japan resistant to reform. Managed trade may temporarily lessen the imbalance but will not bring about a more open economy. Indeed, by providing a short-term cure, the arrangement takes the pressure off the Japanese to reform their markets fundamentally. When the arrangement is eventually cast off, as it will be, Japanese markets will remain as difficult as ever to penetrate.

THE PROBLEMS

Japanese financial markets had undergone considerable reform, with foreign, particularly US, pressure playing a significant, although intermittent, role in the process. Most narrowly, the efforts impacted the timing and pace of reform. They also caused a shift in the MoF's approach to regulation. Foreign banks also learned to use the threat of government intervention to overcome barriers to operations. Citibank was particularly adept at invoking foreign pressure to obtain results. Aware that imperious behavior might incur the wrath of the United States, the MoF took a more deferential approach toward issues of concern to the foreign banking community.[2]

Even more broadly, efforts by the United States and European governments sparked comprehensive change in the Japanese financial system. The efforts permanently fractured the antiquated system of regulation. Interest rate deregulation, an historical source of government control, accelerated. By allowing foreign banks to enter the trust and securities business, the Yen/Dollar Accord effectively destroyed the symmetry that had prevailed since the early 1950s. Efforts to decompartmentalize the financial system began almost contemporaneously with the execution of the Accord.

Reforms in the Euroyen markets, another byproduct of the Accord, eviscerated the domestic bond market. The Euroyen market had the benefit of less regulation and less cost and became the market of choice. By the early 1990s, the MoF had begun casting off restrictions in the domestic market in an effort to lure back bond issuers.

Despite the considerable changes, however, foreign banks continued to feel smothered. Tight government oversight had not dissipated. Daily reports of loan balances to the Bank of Japan were still required, personal visits to the MoF still the norm. The guiding principal of "no surprises" remained unchanged. All major developments needed Ministry approval before implementation, particularly the use of innovative products and novel strategies. In a competitive market that often rewarded the fleet footed, the Ministry continued to tread in a deliberate and methodical fashion.

The core difficulty was the MoF's belief in intervention over market forces. Even in areas that had purportedly been deregulated, the MoF's ubiquitous control remained. In the Euromarket, Japanese banks regularly had to report loans to the government by industry and to explain unusual trends or developments. Restrictions remained on the authority to manage a Euroyen offering by a Japanese company and the amount of a Euroyen bond issue that could be sold to Japanese purchasers.[3] All of the restrictions arose out of guidance imposed by the MoF.

Similarly, concessions made in the domestic financial system did nothing to remove the Ministry's long shadow. Foreign banks were given the authority to engage in trust activities in 1985. The MoF, however, never issued standards for future entry of other foreign banks and, indeed, made clear that there would be no additional licenses for the foreseeable future. Limits remained on securities operations and on the relationship between a trust subsidiary and the bank branch.

Even the success of Citibank did nothing to dispel the appearance of government intervention. Notwithstanding the unique expansion in the retail sector, the bank amounted to an exception. The MoF did not articulate standards or rules that would apply to financial institutions seeking to open additional branches or to buy a Japanese bank. Other foreign banks intending to expand in a comparable fashion would have to obtain the requisite approvals through lengthy face-to-face negotiations with the relevant Ministry officials.

The reasons for the bureaucratic torpor were not particularly Machiavellian or anti-foreign. The problems largely arose from the MoF's historical position in the financial system. Having played a critical role in directing the flow of capital and ensuring economic recovery, the MoF had little interest in relinquishing authority. This was true even though the circumstances requiring such heavy handed intervention had long since passed.

Above all else foreign banks wanted an end to the interventionist approach to regulation, a tall order. That meant that consumers and corporate users, not the MoF, were to become the primary arbiters of the practices and products that would succeed, subject only to certain prudential limitations. Success would require the government to alter an approach to regulation that had existed since the occupation.

While in earlier eras this might have seemed fanciful, the opportunity to induce the MoF to reduce its authority had suddenly become possible. The compensation scandals, the plummeting stock market, and the difficulty in ensuring the solvency of the banking system, all demonstrated the declining hold of the MoF over the financial markets.

Efforts to reduce government intervention would probably accelerate a process already under way in Japan. To work, however, foreign banks needed a more aggressive attitude, greater commitment to the market, and a more unified approach toward unnecessary government restrictions. In addition, the Treasury needed to modify the negotiation process substantially with an eye toward increasing effectiveness. This required sharp changes in the negotiation agenda and a more inclusive approach toward the talks.

THE SYMPTOM

To some degree, the Treasury recognized the problem of bureaucratic intervention but addressed the issue ineffectively. The Yen/Dollar talks from the very beginning emphasized the need for increased transparency. Increased transparency was discussed in the Accord and came up at follow-up meetings, particularly after the compensation scandals. Broadly, transparency meant making regulatory positions more clear and accessible.

To the Treasury, the transparency problem arose out of the system of informal regulation prevalent in Japan. Rather than reduce matters to written regulations, MoF officials typically articulated positions in face-to-face meetings. Lack of personal access – a more significant problem for the foreign banking community – sometimes made it difficult to discern Ministry policies. As Under Secretary of the Treasury Mulford described:

> Foreign firms are not given fair opportunities to engage in the process through which official policies, regulations and administrative guidance are developed by the Ministry of Finance. Some claim it is hard for them to even obtain *clear written statements* of the rules or policies once they are decided. Furthermore, the bureaucracy is empowered to interpret the law as it deems fit creating fears of arbitrary treatment of foreign firms if they question authoritative interpretations by Government officials.[4]

Transparency, therefore, meant reducing the positions to writing both to provide certainty and to eliminate the personal nature of the interpretations.

The focus, however, misjudged the process of regulation in Japan. Emphasis on transparency seemed to suggest a body of hidden rules or arbitrarily determined policies. By requiring "clear written statements," the financial system would somehow become more open. This, however, was at best seriously misleading and at worst simply wrong.

Most Japanese and sophisticated foreign bankers recognized that government positions – to the extent formalized – could be uncovered with perseverance and the right contacts. As was often said, Tokyo had no secrets. The real difficulty arose where the Ministry had not yet formulated a consistent position on an issue. This most commonly occurred when the MoF faced something unusual, particularly something that upset the status quo. Either the matter was unique or the party requesting the advice was unknown. Always afraid of a career ending blunder, MoF officials studied a new matter interminably. A consensus within the Ministry and the affected industry usually needed to develop. No amount of "clear written statements" would eliminate that internal process.

More importantly, the focus on written regulations may have represented an appropriate solution in a legalistic, litigious society like the United States, but not in Japan. Regulations meant little, particularly in the financial sector. The MoF's most effective source of authority had arisen from the ability to prevent banks from invoking legal requirements.

Examples abounded. Japanese law explicitly authorized banks to engage in trust activities. The MoF, however, had decreed otherwise. No Japanese or foreign bank ever tested the ban by actually filing an application.[5] Additional transparency – rules concerning eligibility requirements and timetables for approval – meant nothing if banks could be discouraged from applying in the first instance.[6]

Japanese law also provided that foreign banks could open a representative office without first obtaining Ministry approval; mere notification was enough. Under the statutory scheme, the MoF had no discretion: once

197

the notice was filed the office could be opened. The system was therefore entirely transparent. As a practical matter, however, foreign banks never submitted notices until first receiving informal approval from the MoF. The banks knew that good relations with the MoF were critical to success in the market and a future branch license and were not about to act in a way that would earn disfavor.

"Clear written statements," therefore, meant little if the MoF retained the authority to discourage banks from invoking them. Yet the Treasury expended considerable energy pushing for its definition of greater transparency. When the MoF did give ground on the issue, the victory was Pyrrhic. The fundamental approach to regulation did not change.

Similarly, criticism of the personal relationship between the MoF and industry constituted too simplistic an approach. The relationship in many instances arose out of necessity. With financial markets evolving rapidly, Ministry officials, all hired directly out of university, had no practical experience. Many had graduated from law faculties without adequate training in finance. Even after entering the MoF, officials rotated through various bureaus and did not develop expertise in one area.

Eliminating the contacts between regulator and regulated would deprive Ministry officials of a critical source of education and intelligence about the markets, perhaps making matters worse. This essentially occurred during the compensation scandals. In the immediate aftermath, officials within the Securities Bureau reduced contacts with brokers. The consequences were apparent. The MoF's efforts to halt the stock market's decline seemed either ineffective or counterproductive. Given the symbiotic relationship and lack of alternatives, Ministry officials had no choice but to normalize relations with securities firms gradually.

THE SOLUTION

Transparency, therefore, represented more a symptom than a cause. The real problem was Ministry intervention. Despite immense changes in Japan's economy, the MoF still insisted on micro-managing the financial markets. The result was a stifling degree of oversight that impeded operations. Focusing on bureaucratic discretion, however, posed problems. For one thing, the approach had no easy road map. The core issue involved a reduction in the MoF's proclivity toward intervention in the financial markets. No single change in rules or regulations would solve the problem. The issue was one of attitude and approach. Finally, foreign pressure alone could not compel the shift. At best, foreign influence could add its weight to pressures already existing in Japan.

To succeed, the MoF had to be convinced that it benefited from reduced involvement – a difficult lesson to absorb. The MoF began orchestrating economic growth at a time when the entire country struggled to recover from the war. By exercising complete control, the government ensured solvency of the financial system and directed capital to facilitate economic recovery. Although the formative era had long since passed, the centralized system of regulation remained.

Foreign and Japanese interest in reduced control intersected. The compensation scandals illustrated that the regulatory system protected the financial industry rather than consumers. Interventionist policies also threatened to damage Tokyo's claim as a world financial center. The MoF's efforts to clamp down on the sale of derivative products within Japan simply caused business to move to Singapore.

Increasing dissatisfaction with the MoF's role could be seen within the Japanese banking community. Often frustrated with excessive guidance, Japanese banks developed methods of circumventing Ministry authority. To avoid Ministry disapproval, they sometimes engaged in behavior without informing government officials.[7] Better to risk displeasure when discovered than to ask and receive a negative answer. Banks also seemed increasingly less susceptible to administrative pressure.[8] The MoF had growing difficulty brow beating financial institutions into participating in the rescue of sick banks. Similarly, mere expression of Ministry displeasure no longer seemed sufficient to induce compliance with government inspired policies. Efforts to use guidance to reduce property loans in the late 1980s failed miserably.[9]

Even the decision to create a company to purchase bad loans from banks illustrated the changing attitude. Although inspired by the MoF, the company was funded entirely by banks. Nor did the corporation include any former Ministry officials. A comparable entity set up in 1965 had received funds from the Bank of Japan. While the absence of government funding necessarily meant a reduced scale of operations, it also meant less government control.

Dissatisfaction was not limited only to the private sector. Politicians seemed to be edging closer to confrontation. The Hosokawa government, the first non-LDP government since 1955, targeted bureaucratic over-regulation as one of the key causes of the country's weakened economic condition. While the coalition government lacked the cohesion to seriously challenge the bureaucracy, the tone and approach represented a rare and public display of hostility and suggested less complacency from politicians in the future.

The high level of control also seemed to have become increasingly dysfunctional. Despite their enormous size, Japanese banks lacked the nimbleness needed to dominate markets outside the country, particularly when they were no longer able to compete through razor-thin margins. Prodigious efforts in the United States to pierce the retail market or to achieve a profitable position in the middle market had largely been ineffective.[10] Tight government control contributed to the lack of competitiveness.

The MoF's ability to control the financial markets had fallen since the 1950s. Changes in the financial markets had already eroded a variety of mechanisms used to facilitate control. Deregulation of interest rates and reform of the Euromarkets eviscerated the government's direct authority over bank funding. The elimination of barriers separating classes of financial institutions further removed government leverage, at least over the long term. Foreign pressure also affected behavior. The ubiquitous presence of *gaiatsu* meant that the MoF could not act in an imperious and secretive manner. Even Japanese financial institutions learned that the MoF became more responsive when foreign firms were involved.

Equally important, the MoF's image underwent psychological blows as a result of the collapse of the stock market and the *tobashi* or compensation scandals that erupted over the payment by securities firms to certain corporate clients. The compensation scandals generated a public upbraiding and legislation designed to change the MoF's enforcement authority. Perhaps more long lasting, the falling stock market showed the growing impotence of the Ministry to control large-scale financial disasters. Twice in the past, the MoF confronted a collapsing market: 1965 and 1987. In both instances, the omnipotent regulator was able to stem the fall by inducing securities firms, banks and institutional investors to embark on purchase programs.

By the 1990s, however, much had changed. Because of the compensation scandals, the Ministry no longer had the same relationship with securities firms. Weakening relations and the brokers' economic difficulties made efforts to induce them to buy shares far more problematic. Insurance companies and other institutions also had little interest. They had been large purchasers during the 1980s, when the stock market reached record highs, and had suffered disproportionately from the collapse. They were not interested in vigorously re-entering the markets while the fall was still under way.

Success in the past had raised expectations, both by the public and by the MoF. The Ministry embarked on a host of furtive policies designed to resuscitate the market. The MoF succeeded in stemming the fall and even resuscitating the market a bit. Success, however, came at a price. Reports indicated that much of the stock activity came from trust banks using public pension plan assets under their management, a risky gambit with retirement resources.[11]

As long as the MoF insisted on trying to control market forces – particularly given the volume involved – embarrassments would continue. The MoF had already drawn a line in the sand over bank failures. In an effort to forestall a failure, the MoF allowed banks to obscure bad loans, presented a budget with funds designed to help steady property markets, and engineered increases in stock prices to assist banks in meeting capital standards. When a failure did eventually occur – an inevitability – the responsibility would be clear. As long as the MoF pursued an interventionist approach and continued to project the sense of control, it would be held responsible for any insolvency.

Other longer-term developments suggested the need for the MoF to rethink its role in the financial markets. Two trends seemed likely to generate fundamental changes. First, with decompartmentalization a growing reality, the largest Japanese banks were likely to become more dominant and, as was the case before the war, less susceptible to government pressure.[12] MoF officials would have less ability to micro-manage the banks and otherwise induce them to implement the government's agenda.[13]

In addition, recent elections have ended the Liberal Democratic Party's (LDP's) monopoly on political power. In the short term, this has meant enhanced authority for the MoF. The unstable coalition currently leading Japan does not have the strength to take on the powerful bureaucracy. Thus, initial efforts to spur economic growth struck shoals when MoF Vice Minister Jiro Saito opposed further economic stimulation, particularly tax cuts.

Over the longer term, however, this will change. Japanese politicians must now prepare for an era of increased political competition. As that era dawns, Japanese parties, including the LDP, will probably place greater emphasis on vote-generating policies. In the financial area, this will mean policies with a more pro-consumer orientation. The MoF will find that the premise of stability (i.e. protectionism) must sometimes be replaced by a politically favored policy of consumerism (i.e. competition).[14]

All of this suggests that a prudent MoF should already begin focusing more on the interests of consumers. For one thing, this represents an approach that will continue to provide leverage against Japanese banks, even as they grow larger and more dominant. Second, as the political situation evolves, the MoF will not have all of its interests in one camp but will instead be in a better position to react to the vicissitudes of the political process and maintain its central role in the financial system.[15]

THE ROLE OF FOREIGN PRESSURE

These factors suggest that the MoF has reason to reduce involvement in the financial markets. In some respects, the MoF may already be moving in that direction. The loans from the deposit insurance system to facilitate the bailout of Toyo Shinkin represented the first time that government controlled funds played a direct role in a bank rescue operation. In a country inculcated by a step-by-step approach, the next step would be an outright transfer of funds to rescuing banks and, eventually, a bank failure completely funded by the deposit insurance system. The MoF therefore seemed to be preparing the country for an eventual bank failure, something that would have been unthinkable only a few years before.

Foreign pressure could hasten the process, however, by encouraging the MoF to become less involved in the oversight of the financial system. Reducing intervention and limiting the MoF's discretion will not be easy. Particularly uncomfortable for US negotiators, it does not involve the repeal of any special law or the undoing of any particular regulation. Instead, reform requires a fundamental change in attitude.

In the case of the United States, advancing this goal would necessitate a shift in attitude at the Department of the Treasury. The Department cannot continue to treat with disdain specific problems raised by specific banks. While concerned primarily with macroeconomic issues, the activities of individual banks can advance these goals. This is particularly true in connection with efforts to reduce government interference in the financial markets.

Attempts to employ a more aggressive approach toward advertising represents an example. Citibank tested the barriers to advertising when it began marketing foreign currency accounts. A seemingly small, bank-specific matter that did not advance broad goals, the inability to advertise minimized the value of macro reforms. Small banks with insignificant branch networks (read foreign) had greater difficulty selling innovative products or otherwise publicizing a competitive edge. They could not take full advantage of trust authority or interest rate deregulation if prohibited from effectively getting the word out. The Treasury's support for these types of matters would contribute to more rapid reform and a reduction in Ministry involvement in the financial markets.

As in the case of advertising, resolution of bank-specific issues also have a way of causing broader reform. As banks push against barriers, the mere prospect of a diplomatic fracas will subtly affect the MoF's reaction. Citibank's efforts to join the automated teller machine (ATM) network was facilitated by the looming threat that the matter would become a bilateral trade issue.[16] Nor would Treasury support for specific banking issues preclude the development of a more institutional agenda.

In reducing Ministry intervention, one possibility would be to encourage the division of the bureaucracy. This would mean cleaving off particular areas of regulatory oversight, particularly the financial markets. Independence would decentralize control. Deprived of control over the budget, financial regulators would become less omnipotent. This would probably induce a more realistic attitude toward regulation. In addition, employees would not rotate in and out of different bureaus but would essentially specialize.

This type of proposal would have seemed far fetched, even ludicrous, only a few years ago. Proposals within Japan to remove portions of the MoF's bailiwick have arisen before. They typically involved efforts by politicians to acquire control of the budgetary process and had never been particularly successful.

Events in the 1990s have suddenly made the suggestion seem more rational. During the compensation scandals, serious calls arose to strip away the MoF's regulatory authority over the securities markets. The approach may also find some support within the MoF itself. Further financial crises will only cause further embarrassment. As conditions worsen, the bureaucracy may agree that it is better off without the constant headaches.

Thoughts of seriously dividing the bureaucracy will probably need a catalyst such as a financial scandal or disaster. When this occurs, negotiators will need to throw their weight behind renewed calls for dividing the MoF, something they failed to do during the compensation scandals.

A reduction in the MoF's practice of micro-management could also be facilitated through reforms in the process of developing financial policy. Japan has long considered but never implemented an Administrative Procedures Act, statutes that required agencies to publish rule proposals for public comment.[17] Putting in place an Administrative Procedure Act would change nothing, immediately. Policies would still be developed informally through constant contact between regulator and regulated.

Nonetheless, the procedures would sometimes prove useful, particularly as an alternative whenever the prevailing system ceased to function effectively. During the compensation scandals, relations between the MoF and the securities firms faltered. The MoF, however, had no choice but to resume close contact. Officials lacked expertise about the securities markets and had no other way to obtain the information needed to devise appropriate policies. The Ministry therefore had no choice. A more formal publication and comment process would have provided an alternative.

An Administrative Procedure Act would have other benefits. The close relationship between regulated and regulator has caused concern recently because of the perception that industry interests take precedent over the public's. One way to avoid the perception would be to expand the policy formulation process by including the public – through a formal comment process.[18]

Other steps may not amount to much individually but would collectively contribute to a reduction in Ministry intervention. Providing resources and technical assistance to the new investigatory commission within the MoF would be one. The Securities and Exchange Commission in the United States has been policing securities markets since 1934 and could provide much insight into investigatory practices. The more effective the investigatory commission, the less cozy will be the relationship between regulator and regulated.

Talks could pressure the Ministry into accelerating the process of decompartmentalization. While the Diet has passed the necessary legislation, the MoF has indicated that it will use guidance to ensure that the process moves slowly, on a step-by-step basis. To some degree, therefore, the process actually accentuates Ministry control. Efforts should be made to encourage more rapid removal of the barriers separating categories of financial institutions.[19]

Other areas that provided the MoF with leverage warrant attention. The MoF should be pushed to free in principle the opening and closing of additional branches.[20] Similarly, the MoF should be pressured to deregulate the licensing process for new banks and brokers.[21] With a few anomalous exceptions, the MoF has not granted a new banking license since the end of the occupation.

One of the most significant yet subtle areas for foreign pressure involves the relationship between the MoF and the Bank of Japan. Over the last ten years, the Bank of Japan has gone a long way toward abandoning its interventionist approach toward regulation of the financial markets.[22] Interest rate controls in the interbank market were abandoned in 1989; window guidance in 1991. The central bank has instead preferred to influence financial markets indirectly through changes in interest rates, much the way matters are done in London and Washington.

The more market oriented philosophy of the Bank of Japan sharply contrasts with the interventionist approach of the MoF. The two financial regulators have also diverged on the philosophy underlying regulation. The central bank has tended to view inflation as the most serious threat while the MoF has emphasized economic growth. Although tensions often exist between central banks and the more political treasury or finance departments in other countries, the Bank of Japan suffers from an additional difficulty: direct control by the MoF.

War time legislation gave the MoF the authority to review central bank activities. The authority has never been formally invoked, however. Instead, much of the practical control comes from a more unusual source. With one exception, the practice has arisen since the occupation that governors of the central bank alternate between a career official within the Bank of Japan and a retired official from the MoF. The MoF, therefore, knows that any independent stance of the central bank will be susceptible to change once one of its officials becomes governor.

The rotation system probably made little practical difference through most of the post-war era. The MoF and the Bank of Japan typically acted in tandem. They both shared the same basic approach toward financial regulation. Appointing a former Ministry official as governor therefore caused no fundamental change in the central bank's approach.

Given the divergent views today, however, that is no longer the case. Appointing a former Ministry official as governor will deprive the central bank of critical independence. Efforts to take politically difficult stances on interest or exchange rates will be less likely. Moreover, the former Ministry official will bring a lifetime of interventionist experience, something not consistent with the central bank's reliance on market mechanisms.[23]

Ending the rotation system, therefore, would be beneficial to Japan and weaken another source of Ministry control over the financial markets. The MoF, however, would not give up the position without a struggle. Nevertheless, the stature within Japan of the governor, Mieno and the MoF's difficulties provide a narrow window of opportunity. A statement by Mieno that it would not be wise to appoint a former Ministry official as governor would carry considerable weight. In a consensus oriented society, the cabinet would have a very difficult time appointing a governor over such pronounced objections.

Subtle pressure on Mieno might help induce him to take the step. Another opportunity will not appear for a considerable time. When Mieno steps down in 1994, the next governor will be a former Ministry official.[24] Only after that five year term will another governor from the central bank assume the position and have an opportunity to break the rotation system. Moreover, success will depend at least in part on the relative strength and stature of the central bank and the MoF at the time.

Reducing administrative discretion will also require support from the Japanese private sector. To facilitate support, the Treasury needs an agenda that has greater domestic support within Japan. A confluence of foreign and Japanese domestic interests has, in the past, proved successful. The 1979 decision authorizing certificates of deposit represented one example. Efforts by foreign banks to engage in securities activities also had support among Japanese commercial banks.

Obtaining the support for positions from within the financial community, however, has limits. Japanese banks have tended to favor incremental reform. They also wanted change but not at the expense of their profitable market niches. In general, banks remained comfortable with the MoF's basic approach to regulation.

Foreign negotiators should therefore focus on issues that have the support of other domestic constituencies, particularly consumers. Reducing Ministry control would benefit corporate consumers by en- suring a wider range of financial products. Lessening guidance and allowing the market to function would also permit more competitive returns on pension plan assets, something of growing concern in a country with a rapidly aging population.

Individual consumers, however, represent the most obvious source of support. Appealing to this group, negotiating positions would involve efforts to obtain greater latitude in hours of operations, availability of ATMs, competitiveness in fees charged for basic services, and the availability of a full range of products such as car loans and credit cards. The key would be to obtain the Ministry's understanding that these practices were not subject to guidance but to competitive forces. The Ministry would need to get used to the idea that certain areas within the financial markets should remain outside of its continual oversight.

Consumers have not historically represented an organized or cohesive interest group in Japan. That, however, may be changing, particularly as the advantages of deregulation become apparent. Reform of the Large Store Law as a result of the Structural Impediments Initiative and the opening of Toys R Us stores throughout Japan has been met with considerable success. The favorable response will encourage vote-hungry politicians to be more accepting of comparable reforms in other areas.

Moreover, foreign pressure provides the requisite cover for politicians favoring the changes. By activating politicians, bureaucratic resistance to the policy shifts will become more difficult to sustain.

To the extent that Japanese banks refused to exploit any liberalization – whether out of fear of the MoF's reaction or out of a basic conformist approach – foreign banks would provide the necessary catalyst. Citibank engaged in aggressive advertising despite Ministry concerns. It has pushed against the envelope in the retail sector. The banks would need to know, however, that attempts by the Japanese government to penalize the behavior would result in quick diplomatic repercussions.

This means taking seriously the individual problems of each bank, something the Treasury has so far eschewed. Bureaucrats in Japan need to know that limitations on operations will immediately become topics of bilateral discussion and potential political intrusion. The approach will do more than transform foreign negotiators into spokespeople for the financial industry. It will both benefit foreign banks and demonstrate to the MoF the consequences of continued intervention. Past experience suggests that the MoF will eventually take a more sparing attitude toward restrictions on foreign banks, which will in turn impact the domestic financial system.

STRUCTURAL REFORM

Not all of the problems, however, are in Japan. Those wanting access to the markets likewise need to substantially revise their approach to negotiations. The ineffectiveness of the yen/dollar process since 1986 suggests serious problems with the US approach and the need for something more than changes in the negotiating agenda.

The principal difficulty with the Japanese financial system has been the role of the MoF. Yet the exclusive forum for discussing reforms has been a periodic convocation between the Treasury and the MoF. Thus, in an Alice in Wonderland fashion, the Treasury must annually ask the MoF voluntarily to relinquish its authority. Unsurprisingly, the MoF has not been particularly receptive to the request.

The 1980s proved to be an intriguing experiment in the ability of a single department with substantive expertise to negotiate financial reform with another country. Involving heady matters such as the balance of payments and exchange rates, the financial area required the sensitive, guiding hand of those with the requisite expertise. That meant the Treasury.

The Treasury had little faith in others handling the matter. Officials even resisted categorizing the area as "trade," as if an inappropriate appellation would invite involvement from other agencies or departments. The attitudes were not, of course, unique. Financial ministries worldwide viewed themselves as watchdogs over international monetary matters. Talk of participation by others would send shivers down the collective spines of financial regulators.

The single sector framework initially succeeded. The Department of the Treasury and the financial industry were united on the need for reform. The clamor for access to the Japanese market by brokers and banks coincided with the Treasury's interest in further liberalization of the capital markets.

The process eventually broke down, however. The Treasury promoted open financial markets and free capital flows. Ideologically pure, the view represented a myopic vision. The Department refused to place significant focus on issues designed to improve the market share of foreign banks. Members of the Yen/Dollar Committee during the follow-up period had an almost belligerent attitude. They were not captives of industry and did not see themselves as beacons for banking complaints.

The banking industry began to view the Treasury approach as increasingly irrelevant, even harmful. As a result, the partnership between foreign banks and foreign trade negotiators dissipated. The Treasury lost a critical source of support and information. Communication with industry became an episodic event, something that occurred in a comprehensive fashion only before annual meetings of the Yen/Dollar Committee.

The Department also began to devote less energy to the process. The high level commitment of time and talent so apparent in connection with the Yen/Dollar Accord waned. Without the commitment, the follow-up meetings reflected a less prepared, less sophisticated, understanding of the reform process in Japan.

Other, more systemic problems existed with the Treasury's role, however. The Treasury simply lacked the leverage to induce more than incremental change. With US financial markets essentially open, the Yen/Dollar Committee had little to offer in return for Japanese concessions. Nor could the Treasury make commitments for other agencies and departments. Regulatory matters were within the oversight of the Federal Reserve Board and the Securities and Exchange Commission, neither of which fell under the auspices of the Department of the Treasury.

Problems even existed within the Treasury itself. When commenced in the early 1980s, financial negotiations did not represent a significant portion of the Department's activities. The team negotiating the Yen/Dollar Accord amounted to an *ad hoc* group put together for that one function. By the early 1990s, however, the Treasury found itself immersed in talks involving Canada, Mexico, Japan, and GATT. The time and resources needed increased exponentially.

The Treasury did not, however, create a single bureau or division to handle all of the talks. Instead, responsibilities were divided. In addition to logistical difficulties and problems of consistency, those handling the talks had a variety of other responsibilities. The Treasury did not therefore have a single office that could develop expertise and institutional memory necessary to maximize the negotiation process.

All of these problems hurt effectiveness. One solution would be to eliminate the talks or to reduce them to low level communications between the MoF and Treasury. Issues could still be raised at episodic meetings or convocations at the various economic summits. By disbanding yen/dollar, however, the high profile, politically charged, annual convocation would cease. This might lower political expectations and reduce acrimony.[25]

Elimination represents a second best solution. It would be preferable to the current arrangement. The talks today accomplish little and, even worse, their overbearing nature provides grist for those within Japan claiming that the United States asks for too much or uses the island nation as a scapegoat for its own problems.

The most effective solution would be to broaden the negotiation process. While perhaps for a brief, shining moment Treasury could rightfully claim a monopoly over financial services talks, that began to erode almost immediately. The process requires the addition of other departments and agencies within the executive branch. In particular, the Office of the United States Trade Representative (USTR) should have an opportunity to participate.

Providing a role for the USTR in the yen/dollar process would generate a number of advantages. The Office has one principal area of expertise: negotiating trade agreements. Officials therefore can bring a wealth of practical experience to the process. Responsible for a variety of areas, the USTR also presents the possibility of cross-sectoral trade-offs.

The USTR adds a psychological benefit. Through the use of the inter-agency review process, the positions of the Office would have the force and effect of a unified executive branch position. This would strengthen the hand of US negotiators. Finally, close and continual contact with industry gives positions of the USTR broad domestic support.[26]

Letting the USTR into the process will also head off an inevitable jurisdictional dispute. The MoF, like finance ministries almost everywhere except in the United States, oversees not only the banking system but also the insurance industry. In contrast, the United States has generally left oversight to the states. In international forums, negotiating responsibility over insurance has fallen to the USTR, with reliance on expertise provided by the Department of Commerce.

US negotiators are focusing increasingly upon barriers in Japan to foreign insurance companies. In those circumstances, the USTR will find itself negotiating with the MoF. This will result in two separate forums, each involving a facet of the Japanese financial system, each run by a different US agency or department, and each negotiating with the same Japanese regulator – a clumsy arrangement that minimizes cross-sector compromise. The talks should instead be combined into a single forum including both the Treasury and the USTR.

The presence of the USTR would probably have a dramatic effect on the Japanese side. The MoF use the yen/dollar forum to exclude from participation the Foreign Ministry and the Ministry of International Trade and Industry, ministries with more internationalist views; the very ministries most likely to want to compromise with the United States and, concomitantly, pressure the MoF for greater reform. By breaking the Treasury's monopoly and expanding the process on the US side, other Japanese ministries would likewise have an opportunity to enter the negotiation process. Given that much of the direction of future reform will involve limitations on the MoF's authority, the entry of other actors would increase the likelihood of positive results.

A role for the USTR would not mean a diminished presence for the Treasury. With the requisite expertise, the Treasury would necessarily retain considerable direct involvement in, and have immense ability to influence, any talks on the subject. Yet the USTR would also bring advantages to the table, improving the effectiveness of the process.

CHANGING ATTITUDES

Problems in the approach to Japan have not been limited to the US government. Foreign banks have been unable to pick up the cudgel, despite growing opportunities. J. P. Morgan, Bankers Trust, and Citibank competed aggressively for corporate business, Citibank at the retail level. Few other US financial institutions have done much to take advantage of the lull provided by the host of problems confronting Japanese banks. Operations were not expanded; profits continued to languish.

Banks need a fundamental change in attitude. This requires a renewed commitment to the market. A long-term strategy, they must develop a more sophisticated understanding of the financial markets. Relationships in Japan are still important. Corporate Japan focuses not only on cost in selecting lenders but on other factors including the permanency of the relationship.

Relationship banking means that foreign financial institutions need to have the staff on hand to succeed. That requires officials with adequate linguistic ability who can serve a long enough term in Japan to achieve results. Rotating employees in and out every few years, the common approach today, has become counterproductive.

This would not require a return to the pre-war days when officials served their entire career in a particular country. Some degree of rotation would clearly provide benefits both by teaching new skills and reaffirming the corporate culture. Yet the critical component would be to remain in a particular country long enough to learn the markets and gain expertise.[27]

In some respects, the personnel policies in foreign branches represent a pendulum. While lifetime tenure at a foreign branch has disadvantages, particularly the problem of "going native" when the country becomes the client rather than the bank, rapid turnover has the reverse problem. Employees have no incentive to engage in a time consuming effort to understand the markets, instead opting for short-term, often illusory, gains. The pendulum now needs to swing back.

The need for better trained, better connected employees has another, more subtle purpose. Japan, unlike the United States and other industrial countries, lacks the infrastructure of lobbyists and influence peddlers that provide ready access to the policy-making process. Companies entering Japan lack the necessary connections and, without lobbyists, have little means of obtaining them over the short term.[28] Influence, therefore, must be home grown, developed through employees with adequate sophistication and experience.

More than personnel and training problems have to change, however. Foreign banks need a more aggressive stance toward business opportunities and regulatory restrictions. With Japanese banks in full fledged retreat, lending opportunities have suddenly appeared. While many foreign banks eschew lending activities – whether because of the small margins or because of the lack of capital – the approach is shortsighted. Japanese companies will remember those banks that provided much needed funds when their own lead bank would not. Moreover, it is still the case in Japan that corporations provide lenders with collateral business. Thus, low margin loans may be offset by increased business in other areas such as foreign exchange activity.

A more risky approach but one with more long-term potential would be a greater emphasis on smaller borrowers. The Japanese press is replete with stories of small businesses having protracted difficulties obtaining loans. Whatever hesitancy they might have in dealing with foreign financial institutions, they will be overcome if loans are not otherwise available from domestic sources, as appears to be the case.

This is not a facile solution. The loans are fraught with risk. Smaller companies carry a greater likelihood of default. Credit analysis would be time consuming and costly. It would require both local skills in assessing the viability of a business and skills in assessing the prospect of repayment, particularly if based on cash flows.

While the risks would be great so would the potential payoff. Within the class of small corporate borrowers exists a future group of world class performers. In the early 1960s, Sony and Honda hardly appeared on the map. Close banking relations today will lead to increased business and the necessary business relationship in the future.

Foreign banks also need to develop a more aggressive attitude toward regulatory restrictions. This does not mean a blunderbuss approach. Effectively resisting restrictions requires considerable expertise in knowing where to push. Citibank used the Yen/Dollar Committee and political pressure to open some avenues. The bank obtained support from the MoF to acquire access to the city bank ATM network. Sometimes, however, Citibank just acted, whether through the acquisition of a securities firm with offices in Tokyo or by preventing accounts from balancing, forcing the Bank of Japan to make the discount window available, calculating correctly that the MoF would not undo the activity.

A more aggressive attitude also requires a willingness to see opportunities and take them. Rare opportunities to expand now exist. With some Japanese banks edging toward insolvency, the Ministry has had increasing difficulty finding healthy financial institutions to act as rescuers. Foreign banks would be welcomed if it meant avoiding a failure. Moreover, the MoF has shown increased willingness to expunge some of the non-performing loans from the unhealthy bank. Foreign banks therefore might be able to acquire control without absorbing a mountain of debt.

Finally, subsumed in all of these suggestions is the need for resolve and a long-term commitment to the market. Rightfully, the Japanese financial community, including the MoF, view the fickleness and lack of permanency among foreign banks with concern bordering on disdain. Recent events including cut-backs in the market have done little to dispel this impression. Foreign banks can succeed in Japan but not overnight and not if operations are continuously rearranged to reflect short-term considerations in Tokyo or London or New York.

A QUESTION OF BALANCE

This book illustrates that the problem of trade relations cannot be reduced to a simplistic explanation that puts total blame on Japan. Foreign firms and governments must accept some of the responsibility for the present state of affairs, a conclusion not limited to the financial sector. Resorting to punitive measures as the exclusive method for solving the problem, therefore, will not work. Short-term solutions such as managed trade are not the answer. They involve punishment for practices that, in the end, we helped create.

In addition to creating substantial animosity with trading partners, the approach does nothing to make foreign companies more competitive or to solve their own problems that contribute to the lack of competitiveness. To the extent that short-term solutions shift the focus away from problems with foreign companies, the result may be considerable long-term harm. While that does not and should not preclude continued pressure on the Japanese, it does mean a more balanced approach to the problem and an under-standing of how matters can improve through changes outside Japan.

211

NOTES

1 A QUESTION OF BALANCE

1 Robert Zielinski and Nigel Holloway, *Unequal Equities: Power and Risk in Japan's Stock Market*, Kodansha International, Tokyo and New York, 1991, p. 220.

2 Clyde V. Prestowitz, Jr., *Trading Places: How We Allowed Japan to Take the Lead*, Basic Books, New York, 1988, p. 313.

3 Pat Choate, *Agents of Influence*, Alfred A. Knopf, New York, 1990, p. xiv.

4 See Karel van Wolferen, *The Enigma of Japanese Power: People and Politics in a Stateless Nation*, Alfred A. Knopf, New York, 1989.

5 See Jim Powell, *The Gnomes of Tokyo*, Dodd, Mead, New York, 1988.

6 By the end of 1977, lending by foreign banks had begun a steep decline. With the fall-off in lending went profitability. From 1976 to 1979, the net earnings of foreign banks fell from ¥41 billion to ¥18 billion. Between 1976 and 1979, return on assets fell from 0.93 percent to 0.29 percent. By mid-year 1978, total foreign banking assets in Japan ranked below Bulgaria, Liberia, and Bermuda.

7 The statistics came up in the debate over the Fair Trade in Financial Services Act, reciprocal based legislation designed to penalize the Japanese for the inaccessibility of their financial markets. See 136 Cong. Rec. S-476-77 (noting that the Japanese had 25 percent of the California market; foreign banks in Japan had 1 percent).

8 For a historical overview of the role of Japanese banks, see Edna E. Earlich, *The Role of Banking in Japan's Economic Development*, PhD Dissertation, The New School, 1960.

9 J. P. Morgan officially received a license on December 8, 1968. Continental Illinois had received licenses to operate two branches in Japan in 1964. Not "new" licenses, Continental Illinois had acquired them from Chase, which had in turn acquired them from a departing Dutch bank. In addition, Mercantile Bank received a license to operate a branch in Osaka in 1963.

10 The loans were in the form of banker's acceptances and impact loans. Impact loans were medium-term dollar loans typically converted into yen. Although commonly used to finance specific projects, impact loans were in fact unsecured. Because of guarantees issued by Japanese banks, the foreign banks did not have to do the analysis ordinarily required for project financing, although some foreign banks did.

11 Interview with former Vice Minister for International Affairs, Ministry of Finance,

Tokyo. Consistent with this, J. P. Morgan's officials in Tokyo became interested in upgrading to a branch when they learned from data at the MoF about the profitability of Citibank.

12 The primary vehicle was the Foreign Exchange Control Law. Occupation officials not only knew about but approved the discriminatory potential of the law. They thought that Japan would abandon the protectionist approach once economic recovery had occurred. See Supreme Commander for the Allied Powers, *Historical Monographs, 1945–1951, History of the Non Military Activities of the Occupation of Japan*, volume XVIII, *Commerce*, Monograph 50, "Foreign Trade," 1945 through December 1950, at 110 ("The restrictions in the [Foreign Exchange Control Law] were to be gradually relaxed by cabinet orders and ministerial ordinances as the need for them subsided").

2 ENTRY AND OCCUPATION

1 All of the branches were opened under the appellation of the IBC. In addition to Yokohama in 1902, Kobe opened on August 1, 1904, Tokyo on January 4, 1923, and Osaka on July 31, 1925. Data on branch openings are supplied by Citicorp.

2 Memoir of Henry M. Sperry, Citibank, August 1976. Citibank was the only foreign bank with a branch in Osaka. Interview with Henry M. Sperry, Citibank.

3 James P. Warburg, "American Banks and American Foreign Trade," *Harvard Business Review*, 3 (1924), at 20, 25.

4 "Our Far Eastern Division," National City Bank, No. 8 (January 1927), at 10.

5 Yoshiaki Koyama, "Gaikoku Ginko Shiten," *Ginko-Ho*, Okura Zaimu Kyokai, Tokyo, 1992.

6 Frank H.H. King, *The Hong Kong Bank*, Cambridge University Press, Cambridge, 1987, at 294.

7 The last foreign branches operating in the country – banks associated with Nazi Germany and Vichy France – were closed in the first days of the occupation.

8 Theodore Cohen, *Remaking Japan*, The Free Press, New York, 1987, p. 87. The reach of the Section was extraordinarily broad. As Cohen noted, "[i]ts responsibilities reached into every cranny of Japanese everyday life, and its chief was pulled into almost every problem of significance" (ibid., at 87). Through most of the occupation (1946–52), Major General William F. Marquat headed the Section.

9 Extract of Allocation of Staff Responsibilities for Execution of JCS Directives Published, March 4, 1947, SS Responsibilities in Japan, SCAP Records, Suitland, Maryland. See also Draft Financial Directive for Japan, inter-office communication (for information), Treasury Department, to Secretary Vinson, from Mr White, Assistant Secretary of the Treasury, August 28, 1945, reprinted in *The Financial History of Japan: The Allied Occupation Period, 1945–1952*, Toyo Keizai Shinposha, Tokyo, 1982, 2-23, at 143.

10 Incoming message, Washington radio, WX61967, dated September 9, 1945, General Headquarters, US Army Forces Pacific, Adjunct General's office, SCAP Records, Suitland, Maryland. See also Supreme Commander for the Allied Powers, *Historical Monographs, 1945–1951, History of the Non Military Activities of the Occupation of Japan*, volume XIII, *Finance*, Part C, Monograph 39, "Money and Banking," 1945 through June 1951, at 1 ("The basic Occupation Directives required the Japanese authorities, rather than SCAP, to plan and direct the reform of Japan's banking system so that it could make its full contribution to the development of a democratic, peaceful and stable economy capable of supporting the Japanese people and maintaining trade relations with the free nations of the world").

11 The closing of the financial institutions in the occupied territories was intended to be the first step in economically separating Japan from those countries. See Cincafpac-Adv to Comgen Usafik-Opnl priority, September 29, 1945, SCAP Records, Suitland, Maryland.

12 Closing of Colonial and Foreign Banks and Special Maritime Institutions, Supreme Commander of the Allied Powers, Instructions to the Japanese Government (SCAPIN) 74, September 30, 1945, MacArthur Museum, Norfolk, Virginia. See also Supplemental Instructions pertaining to the Closing of Financial Institutions, SCAPIN 104, October 8, 1945, MacArthur Museum, Norfolk, Virginia (detailing practices with respect to employees of closed institutions).

13 Oral Instructions Given to MoF on 30 Sept. 1945, SCAPIN 73, September 30, 1945, MacArthur Museum, Norfolk, Virginia. See also Appointment of a Liquidator of Branches, SCAPIN 163, October 20, 1945, MacArthur Museum, Norfolk, Virginia (appointing the Bank of Japan as liquidator of closed institutions and directing prompt submission of a plan of liquidation).

14 See Letter from Harrison A. Gerhardt, Colonel, General Staff Corps, Executive to Assistant Secretary of War, September 13, 1945, National Archives, Washington, DC. Informal contacts had apparently occurred even earlier. See Memorandum for the Director, Civil Affairs Division, Attention: Colonel Hilliard. Department of Army Records, Box 117, RG165, CAD, 1945–June 10, 1946, National Archives, Washington, DC ("A request has been received from the National City Bank of New York as to whether General MacArthur desires to re-establish the branch of the National City Bank of New York formerly located in Tokyo, Japan. Can you give me any information on which to reply to this request?").

15 See Letter from Harrison A. Gerhardt, Colonel, General Staff Corps, Executive to Assistant Secretary of War, to Leo N. Shaw, September 21, 1945, Box 117, RG165, CAD, 1945–June 10, 1946, National Archives, Washington, DC.

16 See Cable CA 53 549, October 19, 1949, from SCAP to the War Department, portions of which are reprinted in *Financial History*, at 798 n.1; see also Monograph 39, at 27.

17 Memorandum from L. W. Chamberlain re Report on Closing and Reopening of the National City Bank of New York, Tokyo Branch, July 29, 1946.

18 Memorandum re Resumption of Travel and Commercial Banking Facilities, Japan, to Mr John Groome, Vice President, American Express, from W. L. McAvey, April 18, 1946.

19 Tom Davis, another interned bank official, managed to get back into the country as part of the occupation forces. Interview with Roger Christiansen, Citibank. The bank's influence did not stop at Japan. William Draper, appointed Under Secretary of the Army in 1947, had worked for Citibank after the First World War. Citibank was not the only source of expertise. In need of experience in financial markets, SCAP also "borrowed" employees from other US banks. They typically served in the country for several years before returning to the lending bank.

20 Memorandum re Collusion by SCAP's Economic and Scientific Section with National City Bank, AGAO-C004.2 (19 Aug. 46, WSCA), National Archives, Washington, DC.

21 Memorandum from O. P. Echols, Major General, USA Chief, Civil Affairs Division, WDSCA 004.2 (22 Aug. 1946), National Archives, Washington, DC.

22 Establishment or Re-establishment in Japan of Branches, SWNCC 226-1-D, Memorandum to Secretary, SWNCC, from John D. Hickerson, Acting Chairman, December 2, 1945, reprinted in *Financial History*, 12-2, at 798–9.

23 Incoming Message from Washington to CINCAFPAL, W 82460, March 29, 1946, MacArthur Museum, Norfolk, Virginia. SCAP also indicated that all foreign banks would be subject to the same conditions for entry. Incoming Message from

Washington to CINCAFPAL, W 82130, March 28, 1946, MacArthur Museum, Norfolk, Virginia ("That authority for re-opening of Tokyo Branch of [Citibank] is with provisions that other American banks or banks prepared to operate in Japan under same conditions as those prescribed for [Citibank] would also be authorized to open or re-open branches in Japan").

24 Incoming Message from Washington to CINCAFPAL, W 82130, March 28, 1946, MacArthur Museum, Norfolk, Virginia. See also SWNCC 226-3, authorizing the establishment or re-establishment in Japan of branches of American banks and of banks of other allied powers, March 15, 1946; quoted in Establishment of Commercial and Foreign Trade Banking Facilities in Japan, SWNCC 22/6, June 20, 1947; reprinted in *Financial History*, 12-10, at 804, 805.

25 National City Bank, No. 8, (July–August 1946). The opening was also attended by Ambassador George Atcheson, Jr, Chairman Nu, a member of the Allied Counsel for Japan, Major General L. J. Whitlock, Deputy Chief of Staff in General MacArthur's headquarters, and Major General W. F. Marquat, Chief of the Economic and Scientific Sanction, SCAP.

26 Memorandum from L. W. Chamberlain re Report on Closing and Reopening of the National City Bank of New York, Tokyo branch, July 29, 1946. By March 1948, the number had increased to 120.

27 Letter from F. P. Munson, Colonel, General Staff Corps, Executive to the Assistant Secretary of War, to Mr R. P. A. Everard, Vice President, Bank of America, June 1947, National Archives, Washington, DC.

28 The first private credit for Japan, the credit was for $50 million, half in dollars and half in sterling. Bank of America and J. H. Schroder (New York) had responsibility for the dollar portion. The loan was to the Bank of Japan, subject to the unconditional guarantee of the Japanese government. The funds were used to import raw materials for the production of exports. Incoming Message from War Department to CINCFE, May 28, 1947, SCAP Records, Suitland, Maryland.

29 Memoir of Tom Coughran, Bank of America, April 15, 1989. Bank of America received a license from SCAP on July 22, 1947. Chase National Bank received a license nine days later. Monograph 39, at 29.

30 International Department, Japan (Tokyo Branch), Box 4B16, Chase Manhattan Archives. The number of employees had jumped to 61 by February 1949. As with the Citibank branch, Chase primarily serviced occupation forces. See *The Chase*, February 1948, at 30–1 ("The New Tokyo Branch will offer facilities to assist American business interests and the development of trade with Japan, in line with our Government's objectives, and provide the type of banking services to which they are accustomed to US military and other personnel there").

31 Radiogram from CINCAFPAC to WARCOS (JCOS), May 23, 1946, MacArthur Museum, Norfolk, Virginia.

32 See Report by G. K. Berkey, File No. 2724, American Express, March 26, 1948.

33 See, for example, Minutes of the Meetings of the Board of Directors of National City Bank of New York, July 27, 1948 ("[B]illets previously provided by the Army must be vacated, and that there is now available for purchase two houses in Tokyo and one house in Yokohama which will be adequate for the staff.... Until such time as the Bank is permitted to own property in Japan legal title to all three houses will be taken and held by the Industrial Bank of Japan").

34 In 1949, the bank purchased the building from the Closed Institutions Liquidation Commission, with Chamberlain authorized to pay up to ¥67,992,053 or approximately $190,000 (¥360 = $1). The price included the building and repairs. The land was subject to a long-term lease from Mitsubishi Estates. Some years later, Citibank agreed to give back some of the land in return for an extension on the lease and an agreement by Mitsubishi to build new facilities.

35 Letter from S. S. Wilson, President, to Mr Frank Groves, V.P. & G.M., American Express, Hong Kong, May 6, 1949.

36 Mitsubishi Estates owned much of the land in the Marunouchi district. More than one foreign bank official indicated that, as a quid pro quo for a much coveted lease in the area, Mitsubishi Estates insisted on a loan from the bank, a valuable commodity during a period of capital shortages.

37 See Memorandum to Mr F. A. Howard from A. E. Schumacher, Chase National Bank, October 23, 1947.

38 Memorandum to Mr F. A. Howard from A. E. Schumacher, Chase National Bank, October 23, 1947.

39 See Letter from J. P. Duddy, Chase National Bank, Tokyo, to A. E. Schumacher, VP, Chase National Bank, NY, October 18, 1947 (noting that mail arrived every eight days when not interrupted by typhoons).

40 Apparently, a black market in cables existed. One banker in Japan during the occupation remembers being offered his competitor's cables for $20 or $25.

41 In the summer of 1948, the Board of Directors of Citibank approved the purchase of three homes, two in Tokyo and one in Yokohama, for approximately ¥10 million or about $28,000 (¥360 = $1).

42 Bank of America bought the property in 1948; Chase some years later. According to published sources, Chase ultimately sold the general manager's residence in Japan for $75 million. Bank of America did the same in 1986, earning a profit of $58 million.

43 Chase's office opened on March 14. Chase began operations with "a staff of 20 Japanese, three American girls and the five New York men." Letter from J. P. Duddy to A. E. Schumacher, Vice President, Chase National Bank, March 21, 1949.

44 Citibank had a branch in Kobe before the war. Originally intending to reopen in that city, the bank had difficulty finding adequate space and decided that the port had "not yet shown the development of private foreign trade which we expected . . . ." Memorandum to Mr N. C. Lenfestey, Vice President and Cashier, from George N. Coe, Assistant Vice President, Far Eastern District, National City Bank, July 6, 1949. Citibank instead opted to open in Nagoya. The bank remained the only foreign financial institution in that city for 10 years.

45 See Letter from J. P. Duddy to A. E. Schumacher, Vice President, Chase National Bank, September 14, 1948 ("Leo Chamberlain told me that they would have been satisfied for the present with a branch in Tokyo and one in Osaka, except for the fact that Bank of America is opening in Yokohama and Kobe, and they just were not going to let them take over in those cities . . . ").

46 See Report by G. K. Berkey, File No. 2724, American Express, March 26, 1948.

47 In addition to the three American banks, the foreign banks included The Hong Kong and Shanghai Banking Corporation, The Chartered Bank of India, Australia and China, Mercantile Bank of India Ltd, the Banque de l'Indochine, Nederlandsche Handel Maatschappij, Nationale Handelsbanks, Bank of China, and Bank of India Ltd. See Takeshi Otsuki, "The Banking System of Japan," *The Oriental Economist*, July 7, 1951, at 523 (number of foreign banks operating in Japan as of December 1950). Banque de l'Indochine had opened a representative office in Yokohama in 1936. The MoF approved the upgrading of the office to a branch in 1942 but because of the war the license was only activated in 1947. Information provided by Banque Indosuez Group.

48 Memorandum from Herman Bylandt, Acting Chief, Accounts and Records Branch, to V. L. Rich, Banking and Foreign Exchange Division, ESS, September 8, 1950, SCAP Records, Suitland, Maryland (noting that three foreign banks, including Citibank, submitted reports "irregularly and never on time"); see also

Memorandum from Edward W. Tom, Chief, Internal Audits Branch, to Reginald H. Marlow, Acting Controller, ESS, December 19, 1950, SCAP Records, Suitland, Maryland ("At the present time, reports are required from the several Resident Foreign Banks every ten days by both the Accounts and Records Branch, Banking and Foreign Exchange Division, and the Business Section, Bank of Japan. The banks are rather annoyed by this requirement and are confused as to just what information is required").

49 See Memorandum for Chief of Staff, from W. F. Marquat, Chief, ESS, 335.2 ESS/FIN APO 500, January 26, 1949, SCAP Records, Suitland, Maryland.

50 Memorandum for Chief of Staff, from W. F. Marquat, Chief, ESS 335.2, ESS/FIN APO 500, January 26, 1949, SCAP Records, Suitland, Maryland ("Due to the flexibility of the 'Foreign Exchange Control Law [of 1941],' it was possible to implement [SCAP control] by means of Ministry of Finance Ordinance No. 88 . . . , thus leaving the law in full force and effect and nullifying the provisions of previous Ministerial Ordinances issued under the law which were in conflict . . . ").

51 Interview with Seymour Janow, SCAP. See also Trade Agreements With Foreign Countries, from Frank R. J. Gerard, ESS/BFB, January 19, 1950, check sheet attachment, SCAP Records, Suitland, Maryland ("[T]he present monitor arrangements provide that a particular foreign bank shall be responsible for the handling of all transactions with a certain country, . . . ").

52 Monograph 50, at 181.

53 Monograph 39, at 29. See Memorandum to The Chase National Bank of New York re Amendment to License to Engage in Business in Japan, A6 004.2 (14 Jun. 48) ESS/FIN, June 14, 1948.

54 Establishment of commercial or foreign trade banking facilities in Japan, SWNCC-226/6, June 20, 1947, reprinted in *Financial History*, at 805. The definition of foreign banks did not include those from axis countries (ibid.).

55 Ibid., at 806. A cable to SCAP implemented the recommendations by authorizing foreign banks to act as depositories for proceeds from Japanese exports. Cable From War Department to SCAP proposing expansion functions of foreign banks, from WSCA EASE, to CINCFE, Tokyo, War 98341, May 17, 1947, reprinted in *Financial History*, at 806.

56 Monograph 50, at 192.

57 Monograph 50, at 206.

58 See Memorandum for the Record, WKL/WNR/GPW/YY, ESS, Finance Division, July 14, 1949, SCAP Records, Suitland, Maryland.

59 See Memorandum to R. T. Reed, Pres., from J. F. Begole, Special Representative, American Express, August 18, 1949 ("It appears that the majority of the business of American banks is comprised of Letters of Credit which SCAP farms out to only American banks operating in Japan. Japanese banks are screaming about the practice but doubt that anything will come of it for some time").

60 See Incoming Message from CSCAD ECON to CINCFE, NR: W 94050, January 16, 1948, SCAP Records, Suitland, Maryland ("Add of foreign banks to present domestic Jap banking system would seem to lead toward credit expansion which would not otherwise occur, and attendant inflationary effect").

61 See Proposed Radio to Washington, attached to Memorandum for Chief of Staff, from W. F. Marquat, Chief, ESS, July 15, 1949, SCAP Records, Suitland, Maryland ("Cost of maintaining random, unproven deposit accounts is not attractive to foreign banks and their interest lies in recovery of pre-war and carefully selected new clientele").

62 Memoir of Tom Coughran, Bank of America, April 15, 1989; interview with Tristan Beplat, Chief, Money and Banking Branch, ESS, June 1991.

63 Memorandum for Chief, ESS, from Walter K. LeCount, Chief, Finance Division,

ESS, July 11, 1949, SCAP Records, Suitland, Maryland. In July 1949, SCAP had received a radio call from Washington suggesting the need to return foreign banks to Japanese regulation. See, for example, Memorandum for Chief of Staff, from W. F. Marquat, re Brief of Radio to Washington, July 15, 1949, SCAP Records, Suitland, Maryland.

64 Edwards Mission, Report of the Mission on Japanese Combines, Report prepared for the Department of State and War, January 1946, at 53.

65 See Memorandum for Chief, ESS, 010 (28 May 48) ESS/FIN, May 28, 1948, SCAP Records, Suitland, Maryland ("The Board will be responsible for the formulation and enforcement of all monetary and audit policies of the Government and will regulate and supervise all banks and all other credit and financial institutions . . .").

66 The reforms also targeted discretion exercised by the Bank of Japan. At least one commentator has described the reform as motivated by the "object of 'democratizing' the policy decision by the Bank of Japan." See Tsukumo Shionoya, *Problems Surrounding the Revision of the Bank of Japan Law*, The Beckhart Foundation, Nagoya, 1962, p. 40.

67 Memorandum to Major General W. F. Marquat, Chief, ESS, from Paul M. Atkins, Expert to the Secretary of the Army, October 25, 1948, SCAP Records, Suitland, Maryland.

68 Occupation officials saw in the Policy Board a mechanism for limiting government influence over monetary policies. The Board, however, had no real independence, and became dominated by the Bank of Japan. See Letter to Joseph M. Dodge from W. F. Marquat, Chief, ESS, June 4, 1950, SCAP Records, Suitland, Maryland ("In fact, this Policy Board has proved to be ineffective as a control device and certainly is no substitute for statutory controls as a replacement for arbitrary administrative personal power as exercised primarily by the Governor of the Bank of Japan, and in addition by the Minister of Finance").

69 See Letter to the Hon. W. J. Sebald, Chief, Diplomatic Section, from W. F. Marquat, Chief, ESS (undated), SCAP Records, Suitland, Maryland.

70 See Letter to Joseph M. Dodge from W. F. Marquat, Chief, ESS, June 4, 1950, SCAP Records, Suitland, Maryland ("The existing general banking law and the Bank of Japan law merely stipulate who has general authority over general banking institutions, leaving the way open to arbitrary discrimination among banks as well as permitting unsound practices. New legislation based on statutory limitations rather than administrative discretion is in the course of formulation and is nearing completion. In its draft form, however, this legislation appears to require much study and careful analysis").

71 Letter to the Hon. W. J. Sebald, from W. F. Marquat, Chief, ESS (undated), SCAP Records, Suitland, Maryland.

72 Memorandum for Chief, ESS, from Walter K. LeCount, Chief, Finance Division, ESS, July 11, 1949, SCAP Records, Suitland, Maryland.

73 See Notification of License, Tokyo and Osaka Branch, 1947–1951, Box 405, Chase Manhattan Archives.

74 See, for example, License to Perform Limited Banking Functions for the Occupation, to: The Chase National Bank of the City of New York, AG004.2 (23 June 1950) ESS/BFB, SCAP Records, Suitland, Maryland.

75 For example, the US banks wanted to remain open on American holidays but close on Japanese, Christmas being the only exception. The banks had to apply to the military for approval to close on Japanese holidays and to the MoF to close at Christmas. See Memorandum from ESS to C/S, 004.2 (13 Mar. 51) ESS/FIN, March 29, 1951, SCAP Records, Suitland, Maryland.

3 BEHIND THE SHOJI CURTAIN

1 Data provided to SCAP during the occupation showed that, before the war, bank financing had become increasingly less important, a trend only reversed once the conflict began. While 74.5 percent of externally raised corporate funds came from banks in 1918, the percentage had fallen to 23.7 percent in 1935. The bulk of the funds – 41.5 percent – came from the sale of stock. By 1937, however, bank financing had increased to 38.8 percent, finally peaking at 90.7 percent in 1945. Necessity for Industrial Credit Institution in Japan, October 5, 1948, SCAP Records, Suitland, Maryland.
2 Some officials within SCAP argued for the dismantling of the largest Japanese banks. Although never done, the Finance Division within the Economic and Scientific Section (ESS) opted to increase competition by creating new classes of financial institutions. Among other things, additional entrants would increase the accessibility of credit. See Letter from W. F. Marquat, Chief, ESS, to the Hon. W. J. Sebald, Chief, Diplomatic Section (undated), SCAP Records, Suitland, Maryland. SCAP therefore encouraged the creation of new classes of banks. The division of financial institutions into compartments was largely intended to prevent their absorption by city banks. In many ways, therefore, SCAP encouraged compartmentalization, an attribute that had existed in Japan since before the war.
3 Occupation officials first intended to liquidate the pre-war special banks with debenture issuing authority, including the Industrial Bank of Japan. See Memorandum from J. R. Allison, Director of Finance (acting), to Chief, ESS, March 29, 1950, SCAP Records, Suitland, Maryland. Eventually SCAP decided to convert them to ordinary commercial banks, which occurred with the adoption of the Law Concerning Debenture Issues of Banks. With the stock market not recovering and the Japanese companies having difficulty obtaining long-term funds, SCAP had embarrassingly to reverse direction and permit the creation of a class of long-term-credit banks. See Memorandum from Joseph M. Dodge to Major General W. F. Marquat, Re: Industrial Financing, December 3, 1950, SCAP Records, Suitland, Maryland. This was officially confirmed with the adoption of the Long Term Credit Law in 1952.
4 Most trust banks were trust companies that had converted to banks during the occupation. Commercial banks had received the authority to engage in trust activities during the war. See Commercial Banks Additional Operation of Trust and Savings Bank Business Act, Law No. 43, 1943. To prevent untoward competition with the fledgling trust banks, the MoF used administrative guidance to force most city and regional banks out of the trust area. Interview with Tristan Beplat, Chief, Money and Banking Branch, ESS, June 1991; see also *The Banking System in Japan*, Federation of Bankers Associations of Japan (Zenginkyo), 1989, at 15 ("After the war, however, the GHQ and the Ministry of Finance intervened with the policy that once again separated banking and trust businesses").
5 The MoF did this in large part by limiting the number of trust bank branches.
6 Before the war, the MoF encouraged consolidation of regional banks under the principle of "one prefecture, one bank." SCAP tried to encourage greater competition among regional banks but was not particularly successful.
7 Although imported from the United States, the purpose of the separation was entirely different. The separation of securities and banking functions in the United States arose in part out of the belief that the intertwining of the two led to the abuses that caused the Great Depression. In Japan, the United States separated the two industries entirely to prevent city banks from monopolizing the brokerage business, thereby creating an additional class of competitors. Interview with Tristan Beplat, Chief, Money and Banking Branch, ESS, June 1991.

8 Almost from the very beginning, the MoF and the Bank of Japan indicated concern with the ability of foreign banks to circumvent the highly regulated financial system in the country. See *The Oriental Economist*, July 14, 1951, at 555 ("The Bank of Japan and the Ministry of Finance are apparently much concerned about this for the following reasons: (1) Such liberal financing by foreign banks will stimulate the note circulation and the inflation spiral, (2) foreign banks will weaken the controlling influence of the Bank of Japan, and (3) it is highly problematical whether or not foreign capital should be invited through this kind of channel under the current dollar position").

9 The United States tried throughout the occupation to get Japan most favored nation status and membership in GATT. The efforts generated considerable opposition, particularly from Great Britain. A harbinger of things to come, allies had concern over Japanese trading practices. As one US official described: "[According to our allies,] [t]he Japanese were quite unethical in many of their trade practices before the war, and countries who compete with them in world trade still do not trust them." Letter from David M. Maynard, US Delegation to the 3rd Session of GATT, to General W. F. Marquat, Chief, ESS, April 23, 1949, National Archives, Suitland, Maryland.

10 The need for compensating balances was not limited to Japan. They were also common in other countries, including the United States.

11 One of the great ironies was the role played by SCAP in developing the foreign exchange controls used so effectively by the MoF to limit foreign banking operations and foreign investment. Not only encouraging the policy, SCAP did so over the opposition of many Japanese who wanted greater foreign investment. It did so at least in part in an effort to wean Japan from US aid. See Letter from Douglas MacArthur, SCAP, to Prime Minister Shigeru Yoshida, March 9, 1950, National Archives, Suitland, Maryland ("There is serious doubt, however, whether unrestricted foreign investment, accompanied by uncontrolled remittance of interest and profits up to a certain amount is feasible under the existing conditions of foreign exchange stringency. In effect this would be tantamount to according priority to unregulated future investments above the prime demand for foreign exchange to reduce United States appropriations and to meet existing obligations").

12 Swap ceilings clearly restricted the ability of foreign banks to raise yen, limiting their role in the domestic economy. They also had a less subterranean purpose, however. Dollars converted into yen had to be reconverted sometime in the future. Reconversion reduced reserves. Until the end of the 1960s, Japan lived on the edge, with the barest supply of reserves. Without the ceilings, the MoF would not have been able to manage the reserves as effectively.

13 Interview with Official at the Bank of Tokyo. These were all places in which the Yokohama Specie Bank had operated branches before the war. By 1956, the Bank of Tokyo had an extensive network abroad, with branches in nine countries including Argentina, Brazil, China, Egypt, England, India, Pakistan, the United States, and West Germany.

14 The MoF essentially permitted the four largest banks – Fuji, Sumitomo, Mitsui, and Mitsubishi – to open offices abroad at the same pace. They placed early emphasis on offices in London, New York, and, to a lesser extent, California. In 1952, the MoF approved the first international offices for city banks, with Mitsubishi and Sumitomo opening in New York and Mitsui and Fuji in London. The same year, Sanwa set up a branch in San Francisco and Sumitomo resumed war-interrupted operations in California.

15 In the international area, dollar deposits represented another form of control. Although usually placed with foreign banks, reserves deposited with Japanese

banks provided the dollars needed to expand abroad. The scarce dollars paid the expense of setting up the branch. Without the deposits, foreign expansion would have been far more difficult. By the mid to late 1960s, this became less important as Japanese banks obtained the ability to tap international capital markets directly.

16 Policy for Future Business with Japan, International Banking Department No. 661, Bank of America, San Francisco, Headquarters, May 15, 1952, at 1–2.

17 "Japan's Swing to Deficit," *The Economist*, September 30, 1961, at 1283. The deficit resulted from an import surge due to heavy domestic growth (ibid.).

18 See International Banking Activities – Japan, Far Eastern Branch Managers' Conference, Bank of America, November 16, 1952 (officials of Bank of America noting that domestic competition with Japanese banks should be avoided because "it would mean competing with Japanese banks, antagonize them and thus strain the good relationship which is being maintained").

19 In the early 1960s, Citibank's profits in Japan ranked third in its entire international branch network, behind only London and Manila, and its four branches were more profitable than Fuji Bank, Japan's largest. Interview with former Vice Minister for International Affairs, MoF. For Bank of America, the Japanese branches were the most important international outposts. See, for example, "Market Penetration by the Bank of America in the International Sector," attached to a memorandum from D. L. Grove, Economist, Economics Department, to Mr F. C. Beise, President, Mr Roland Pierotti, Assistant to the President, Mr J. W. Tapp, Chairman of the Board, L. A. Headquarters, Bank of America, Bank of America Archives ("Among the individual foreign countries in which the Bank of America is doing business, Japan is the most important in terms of the over-all amount of business which has been generated . . . . The Tokyo branch is, by a considerable margin, the largest foreign branch operated by either Bank of America N.T. & S.A. or Bank of America – New York").

20 Beplat's influence could be seen even before the occupation ended. By late 1950, Manufacturers had the fourth largest account balance with the Foreign Exchange Control Board, behind only Citibank, Chase, and Bank of America. Memorandum re Report on Status of Bank Accounts and Liabilities – FECB Account, December 19, 1950, SCAP Records, Suitland, Maryland.

21 See Report by G. K. Berkey, File No. 2724, American Express, March 26, 1948 ("[Tristan Beplat of SCAP] said that he hoped we did not expect to engage in a general banking business because already there are more foreign banks in Japan than there is international business").

22 American Express made the request in December 1951 and received approval from SCAP for a license to operate a military banking facility at Misawa Airforce Base on February 11, 1952.

23 The license was granted in October 1953. Operations began on March 1, 1954. MoF officials did not want to give American Express the license. In the end, the company received it because the Banking Bureau, without consultation with other Ministry officials, gave licenses to all banks operating in Okinawa, including American Express. Interview with Gengo Suzuki, MoF.

24 Letter from W. D. Murray, Inspector, to Frank Groves, Vice President, The American Express Co., Inc., April 8, 1954.

25 Ibid.

26 Continental Illinois purchased two branches from a Dutch bank in 1964. The Mercantile Bank represented the only exception, obtaining the right to open a branch in Nagoya in February 1963.

27 Sarkis J. Khoury, *Dynamics of International Banking*, Praeger, New York, 1988, p. 40.

28 As of December 30, 1950, only four national banks in the US had branches

abroad. The only one not represented in Japan was First National Bank of Boston, which had branches in Argentina, Brazil, and Cuba. See 88th Annual Report of the Comptroller of the Currency, 1950, at 114.

29 Bank of Montreal (1962); Bank of Nova Scotia (1962).

30 Swiss Bank Corporation (1965); Union Bank of Switzerland (1966); Banque Nationale de Paris (1968).

31 See Article 52 of the Banking Law of 1927; see also *The Banking System in Japan*, Federation of Bankers Associations of Japan (Zenginkyo), 1989, at 1–2.

32 In the midst of an international expansion effort abroad, the bank wanted a presence in Japan. Continental Illinois even considered buying all five Handelsbank branches. With only one international outpost, a small branch in London, however, Continental Illinois ultimately decided to curb its appetite and purchase just the two branches in Japan. Interview with Leo C. de Grijs, Continental Illinois.

33 Some bankers indicated that Continental Illinois paid for the two branches a price roughly equal to what Chase paid Handelsbank for all five.

34 Nineteen Japanese trading companies and the Bank of Tokyo each owned 5 percent of the bank, with the Bank of Tokyo responsible for operating the bank. This type of convoluted structure would become unnecessary in 1973 when the Illinois legislature permitted foreign banks to open branches in the loop.

35 Information provided by J. P. Morgan. The Glass–Steagall Act, adopted in 1933, forced J. P. Morgan to divide its banking and securities business. In 1935, J. P. Morgan elected to continue to operate as a commercial bank. A separate entity, Morgan Stanley, was formed to act as a securities firm. The two have remained distinct entities although the separation of banking and securities functions has eroded.

36 J. P. Morgan had a long presence in these centers. Offices were opened in London in 1838 and Paris in 1868. In addition, Guaranty Trust Company had opened a representative office in London in 1892 and a branch five years later. The office in Brussels opened in 1919.

37 The First National Bank of Chicago received a branch license in 1972. Other similarly situated banks had received licenses a year earlier.

38 Married to a daughter of former Prime Minister Fukuda, Ochi ultimately left MoF and embarked on a long career within the Liberal Democratic Party. He served as head of the Economic Planning Agency.

39 Steve Lohr, "Morgan Stanley's Man in Tokyo," *New York Times*, May 30, 1982, § 3, p. 6, col. 3. Phillips started his career with J. P. Morgan and ended it with Morgan Stanley.

40 Interview with Yusuke Kashiwagi, MoF.

41 From 1965 through 1970, the Bangkok Bank, alone of all foreign banks in Japan, opened an additional branch. With one branch in Tokyo, the bank received the authority to open another in Osaka. "Foreign Banks in Japan," *The Oriental Economist*, March 1971, at 14.

4 FOREIGN PENETRATION IN THE 1970s

1 Apparently after learning about J. P. Morgan's negotiations with the MoF, a banker in 1968 tried to obtain a branch for a US financial institution without first setting up a representative office. He arranged a meeting with Finance Minister Mikio Mizuta to discuss the matter. He was politely told that a representative office was a precondition to opening a branch.

2 This included those not in the mainstream of Japanese practices such as employees without a university degree or who had obtained a divorce.

3 See Ray Vicker, "Jailed Chief of UCB's Swiss Unit Talks of Huge Commodities Gamble That Failed," *Wall Street Journal*, October 8, 1970, at 1, col. 1 (reporting losses in excess of $30 million; Swiss subsidiary ultimately liquidated).

4 One former United California official thought, but was not sure, that it was Toyoo Gyohten, who later became Vice Minister for International Affairs at the MoF.

5 Mitsubishi, Sanwa, Mitsui, Tokai, and Nippon Kangyo were all apparently seeking licenses. See *The Oriental Economist*, March 1971, at 33. A number of bankers familiar with the story identified Tokai Bank as the key financial institution that had the most immediate interest in obtaining a state issued license and, therefore, the one most affected by the shift in policy.

6 Reciprocity continues to remain the policy of the MoF with respect to branch licenses. See Yoshiaki Koyama, "Gaikoku Ginko Shiten," *Ginko-Ho*, Okura Zaimu Kyokai, Tokyo, 1992.

7 Union Bank of Switzerland opened a representative office in Japan in 1966, a year after Swiss Bank.

8 Switzerland abandoned the strict one for one approach in February 1984. This occurred in part because Japanese banks had entered the country through finance companies, entities not regulated by banking authorities. By issuing bank licenses, Swiss banking authorities obtained a greater supervisory role over the Japanese banks.

9 JCIF Policy Study Series 10, at 105–10.

10 Despite the new entrants, the US banks in Japan since the occupation continued to dominate the market. Citibank headed the list, with 330 employees and pre-tax profits of ¥12 million, double that of the next competitor. Chase, Bank of America, Hong Kong and Shanghai, Continental Illinois, and Banque de l'Indochine all had a profitable presence. Other than Continental Illinois, J. P. Morgan was the only non-occupation bank to make the list. See "Change of Present System is Only Means for Improvement," *Japan Economic Journal*, June 20, 1978, at 24, col. 1 (57 foreign banks by September 1977).

11 This was not always the most direct way of achieving results. Officials in the International Finance Bureau had to obtain the consent of other bureaus within the Ministry affected by the decision. As a practical matter, therefore, that meant consultation with the Banking Bureau.

12 "Both Japan and US Tighten Control on Foreign Banking," *Japan Economic Journal*, August 30, 1977, at 3, col. 4.

13 Interview with Official from Bank of Japan. See also Interview with Haruo Mayekawa, Governor, Bank of Japan, *Euromoney*, January 1981, 56–7.

14 The Bank of Japan used guidance to prohibit banks from being both a borrower and a lender simultaneously in the call market. See Haruhiko Kuroda, "The Changing Structure of International Banking," *Euromoney*, March 1974, at 28.

15 "Foreign Banks Chafe at Official Controls," *Business Week*, February 6, 1978, at 54.

16 Interview with Walter Wriston, Citibank.

17 This was not the only source of profits. US banks also made large sums on transactions booked overseas. Particularly during the first oil crisis, dollar loans to Japanese banks carried very high margins.

18 Bank of Japan, *Economic Statistics Annual 1974*. Of course, by the 1970s, the gross amount of borrowing was substantially higher.

19 According to one source, Sumitomo alone absorbed $818 million in losses from Ataka. Stephen Bronte, "Sumitomo's Hunger for Profits," *Euromoney*, September 1980, at 29. For an extensive discussion of the bailout and the role of the government, see Zushi Saburo, "How To Go Bankrupt and Still Stay Afloat," in Murakami Hyoe and Johannes Hirschmeier (eds) *Politics and Economics in Contemporary Japan*, Japan Culture Institute, 1979, at 204.

20 Loans had to be converted into yen when made and reconverted to dollars when repaid. Exchange fees could transform a marginal impact loan into a profitable one.

21 A number of joint leasing ventures occurred, including General Lease Co. (Bank of America/Sumitomo); Fuyo General Lease Co. (Citibank/Fuji); Diamond Leasing (Mitsubishi/Chase). Bankers Trust formed a relationship with Mitsui and Dai-Ichi with Manufacturers Hanover. Finally, Sanwa Bank entered into a leasing venture with Euro Finance.

22 For a discussion of the types of problems incurred by foreign banks seeking the authority to open a leasing company, see Jackson N. Huddleston, Jr., *Gaijin Kaisha: Running A Foreign Business in Japan*, M. E. Sharpe, Armonk, NY, 1990, pp. 97–100.

23 Yoh Kurosawa, "The Growth of Foreign Banking Operations in Tokyo," *Euromoney*, March 1976, at xiii.

24 Citibank (¥12,423 million); Chase Manhattan (¥6,142 million); Bank of America (¥5,694 million); and J. P. Morgan (¥2,771 million).

25 Louis W. Pauly, *Opening Financial Markets: Banking Politics on the Pacific Rim*, Cornell University Press, Ithaca, NY, 1988, p. 71.

26 The limitations on yen funding led to anomalous results. In the early 1970s, most foreign branches of US banks were net borrowers in the country of location, usually relying on the local interbank market. In contrast, branches in Japan tended to be net borrowers from overseas offices. See "Recent Activities of Foreign Branches of US Banks", *Federal Reserve Bulletin*, 58 (October 1972), 855.

27 Although banks typically had representatives on the board, they did not use existing employees. Instead, they relied upon employees who had "retired" from the bank.

28 "The Moneylenders' Victims Welcome American Competition," *Euromoney*, January 1981, at 60 (statement by Richard L. Huber of Citibank).

29 According to one bank official, some sarakin even wrote manuals on how to apply for a loan from foreign finance companies.

30 See "Little Effect Expected from Cancellation of Leasing Plan," *Aviation Week and Space Technology*, May 21, 1979, at 43 (Ex–Im Bank made loans at 6 percent, while leasing companies obtained 8.25 percent on aircraft leases).

31 "Bank of Japan Rebuts Charges by Foreign Banks," *Japan Economic Journal*, May 9, 1978, at 1, col. 1.

32 Japanese banks echoed these views. Masahiko Seki, "Internationalization of Japanese Finance is Crucial to Economy," *American Banker*, May 11, 1979, at 9 (speech by president, Mitsui Bank Ltd, and chairman, Federation of Bankers Associations of Japan) ("Turning to the question of whether there is discrimination against foreign banks in Japan, regarding establishment of branches, participation in the call and bill markets, or a takeover of Japanese banking institutions, I wish to stress that such criticism is totally improper. There is no discrimination whatsoever between foreign and Japanese banks").

33 Kinyu Saido Chosukai, 1979, ch. 8, pt. 4, para. 3, reprinted and translated in Pauly, *Opening Financial Markets*, at 77.

34 See The Fair Trade in Financial Services Act of 1990, Hearing before the Committee on Banking, Housing and Urban Affairs, United States Senate, 101st Cong., 2nd Sess., at 76 (April 5, 1990) (statement of Eric W. Hayden, President, Investors Bank & Trust Co.).

35 Department of the Treasury, *Report to Congress on Foreign Government Treatment of US Commercial Banking Operations*, Department of the Treasury, Washington, DC, 1979, 77, 132–3.

5 BREAKDOWN OF CONSENSUS: REFORM OF THE JAPANESE FINANCIAL MARKETS

1 A class of smaller banks, resembling savings and loans in the United States, sogo banks converted to ordinary commercial banks in the late 1980s. They are now referred to as second tier regional banks.

2 Following an unprecedented *fall* in gross national product in 1974, the economy expanded by about 4 percent a year over the next decade. This compared with an average of 10 percent before the oil crisis. The oil crisis was probably not the sole explanation for the decline in growth rate. Japan had by that point largely "caught up" to the West and could no longer sustain the same rate of growth.

3 Samuels has undertaken perhaps the most thoughtful discussion of the interrelationship between the bureaucracy and industry. Richard J. Samuels, *The Business of the Japanese State: Energy Markets in Comparative and Historical Perspective*, Cornell University Press, Ithaca, NY, 1987. Contesting the general view that the bureaucracy represented the center of power, he concluded that Ministry officials operated under a system of "reciprocal consent." Bureaucratic authority could only be understood as part of a continuing process of negotiation with private sector interest groups.

4 For a discussion of these reforms, see Chapter 2.

5 See Draft of the Law Concerning Banks, Banking Bureau, MoF, the Japanese Government, November 12, 1950, SCAP Records, Suitland, Maryland.

6 Sumita represented an interesting choice to lead the reform movement. A protégé of then Finance Minister Takeo Fukuda, Sumita came to the post of director general of the Banking Bureau without prior banking experience. His success, however, eventually led to his appointment as jikan or administrative vice minister, only the third time a director general from the Banking Bureau had risen to that position in the post-war era.

7 The provisions were contained in the Merger and Conversion Law, Gappei Tenkan Ho, or Gatten Ho.

8 Initial capitalization was ¥455 million, with approximately one-third coming from the Bank of Japan, one-third from the government, and one-third from private sector financial institutions. See *The Banking System in Japan*, Federation of Bankers Associations of Japan (Zenginkyo), 1989, at 33. Banks paid a relatively paltry sum for the insurance, 0.012 percent of deposits.

9 For a detailed overview of the impact of the floating of exchange rates on Japan, see Robert C. Angel, *Explaining Economic Policy Failure: Japan in the 1969 and 1971 International Monetary Crisis*, Columbia University Press, New York, 1991.

10 Takeji, Yamashita, *Japan's Securities Markets: A Practitioner's Guide*, Butterworths, Singapore, 1989, at 217–18. Most of the sellers in the market were securities firms. Most of the buyers were corporations. See Yoshio Suzuki (ed.) *The Japanese Financial System*, Clarendon Press, Oxford, 1992, at 119–20. Attractive as long as alternatives did not exist, the *gensaki* market declined after the introduction of certificates of deposit. The *gensaki* market only applied to certain securities and was subject to a transfer tax. Yamashita, *Japan's Securities Markets*, at 219.

11 During a 21 month period ending September 1974, Japanese banks borrowed $16 billion. Quek Pec Lim, "The Year of the Samurai," *Euromoney*, February 1978, at 10.

12 Lending fell from $10 billion in the nine month period before the limitations, to $280 million in 1975 and $300 million in 1976. See "A Yen to Lend Abroad," *The Economist*, March 4, 1978, at 20.

13 Dodge, a banker from Detroit, was invited to Japan during the occupation to help

devise programs designed to end inflation and promote economic recovery. He also played a critical role in pegging the US–Japan exchange rate at ¥360 to the dollar. Dodge often receives credit for creating the economic foundation that facilitated the country's rapid post-war growth.

14 In addition to regional, city, trust, and long-term-credit banks, the syndicate included sogo (mutual) banks, credit cooperatives, agricultural banks, life insurance companies, and securities firms.

15 The Bank of Japan ultimately acquired 98 percent of the bonds. Eisuke Sakakibara and Yorikuki Nagao (eds) "Study on the Tokyo Capital Markets," JCIF Policy Studies Series 2, p. 40.

16 The system created conflicts within the MoF. The Finance Bureau had as its primary goal the financing of the government deficit, which meant keeping down the costs of debt. That goal brought it into conflict with the Banking Bureau, which to some degree sought to regulate and advance the goals of Japanese banks.

17 The numbers told the story. From ¥1.97 billion in 1965, government bond sales inched up to ¥3.427 billion by 1970. In 1975, the number increased to ¥52.80 billion, climbing to ¥141.7 billion in 1980. See also GAO, United States–Japan Trade: Issues and Problems, September 1979, p. 156 ("According to the Japanese Government, the deficit for the fiscal year, April 1, 1979 to March 31, 1980, amounts in dollar value to the administration proposed deficits of the United States, United Kingdom, France and Germany combined. It is a budgetary deficit of 40 percent amounting to 7 percent of GNP").

18 The MoF had authorized the issuance of certificates of deposit in London in May 1972.

19 Regional banks underwent a more modest decline. They fell from 20.4 percent in 1953 to 17.1 percent in 1973.

20 Trust banks went from 1.9 percent in 1953 to 3.1 percent in 1973. Long-term-credit banks increased from 4.8 percent to 6.8 percent over the same period. Credit associations and cooperatives saw similar increases. Associations went from 4.6 percent in 1953 to 10.1 percent in 1973, cooperatives from 0.4 percent to 2.1 percent. See Henry C. Wallich and Mable I. Wallich, "Banking and Finance," in Hugh Patrick and Henry Rosovsky (eds) *Asia's New Giant*, The Brookings Institution, Washington, DC, 1976, p. 281.

21 In the end, the opposition came from those institutions that had increased market share at the expense of the city banks. Unsurprisingly, they had no interest in a new instrument that might enhance the position of the city banks.

22 The largest financial institution was the Postal Savings System.

23 R. Taggart Murphy, "Power Without Purpose: The Crisis of Japan's Global Financial Dominance," *Harvard Business Review*, March–April 1989, 71, 73 ("According to widespread rumors in Tokyo, the MOF engineered a halt to sliding equity prices by leaning on the so-called Big Four . . . to support the market").

24 Following financial reforms adopted in 1992, the MoF agreed to phase out the Three Bureaus Agreement over a five year period.

25 Ironically, banks actually had considerable legal latitude in the area. Article 65(2) permitted financial institutions to sell government securities. As a practical matter, however, the MoF did not permit the resale of the bonds by banks. It took amendments in 1981 to the Banking Law to clarify the authority.

26 Masahiko Ishizuka, "New Bank Law To Be Finally Passed, But Bankers Are Still Feeling Bitter," *Japan Economic Journal*, May 19, 1981, at 15.

27 Ohira joined the Ministry in 1936. He served as the private secretary to the Minister of Finance before obtaining a seat in the Diet in 1952. He became Minister of Finance in 1974.

28 The director general of the Banking Bureau, Yasutaka Miyamoto, went to great lengths to placate banks following adoption of the reforms. He solicited views and otherwise maintained open communications with banks in devising language in Cabinet and Ministry orders ancillary to the new legislation. See Kuribayashi Yoshimitsu, *Okura Sho Ginko Kyoku* Kodansha: 1988.

6 THE YEN/DOLLAR ACCORD

1 *Report on Yen/Dollar Exchange Rate Issues* by the Japanese Ministry of Finance–U.S. Department of the Treasury Working Group, to Japanese Minister of Finance Noboru Takeshita and U.S. Secretary of the Treasury Donald T. Regan, Department of the Treasury, May 1984.

2 The early attempt to characterize undervaluation of the yen as some type of intentional behavior by the Japanese met strong opposition from the Reagan Administration. See Statement of Beryl W. Sprinkel, Under Secretary for Monetary Affairs, US Treasury Department, before the Subcommittee on Trade, House, Ways and Means Committee, April 21, 1983 ("We had found no evidence that the Japanese authorities were manipulating markets to weaken the yen. To the contrary, Japanese macroeconomic policy objectives, foreign exchange market intervention, and reluctance to lower the official discount rate all suggested that the Japanese authorities sought a stronger yen").

3 David C. Murchison and Ezra Solomon, "The Misalignment of the US Dollar and the Japanese Yen: The Problem and Its Solution," Private study, September 19, 1983.

4 He had also made similar statements in testimony before Congress. See US Economic Relations with Japan, Hearing before the Senate Committee on Foreign Relations, S. Hrg. 98-67, 98th Cong., 1st Sess. on the Impact of the Yen–Dollar Exchange Rate, at 16 (April 7, 1983) (Testimony by Lee Morgan).

5 They did not, for example, take into account the mediocre profitability of most of the assets.

6 In 1980, total profits had fallen to ¥229 million. After an upswing the following year to ¥528 million, they fell to ¥271 million in 1982, ¥238 million in 1983, ¥211 million in 1984, ¥141 million in 1985, ¥303 million in 1986, and ¥187 million in 1987. JCIF Policy Study Series 10, at 103.

7 JCIF Policy Study Series 10, at 103. Even those numbers represented somewhat of an improvement over prior years. In 1985, 76 banks had average profits of only 1.8 percent, with 23 actually showing losses (ibid.).

8 Interview with Walter Wriston, Citibank.

9 James V. Houpt, "International Trends for US Banks and Banking Markets," Staff Study, Federal Reserve Board, Washington, DC, May 1988, at 7.

10 From 1975 through 1986, overseas branches increased by 70 percent, to 218. Assets underwent similar growth. The growth, however, occurred primarily in Hong Kong and Singapore. The number of branches and assets in Japan during the same period remained largely unchanged. Houpt, "International Trends," at 9.

11 Houpt, "International Trends," at 33. Other popular destinations included Portland (one branch, one representative office); Washington, DC (two representative offices); Houston (three branches, eight representative offices); Miami (one branch, one representative office); Boston (one branch); and Honolulu (one branch). See *The Banking System in Japan*, Federation of Bankers Associations of Japan (Zenginkyo), 1989, at Appendix II, 6–7.

12 Interview with R. Timothy McNamar, Department of the Treasury.

13 Specifically, Under Secretary of the Treasury Sprinkel and Vice Minister of International Finance Tomomitsu Oba were assigned to co-chair the Working Group.

14 The other was the administrative vice minister or *jikan*. The highest ranking career position within the MoF, most *jikans* in the post-war era served as director general of the Budget Bureau before promotion, illustrating the domestic focus of the position.

15 The bureaus include Budget, Tax, Finance, Banking, International Finance, Securities, and Customs. In general, the Budget Bureau is considered the most powerful.

16 Stephen Bronte, "The Most Powerful Man in Japan," *Euromoney*, June 1979, at 24 (attributing statement to manager of a Japanese securities firm). Once a consensus emerged, however, the disharmony disappeared. Instead, the MoF spoke with one voice. This included ex-Ministry officials, the "Old Boys." Dissension would weaken the Ministry's position, something that could not be tolerated.

17 The United States did not always succeed in convincing some of the more domestically oriented bureaus to agree to reform. The yen/dollar team wanted the removal of barriers to investments in Japan, including mandatory withholding on earnings from securities. Despite much lobbying, the Tax Bureau refused to budge on the issue. Essentially the Bureau saw no reason to treat withholding on particular categories of assets in a unique fashion.

18 February 23–24 (Tokyo); March 22–23 (Tokyo); April 16–17 (Washington); May 6–7 (Hawaii); May 9–11 (Tokyo); and May 21 (Rome).

19 The Japanese government had been trying to get foreign banks to form an association since the late 1960s. Associations could act as conduits and disseminators of government "guidance" on various issues. An association of foreign banks did ultimately form, although the members generally avoided acting as a conduit for MoF-inspired policies.

20 *See* Office Correspondence, Re: Japanese Financial-Market, Board of Governors, Federal Reserve System, March 19, 1984, obtained under the Freedom of Information Act (noting that, following February meetings, Sprinkel requested that the Japanese authorities "present a specific agenda and timetable for further steps").

21 Remarks of President Reagan and Prime Minister Yasuhiro Nakasone in Joint Statement, November 16, 1983.

22 Following the compensation scandals in 1990, Aida became chairman of Nomura.

23 The reaction surprised Oba and others on the Japanese side. In their eyes, progress had continued, with the final negotiation session scheduled for the end of that month. They thought that Regan's anger reflected a breakdown in communication between the Secretary and the negotiating team.

24 The gesture did surprise Oba, however. He and Mulford had negotiated a number of matters in a meeting in Amsterdam a few weeks before. In his mind, there was little to accomplish in Hawaii and little reason to send the upper echelon of the Ministry on a trip out of Japan.

25 The Japanese agreed to negotiate the final document in English. This meant that there would be fewer subsequent battles over the precise meaning of language used in the Accord.

7 REFORM AND FOREIGN PRESSURE

1 During the 1980s, the Yen/Dollar Committee met seven times: November 1984; June 1985; December 1985; September 1986; May 1987; April 1988; November 1989.

NOTES

2 See JCIF Policy Study Series 10, pp. 40–59.
3 The Yen/Dollar Accord, *Report on Yen/Dollar Exchange Rate Issues* by the Japanese Ministry of Finance–US Department of the Treasury Working Group to Japanese Minister of Finance Noboru Takeshita and US Secretary of the Treasury Donald T. Regan, Department of the Treasury, May 1984, at 25.
4 Ibid.
5 "It is noted that there will be relaxation on the scope of non-resident issuers to be operative from April 1, 1985, which will have the effect of qualifying corporations with a credit rating of AA or better, as well as a reasonable portion of the universe of world corporations whose outstanding debt would be rated A" (The Yen/Dollar Accord, at 27).
6 The Sears deal occurred at 2:00 a.m. on December 1, with Dow's taking place later in the day. The early hour enabled Daiwa Securities to have the distinction of becoming the first lead manager for a Euroyen bond deal for a foreign company.
7 Shogun bonds, or foreign currency denominated bonds sold in Japan, were marketed for the first time in August 1985 when the World Bank raised $300 million.
8 Foreign banks were eligible to issue the bonds beginning June 1, 1986.
9 Samurai bonds are yen denominated bonds issued by foreign entities in Japan.
10 The Yen/Dollar Accord, at 18.
11 "Japan: Euromoney 20 Years Scrapbook: 1984 – Japanese Companies Permitted to do Swaps and Profit as a Result," *Euromoney Supplement*, June 27, 1989.
12 The converse was also true. Long-term-credit banks could use swaps to obtain short-term funds.
13 The Yen/Dollar Accord, at 14. *See* also New Japanese Financial – Market Measures, Memorandum of the Federal Reserve Board, Nov. 18, 1983, obtained under the Freedom of Information Act (noting that smaller regional banks opposed the lowering of the minimum size for certificates of deposit, fearing that this would "draw funds away from small-scale time and savings deposits").
14 Gradually, the MoF lowered the ceilings on unregulated accounts. By September 1986, the minimum denomination had fallen to ¥300 million. By October 1989, minimum amounts for certificates of deposit and money market certificates had fallen to ¥10 million and ¥3 million respectively. Moreover, the MoF indicated that complete decontrol would occur by 1994.
15 Removing controls on rates did not automatically lead to increased competition. The Federation of Bankers Associations of Japan had a "voluntary" rule prohibiting the advertisement of rates on deposits. The rule was only repealed in April 1993.
16 The Yen/Dollar Accord, at 22.
17 Ibid.
18 Ibid.
19 The MoF made no secret of the limitation. When the eligibility requirements for foreign trust banks were announced in December 1984, the conditions provided that the maximum number of licenses would be eight. *See* Attachment II to Letter from Makoto Utsumi, Minister, Embassy of Japan, December 20, 1984, obtained under the Freedom of Information Act. The most significant restriction was that the applying foreign banks engage in pension fund management in their home country and that the assets under management exceed the corresponding average of the Japanese trust banks (¥1.2 trillion yen). *Id.* The licenses were obtained by six American, as well as two Swiss and one British, banks. These included J. P. Morgan Trust, Japan Bankers Trust, Chase Manhattan Trust, Citi Trust, Chemical Trust, and Manufacturers Hanover Trust. The other three licenses

went to Union Bank (Switzerland), Credit Suisse (Switzerland), and Barclays Trust (United Kingdom).

20 In 1991, the MoF did approve the sale of a trust bank owned by Manufacturers Hanover to State Street Boston Bank.

21 The duplication could have been avoided by closing the branch and operating only a trust bank. The MoF would not allow a branch to operate as a trust bank, however.

22 The financial scandals in the early 1990s would demonstrate other reasons for the lack of progress. Japanese securities firms were guaranteeing principal and interest payments, something US trust banks would not do.

23 In 1984, Merrill Lynch put a bid in for a vacant seat. A Japanese securities firm, however, acquired the seat.

24 The Yen/Dollar Accord, at 22.

25 They included Merrill Lynch, Morgan Stanley, Goldman Sachs, Vickers da Costa, Jardine Fleming, and S. G. Warburg. The honor did not come cheaply. Each broker paid around $5 million for the seat on the Tokyo Stock Exchange.

26 American Express, however, may have had other reasons for closing the branch. Citicorp's acquisition of Vickers demonstrated that the MoF would simultaneously permit the operation of a bank branch and securities firm. The American Express branch, however, had a number of problems, including continued difficulties with the union, Gai Gin Ro. Opening the Shearson office gave the company a clean way to justify closing the branch.

27 In allowing the office to remain open, the MoF rationalized that the purchase had been by a subsidiary of the holding company and would therefore not be subject to the bank's control.

28 J. P. Morgan entered into the venture with Bechtel; Manufacturers with Chrysler; and Chemical with a British investor.

29 Part of the reason was cost. By 1990, when the Tokyo Stock Exchange seemed willing to let in Chase, the cost of a seat had risen to almost $10 million, 20 times the cost of a seat on the New York Stock Exchange.

30 The Yen/Dollar Accord, at 16.

31 The two year limitation was scrapped a year later.

32 Rich Miller, "Japan Warns U.S. Should Not Raise Hopes For Talks," *Reuters*, January 14, 1988.

33 The Accord also called for a study of the viability of a banker's acceptance market in Japan. The market was eventually implemented but never became particularly effective.

34 The MoF also kept securities firms out, limiting the market to banks and Tanshi brokers.

35 While theoretically decontrolled, the Bank of Japan through the Tanshi brokers tended to have heavy influence on the rates.

36 Beginning in June 1988, the higher open market rates caused funds to leave the interbank market. Because the Bank of Japan relied upon the market to exert monetary control, the drop caused concern. The reforms were intended to bring funds back into the market. See *Mitsubishi Bank Review*, 20 (March 1989), at 1155.

37 See Press Conference of David Mulford, Under Secretary for International Affairs, Department of the Treasury, and Makoto Utsumi, Vice Minister, MoF, Federal News Service, November 8, 1989.

38 Basel Supervisors Committee, International Convergence of Capital Measurement and Capital Standards (July 1988).

39 Peter C. Hayward, "Prospects for International Cooperation by Bank Supervisors," *International Lawyer*, 24 (Fall 1990), 787.

40 The US and British negotiators had initially opposed the inclusion of any portion of unrealized appreciation on stock.

8 TREASURY VERSUS UNITED STATES TRADE REPRESENTATIVE

1 Diehl also served in the position of Financial Counselor to the Supreme Commander of the Allied Powers and joined the staff of Joseph Dodge in 1949.
2 See Trade Expansion Act of 1962, Pub. L. 87–794, § 241, 76 Stat. 878; see also Exec. Order No. 11075, 28 F.R. 473 (1963).
3 Trade Reform Act of 1974, Pub. L. 93–618, § 141, 88 Stat. 1978, 2009-11 (1975), codified at 19 U.S.C. § 2101.
4 See Executive Order 12188 (January 2, 1980), 45 F.R. 989.
5 15 C.F.R. § 2001.2.
6 15 C.F.R. § 2001.2. All major executive branch agencies had representation, including Commerce, State, Treasury, and Defense. Other represented offices included Agriculture, Labor, Justice, Interior, Transportation, Energy, OMB, The Council for Economic Advisors, and the International Development Cooperation Agency. See Executive Order No. 12188 (January 2, 1980); see also USTR, Twenty-Fifth Annual Report, at 28.
7 The Trade Policy Staff Committee handled most issues. The Committee had over 40 subcommittees that addressed specific issues or geographic areas. Disagreements or important policy issues were addressed by the Trade Policy Review Group, populated by officials at the Assistant Secretary level. The last step involved cabinet level review of issues. USTR, Twenty-Fifth Annual Report, at 28.
8 Ironically, the US government at one time proposed reforms that would have fundamentally altered the effectiveness of the USTR. The Reagan Administration considered the creation of a Department of International Trade, a combination of the USTR and a streamlined Department of Commerce. The Administration apparently had the Ministry of International Trade and Industry as a model. The proposal generated considerable criticism, because of both the expected dilution of the trade focus and the turf battles over trade that were likely to emerge. The Senate ultimately voted down the proposal. Nonetheless, these proposals still occasionally surface, reflecting continued US fascination with the MITI model.
9 USTR, Twenty-Fifth Annual Report, at 30. The system includes an Advisory Committee for Trade Negotiations with 45 members appointed by the President from "various elements of the US economy that have trade interests" (Twenty-Sixth Report, at 184). Beneath the Committee are other advisory committees that divide into specific industry sectors, including a Services Policy Advisory Committee and an Investment Policy Advisory Committee.
10 See also *Japanese Barriers to US Trade and Recent Japanese Trade Initiatives*, USTR, November 1982, at 38–40 (discussing financial issues).
11 Study Prepared by the Office of the USTR for Submission by the US Government to GATT (Washington, DC, December 1983).
12 The Securities and Exchange Commission sent a representative to one of the meetings.
13 The Treasury did typically coordinate with other agencies responsible for implementation of any agreement.
14 United States–Canada Free Trade Agreement Implementation Act of 1988, 100th Cong., 2nd Sess., Rept 100-816, at 2 (August 5, 1988).

9 BREAKING THE LOG JAM: THE REFORM PROCESS AND THE MINISTRY OF FINANCE

1 Consensus does not mean affirmative support from all participants but an absence of opposition.

2 Richard J. Samuels, *The Business of the Japanese State: Energy Markets in Comparative and Historical Perspective*, Cornell University Press, Ithaca, NY, 1987.

3 The policy of "encouraging" city banks to cease trust activities actually began during the occupation at the insistence of the Supreme Commander of the Allied Forces. Officials wanted to ensure that the trust banks were not absorbed by larger Japanese banks. Interview with Tristan Beplat, Chief, Money and Banking Section, ESS, June 1991. See also *The Banking System in Japan*, Federation of Bankers Associations of Japan (Zenginkyo), 1989, at 15 ("After the war, however, the GHQ and the Ministry of Finance intervened with the policy that once again separated banking and trust businesses").

4 The bank formed from the trust departments of Sanwa Bank and Kobe Bank and the securities transfer agency business of Nomura Securities.

5 The trust bank formed from the trust activities of Tokai Bank and Dai-Ichi Bank and the transfer agency business of the Industrial Bank of Japan.

6 Daiwa remained in the bottom tier of city banks, a condition attributed by some in the financial sector, to MoF's refusal to permit the opening of a sufficient number of branches. Other examples exist. When Mitsui and Taiyo Kobe merged, one reason given was the need of Mitsui to circumvent MoF-imposed limitations on additional branches. Approvals were slow because Mitsui had violated the Ministry's guidance on lending to large clients. See Jathon Sapsford, "Merged Japan Superbank Facing Jumbo Problems, Analysts Say," *The Reuters Business Report*, March 30, 1990.

7 Efforts by securities firms to edge into banking also generated strong opposition. When the 1982 decision of Nomura and J. P. Morgan to form a trust company became public, banks immediately opposed the efforts. While J. P. Morgan's entry into the trust area was a concern, the primary objection was the attempt by a securities firm to cross into an area within the purview of banks (and insurance companies).

8 The MoF was careful to allow foreign banks into the trust area while keeping Japanese securities firms out. Nomura was subtly informed that continued pressure for a trust company would result in fixed commissions becoming an issue at the yen/dollar talks. The large securities firm got the message and gave up the effort to obtain trust authority.

9 Chalmers Johnson, *MITI and the Japanese Miracle: The Growth of Industrial Policy, 1925–1975*, Stanford University Press, Stanford, CA, 1982.

10 Efforts in 1991 to amend the Securities and Exchange Act to address securitization of assets by banks and finance companies foundered when the MoF and the Ministry of International Trade and Industry could not resolve their differences.

11 Ikeda, Ohira, Fukuda, and Miyazawa all started their careers in the MoF before becoming Prime Minister.

10 PUSHING AGAINST THE ENVELOPE: CITIBANK IN JAPAN

1 Even after the purchase in 1915, Citibank continued to open branches under the IBC name. By 1927, however, the practice had ceased and most of the IBC branches had been converted to the Citibank (then known as National City) name.

2 "Our Far Eastern Division," National City Bank, No. 8 (January 1927), at 10.

3 The IBC was not the only bank to recognize the importance of the Far East. Guaranty Trust Company, which would later merge with J. P. Morgan, opened a branch in Manila in 1901. The Company subsequently opened agencies in Hong Kong and Shanghai. The National Park Bank of New York and Union Bank of

Canada jointly operated Park Union Foreign Banking Corporation which, for a time, had offices in Yokohama and Tokyo.

4 In addition to additional branches in China, Japan, and the Philippines, the IBC opened offices in Calcutta in 1903 and Bombay in 1904; Malaysia in 1904; Batavia (Jakarta) in 1918; Rangoon in 1919. The IBC also opened offices in South and Central America, including Columbia, Mexico, Panama, Haiti, and the Dominican Republic.

5 Citibank had offices in Moscow, St Petersburg and Vladivostok.

6 The IBC had a branch in Mexico City that closed in 1915. Citibank reopened in 1929. In Haiti, the bank acquired the Banque Nationale de la Republique d'Haiti in 1922, with 12 branches, but sold it to the Haitian government in 1935. A branch in Cape Town opened in 1920 but closed two years later.

7 Although wanting single people, marrying locally was frowned upon and through the 1950s, grounds for dismissal. The bank hired the first married official (Robert Grant) for an overseas assignment after the Second World War. As part of the process, the bank also interviewed his wife. Shirley Syaru Lin, *Citicorp in China*, Citicorp/Citibank, New York, 1989, at 33.

8 Interview with George Scott, Citibank.

9 "Mr. Holbrook and Mr. Morse Lost in the Japanese Disaster," National City Bank, No. 8 (September 1923), at 5.

10 "Japan Looks Forward," National City Bank, No. 8 (October 1951).

11 Letter from Richard M. Henry, Citibank, November 18, 1991.

12 See Memorandum on Foreign Investment in Japan, ESS, RPD, Price Survey Unity, October 7, 1948, SCAP Records, Suitland, Maryland.

13 Memoir of George Scott, Citibank.

14 The closing dates for the branches were as follows: Moukden, May 31, 1935; Hankow, December 12, 1940; Harbin, February 15, 1941; Canton, August 31, 1941; Shanghai, December 8, 1941; Tientsin, December 8, 1941; Hong Kong, December 25, 1941. Information provided by Citicorp. The bank had also opened a branch under the IBC banner in Tsingtao in 1919 but it was closed two years later.

15 Memorandum concerning liquidation of foreign banks in Japan and statements of the National City Bank of New York, Tokyo Branch, AG 004.2 (8 Nov. 45), ESS/FI, SCAP Records, Suitland, Maryland.

16 Report on Closing and Reopening of the National City Bank of New York, Tokyo Branch, by L. W. Chamberlain, Manager, July 29, 1946.

17 Interview with Henry M. Sperry, Citibank.

18 Interview with Henry M. Sperry, Citibank.

19 In addition, the camp contained family members caught in the country when the city fell. "Thirteen Citibankers in Manila," National City Bank, No. 8 (April 1942), at 8.

20 In Asia, only the Citibank branch in Bombay stayed open for the duration of the war.

21 "What Happened to the National City's Far Eastern Staff After the Attack on Pearl Harbor," National City Bank, Supplement, No. 8 (September 1942).

22 Max Hill, *Exchange Ship*, Farrar & Rinehart, New York, 1942, at 35, 63.

23 Memoir of Richard Henry, Citibank, June 1, 1972. The voyage even had a light moment or two. The ship had a fully stocked bar which was empty by voyage end. Reed, the Citibank manager of the Shanghai branch, had one of his staff bribe a ship steward for a daily bottle of scotch. When the ship ultimately docked, the Japanese captain wanted to toast the returning detainees, only to find his personal stash of scotch gone. Interview with Richard M. Henry, Citibank.

24 Citibank apparently initiated the process. The bank contacted the War

Department some time in late 1945 which generated a cable to SCAP concerning the reestablishment of the Tokyo branch. See WARX 76093, October 15, 1945, from the War Department to SCAP, discussed in *The Financial History of Japan: The Allied Occupation Period, 1945–1952*, Toyo Keizai Shinposha, Tokyo, 1982, at 798 n.1.

25 Tientsin closed in 1948. The bank would only return to the Peoples Republic of China in the 1980s, with the opening of a representative office in Shenzhen, a city near Hong Kong, in 1983. The office became a branch in 1988.

26 The office opened in 1948 and converted to the Citibank name four years later.

27 Other than Paris and London, Citibank's only other outpost in the 1950s in Europe was a representative office in Frankfurt.

28 When the Tokyo branch reopened, 15 of the 70 Japanese employees had worked for the bank before the war. Japanese officials who would play an important role in the bank's post-war operations – Eda, Koshitaka, and Umezono – all joined or rejoined the bank during the occupation.

29 The only change was the opening of a branch in Nagoya rather than Kobe. For the reasons underlying this shift, see Chapter 2.

30 See Letter from Leo Chamberlain, Resident Vice President, Tokyo, The National City Bank of New York, to J. A. MacKay, Vice President, New York, July 18, 1949 ("My immediate plan is to get Cullings back here as soon as possible to take over office supervision so I can get out and circulate around. I need some time to talk and discuss all sorts of things with all sorts of people. Bank of Japan, Foreign Exchange Control Board, SCAP and Japanese government officials, commercial banks, etc.").

31 In particular, Chamberlain maintained relations with the MoF, although views of him within the MoF varied considerably. During the occupation, he represented one of the few non-SCAP sources of information about financial and economic developments in the United States. The liaison office at the Ministry, therefore, routinely consulted with him. Some MoF officials, however, viewed his demeanor as haughty.

32 Until 1975, a country head was known as the senior officer in the field, or SENOF.

33 This was not, however, a practice instituted by Wriston but more accurately reflected the corporate culture of the bank. Citibank always had a strict policy toward accuracy and toward credit risks. One official remembers that, after a single $100 bounced check in Hong Kong in 1948, he was told either to book the loss, with the clear implication that it would be remembered at raise time, or to repay the amount from his salary.

34 The IBC had opened a branch in Penang, Malaysia, in 1904 but closed it in 1909, before Citibank acquired the bank.

35 Ending the guarantees also meant lending based upon cash flow, something common in the United States but uncommon in Japan.

36 Citibank had been considering expansion since the 1950s. The early efforts were not part of a nascent retail strategy. In the early part of the 1960s, bank officials wanted additional branches in cities like Kobe. These branches were not intended to be retail facilities but as additional sources of wholesale banking activity.

37 See "US Banks Wishing to Enter Japan," *Japan Economic Journal*, November 14, 1967, p. 1, 6, col. 5 ("Japanese banking quarters are viewing [Citibank's] intention to create a new branch with caution. They feel that it represents a move on its part to expand its branch network with the aim of bringing it in closer contact with the public, though officials of the US bank hold that the branch simply is intended for insuring its ties with its past clients").

38 The bank delivered a "memorandum of intention" rather than an actual application. Applications in Japan were only submitted after MoF officials had given unofficial approval to the requested action.

234

39 Interview with Richard Wheeler, Citibank.
40 The venture was between Fuji, a Fuji affiliate, Nihon-Bashi Kogyo Co., and Citicorp Realty Consultants, with each having a half interest.
41 In addition to Fuji and APCO, Mitsubishi joined Orion Banking Group, Sumitomo the Société Financière Européenne, and the Industrial Bank of Japan joined Rothschild.
42 As a recruitment technique, the bank invited students to spend a week playing the Bourse Game, a computer game simulating exchange trading, with the winning team receiving an all expense paid trip to New York. The game gave university students some insight into bank activities and gave the bank insight into the students' ability.
43 Citibank also pressed for the authority to sell unsecured yen bonds. Bonds provided an alternative to deposits and would have to some degree solved the inability of foreign banks to obtain necessary lending funds. The request, however, challenged the separation between long-term-credit and commercial banks. The MoF said no.
44 Initially, Information Systems supplied the data free of charge. Headquarters in the United States, however, insisted on profitability, including the imposition of charges for the information. This misread the local market. In Japan, companies typically did not buy information. Instead, they reciprocated through additional business in the form of increased deposits or borrowings. In part this was cultural, in part practical. The employee within a company using the service could typically increase deposits or borrow small amounts without a supervisor's approval. Buying the service, however, did require approval, something employees were less willing to do.
45 Japanese banks did not receive comparable authority until 1990.
46 Most banks closed at 3:00 p.m. during the week, noon on Saturday. ATMs ceased operating at 7:00 p.m. on weekdays and 2:00 p.m. on Saturdays. All banking operations including ATMs were closed on Sunday. *The Banking System in Japan*, Federation of Bankers Associations of Japan (Zenginkyo), 1989, p. 46.
47 Other more "unique" reasons sometimes explained the edge. One Citibank official remembers visiting the Japanese bank tellers who sold travelers' checks and slipping them a Kennedy half dollar. This dramatically increased the number of travelers' checks sold.
48 According to some familiar with the venture, Nippon Shinpan expected Citibank to lend the operation funds needed for lending and was sorely disappointed when the bank did not.
49 The initials stood for Citicorp Credit Kabushiki Kaisha.
50 The new branches were in Tokyo and Kobe. Information provided by Citicorp on branch openings.
51 Reports indicated that Citibank studied Kokumin and Dai-Ichi Sogo Bank. See "Citibank Reported to be Aiming to Buy Japanese Bank," *Kyodo News Service*, February 7, 1986. The failure to acquire the banks may have been a blessing. In particular, Dai-Ichi, which changed its name to Taiheiyo, had severe financial difficulties and was taken over by the government before a bailout by Japanese banks could be arranged.
52 "Citibank to Take Over Heiwa Sogo?," *Japan Economic Journal*, January 11, 1986, at 1.
53 As part of the expansion effort, Citibank explored innovative approaches that pushed up against other conventions and limits. Mitsubishi Bank agreed to rent Citibank space for a branch office in Osaka and for ten other locations. The MoF had previously frowned upon these types of office sharing agreements, ostensibly because of the potential for creating confusion among bank customers.
54 Interview with Masamoto Yashiro, Citibank. See also Masamoto Yashiro,

"Citibank Builds Full-Service Strategy in Japan," *The Banker's Magazine*, July–August 1990, at 32, 34.

55 Data provided by Citibank, Tokyo Branch, April 20, 1993.

56 In place since the 1950s, the rules prohibited advertisement of rates, use of television, and sponsorship of events and limited the size of any newspaper advertisements. By April 1993, most of these restrictions had been lifted.

57 While the rules emanated from the Federation of Bankers Associations of Japan, they reflected the MoF's policy toward advertising. Thus, while "voluntary," Japanese banks accepted them as mandatory. Similarly, foreign banks – which were not even members of the Federation – also adhered to the limitation.

58 Initially dividing clients into corporate, consumer, and world banking, by the latter half of the 1970s the system became the five Is: insurance, information, industry, individual, and investment.

59 Because of the small volume, the bank had relied on a third party, to administer the program. Yashiro, however, decided to bring credit card administration in house, transferring it to the Citibank Singapore Regional Center.

60 Yashiro's predecessor, James Collins, acquired the site. The building was completed during Yashiro's tenure, however.

11 THE OPPORTUNITIES

1 The discount rate stood at 9 percent on March 19, 1980. It fell steadily thereafter, finally reaching 2.5 percent on February 23, 1987. *Financial Statistics of Japan*, Institute of Fiscal and Monetary Policy, MoF. As Japan's economy continued to deteriorate, the Central Bank lowered the rate to 1.75 percent in the fall of 1993, a post-war low.

2 Market capitalization of the Tokyo Stock Exchange exceeded that of the New York Stock Exchange in April 1987. By the end of 1989, the Tokyo Stock Exchange had a market capitalization of about $4.2 billion compared with $3 billion for the New York Stock Exchange. As evidence of excessive liquidity, the rise in market capitalization and land values overstated the case. Much of the increase came from changes in exchange rates.

3 The Nikkei Index hit an all time high of 38,915.87 in December 1989.

4 See "Profit Worries Could Cause Banks to Dump Some Clients," *The Nikkei Weekly*, June 1, 1991, at 19, col. 1. The practice cut both ways. Companies in need of capital also began selling shares, particularly bank shares.

5 The losses came from the payment of taxes on the gain.

6 Foreign banks had already begun to test the restriction. In the late 1980s, Citibank began selling corporate loans to other banks.

7 A study by Mitsubishi Bank of 100 corporate accounts showed that some were unprofitable while other marginally profitable accounts shifted into the red when dividends and paper losses on stock were taken into account.

8 "Regional Banks Post Lower Profits," *Japan Economic Journal*, December 15, 1990, at 24. The Bank of Yokohama saw the least decline, Gunma the largest.

9 Their profits on a pre-tax basis fell 39.4 percent, while those of the long-term-credit banks fell 31.5 percent. Tomio Shida and Hidedtaka Tomomatsu, "Banks' Profits Fall Sharply," *Japan Economic Journal*, December 1, 1990, at 32. The data were from the six month period ending September 30, 1990.

10 In fiscal 1992, city banks saw profits fall by an average of 14 percent, with Daiwa down almost twice that amount. Only Bank of Tokyo showed an increase, with pretax profits up 0.1 percent.

11 Moreover, four of the trust banks would have shown net losses but for the sale of stock from inventory.

12 Writing off a loan required Ministry approval. As one Japanese bank employee described: "We send the data [on loans] in pencil, the MoF returns the revised figures in ink." Tony Shale, "Japan: MoF and the Banks Have Vested Interests in Keeping Disclosed Bad Debt Figures Low," *Euromoney*, July 13, 1992.

13 Including automated teller machine locations, Sanwa actually surpassed Sakura Bank. The opening of an office in Fujisawa in Kanagawa prefecture in 1993 gave Sanwa a total of 1,000, compared with 978 for Sakura.

14 The combination was renamed Asahi Bank.

15 Naoyuki Isono, "Giant Mitsui Taiyo Kobe Bank Faces Huge Capital Worry," *The Nikkei Weekly*, June 8, 1991, at 19, col. 1.

16 The prospect of increased branches was a critical motivation. The Banking Bureau both issued branch licenses and supervised the rescues. The Bureau historically had taken a penurious approach toward new branch licenses for city banks. See "Banking Power Balance Shift," *The Oriental Economist*, Nov. 1964. With banks eager for additional offices to attract retail deposits, acquiring a sick bank effectively circumvented the restrictions.

17 JEI Report No. 15B, April 19, 1991, p. 3.

18 Formerly Dai-Ichi Sogo, Taiheiyo converted to a second tier regional bank and changed its name in October 1989. Fuji, Tokai, and Sanwa also contributed to the rescue.

19 Indeed, during the occupation, the Bank of Japan suggested the "elimination of approximately one-third of the total number of security dealers . . . ." Memorandum from the Bank of Japan, to Banking and Foreign Exchange Division, ESS, SCAP, Re: Problems Concerning Security Dealers, July 14, 1950, SCAP Records, Suitland, Maryland.

20 Bank of Tokyo substantially increased its interest in the ailing Dainana Securities in April 1992.

21 See "Matsuno Explains Bank-Securities Policy," *Comline*, March 30, 1992 (noting that banks rescuing unhealthy securities firms would be allowed to engage in brokerage activity). In August 1993, Daiwa Bank took control of ailing Cosmo Securities. True to form, the rescue enabled Daiwa to perform a broader range of securities activities.

22 Underwriting by banks was to be approved on a case by case basis. Keno Cacao, "Banks Lukewarm on Finance Reform Bill," *The Nikkei Weekly*, March 28, 1992, at 14, col. 3.

23 The MoF, for example, ordered Nikko Securities to implement a "halt in all business activities . . . for a period of four days between July 10 (Wed.), and July 15 (Mon.), 1991 at the corporate finance sections of all branches, and at the company's main headquarters." The MoF also ordered the implementation of "a method of insuring that these rules are always followed in the future" and a "concrete education program . . . " (ibid.). In addition to implementing the orders, Nikko expressed "our deep apologies for the events which have led to this loss of trust" and ordered six directors to forfeit half a year's salary. Documents obtained from the Securities and Exchange Commission under the Freedom of Information Act.

24 As a result of trade activities with persons linked to organized crime, Nikko expressed "deepest apologies" over the activities, fired the president, forfeited all bonuses paid to the board of directors, and punished 19 employees involved in, or responsible for, the transactions, with the punishments ranging from severe warnings, to salary cuts, to resignation or

demotion. Documents obtained from the Securities and Exchange Com-mission pursuant to the Freedom of Information Act.

25 See Clay Chandler and Masayoshi Kanabayashi, "Japan's Securities Flap Causes Tension Between Big Brokers, Finance Ministry," *Wall Street Journal*, July 1, 1991, at A10, col. 5; see also Henny Sender, "The Humbling of Nomura," *Institutional Investor*, February 1992, at 49 ("At Nomura's annual shareholder meeting on June 28, President Tabuchi stunned his audience by asserting that the Finance Ministry knew of, and therefore implicitly condoned, the firm's practice of compensating its best clients").

26 Masahiko Ishizuka, "Securities 'Scandal' Should Be A Right of Passage," *The Nikkei Weekly*, July 27, 1991, at 6.

27 Uko Inoue, "'Retirement' – A Gold Mine for Bureaucrats," *Japan Economic Journal*, May 14, 1988, at 24 ("As of December 1983, 38 percent of the total 754 known MoF officials who left the Ministry and sought a second career assumed posts in prestigious financial organizations").

28 Perhaps motivated by a desire to get to the root of the scandal, the problems also provided the Prime Minister with an opportunity to further embarrass the Finance Minister, a political rival.

29 Earlier efforts by politicians to divide the MoF had focused primarily on the removal of budget authority.

12 THE OPPORTUNITIES FORGONE

1 Manufacturers Hanover created the first investment advisory subsidiary in 1985. Credit Suisse became the first foreign bank to engage in investment trust (mutual fund) management.

2 A host of practical problems existed including the absence of companies specializing in direct mail campaigns, making customer solicitations more difficult. Still, at least the prospect of expanding operations now existed.

3 Japanese banks only received comparable authority following reforms enacted in 1992.

4 Even then the MoF imposed limitations on subsidiaries of Japanese banks, including a prohibition on retail brokerage activity. Foreign subsidiaries were not subject to the same restrictions.

5 This was particularly true of the US banks. Europeans, in general, fared better.

6 Interview with Walter Wriston, Citibank. In contrast to the almost universal attitude of retrenchment among US banks, a select group of European financial institutions were actually expanding in Japan. Largely government owned, the banks did not have the same pressure to maintain a healthy return on assets. They could therefore increase their book of business with less regard for margins.

7 Report of the Subcommittee on Financial Institution Supervision, Regulation and Insurance, Task Force on the International Competitiveness of US Financial Institutions, of the House Committee on Banking, Finance and Urban Affairs, Committee Print No. 101-7, 101st Cong., 2nd Sess., at 35 (October 1990).

8 The only significant legal restraint concerned the inability of foreign banks to obtain deposit insurance. This had not become a bilateral trade topic, however, largely because US banks in Japan are not sure they want to incur the costs of participating in the insurance system.

9 1990 Report on Foreign Treatment of US Financial Institutions.

10 Ibid.

11 1990 Report on Foreign Treatment of US Financial Institutions. The Study suggested that the absence of deregulation provided Japanese banks with a

competitive advantage, something the Japanese disputed. See Tomio S. Shida, "US Called Wrong in Its Criticisms of Japanese Banking," *Japan Economic Journal*, January 12, 1991, at 1 (interview with Tadao Chino, director general of the International Finance Bureau, MoF) (noting that "almost all financial resources for Japanese-owned banks operating in the US are raised either on the Euromarket or in the US, so Japanese banks' competitive opportunities with respect to the cost of funds are equal to those of US banks").

12 James Sterngold, "Treasury Official Rebukes Japan," *New York Times*, October 18, 1991, Sec. D, p. 1, col. 3.

13 Other bills had an equally anti-Japanese intent. See The Foreign Capital and Securities Markets Study Act of 1993, S.163, 1993.

13 SHARED RESPONSIBILITY

1 The Federation of Bankers Associations repealed the rule governing advertisements, in April 1993.

2 In at least one instance, officials from the Banking Bureau intervened to affirmatively assist Citibank's efforts. This occurred when the financial institution tried to obtain access to the automated teller machine system for city banks. Access was permitted but only after behind the scenes pressure from the MoF.

3 The restrictions on management of Euroyen offerings emanated from the Three Bureaus Agreement executed in 1975. The MoF did agree, following legislative changes in 1992, to phase out the limitations on lead managing over five years.

4 136 Cong. Rec. S-479 (emphasis added).

5 Nomura and J. P. Morgan came close in 1982. MoF officials, however, asked the companies not to file an application and they complied. Interview with official from J. P. Morgan.

6 The same was true of Citibank's efforts in the 1960s to obtain additional branches. The bank never filed an application, only a "memorandum of intention." The bank therefore did not actually trigger application of the Banking Law, but instead relied on a process of informal and ultimately unsuccessful negotiations with the MoF.

7 This was particularly true of activities abroad. A rare example in the Euromarket surfaced publicly in the late 1980s. The British subsidiary of the Industrial Bank of Japan began dealing in stocks of Japanese companies, apparently without prior approval from the MoF. The action represented a foray across the line separating banking and securities activities. Upon becoming aware, the MoF put a stop to the activity.

8 Banks were not the only ones chafing under government regulation. See Peter F. Drucker, "The End of Japan, Inc.?" *Foreign Affairs* 10, 13 (1993)("Japanese business leaders are disenchanted with 'administrative guidance,' which committed them in the last ten years to such strategic blunders as the emphasis on mainframe and supercomputers and the maintenance of the monopolies in telecommunications equipment").

9 Imposed in 1987, banks had to restrict loans to real estate companies. After a one year decline, the proportion of real estate loans began a brisk increase, Ministry guidance notwithstanding.

10 California represents the only state to have a significant Japanese retail presence. In general, the Japanese owned banks have not done particularly well, the Bank of Tokyo's subsidiary, Union Bank, the possible exception. Moreover, the activities of these banks are still dwarfed by the largest domestic banks in the state, particularly Bank of America and Wells Fargo. At the end of 1992, Bank of

America's total assets in California were $133 billion compared with about $17 for Union Bank, the largest Japanese owned subsidiary.

11 Ironically, critical buying that helped shore up the market also came from overseas investors.

12 In the pre-war era, five entities dominated the banking sector. By 1944, Fuji, Mitsui, Sumitomo, Mitsubishi, and Dai Ichi accounted for 74.9 percent of all bank loans. Kozo Yamamura, *Economic Policy in Post-War Japan: Growth Versus Economic Democracy*, University of California Press, Berkeley, CA, 1967, at 112. To some degree, these banks represented counterweights to government influence. Not dependent upon the Bank of Japan for funds, the banks had considerable practical independence from government oversight. Some even viewed the Ministry as a captive of the large banks. See Samuel E. Neel and Raymond Vernon, "Japan Has a Bank Problem," *Banking*, October 1946, at 45, 118.

13 Even today, the former zaibatsu banks have studiously resisted the MoF's influence, refusing to accept retiring government officials. With one exception, no former zaibatsu bank has given employment to a retiring Ministry official. Sumitomo took an official in the 1980s but has not repeated the experiment.

14 During the election campaign in the summer of 1993, MoF officials repeatedly ruled out tax cuts as a method of stimulating the economy. Only with the further deterioration of the economy did MoF's views begin to soften. Moreover, the Ministry favored an income tax cut only if coupled with an increase in the consumption tax. As the discussion in Chapter 9 notes, the MoF has remained powerful in part through the ability to operate within the broad parameters set by politicians. If the parameters change, the Ministry's policies will also have to evolve.

15 In many respects, the Ministry of International Trade and Industry (MITI) has begun to do the same thing. Pressured to reduce trade barriers, the Ministry can no longer be considered an unequivocal proponent of Japanese industry. By promoting the interests of consumers, for example by favoring changes in the laws that prohibited large stores, MITI has found a new constituency and has been able to remain influential.

16 Perhaps aware of the Treasury's hesitancy to promote these types of issues, the matter was apparently brought to the attention of the Office of the United States Trade Representative.

17 The topic was addressed briefly and to little effect in the Structural Impediments Initiative talks.

18 This does not suggest that a formal comment process is inherently superior to a face-to-face process. It is, however, more inclusive.

19 Pressure could be applied to ensure that foreign firms received broad operating authority. As past efforts have shown, this would act as a catalyst and cause Japanese financial institutions to clamor for comparable authority. For a discussion of this approach in connection with investment advisory services, see J. Robert Brown, Jr., "How to Open Japan's Pension Markets," *Asian Wall Street Journal*, Nov. 29 1993.

20 The MoF has announced a loosening of restrictions on branch licenses for regional banks. They apparently remain in place, however, for city banks. Given current economic circumstances, city banks have little interest in expansion. Absent repeal of the provision in the Banking Law requiring approval to open, close, or move a branch, the MoF can always reimpose the restrictions.

21 In the United States, for example, brokers need only register. They do not have to obtain a license and official government approval.

22 Deregulation, however, has only gone so far. Banks still must make daily reports on loan volume.

23 The differing philosophy surfaced visibly in early 1993. Unhappy with long-term interest rates and the central bank's stubborn refusal to drop the discount rate, the MoF announced its intention to begin purchasing bonds in the secondary market in an effort to force down interest rates. The Bank of Japan responded by lowering the discount rate.

24 According to some published reports, Mitsuhide Yamaguchi, former Vice Minister of the MoF and current governor of the Export–Import Bank, apparently has been anointed as Mieno's successor.

25 Indeed, some members of the original Yen/Dollar Committee thought that the talks should have ended upon the signing of the Accord and the immediate follow-up meetings necessary for implementation.

26 The USTR had increasingly focused on and developed expertise in trade barriers to the financial services sector. The *1993 National Trade Estimate Report on Foreign Trade Barriers* devoted 37 pages to the subject.

27 The most successful US banks inevitably seemed to have people with considerable long-term experience with the Japanese financial markets. J. P. Morgan had its Wynn and Loughran; Citibank its Kathe; Manufacturers its Beplat.

28 Foreign banks and companies sometimes hire retired government officials to provide insight into the policy process. This represents a limited solution, however. Most high ranking career officials prefer not to embark on second careers with foreign firms. Moreover, once hired, questions of loyalty remain open, with retired officials often believed to act in the best interests not of the company but of the official's bureaucracy.

INTERVIEWS

In general, the list does not include current employers but the employers of the interviewee relevant to the book.

Abbott, John. Department of the Treasury. Interview by author, October 1991.
Adachi, Barbara. SCAP. Interview by author, August 1991.
Adams, George A. American Express. Interview by author, December 1991.
Adewusi, Adebayo. Japan Center for International Finance. Interview by author, March 1992.
Ahmad, A.S.I (Butch). National Bank of New York. Interview by author, November 1991.
Allen, Dwight G. Manufacturers Hanover. Interview by author, November 1991.
Arakawa, Ayako. Federation of Bankers Associations of Japan. Interview by author, March 1992.
Awamura, Minoru. Japan Center for International Finance. Interview by author, March 1992.
Bacigalupi, Frank. Bank of America. Interview by author, November 1991.
Baker, Steven K. Citibank. Information from correspondence, December 1991.
Ballon, Robert J. Sophia University. Interview by author, March 1992.
Barker, Norman. United California. Interview by author, March 1992.
Barrand, Henry P., Jr. Manufacturers Hanover. Interview by author, February 1992.
Beplat, Tristan E. SCAP; Manufacturers Hanover. Interview by author, March 1991, June 1991, October 1991, January 1992, March 1992.
Berzin, Walter B. Chemical Bank. Information from correspondence. November 1992.
Boege, Sheldon. Citibank. Information from correspondence, January 1992.
Brenn, Bruce M. Citibank. Interview by author, May 1992.
Calhoun, Alexander D. Graham & James. Interview by author, August 1991.
Campbell, Carl C. SCAP. Interview by author, November 1991.
Casse, Marshall. Department of State. Interview by author, May 1992.
Cavelti, Reto A. Swiss Bank. Interview by author, May 1993.
Chew, Eng Hwa. Overseas Union Bank. Information from correspondence, October 1991.
Christiansen, Roger. Citibank. Interview by author, November 1991.
Clark, Brian C. American Express. Interview by author, February 1992.
Clark, Ian. J. P. Morgan. Interview by author, January 1993.
Collins, James J. Citibank. Interview by author, November 1991.
Coughran, Thomas B. Bank of America. Interview by author, November 1991.

Crouse, Thomas C. Citibank; Wells Fargo. Interview by author, November 1991.

Curran, George. Bank of America. Interview by author, August 1991.

Dallara, Charles H. Department of the Treasury. Interview by author, November 1991.

Deguchi, Haruaki. Nippon Life Insurance Co. Interview by author, March 1992.

Dempsey, Louis F. Northern Trust Company. Interview by author, January 1992.

Diehl, William W. SCAP; Department of the Treasury. Interview by author, May 1992.

Draughn, Paul. United California. Interview by author, November 1991, February 1992.

Fauver, Robert C. Department of the Treasury. Interview by author, June 1992.

Fine, Sherwood. SCAP. Interview by author, November 1991.

Finn, Richard B. Department of State. Interview by author, February 1991.

Freytag, Richard A. Citibank. Interview by author, January 1992.

Fujita, Koichi. Citibank. Interview by author, March 1992.

Funakoshi, Takehiro. Ministry of Finance. Interview by author, March 1992.

Geithner, Timothy F. Department of the Treasury. Interview by author, March 1992.

Goodhue, Frank W. First Chicago. Interview by author, May 1993.

de Got, Stephen Pare. Chase Manhattan. Interview by author, November 1991.

Goto, Keizo. Ministry of Finance. Interview by author, November 1991, June 1992.

de Grijs, Leo C. Nederlandsche Handel Maatschappis; Continental Illinois. Interview by author, December 1991

Grossberg, Kenneth A. Citibank. Interview by author, February 1992.

Grove, Wesley J. Texas Commerce Bank. Interview by author, December 1991.

Hadley, Eleanor M. SCAP. Interview by author, October 1991.

Harshfield, Edward G. Citibank. Interview by author, April 1992.

Hayamizu, Terumi. Citibank. Interview by author, March 1992.

Heck, Gerald L. Citibank; Detroit Bank & Trust; Wells Fargo. Information from correspondence, November 1991.

Henry, Richard M. Citibank. Interview by author, November 1991; Memoir, June 1, 1972.

Herman, Frederick. Denver Investment Advisor. Interview by author, February 1992.

Howell, Peter. Citibank. Interview by author, July 1991.

Huber, Richard L. Citibank. Interview by author, February 1992.

Huddleston, Jackson N. Chemical Bank; American Express. Interview by author, November 1991, March 1993.

Inouye, Minoru. Bank of Tokyo. Interview by author, March 1992.

Ito, Hiroshi. Japan Center for International Finance. Interview by author, June 1992.

Itoh, Seishichi. Bank of Tokyo. Interview by author, March 1992.

Janow, Seymour S. SCAP. Interview by author, October 1991.

Jansma, Andries, H.J. Handelsbank; Continental Bank. Interview by author, December 1991.

Jeannin, Gerard. Banque Indosuez Group. Information from correspondence, October 1991.

Johnson, W.J., Jr. Bank of America. Interview by author, July 1991.

Kanda, Hideki. University of Tokyo. Interview by author, March 1992.

Kashiwagi, Yusuke. Ministry of Finance; Bank of Tokyo. Interview by author, March 1992.

Kathe, Raymond A. Citibank. Interview by author, August 1991, May 1993.

Kato, Takatoshi. Ministry of Finance. Interview by author, March 1992.

Kellogg, David M. Citibank. Interview by author, December 1991.

Kimura, Yuji. Industrial Bank of Japan. Interview by author, March 1992.

Korenaga, George J. Citibank; Sanwa Bank; Bank of Nova Scotia. Interview by author, March 1992.

Koyama, Yoshiaki. Ministry of Finance. Interview by author, March 1992.

Kruse, Douglas C. Department of the Treasury. Interview by author, March 1993.

van Leijenhorst, Jan J. Continental Illinois. Information from correspondence, April 1993.

Leland, Marc E. Department of the Treasury. Interview by author, January 1992.

Leonard, Mathew. Citibank. Interview by author, November 1991.

Lindstedt, Olaf D. First Chicago; Chemical Bank. Interview by author, January 1992.

Loughran, John F. (Jack). J. P. Morgan. Interview by author, October 9 and 16, 1991, January 1992, February 1992, June 1993.

Machol, Margot E. Department of the Treasury. Interview by author, October 1991.

Maehara, Yasuhiro. Bank of Japan. Interview by author, June 1992.

Mano, Teruhiko. Bank of Tokyo. Interview by author, March 1992.

Matsumara, Tomokuni (Tom). First Interstate Bank. Interview by author, August 1991.

McCamey, William. Department of the Treasury. Interview by author, February 1992.

McNamar, R. Timothy. Department of the Treasury. Interview by author, February 1992.

Milby, James D. Citibank. Information from correspondence, April and May 1993.

Miyazawa, Yoichi. Ministry of Finance. Interview by author, November 1991.

Mizuno, Takanorie. Michinoku Bank. Interview by author, June 1992.

Morehouse, Robert H. Citibank; Bankers Trust. Interview by author, February 1992, April 1992.

Mulford, David C. Department of the Treasury. Interview by author, June 1992.

Munk, Russell. Department of the Treasury. Inverview by author, June 1992.

Muraoka, Sadao. Japan Center for International Finance. Interview by author, March 1992.

Murphy, Peter. Office of the United States Trade Representative. Interview by author, May 1992.

Muto, Haruo. Bank of Tokyo; Union Bank. Interview by author, August 15, 1991, March 1992.

Newman, Barry S. Department of the Treasury. Interview by author, June 1992.

Nielson, Ronald. United California. Interview by author, April 1992.

Niu, Masao. Citibank. Interview by author, March 1992.

Nunami, Tadashi. Bank of Japan. Interview by author, November 1991, June 1992.

Oba, Tomomitsu. Ministry of Finance. Interview by author, March 1992.

Odaka, Yasuo. Citibank. Interview by author, March 1992.

Ogata, Shijuro. Bank of Japan. Interview by author, March 1992.

O'Malley, Fred. Citibank. Information from correspondence, November 1991.

Osugi, Kazuhito. Bank of Japan. Interview by author, March 1992.

Peterson, Rudolph A. Bank of America. Interview by author, August 1991.

Rabinowitz, Richard. Anderson, Mori & Rabinowitz. Interview by author, January 1992.

Rapp, William V. J. P. Morgan; Bank of America; Department of Commerce. Interview by author, November 1991.

Reeves, Douglas F. SCAP. Interview by author, November 1991.

Regan, Donald. Department of the Treasury. Interview by author, April 1992.

Richardson, Bonnie. Office of the United States Trade Representative. Interview by author, June 1992.

Roberts, Daniel. American Express. Information from correspondence, November 1991.

Roberts, Edward. Marine Midland. Interview by author, February 1992.

de Rochefort, Jean. Irving Trust. Interview by author, December 1991.

Scott, George C. Citibank. Interview by author, December 1991.

Scott, John. Chartered Bank. Interview by author, December 1991.

Sebastian, Robert F. Continental Illinois. Interview by author, November 1991.

Sheville, Henry. SCAP. Interview by author, November 1991.

Shimizu, Brinda. Industrial Bank of Japan. Interview by author, July 1991.

Sonoda, Naruaki. Nikko Research Center. Interview by author, March 1992.

Sperry, Henry M. Citibank. Interview by author, February 1991; Memoir, August 1976.

Sprinkel, Beryl W. Department of the Treasury. Interview by author, October 1991, February 1992.

Stankard, Francis X. Chase Manhattan Bank. Interview by author, July 1991.

Stewart, Carleton M. Citibank. Information from correspondence, November 1991, April 1993.

Sumino, Hiroshi. Citibank. Interview by author, March 1992.

Suzuki, Gengo. Ministry of Finance. Interview by author, March 1992, March 1993.

Suzuki, Hideo. Ministry of Finance. Interview by author, March 1992.

Takada, Teruo. Federation of Bankers Associations of Japan. Interview by author, March 1992.

Takata, Ryouichi (Roy), Jr. Bank of Tokyo. Interview by author, June 1992.

Tatsuuma, Fujio. Mitsubishi Bank. Interview by author, March 1992.

Toba, Osamu. J. P. Morgan. Interview by author, January and February 1992.

Torii, Osamu. Citibank. Interview by author, March 1992.

Toyama, Haruyuki. Bank of Japan. Interview by author, March 17, 1992.

Umezono, Tatsuo M. Citibank. Interview by author, March 1992.

Usuki, Masaharu. Long Term Credit Bank. Interview by author, March 1992.

Utsumi, Makoto. Ministry of Finance. Interview by author, March 1993.

Vojta, George J. Citibank; Bankers Trust. Interview by author, July 1991.

Wallis, Allen. Department of State. Interview by author, March 1992.

Walsh, Helen. Department of the Treasury. Interview by author, September 1992.

Walsh, John G. Senate Committee on Banking, Housing and Urban Affairs, Subcommittee on International Finance and Monetary Policy. Interview by author, June 1992.

Watanabe, Masahiro. Industrial Bank of Japan. Interview by author, June 1992.

Watanabe, Takeshi. Ministry of Finance. Interview by author, March 1992.

Weadock, James J. Citibank. Interview by author, March 1992.

Weber, Alan. Citibank. Interview by author, December 1991.

Wheeler, Richard W. Citibank. Interview by author, September 1991, December 1991.

Williams, S. Linn. Office of the United States Trade Representative. Interview by author, November 1991.

Wilson, Bruce. Office of the United States Trade Representative. Interview by author, May 1992.

Woodworth, Richard H. Department of the Treasury. Interview by author, March 1992.

Wriston, Walter B. Citibank. Interview by author, July 1991.

Wynn, Robert J. J. P. Morgan. Interview by author, December 1991.

Yamada, Osmau (Sam). Mitsubishi Bank; Bank of California. Interview by author, July 1991.

Yamamoto, Kenzo. Bank of Japan. Interview by author, March 1992.

Yamamoto, Shigeru. Industrial Bank of Japan. Interview by author, March 1992.

Yashiro, Masamoto. Citibank. Interview by author, March 1992.

Yokota, Tadashi. Dai-Ichi Bank. Interview by author, March 1992.

Yoneda, Yasuharu. Industrial Bank of Japan. Interview by author, July 1991.

Yoshida, Tatsuo. Industrial Bank of Japan. Interview by author, March 1992.

Yoshizawa, Kenji (Peter). Bank of Tokyo. Interview by author, March 13, 1992.

BIBLIOGRAPHY

Aberbach, Joel D., Putnam, Robert D. and Rockman, Bert A. *Bureaucrats and Politicians in Western Democracies.* Cambridge, MA: Harvard University Press, 1981.

Adams, Thomas Francis M. and Hoshii, I. *A Financial History of the New Japan.* Tokyo: Kodansha, 1972.

Allen, George C. *A Short Economic History of Modern Japan.* New York: St Martin's Press, 1981.

—— *Japan's Economic Recovery.* Oxford: Oxford University Press, 1982.

Allison, Graham T. *Essence of Decision: Explaining the Cuban Missile Crisis.* Boston, MA: Little, Brown, 1971.

Angel, Robert C. *Explaining Economic Policy Failure: Japan in the 1969 and 1971 International Monetary Crisis.* New York: Columbia University Press, 1991.

—— "Banking Power Balance Shift," *The Oriental Economist,* Nov. 1964.

The Banking System in Japan. Federation of Bankers Associations of Japan (Zenginkyo), 1989.

Banyai, Richard A. *Money and Banking in China and Southeast Asia During the Japanese Military Occupation 1937-1945.* Taipei: Tai Wan Enterprises, 1974.

Bieda, Ken. *The Structure and Operation of the Japanese Economy.* Sidney, NY: Wiley, 1970.

Bronte, Stephen. "The Most Powerful Man in Japan," *Euromoney,* June 1979.

—— "Sumitomo's Hunger for Profits," *Euromoney,* September 1980.

Brown, Jr., Robert, J. "Bureaucratic Practices in the United States and Japan and the Regulation of Advertisements by Investment Advisors," *UCLA Pacific Basin Law Journal,* 1994.

—— "How to Open Japan's Pension Markets," *Asian Wall Street Journal,* November 29, 1993.

—— "Industrial Policy and the Dangers of Emulating Japan," *George Washington Journal of International Law and Economics,* 1994.

—— "Japanese Banking Reform and the Occupation Legacy: Decompartmentalization, Deregulation, and Decentralization," *Denver Journal of International Law,* v. 21, Winter 1993, at 361.

—— "Towards a More Independent Bank of Japan," *Asian Wall Street Journal,* March 8, 1993, at 10.

Cacao, Keno. "Banks Lukewarm on Finance Reform Bill," *The Nikkei Weekly,* March 28, 1992, 14, col. 3.

Calder, Kent E. *Crisis and Compensation: Public Policy and Political Stability in Japan: 1949–1986.* Princeton, NJ: Princeton University Press, 1988.

246

Campbell, John Creighton. *Contemporary Japanese Budget Politics*. Berkeley, CA: University of California Press, 1977.

Cargill, Thomas F. *Financial Deregulation and Monetary Control: Historical Perspective and Impact of the 1980 Act*. Englewood Cliffs, NJ: Prentice Hall, 1982.

—— *The Transition of Finance in Japan and the United States: A Comparative Perspective*. Stanford, CA: Hoover Institution Press, 1988.

Chandler, Clay and Kanabayashi, Masayoshi. "Japan's Securities Flap Causes Tension Between Big Brokers, Finance Ministry," *Wall Street Journal*, July 1, 1991, A10, col. 5.

Chernow, Ron. *The House of Morgan: An American Banking Dynasty and the Rise of Modern Finance*. New York: Simon & Schuster, 1990.

Choate, Pat. *Agents of Influence*. New York: Alfred A. Knopf, 1990.

Cleveland, Harold van B. and Huertas, Thomas F. *Citibank 1812–1970*. Cambridge, MA: Harvard University Press, 1985.

Cohen, Jerome B. *Economic Problems of Free Japan*. Washington, DC: Center of International Studies, 1952.

Cohen, Stephen D. *The Making of United States International Economic Policy: Principles, Problems, and Proposals for Reform*. New York: Praeger, 1977.

Cohen, Theodore. *Remaking Japan*. New York: Free Press, 1987.

Drucker, Peter F. "The End of Japan, Inc.?" *Foreign Affairs*, 10, 1993, 13.

Earlich, Edna E. *The Role of Banking in Japan's Economic Development*. PhD Dissertation, The New School, 1960.

Fearey, Robert A. *The Occupation of Japan Second Phase: 1948-50*. New York: Macmillan, 1950.

The Financial History of Japan: The Allied Occupation Period, 1945–1952, vol. 20. Tokyo: Toyo Keizai Shinposha, 1982.

Financial Statistics of Japan. Institute of Fiscal and Monetary Policy, Tokyo: Ministry of Finance, 1991.

Finn, Richard B. *Winners in Peace: MacArthur, Yoshida, and Postwar Japan*. Berkeley, CA: University of California Press, 1992.

Frank, Isaiah (ed.). *The Japanese Economy in International Perspective*. Baltimore, MD: Johns Hopkins University Press, 1975.

Frankel, Jeffrey A. *The Yen/Dollar Agreement: Liberalizing Japanese Capital Markets*. Washington, DC: Institute for International Economics, 1984.

Goldsmith, Raymond W. *The Financial Development of Japan, 1868–1977*. New Haven, CT: Yale University Press, 1983.

Hadley, Eleanor, M. *Antitrust in Japan*. Princeton, NJ: Princeton University Press, 1970.

Haitani, Kanji. *The Japanese Economic System*. Lexington, MA: Lexington Books, D. C. Heath, 1976.

Hayward, Peter C. "Prospects for International Cooperation by Bank Supervisors," *International Lawyer*, 24, Fall 1990, 787.

Henderson, Dan Fenno. *Foreign Enterprise in Japan: Laws and Policies*. Chapel Hill, NC: University of North Carolina Press, 1973.

Hill, Max. *Exchange Ship*. New York: Farrar & Rinehart, 1942.

Horne, James. *Japan's Financial Markets*. Boston, MA: George Allen & Unwin, 1985.

Houpt, James V. "International Trends for US Banks and Banking Markets," Staff Study. Washington, DC: Federal Reserve Board, May 1988.

Huddleston, Jackson N., Jr. *Gaijin Kaisha: Running A Foreign Business in Japan*. Armonk, NY: M. E. Sharpe, 1990.

Ikenberry, John G., Lake, David A. and Mastanduno, Michael (eds). *The State and American Foreign Economic Policy*. Ithaca, NY: Cornell University Press, 1988.

Ikko, Jin. *Okura Kanryo – Cho Erito Shudan No Jinmiyaku To Yabo (MoF Bureau-*

crats: The Connections and Ambitions of the Elitest Group). Tokyo: Kodansha, 1992.

Inoue, Uko. "'Retirement' – A Gold Mine for Bureaucrats," *Japan Economic Journal*, May 14, 1988.

Ishizuka, Masahiko. "New Bank Law To Be Finally Passed, But Bankers Are Still Feeling Bitter," *Japan Economic Journal*, May 19, 1981.

––––– "Securities 'Scandal' Should Be A Right of Passage," *The Nikkei Weekly*, July 27, 1991.

Isono, Naoyuki. "Giant Mitsui Taiyo Kobe Bank Faces Huge Capital Worry," *The Nikkei Weekly*, June 8, 1991, 19, col. 1.

Johnson, Chalmers A. *MITI and the Japanese Miracle: The Growth of Industrial Policy, 1925–1975*. Stanford, CA: Stanford University Press, 1982.

Kawaguchi, Hiroshi. "The 'Dual Structure' of Finance in Post-War Japan," *Developing Economies*, 5(2), June 1967, 301.

Kester, W. Carl. *Japanese Takeovers: The Global Contest for Corporate Control*. Boston, MA: Harvard Business School Press, 1991.

Khoury, Sarkis J. *Dynamics of International Banking*. New York: Praeger, 1988.

King, Frank H. H. *The Hong Kong Bank*. Cambridge: Cambridge University Press, 1987.

Koh, B. C. *Japan's Administrative Elite*. Berkeley, CA: University of California Press, 1989.

Koyama, Yoshiaki. *Ginko-Ho (The Banking Law)*. Tokyo: Okura Zaimu Kyokai, 1992.

Kure, Binji. *Window Guidance of the Bank of Japan*. Japanese Economic Studies, 1988.

Kuroda, Haruhiko. "The Changing Structure of International Banking," *Euromoney*, March 1974.

Kurosawa, Yoh. "The Growth of Foreign Banking Operations in Tokyo," *Euromoney*, March 1976.

Laws, Rules and Regulations Concerning the Reconstruction and Democratization of Japanese Economy, The Holding Company Liquidation Commission. Tokyo: Kaiguchi Publishing, 1949.

Lim, Quek Pec. "The Year of the Samurai," *Euromoney*, February 1978.

Lin, Shirley Syaru. *Citicorp in China*. New York: Citicorp Publications, 1989.

Lohr, Steve. "Morgan Stanley's Man in Tokyo," *New York Times*, May 30, 1982, S 3, p. 6, col. 3.

McKenzie, Colin and Stutchbury, Michael (eds). *Japanese Financial Markets and the Role of the Yen*. Australia: Allen & Unwin, 1992.

Miller, Rich. "Japan Warns U.S. Should Not Raise Hopes For Talks," *Reuters*, January 14, 1988.

Murchison, David C. and Solomon, Ezra. "The Misalignment of the U.S. Dollar and the Japanese Yen: The Problem and Its Solution," Private study, September 19, 1983.

Murphy, R. Taggart. "Power Without Purpose: The Crisis of Japan's Global Financial Dominance," *Harvard Business Review*, March–April 1989.

Nakamura, Takafusa. *The Postwar Japanese Economy: Its Development and Structure*. Tokyo: University of Tokyo Press, 1981.

––––– *Economic Development of Modern Japan: The Development and Structure*. Tokyo: Ministry of Foreign Affairs, 1985.

Nakao, Masaaki and Horii, Akinari. *The Process of Decision-Making and Implementation of Monetary Policy in Japan*. Special Paper 198, Bank of Japan, March 1991.

Neel, Samuel E. and Vernon, Raymond. "Japan Has a Bank Problem," *Banking*, October 1946.

The New Regional Banks of Japan. Tokyo: The Second Association of Regional Banks, 1991.

Odate, Gyoju. *Japan's Financial Relations with the United States.* New York: Columbia University Press, 1922.

Okimoto, Daniel I. *Between MITI and the Market: Japanese Industrial Policy.* Stanford, CA: Stanford University Press, 1989.

Otsuki, Takeshi. "The Banking System of Japan," *The Oriental Economist,* July 7, 1951.

The Past and Present of the Deregulation and Internationalization of the Tokyo Money and Capital Market, JCIF Policy Study Series 10, Japan Center for International Finance, April 1988.

Pauly, Louis W. *Opening Financial Markets: Banking Politics on the Pacific Rim.* Ithaca, NY: Cornell University Press, 1988.

Pepper, Thomas, Janow, Merit E. and Wheeler, Jimmy W. *The Competition: Dealing with Japan.* New York: Praeger, 1985.

Powell, Jim. *The Gnomes of Tokyo.* New York: Dodd, Mead, 1988.

Prestowitz, Clyde V., Jr. *Trading Places: How We Allowed Japan to Take the Lead.* New York: Basic Books, 1988.

Prindl, Andreas. *Japanese Finance.* New York: Wiley, 1982.

Rosenbluth, Frances M. *Financial Politics in Contemporary Japan.* Ithaca, NY: Cornell University Press, 1989.

Rugman, Alan M. *New Theories of the Multinational Enterprise.* New York: St Martins Press, 1982.

Saburo, Zushi. "How To Go Bankrupt and Still Stay Afloat," in Murakami Hyoe and Johannes Hirschmeier (eds) *Politics and Economics in Contemporary Japan,* Japan Culture Institute, 1979.

Sakakibara, Eisuke and Nagao, Yorikuki (eds). "Study on the Tokyo Capital Markets," JCIF Policy Studies Series 2.

Salvatore, Dominick. *The Japanese Trade Challenge and U.S. Response.* Economic Policy Institute, 1990.

Samuels, Richard J. *The Business of the Japanese State: Energy Markets in Comparative and Historical Perspective.* Ithaca, NY: Cornell University Press, 1987.

Sapsford, Jathon. "Merged Japan Superbank Facing Jumbo Problems, Analysts Say," *Reuters Business Report,* March 30, 1990.

Seidensticker, Edward. *Low City, High City.* Cambridge, MA: Harvard University Press, 1991.

Seki, Masahiko. "Internationalization of Japanese Finance is Crucial to Economy," *American Banker,* May 11, 1979.

Sender, Henny. "The Humbling of Nomura," *Institutional Investor,* February 1992.

Shale, Tony. "Japan: Ministry of Finance and the Banks Have Vested Interests in Keeping Disclosed Bad Debt Figures Low," *Euromoney,* July 13, 1992.

Shida, Tomio S. "U.S. Called Wrong in Its Criticisms of Japanese Banking," *Japan Economic Journal,* January 12, 1991.

Shida, Tomio S. and Tomomatsu, Hidedtaka. "Banks' Profits Fall Sharply," *Japan Economic Journal,* December 1, 1990.

Shionoya, Tsukumo. *Problems Surrounding the Revision of the Bank of Japan Law.* Nagoya: The Beckhart Foundation, 1962.

Skully, Michael T. and Viksnins, George J. *Financing East Asia's Success: Comparative Financing Development in Eight Asian Countries.* New York: St Martin's Press, 1987.

Sterngold, James. "Treasury Official Rebukes Japan," *New York Times,* October 18, 1991, Sec. D, p. 1, col. 3.

249

Suzuki, Yoshio. *Money and Banking in Contemporary Japan: The Theoretical Setting and Its Application.* New Haven, CT: Yale University Press, 1991.

—— (ed.). *The Japanese Financial System.* Oxford: Clarendon Press, 1992.

Takenaka, Heizo. *Contemporary Japanese Economy and Economic Policy.* Ann Arbor, MI: University of Michigan Press, 1991.

Terrell, Henry S., Dohner, Robert C. and Lowrey, Barbara R. "The Activities of Japanese Banks in the United Kingdom and in the United States, 1980–88," *Federal Reserve Bulletin,* 76, February 1990, 39.

Thayer, Nathaniel B. *How the Conservatives Rule Japan.* Princeton, NJ: Princeton University Press, 1969.

Tschoegl, Adrian E. "Foreign Bank Entry into Japan and California," in Alan M. Rugman (ed.) *New Theories of the Multinational Enterprise,* New York: St Martins Press, 1982.

Tsuji, Kiyoaki (ed.). *Public Administration in Japan.* Tokyo: University of Tokyo Press, 1984.

Tsutsui, William M. *Banking Policy in Japan: American Efforts at Reform During the Occupation.* New York: New York University Press, 1988.

Uchino, Tatsuor. *Japan's Postwar Economy.* Tokyo: Kodansha, 1978.

Umegaki, Michio. *After the Restoration: The Beginning of Japan's Modern State.* New York: New York University Press, 1988.

Upham, Frank K. *Law and Social Change in Postwar Japan.* Cambridge, MA: Harvard University Press, 1987.

Vasey, Lloyd R. and Viksnins, George J. (eds). *The Economic and Political Growth Pattern of Asia-Pacific.* Honolulu: Institute of Southeast Asian Studies, 1976.

Vicker, Ray. "Jailed Chief of UCB's Swiss Unit Talks of Huge Commodities Gamble That Failed," *Wall Street Journal,* October 8, 1970, 1.

Wallich, Henry C. and Wallich, Mabel I. "Banking and Finance," in Hugh Patrick and Henry Rosovsky (eds) *Asia's New Giant,* Washington, DC: The Brookings Institution, 1976.

Walter, Ingo. *Global Competition in Financial Services.* Washington, DC: American Enterprise Institute, 1988.

Warburg, James P. "American Banks and American Foreign Trade," *Harvard Business Review,* 3, 1924.

Watanabe, Takeshi. *Towards A New Asia.* Singapore: Times Printers, 1977.

Wikawa, Tadao, "The Banking System of Japan," in Parker H. Willis and B.H. Bechhart (eds) *Foreign Banking Systems,* London: Pitman, 1929.

Williams, Justin, Sr. *Japan's Political Revolution Under MacArthur: A Participant's Account.* Athens, GA: University of Georgia Press, 1979.

van Wolferen, Karel. *The Enigma of Japanese Power: People and Politics in a Stateless Nation.* New York: Alfred A. Knopf, 1989.

Yamamura, Kozo. *Economic Policy in Post-War Japan: Growth Versus Economic Democracy.* Berkeley, CA: University of California Press, 1967.

Yamashita, Takeji. *Japan's Securities Markets: A Practitioner's Guide.* Singapore: Butterworths, 1989.

Yashiro, Masamoto. "Citibank Builds Full-Service Strategy in Japan," *The Banker's Magazine,* July–August 1990.

Yoshimitsu, Kuribayashi. *Okura Sho Ginko Kyoku (MoF Banking Bureau).* Tokyo: Kodansha, 1988.

Yoshino, Toshihiko. "Economic Recovery and Banking System," *Contemporary Japan,* 24(1), April 1957, 570.

Zielinski, Robert and Holloway, Nigel. *Unequal Equities: Power and Risk in Japan's Stock Market.* Tokyo: Kodansha, 1991.

INDEX

251

bankers acceptances 34, 59, 109, 118, 150, 212, 230
Bankers Trust Company 35, 49, 115, 185, 205, 208, 224, 229, 243–4
banking, Japanese 7–8, 11, 26, 29, 33, 39, 51, 52, 66, 72, 104, 120, 155, 166, 177, 199, 212, 214, 215; insurance companies and 89, 137, 151, 173, 226; overseas expansion 3, 22, 49, 59, 74, 88, 189, 220; positions of foreign banks 2–4, 11, 41, 59, 63, 65, 114, 157, 191, 203, 212, 216; securities companies and 63, 73, 81, 91, 114, 180, 219; structure and regulation of 4, 24, 26–8, 30, 39, 52, 59, 60, 76, 82, 121, 139, 171, 213, 219; trust companies and 38, 91, 111, 185, 189
banking, United States 5, 11–12, 15, 144, 213; acquisitions 42–4, 145, 187, 230; antitrust policies and 13; foreign banks growth 3, 11, 16, 20, 22, 45, 55, 88, 212, 215, 217; interstate branching 161, 164; regional 29, 31, 72, 79, 80, 88, 117, 164, 168, 175, 187, 219, 225, 226, 236; structure and regulation of 27, 68, 122
Banking Act, United States 70, 122
Banking Bureau, MoF 47, 49, 62, 69, 71, 74, 82, 90, 112, 118, 156, 162, 165, 174, 221, 223, 225–7, 236, 238
Banking Law, Japan; of 1927 40, 41, 59, 69, 74, 82, 222; of 1981 139, 226, 239, 240
Banow National; de la Republique of Haiti 232
Banque Bruxelles Lambert 35
Banque de L'Indochine 216, 223
Banque Nationale de Paris 222
Barclays Trust 229
Basel Accord 120, 170–3, 187, 200, 230
Beplat, Tristan 38, 49, 218, 219, 221, 231, 240–1
Bombay 32, 232–3
bond syndicate 7, 95, 116; formation 95, 106; membership 89, 189–90; reform 104, 116, 118, 190; relations with MoF 7, 89, 104, 117, 190
bonds 29, 45, 81–2, 108, 174–5, 226, 234; auctions 77, 117; deep discount 107; duel currency 107; European 95, 103, 106–7, 229; government 12, 73, 77–8, 80, 82–3, 89, 106, 108, 117–18, 190;

guarantees, Bank of Japan 78; secondary markets 77–8, 82, 89, 116, 240; zero coupon 107, 186
Boxer Rebellion 145
branch; closings 12, 14, 42, 145–8, 186, 213, 215, 230, 232; MoF policies 3, 4, 25, 30, 52, 58, 112, 114, 192, 198, 232, 233; openings 4, 11, 15–17, 20, 28, 32, 40, 45, 55, 57, 89, 142, 145, 149, 161, 212–16, 220, 221, 235, 240
Bretton Woods 122
Britain see United Kingdom
brokers see Securities firms
Brussels 46, 152, 222
bubble 172
Budget Bureau, MoF 95, 228, 234
Bulgaria 65, 212
bureaucratic squabbles, US 6, 9, 121, 124, 125, 129, 193

cabinet 125, 135, 137, 139, 213, 227, 231
Calcutta 32, 232
Calhoun, Alexander 146, 242
California First 91
California, state of 56, 87–8, 91, 187, 193, 212, 220, 239
Canada 57, 128–30, 187, 207, 231
Canton 147, 233
capital adequacy see Basel Accord
car loans 159–60, 174, 186, 205
Caribbean 152
Caterpillar Tractor Company 87
certificates of deposit 69, 71, 73, 76, 78–80, 109–10, 157, 205, 225–6, 229
Chamberlain, Leo 14–15, 17, 147–9, 168, 214–16, 233–4
Chartered Bank of India, Australia and China 216
Chartered Bank, United Kingdom 11–12, 244
Chase Manhattan Bank 16, 23, 32, 36, 42, 215, 221, 223–4; closing offices 42, 186; National City Bank 213–16, 232–3; opening in Japan 10, 16, 17–18, 20, 40–4, 59, 212, 215–17, 222, 227; securities activities 115–16, 230; union problems 55
Chemical Bank 186
Chemical Securities 186
Chicago 42–3, 58
Chicago–Tokyo Bank 44
China 11, 16, 21, 147–9, 152, 220, 223–4, 232–3, 245, 247